THE ANCIENT LANG

This book, derived from the acclaimed *Cambridge Encyclopedia of the World's Ancient Languages*, describes the ancient languages of Europe, for the convenience of students and specialists working in that area. Each chapter of the work focuses on an individual language or, in some instances, a set of closely related varieties of a language. Providing a full descriptive presentation, each of these chapters examines the writing system(s), phonology, morphology, syntax, and lexicon of that language, and places the language within its proper linguistic and historical context. The volume brings together an international array of scholars, each a leading specialist in ancient language study. While designed primarily for scholars and students of linguistics, this work will prove invaluable to all whose studies take them into the realm of ancient language.

Roger D. Woodard is the Andrew Van Vranken Raymond Professor of the Classics at the University of Buffalo. His chief research interests lie generally within the areas of Greek and Roman myth and religion, Indo-European culture and linguistics, the origin and development of writing among the Greeks, and the interaction between Greece and the ancient Near East. His other books include *The Cambridge Companion to Greek Mythology* (2007), *Indo-European Sacred Space* (2006), *The Cambridge Encyclopedia of the World's Ancient Languages* (2004), *Ovid's Fasti* (with A. J. Boyle, 2000), *Greek Writing from Knossos to Homer: A Linguistic Interpretation of the Origins of the Greek Alphabet* (1997), and *On Interpreting Morphological Change* (1990). He has also published numerous articles and served as President of the Society for the Study of Greek and Latin Language and Linguistics from 1992 to 2001.

The Ancient
Languages of Europe

Edited by
ROGER D. WOODARD

CAMBRIDGE
UNIVERSITY PRESS

CAMBRIDGE UNIVERSITY PRESS

Cambridge, New York, Melbourne, Madrid, Cape Town, Singapore, São Paulo,
Delhi, Dubai, Tokyo, Mexico City

Cambridge University Press
The Edinburgh Building, Cambridge CB2 8RU, UK

Published in the United States of America by Cambridge University Press, New York

www.cambridge.org
Information on this title: www.cambridge.org/9780521684958

© Cambridge University Press 2008

This publication is in copyright. Subject to statutory exception
and to the provisions of relevant collective licensing agreements,
no reproduction of any part may take place without
the written permission of Cambridge University Press.

Previously published in 2004 as chapters 17, 24, 25, 32–7 and 39 of Woodard, Roger D.,
The Cambridge Encyclopedia of the World's Ancient Languages
© Cambridge University Press 2004

First published 2008
Reprinted 2010

Printed in the United Kingdom at the University Press, Cambridge

A catalogue record for this publication is available from the British Library

ISBN 978-0-521-68495-8 paperback

Cambridge University Press has no responsibility for the persistence or
accuracy of URLs for external or third-party internet websites referred to
in this publication, and does not guarantee that any content on such
websites is, or will remain, accurate or appropriate.

Contents

Figures

Tables

Maps

Contributors

JAMES P. T. CLACKSON   University of Cambridge

JOSEPH F. ESKA   Virginia Polytechnic Institute and State University

JAN TERJE FAARLUND   Universitetet I Oslo

HENRY M. HOENIGSWALD[†]   University of Pennsylvania

JAY H. JASANOFF   Harvard University

HELMUT RIX   Albert-Ludwigs-Universität Freiburg

REX E. WALLACE   University of Massachusetts at Amherst

ROGER D. WOODARD   University of Buffalo (The State University of New York)

Notes on numbering and cross-referencing

This volume is one of five paperbacks derived from *The Cambridge Encyclopedia of the World's Ancient Languages* (*WAL*), with the content now organized by region for the convenience of students and specialists wishing to focus on a given area of the ancient world.

Cross-references to material within this volume use its own internal chapter numbers. Any cross-references to other chapters of the original *WAL* refer to the chapter numbers in that work, and are prefixed by *WAL*. The contents list of *WAL* is reproduced at the back of this volume, as are the contents of the respective volumes of the paperback series derived from it.

Abbreviations

Any abbreviation that deviates from the form given below is noted within the text of the individual chapter or within a chapter-specific list.

Linguistic terms

abl.	ablative
abs.	absolutive
acc.	accusative
act.	active
adj.	adjective
adv.	adverb (adverbial)
all.	allative
anim.	animate
aor.	aorist
art.	article
asp.	aspirated
aux.	auxiliary (verb)
caus.	causative
cl.	clause
coll.	collective
com.	common
comp.	comparative
comt.	comitative
conj.	conjunction
conjv.	conjunctive
conn.	connective
cons.	consonant
constr.	construct (state)
cont.	continuant
cop.	copula
dat.	dative
def. art.	definite article
dem.	demonstrative
det.	determinate
detv.	determinative
dial.	dialect
dir.	directive
dir. obj.	direct object
disj.	disjunctive
du.	dual
dur.	durative
emph.-pcl.	emphatic particle
encl.	enclitic
eq.	equative
erg.	ergative
ext.	extended
fem.	feminine
final-pcl.	final-particle
fut.	future
gdve.	gerundive
gen.	genitive
ger.	gerund
impf.	imperfect
impftv.	imperfective
impv.	imperative
inan.	inanimate
inc.	inclusive
indef. art.	indefinite article
indet.	indeterminate
indic.	indicative
inf.	infinitive
instr.	instrumental
interr.	interrogative
intr.	intransitive
iter.	iterative
juss.	jussive
loc.	locative
mediopass.	mediopassive
mid.	middle

N.	noun	top.	topicalizer
neg.	negative	tr.	transitive
neut.	neuter	V.	verb
nom.	nominative	var.	variant
NP	noun phrase	vent.	ventive
num.	number	voc.	vocative
obj.	object	vow.	vowel
obl.	oblique	VP	verbal phrase
opt.	optative		
part.	participle	**Languages**	
pass.	passive		
pcl.	particle	Akk.	Akkadian
per.	person	Ar.	Arabic
perf.	perfect	Ass.	Assyrian
perfv.	perfective	Av.	Avestan
perfvz.	perfectivizer	Bab.	Babylonian
pert.	pertinentive	Cis. Gaul.	Cisalpine Gaulish
pl.	plural	Eg.	Egyptian (Old, Late, Earlier)
pluperf.	pluperfect	Eng.	English
poss. suff.	possessive suffix	Etr.	Etruscan
postp.	postposition	Gk.	Greek
PP	prepositional phrase	Gmc.	Germanic
prec.	precative	Go.	Gothic
preC.	preconsonantal	Hisp.-Celt.	Hispano-Celtic
pref.	prefix	Hitt.	Hittite
prep.	preposition	IE	Indo-European
pres.	present	Lat.	Latin
pret.	preterite	Lep.	Lepontic
preV.	prevocalic	Luv.	Luvian
pro.	pronoun	Lyc.	Lycian
prosp.	prospective	MA	Middle Assyrian
quot.	quotative particle	MB	Middle Babylonian
refl.	reflexive	NA	Neo-Assyrian
rel. pro.	relative (pronoun)	NB	Neo-Babylonian
rel./connec.	relative/connective	OA	Old Assyrian
sg.	singular	O. Akk.	Old Akkadian
soc.	sociative case	O. Av.	Old Avestan
SOV	Subject–Object–Verb (word order)	OB	Old Babylonian
		OHG	Old High German
spec.	specifier	OP	Old Persian
splv.	superlative	PG	Proto-Greek
stat.	stative	PGmc.	Proto-Germanic
subj.	subject	PIE	Proto-Indo-European
subjunc.	subjunctive	PIIr.	Proto-Indo-Iranian
subord.	subordinate/subordinator/ subordination marker	PIr.	Proto-Iranian
		PMS	Proto-Mije-Sokean
subord.-pcl.	subordinating particle	PS	Proto-Semitic
suff.	suffix	PSo.	Proto-Sokean
s.v.	*sub voce*	SB	Standard Babylonian

Skt.	Sanskrit	dict.	dictionary
Sum.	Sumerian	intro.	introduction
Y. Av.	Young Avestan	lit.	literally
		NA	not applicable
		NS	new series
Other		trad.	traditional
abbr.	abbreviation	translit.	transliteration

Preface

Preliminary remarks

What makes a language ancient? The term conjures up images, often romantic, of archeologists feverishly copying hieroglyphs by torchlight in a freshly discovered burial chamber; of philologists dangling over a precipice in some remote corner of the earth, taking impressions of an inscription carved in a cliff-face; of a solitary scholar working far into the night, puzzling out some ancient secret, long forgotten by humankind, from a brittle-leafed manuscript or patina-encrusted tablet. The allure is undeniable, and the literary and film worlds have made full use of it.

An ancient language is indeed a thing of wonder – but so is every other language, all remarkable systems of conveying thoughts and ideas across time and space. And ancient languages, as far back as the very earliest attested, operate just like those to which the linguist has more immediate access, all with the same familiar elements – phonological, morphological, syntactic – and no perceptible vestiges of Neanderthal oddities. If there was a time when human language was characterized by features and strategies fundamentally unlike those we presently know, it was a time prior to the development of any attested or reconstructed language of antiquity. Perhaps, then, what makes an ancient language different is our awareness that it has outlived those for whom it was an intimate element of the psyche, not so unlike those rays of light now reaching our eyes that were emitted by their long-extinguished source when dinosaurs still roamed across the earth (or earlier) – both phantasms of energy flying to our senses from distant sources, long gone out.

That being said, and rightly enough, we must return to the question of what counts as an ancient language. As *ancient* the editor chose the upward delimitation of the fifth century AD. This *terminus ante quem* is one which is admittedly "traditional"; the fifth is the century of the fall of the western Roman Empire (AD 476), a benchmark which has been commonly (though certainly not unanimously) identified as marking the end of the historical period of *antiquity*. Any such chronological demarcation is of necessity arbitrary – far too arbitrary – as linguists accustomed to making such diachronic distinctions as *Old English, Middle English, Modern English* or *Old Hittite, Middle Hittite, Neo-Hittite* are keenly aware. Linguistic divisions of this sort are commonly based upon significant political events and clearly perceptible cultural shifts rather than upon language phenomena (though they are surely not without linguistic import as every historical linguist knows). The choice of the boundary in the present concern – the ancient-language boundary – is, likewise (as has already been confessed), not mandated by linguistic features and characteristics of the languages concerned.

However, this arbitrary choice, establishing a *terminus ante quem* of the fifth century, is somewhat buttressed by quite pragmatic linguistic considerations (themselves consequent to the whim of historical accident), namely the co-occurrence of a watershed in language documentation. Several early languages first make a significant appearance in the historical record in the fourth/fifth century: thus, Gothic (fourth century; see Ch. 9), Ge'ez (fourth/fifth century; see *WAL* Ch. 14, §1.3.1), Classical Armenian (fifth century; see *WAL* Ch. 38), Early Old Georgian (fifth century; see *WAL* Ch. 40). What newly comes into clear light in the sixth century is a bit more meager – Tocharian and perhaps the very earliest Old Kannada and Old Telegu from the end of the century. Moreover, the dating of these languages to the sixth century cannot be made precisely (not to suggest this is an especially unusual state of affairs) and it is equally possible that the earliest attestation of all three should be dated to the seventh century. Beginning with the seventh century the pace of language attestation begins to accelerate, with languages documented such as Old English, Old Khmer, and Classical Arabic (though a few earlier inscriptions preserving a "transitional" form of Arabic are known; see *WAL* Ch. 16, §1.1.1). The ensuing centuries bring an avalanche of medieval European languages and their Asian contemporaries into view. Aside from the matter of a culturally dependent analytic scheme of historical periodization, there are thus considerations of language history that motivate the upper boundary of the fifth century.

On the other hand, identifying a *terminus post quem* for the inclusion of a language in the present volume was a completely straightforward and noncontroversial procedure. The low boundary is determined by the appearance of writing in human society, a graphic means for recording human speech. A system of writing appears to have been first developed by the Sumerians of southern Mesopotamia in the late fourth millennium BC (see *WAL* Ch. 2, §§1.2; 2). Not much later (beginning in about 3100 BC), a people of ancient Iran began to record their still undeciphered language of Proto-Elamite on clay tablets (see *WAL* Ch. 3, §2.1). From roughly the same period, the Egyptian hieroglyphic writing system emerges in the historical record (see *WAL* Ch. 7, §2). Hence, Sumerian and Egyptian are the earliest attested, understood languages and, *ipso facto*, the earliest languages treated in this volume.

It is conjectured that humans have been speaking and understanding language for at least 100,000 years. If in the great gulf of time which separates the advent of language and the appearance of Sumerian, Proto-Elamite, and Egyptian societies, there were any people giving written expression to their spoken language, all evidence of such records and the language or languages they record has fallen victim to the decay of time. Or the evidence has at least eluded the archeologists.

Format and conventions

Each chapter, with only the occasional exception, adheres to a common format. The chapter begins with an overview of the history (including prehistory) of the language, at least up to the latest stage of the language treated in the chapter, and of those peoples who spoke the language (§1, HISTORICAL AND CULTURAL CONTEXTS). Then follows a discussion of the development and use of the script(s) in which the language is recorded (§2, WRITING SYSTEMS); note that the complex Mesopotamian cuneiform script, which is utilized for several languages of the ancient Near East – Sumerian (*WAL* Ch. 2), Elamite (*WAL* Ch. 3), Hurrian (*WAL* Ch. 4), Urartian (*WAL* Ch. 5), Akkadian and Eblaite (*WAL* Ch. 8), Hittite (*WAL* Ch. 18), Luvian (*WAL* Ch. 19) – and which provides the inspiration and graphic raw materials for others – Ugaritic (*WAL* Ch. 9) and Old Persian (*WAL* Ch. 28) – is treated in most detail in *WAL* Chapter 8, §2. The next section presents a discussion of phonological elements of the language (§3, PHONOLOGY), identifying consonant and vowel phonemes, and treating matters such as allophonic and morphophonemic variation, syllable structure and phonotaxis, segmental length, accent (pitch and stress), and synchronic and diachronic phonological processes. Following next is discussion of morphological phenomena (§4, MORPHOLOGY), focusing on topics such as word structure, nominal and pronominal categories and systems, the categories and systems of finite verbs and other verbal elements (for explanation of the system of classifying Semitic verb stems – G stem, etc. – see *WAL* Ch. 6, §3.3.5.2), compounds, diachronic morphology, and the system of numerals. Treatment of syntactic matters then follows (§5, SYNTAX), presenting discussion of word order and coordinate and subordinate clause structure, and phenomena such as agreement, cliticism and various other syntactic processes, both synchronic and diachronic. The description of the grammar closes with a consideration of the lexical component (§6, LEXICON); and the chapter comes to an end with a list of references cited in the chapter and of other pertinent works (BIBLIOGRAPHY).

To a great extent, the linguistic presentations in the ensuing chapters have remained faithful to the grammatical conventions of the various language disciplines. From discipline to discipline, the most obvious variation lies in the methods of transcribing sounds. Thus, for example, the symbols ś, ṣ, and ṭ in the traditional orthography of Indic language scholarship represent, respectively, a voiceless palatal (palato-alveolar) fricative, a voiceless retroflex fricative, and a voiceless retroflex stop. In Semitic studies, however, the same symbols are used to denote very different phonetic realities: ś represents a voiceless lateral fricative while ṣ and ṭ transcribe two of the so-called emphatic consonants – the latter a voiceless stop produced with a secondary articulation (velarization, pharyngealization, or glottalization), the former either a voiceless fricative or affricate, also with a secondary articulation. Such conventional symbols are employed herein, but for any given language, the reader can readily determine phonetic values of these symbols by consulting the discussion of consonant and vowel sounds in the relevant phonology section.

Broad phonetic transcription is accomplished by means of a slightly modified form of the International Phonetic Alphabet (IPA). Most notably, the IPA symbols for the palato-alveolar fricatives and affricates, voiceless [ʃ] and [tʃ] and voiced [ʒ] and [dʒ], have been replaced by the more familiar [š], [č], [ž], and [ǰ] respectively. Similarly, [y] is used for the palatal glide rather than [j]. Long vowels are marked by either a macron or a colon.

In the phonology sections, phonemic transcription, in keeping with standard phonological practice, is placed within slashes (e.g., /p/) and phonetic transcription within square brackets (e.g., [p]; note that square brackets are also used to fill out the meaning of a gloss and are employed as an element of the transcription and transliteration conventions for certain languages, such as Elamite [*WAL* Ch. 3] and Pahlavi [*WAL* Ch. 30]). The general treatment adopted in phonological discussions has been to present transcriptions as phonetic rather than phonemic, except in those instances in which explicit reference is made to the phonemic level. Outside of the phonological sections, transcriptions are usually presented using the conventional orthography of the pertinent language discipline. When potential for confusion would seem to exist, transcriptions are enclosed within angled brackets (e.g., <p>) to make clear to the reader that what is being specified is the *spelling* of a word and not its *pronunciation*.

Further acknowledgments

The enthusiastic reception of the first edition of this work – and the broad interest in the ancient languages of humankind that it demonstrates – has been and remains immensely gratifying to both editor and contributors. The editor would like to take this opportunity, on behalf of all the contributors, to express his deepest appreciation to all who have had a hand in the success of the first edition. We wish too to acknowledge our debt of gratitude to Cambridge University Press and to Dr. Kate Brett for continued support of this project and for making possible the publication of this new multivolume edition and the increased accessibility to the work that it will inevitably provide. Thanks also go to the many kind readers who have provided positive and helpful feedback since the publication of the first edition, and to the editors of *CHOICE* for bestowing upon the work the designation of Outstanding Academic Title of 2006.

Roger D. Woodard
Vernal Equinox 2007

Preface to the first edition

In the following pages, the reader will discover what is, in effect, a linguistic description of all known ancient languages. Never before in the history of language study has such a collection appeared within the covers of a single work. This volume brings to student and to scholar convenient, systematic presentations of grammars which, in the best of cases, were heretofore accessible only by consulting multiple sources, and which in all too many instances could only be retrieved from scattered, out-of-the-way, disparate treatments. For some languages, the only existing comprehensive grammatical description is to be found herein.

This work has come to fruition through the efforts and encouragement of many, to all of whom the editor wishes to express his heartfelt gratitude. To attempt to list all – colleagues, students, friends – would, however, certainly result in the unintentional and unhappy neglect of some, and so only a much more modest attempt at acknowledgments will be made. Among those to whom special thanks are due are first and foremost the contributors to this volume, scholars who have devoted their lives to the study of the languages of ancient humanity, without whose expertise and dedication this work would still be only a *desideratum*. Very special thanks also go to Dr. Kate Brett of Cambridge University Press for her professionalism, her wise and expert guidance, and her unending patience, also to her predecessor, Judith Ayling, for permitting me to persuade her of the project's importance. I cannot neglect mentioning my former colleague, Professor Bernard Comrie, now of the Max Planck Institute, for his unflagging friendship and support. Kudos to those who masterfully translated the chapters that were written in languages other than English: Karine Megardoomian for Phrygian, Dr. Margaret Whatmough for Etruscan, Professor John Huehnergard for Ancient South Arabian. Last of all, but not least of all, I wish to thank Katherine and Paul – my inspiration, my joy.

Roger D. Woodard
Christmas Eve 2002

CHAPTER 1

Language in ancient Europe: an introduction

ROGER D. WOODARD

The *Sanscrit* language, whatever be its antiquity, is of a wonderful structure; more perfect than the *Greek*, more copious than the *Latin*, and more exquisitely refined than either, yet bearing to both of them a stronger affinity, both in the roots of verbs and in the forms of grammar, than could possibly have been produced by accident; so strong, indeed, that no philologer could examine them all three, without believing them to have sprung from some common source, which, perhaps, no longer exists: there is a similar reason, though not quite so forcible, for supposing that both the *Gothik* and the *Celtick*, though blended with a very different idiom, had the same origin with the *Sanscrit*; and the old *Persian* might be added to the same family.

Asiatick Researches 1:442–443

In recent years, these words of an English jurist, Sir William Jones, have been frequently quoted (at times in truncated form) in works dealing with Indo-European linguistic origins. And appropriately so. They are words of historic proportion, spoken in Calcutta, 2 February 1786, at a meeting of the Asiatick Society, an organization that Jones had founded soon after his arrival in India in 1783 (on Jones, see, *inter alia*, Edgerton 1967). If Jones was not the first scholar to recognize the genetic relatedness of languages (see, *inter alia*, the discussion in Mallory 1989:9–11) and if history has treated Jones with greater kindness than other pioneers of comparative linguistic investigation, the foundational remarks were *his* that produced sufficient awareness, garnered sufficient attention – sustained or recollected – to mark an identifiable beginning of the study of comparative linguistics and the study of that great language family of which Sanskrit, Greek, Latin, Gothic, Celtic, and Old Persian are members – and are but a few of its members.

All of the chapters that follow are devoted to languages belonging to the Indo-European language family – with one exception: Etruscan. This is not by editorial design, but by historical accident. Many of these are languages whose speakers clustered at points along the northern rim of the central Mediterranean basin. Over half are languages spoken wholly or partially within the space of the Italian Peninsula.

There were languages spoken in Europe prior to the expansion of the Indo-European peoples across the European continent – an event that unfolded over a period of millennia, likely having its inception in about the middle of the fifth millennium BC. For the most part, evidence of those "Old European" languages survives only as shadows cast across the grammars and lexica of the Indo-European languages: they were simply spoken too early in Europe's history to have had the opportunity to achieve a written form that would survive in the historical record.

The earliest documented Indo-European languages of Europe were those that had the good fortune to be spoken in a time after the advent of writing systems suitable for their recording and in places in which those writing systems were created – or to which their

1

Figure 1.1 Cretan hieroglyphic inscription and portrait stamped on a sealing

use expanded – and to be written on materials that escaped decay within the natural environment in which they were produced and deposited. For most – though not all – of the Indo-European languages of Europe, a single writing system provided the key – directly or indirectly, immediately or through some evolutionary chain – to epigraphic survival. That writing system was not, however, the "Indo-Europeans' gift to Europe." It was, on the contrary, the adaptation by one particular Indo-European people of a pre-existing writing system of southwest Asia, whose roots can be traced now with some certainty to Egypt (see the Introduction to the companion volume entitled *The Ancient Languages of Syria-Palestine and Arabia*). That writing system was, of course, the Greek alphabet (see Ch. 2, §2).

And what of the residue – i.e. those languages of ancient Europe that have been preserved using something other than alphabetic writing? The Greeks – the very designers of the "alphabet" – had prior to the time of its creation, during the Mycenaean era, recorded their language on clay tablets using the *syllabic* script that Sir Arthur Evans, the distinguished British archeologist (1851–1941), dubbed *Linear B*; and among the Greeks of Cyprus, a related script – the *Cypriot syllabary* – remained in use long after the creation of the alphabet. Aside from these varieties of Greek, the languages of Europe that were written with a non-alphabetic script are at the present time poorly understood – if at all. The inverse corollary holds only in part, for some of the ancient languages of Europe, though indeed written in a script based upon the Greek alphabet – sometimes only slightly modified – remain undeciphered.

The Linear B syllabary of the Mycenaean Greeks was almost certainly based on the Cretan script that Evans called *Linear A* (see more on this below) – a still undeciphered writing system. In fact, three different undeciphered scripts have survived in the remains of the pre-Greek, Minoan civilization (as also named by Evans) of ancient Crete. The oldest of these is called *Cretan Hieroglyphic* or *Cretan Pictographic* (see Fig. 1.1) and its use is dated to the period 2000–1600 BC, seal stones providing the bulk of examples. The pictographic symbols making up the script probably have a syllabic value.

The second of the undeciphered Cretan scripts is known from only a single document, the *Phaistos Disk* (dated to about 1700 BC; see Fig. 1.2). The disk has been the object of repeated attempts at decipherment since its discovery in the early twentieth century. While success has often been claimed, none of the proposed decipherments carries conviction.

Linear A, the third of the Minoan scripts, is the best represented of the three. Dating from about the mid nineteenth to mid fifteenth centuries BC, Linear A documents partially overlap chronologically with those written in Cretan Hieroglyphic, though in terms of historical development, the former may trace its origins to the latter. Linear A, in turn,

Figure 1.2 The Phaistos Disk (side A)

appears to be the source of the Mycenaean Greek script, Linear B (see Ch. 3, §§1.1; 1.2; 2.1), though a simple direct linear descent is not probable. Of the three Minoan scripts, Linear A holds the greatest hope for decipherment. Recent work by Brown (1990) and Finkelberg (1990–1991) has taken up a notion proposed by Palmer in the middle of the twentieth century (e.g., Palmer 1968) which would identify the Linear A language as a member of the Anatolian subfamily of Indo-European. On the Cretan scripts see, *inter alia*, Chadwick 1990; Palaima 1988; Woodard 1997.

Mention should also be made of the undeciphered language called *Eteo-Cretan*. Much later than the three Bronze Age Minoan scripts, Eteo-Cretan is preserved in inscriptions written in the Greek alphabet. On Eteo-Cretan, see Duhoux 1982.

Prior to the emergence of Greek writing on Cyprus, attested by about the middle of the eleventh century BC (and the somewhat later appearance of Phoenician; see *WAL* Ch. 11, §1.2; Ch. 2, §2), the island was inhabited by a people, or by groups of people, who were recording their speech in the undeciphered set of scripts called *Cypro-Minoan* (see Table 1.1). As the name suggests, these Cypriot writing systems appear to have their origin in a writing system of Minoan Crete, Linear A being the likely candidate. *Archaic Cypro-Minoan* is the name given to the script found on only a single inscription, dated to about 1500 BC. This script has been analyzed as the likely ancestor of the more widely attested *Cypro-Minoan 1*, found in use between approximately the late sixteenth and twelfth centuries BC. A distinct script, *Cypro-Minoan 2*, has been found on thirteenth-century documents from the site of Enkomi. Yet a third, *Cypro-Minoan 3*, dating also to the thirteenth century BC, has turned up not on Cyprus but in the remains of the ancient Syrian city of Ugarit (see *WAL* Ch. 9, §1; on the Cypro-Minoan scripts, see especially E. Masson 1974, 1977; Palaima 1989). Cypro-Minoan remains undeciphered.

Table 1.1	A partial inventory of Cypro-Minoan characters				
I	⊢	∧	⟦	⊟	⋇
⊢	⋎	⋀	⫴	⊟	⋈
+	‖	A	⫫	□	
‡	M	⟰	∨	⊶	
⊥	⊨	⟨	⊔	⊓	
⌀	⊿	∧	⌣	⋀⊤	
/	⊾	⋏	H	∧⊦	
∧	⊤	⋀	⊟	⊬⊦	
⋏	⊦	⫿	⊟	⋇	

Cypro-Minoan 1 appears to have provided the graphic model for the Greek syllabary of Cyprus (see Ch. 3, §2.2). This Greek syllabic script was in turn not only used for writing Greek but also adopted for some other language of Cyprus, as yet undeciphered, dubbed *Eteo-Cypriot*. The Eteo-Cypriot inscriptions are commonly regarded as the documentary remains of an indigenous people of Cyprus who had withstood assimilation to the communities of Greek and Phoenician settlers. After Greek and Phoenician settlement of Cyprus, Eteo-Cypriots appear to have concentrated particularly in the area of Amathus (on the Eteo-Cypriot inscriptions, see O. Masson 1983:85–87).

From Portugal and Spain come ancient inscriptions recorded in those scripts called *Iberian*, broadly divided into two groups, Northeast and South Iberian. The latter group includes the variety of the script called *Turdetan*, after the ancient Turdetanians, of whom the Greek geographer Strabo wrote: "These are counted the wisest people among the Iberians; they write with an alphabet and possess prose works and poetry of ancient heritage, and laws composed in meter, six thousand years old, so they say" (*Geography* 3.1.6). One form of the Northeast Iberian writing system was adopted by speakers of Celtic for recording their own language (*Hispano-Celtic* or *Celtiberian*; see Ch. 8, especially §2.1), and these Celtic documents are interpretable (for the language, see Ch. 8, especially §§3.1; 3.4; 4.2.1.1; 4.3.6; 5.1). However, the Iberian scripts were used principally for a language or languages which are not understood, in spite of the fact that there also occur Iberian-language (*Old Hispanic*) inscriptions written with the Greek and Roman alphabets, and even bilingual texts. On the Iberian scripts and language(s) see, *inter alia*, Untermann 1975, 1980, 1990, 1997; Swiggers 1996; Diringer 1968:193–195.

While the South Picene language of eastern coastal Italy appears to be demonstrably Indo-European (belonging to the Sabellian branch of Italic; see Ch. 5), the genetic affiliation of its meagerly attested northern neighbor, North Picene, remains uncertain (though the two were formerly lumped together under the name *East Italic* or *Old Sabellian*). Though completely readable (being written in an Etruscan-based alphabet), North Picene remains largely impenetrable, in spite of the fact that a Latin – North Picene bilingual exists (a brief inscription, the identity of the non-Latin portion of which has been disputed). For an examination toward a tentative translation of the long North Picene inscription, the *Novilara Stele*, see Poultney 1979 (providing a summary of earlier attempts at interpretation).

The documentation of Insular Celtic – the Celtic languages of Ireland and Britain – (as opposed to Continental Celtic; see Ch. 8) which has survived from antiquity is very meager indeed, and is limited to Irish. The script used in recording this early Irish is the unusual alphabetic system called Ogham (see Table 1.2); most of its characters consist of slashing

Table 1.2 Irish Ogham (Craobh-Ruadh); font courtesy of Michael Everson					
Symbol	Transcription	Name	Symbol	Transcription	Name
⊤	b	beithe	⊥	h	úath
⊤⊤	l	luis	⊥⊥	d	dair
⊤⊤⊤	f	fern	⊥⊥⊥	t	tinne
⊤⊤⊤⊤	s	sail	⊥⊥⊥⊥	c	coll
⊤⊤⊤⊤⊤	n	nin	⊥⊥⊥⊥⊥	q	ceirt
+	m	muin	•+	a	ailm
++	g	gort	••+	o	onn
+++	ng	gétal	•••+	u	úr
++++	z	straif	••••+	e	edad
+++++	r	ruis	•••••+	i	idad
✳	ea	ébad	◇	oi	ór
✳✳	ia	iphín	⌂	ui	uilen
▦	ae	emancholl			

lines, longer and shorter (notches being used at times for vowel characters), giving the impression that it was originally designed to be "written" by means of an ax or some similar sharp instrument, with wood serving as a medium. The Ogham inscriptions, which date as early as the fourth century AD (and perhaps as early as the second century), can be read (owing to our knowledge of later Irish) but consist largely of personal names and provide little data on which can be constructed a linguistic description of Ogham Irish. For such descriptions of Insular Celtic, the linguist must await the appearance of Old Irish and Old Welsh manuscripts in about the eighth century AD (and hence Ogham Irish is not treated in the present volume).

There is, however, a second ancient language of Britain which is written with a variety of Ogham, the language of *Pictish*. The Picts, who receive their name from Latin *Picti* "painted ones" (presumably referring to the practice of tattooing, though other etymologies have been proposed), inhabited portions of modern Scotland, along with the Scots, a Celtic people of Irish origin. A much broader, earlier distribution of the Picts has also been claimed. The Picts are known for their production of stone monuments on which are engraved intriguing images of animals and other designs, at times accompanied by Ogham inscriptions. The language of the Pictish Ogham inscriptions is not understood; it is not Celtic and probably not Indo-European. On the Pictish language, see Jackson 1980; for Ogham generally, see McMannus 1991.

In addition to the above enumerated poorly understood ancient languages of Europe (non-Greek Cretan and Cypriot languages, Iberian, North Picene, and Pictish), several other European languages are attested that are somewhat better known, though too meagerly so, it was judged, to be assigned individual chapters in this volume of grammatical descriptions. Brief discussion of these – many of which were spoken in or near Italy – now follows.

1. SICEL

From Sicily come several inscriptions written in a language which appears to be Indo-European; a number of glosses are claimed as well (see Conway, Whatmough, and Johnson

1933 II:449–458; on Sicel generally, see Pulgram 1978:71–73 with references). The name assigned to the language, Sicel or Siculan, is that given by Greek colonists to the native peoples of Sicily whom they there encountered in the eighth century BC. Little is known about the ethnicity of these Siceli. The form *esti* occurs in Sicel, seemingly the archetypal Indo-European "(s)he is." Interpretations of other inscriptional forms show considerable variation. Tradition held that the Siceli had migrated to Sicily from the Italian peninsula: thus, Varro (*On the Latin Language* 5.101) writes that they came from Rome; Diodorus Siculus (*Library of History* 5.6.3–4) records that the Siceli had come from Italy and settled in the region of Sicily formerly occupied by a people called the Sicani. On the basis of the available linguistic evidence, however, Sicel cannot be demonstrated to be a member of the Italic subfamily of Indo-European (see Ch. 4, §1).

On the inscriptional fragments from western Sicily identified as *Elymian*, see Cowgill and Mayrhofer 1986:58 with references.

2. RAETIC AND LEMNIAN

From the eastern Alps, homeland of the tribes called Raeti by the Romans, come a very few inscriptions in a language which has been claimed to bear certain Indo-European characteristics. For example, from an inscription carved on a bronze pot (the Caslir Situla; see Fig. 1.3) comes the Raetic form *-talina* which has been compared to Latin *tollo* "I raise"

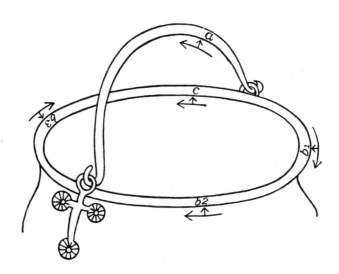

a **lavisešeli**

b 1, 2 **velχanu | lup·nu pitiave |**

  3 **kusenkustrinaχe**

c **φelna vinutalina.**

Figure 1.3 The Caslir Situla

(see Pulgram 1978:40 with additional references). However, similarities to Etruscan have also been identified and the two are perhaps to be placed in a single language family, along with a language attested on the island of Lemnos in the north of the Aegean Sea. Lemnian is known principally from a single inscribed stele bearing the engraved image of a warrior, dated to the sixth century BC. On these connections, see Chapter 7, §1.

Of the Raeti, the Roman historian Livy (*History* 5.33.11) writes, following upon his discussion of the Etruscans: "Undoubtedly the Alpine tribes also have the same origin, particularly the Raeti, who have been made wild by the very place where they live, preserving nothing of their ancient ways except their language – and not even it without corruptions."

3. LIGURIAN

The Ligurians were an ancient people of northwestern Italy. Writing in the second century BC, the Greek historian Polybius (*Histories* 2.16.1–2) situates the Ligurians on the slopes of the Apennines, extending from the Alpine junction above Marseilles around to Pisa on the seaward slopes and to Arezzo on the inland side. Another Greek, Diodorus Siculus (*Library of History* 5.39.1–8), writes of the Ligurians eking out a life of hardship in their heavily forested, rock-strewn, snow-covered homeland and of the extraordinary stamina and strength which this lifestyle engendered in both men and women.

The Ligurian language appears to be attested in certain place names and glosses, some of which have been assigned Indo-European etymologies. For example, Pliny the Elder, a Roman author of the first century AD, in describing the grain called *secale* in Latin, noted that its Ligurian name (the name among the Taurini) is *asia* (*Natural History* 18.141). If the Ligurian form was once *sasia* (see Conway, Whatmough, and Johnson 1933 II:158), then, it has been proposed, the word may find relatives in Celtic – Welsh *haidd* and Breton *heiz* "barley." The location of its speakers, abutting Celtic areas (and Strabo writes of Celtoligurians; *Geography* 4.6.3), might itself be taken to suggest an affiliation with the Indo-European family, but such a relationship cannot be confirmed by the available linguistic evidence.

4. ILLYRIAN

The historical peoples called Illyrian occupied a broad area of the northwest Balkans. Evidence for an Indo-European intrusion into the region can be identified by the late third millennium BC; an identifiable "Illyrian" culture appears only in the Iron Age (see, *inter alia*, Wilkes 1992:28–66). By the first century AD, the Greek geographer Strabo, in describing that part of Europe south of the Ister (the Danube), can identify as Illyrian those people inhabiting the region bounded on the east by the meandering Ister, on the west by the Adriatic Sea, and lying above ancient Epirus (*Geography* 7.5.1). For the Romans, the province of *Illyricum* denotes a rather larger administrative area. The term "Illyrian" can, however, be used by classical authors to designate a variety of peoples in and beyond the Balkans (see the discussion in Katičić 1976:156–163).

Within the northwestern Balkan region itself there was considerable cultural diversity, with not only the so-called Illyrian tribes being present, but Celts as well, by at least the third century BC. Strabo writes of the Iapodes dwelling near Mount Ocra (close to the border of modern Slovenia and Croatia) whom he calls a mixed Celtic and Illyrian tribe (*Geography* 4.6.10) and who, he adds, use Celtic armor but are tattooed like the Illyrians and Thracians

(*Geography* 7.5.4; on the Thracians see below). In his account of the wars which various Illyrian tribes waged against one another and against the Romans, the Greek historian and Roman citizen, Appian of Alexandria, writing in the second century AD, preserves a tradition in which one hears echoes of such Balkan ethnic diversity. Appian (*Roman History* 10.2) records that the Illyrians received their name from Illyrius, a son of Polyphemus (the cyclops of Homer's *Odyssey*) and the nymph Galatea, and that Illyrius has two brothers, Celtus and Galas, namesakes of the Celts and the Galatae (the latter commonly being synonymous with "Celt" and perhaps used here to invoke descent from Galatea).

The Illyrian language presents an unusual case. While the Illyrians are a well-documented people of antiquity, not a single verifiable inscription has survived written in the Illyrian language (on two proposed Illyrian inscriptions, one demonstrably Byzantine Greek, see Katičić 1976:169–170). Even so, much linguistic attention (perhaps a disproportionately large amount) has been paid to the language of the Illyrians. Chiefly on the basis of Illyrian place and personal names, the language is commonly identified as Indo-European. To provide but two examples, the frequently attested name *Vescleves* has been etymologized as a reflex of Proto-Indo-European *wesu-ḱlewes* ("good fame"), with Sanskrit *Vasuśravas* being drawn into the analysis; the place name *Birziminium*, interpreted as meaning "hillock," has been traced to the Proto-Indo-European root *$b^h erĝ^h$-*, source of, *inter alia*, Germanic forms such as Old English *beorg* "hill" (see Katičić 1976:172–176 for discussion). This onomastic evidence is supplemented by the survival of just a very few glosses of Illyrian words; for example, the Illyrian word for "mist" is cited as *rhinos* (ῥινός) in one of the scholia on Homer; see Katičić 1976:170–171, who compares Albanian *re*, earlier *ren*, "cloud." Extensive study of Illyrian was undertaken by Hans Krahe in the middle decades of the twentieth century, who, along with other scholars, argued for a broad distribution of Illyrian peoples considerably beyond the Balkans (see, for example, Krahe 1940); though in his later work, Krahe curbed his view of the extent of Illyrian settlement (see, for example, Krahe 1955). Radoslav Katičić (1976:179–180) has argued, on the basis of a careful study of the onomastic evidence, that the core onomastic area of Illyrian proper is to be located in the southeast of that Balkan region traditionally associated with the Illyrians (centered in modern Albania).

The modern Albanian language, it has been conjectured, is descended directly from ancient Illyrian. Albanian is not attested until the fifteenth century AD and in its historical development has been influenced heavily by Latin, Greek, Turkish, and Slavic languages, so much so that it was quite late in being identified as an Indo-European language. Its possible affiliation with the scantily attested Illyrian, though not unreasonable on historical and linguistic grounds, can be considered little more than conjecture barring the discovery of additional Illyrian evidence.

5. THRACIAN

At the northern end of the Aegean Sea, stretching upward to the Danube, lived in antiquity people speaking the Indo-European language of Thracian. The ancestors of the Iron Age Thracians had probably arrived in the Balkans as a part of the movement which brought the forebears of the Illyrians. For the Greeks, Thrace was a place wild and uncultivated, home to both savage Ares and Dionysus, god of wine who inspired frenzy and brutality in his worshipers. Herodotus (*Histories* 5.3; 9.119) writes of the Thracian practices of human sacrifice and widow immolation, and of the enormous population of the Thracians (second only to the Indians) and their lack of political unity. Were they unified, surmises the historian, they would be the most powerful people on the face of the earth.

Though the Thracian language is not well preserved, its attestation, unlike that of Illyrian, is sufficient to place its membership in the Indo-European family practically beyond doubt. A few short Thracian inscriptions survive (see Brixhe and Panayotou 1994a:185–188), but more valuable are the numerous glosses (e.g., *bólinthos* "European bison," cf. Old Norse *boli* "bull"; *brûtos* "beer," cf. Old English *breowan* "to brew") coupled with the evidence of place and personal names. For a summary of the evidence see Katičić 1976:138–142; Brixhe and Panayotou 1994a:188–189; see also Cowgill and Mayrhofer 1986:54–55, with references. Onomastic evidence may suggest the occurrence of a language boundary within the Thracian area, demarcated by Mount Haemus. South of this boundary the language evidenced has been distinguished as Thracian, while that to the north has been called Daco-Mysian.

According to Greek tradition, the Phrygians of Anatolia had migrated from the Balkans (see Herodotus, *Histories* 7.73, who writes that the Phrygians were formerly called the Briges and had been neighbors of the Macedonians; on the Macedonians see below), a view with which modern scholarship is generally in agreement. The Phrygian language does show certain similarities to Thracian, and some linguists have argued for linking the two in a single linguistic unit (Thraco-Phrygian). The appropriateness of the subgrouping is, however, uncertain; see *WAL* Chapter 31, §1.5.

6. MACEDONIAN

North of the Greeks, bracketed by Illyrians and Thracians, lived the Macedonians. Much uncertainty surrounds the linguistic status of the Macedonian peoples. Though, under the patronage of Macedonian kings, Philip the Second and his son Alexander the Great, Greek culture would be spread across the Mediterranean and Near Eastern world and the Greek language would become a lingua franca (the Attic-based Koine dialect; see Ch. 2, §1) spoken from Italy to India, it remains unclear if Greek was the native language of the Macedonians (see Brixhe and Panayotou 1994b:206–207 for a synopsis of ideas about the identity of Macedonian).

To be sure, the Greek orator Demosthenes, in the fourth century BC, can revile and lambaste Philip as one of the *barbaroi* ("barbarians," those who do not speak Greek, i.e., those who *babble*; *Orations* 3.17) and rehearse how in the old days the Macedonian king had been rightly subject to the Greeks, as *barbaroi* should be (*Orations* 3.24). He can skewer Philip with the charge that, not only is he not a Greek and unrelated to the Greeks, he is not even a *barbaros* from some worthwhile place, but he is a plague out of Macedonia – a place from which you cannot even acquire a good slave (*Orations* 9.31). A century earlier, Herodotus had told the story of an ancestor of Philip, Alexander the First (a contemporary of Herodotus), who had been allowed to compete in games at Olympia – though *barbaroi* were excluded from the competition – because he was able to demonstrate satisfactorily that he himself was descended from a Greek banished from Argos (*Histories* 5.22; 8.137–139).

Explicit references to "Macedonian speech" exist. Plutarch, the Greek savant of the first and second centuries AD, when writing of Cleopatra (*Life of Antony* 27.3–4), the last of the Ptolemies (the Macedonian kings of Egypt), lauds her linguistic abilities, reporting that she could speak the languages of the Ethiopians, Troglodytes, Hebrews, Arabs, Syrians, Medes, and Parthians. In contrast, her male predecessors had not even learned Egyptian and some had even "ceased to speak Macedonian" (μακεδονίζειν ἐκλιπόντων). Presumably they had continued to speak Greek (i.e., had not taken a vow of silence). Athenaeus, a Greek writer of the later second century AD, in his account of a "Learned Banquet" (*Deipnosophistae*

3.121f–122a), places on the lips of one of the guests, the cynic Cynulcus, a Latin word *decocta* (a kind of drink made by boiling and then rapidly cooling a liquid); in turn, Athenaeus has another guest, Ulpian (an "Atticist," promoting the use of untainted Attic Greek), rebuke Cynulcus for uttering a barbarism (!). Cynulcus fires back, retorting that even in the best old Greek one finds Persian loanwords and that he knows many Attic Greeks "using Macedonian speech" (μακεδονίζοντας; a participle from Plutarch's verb). Elsewhere, Plutarch uses an adverb *makedonistí* (μακεδονιστί) having the same sense. For example, in his *Life of Alexander* (51.4), Plutarch recounts how the Macedonian conqueror, in a fit of rage, refusing to be quieted by his body guards, shouted out for the *hypaspistai* (Macedonian infantry troops, one contingent of the army of Alexander), "calling *in Macedonian* – and this was a sign of a great disturbance." The precise sense of "speaking Macedonian" in these and other passages can be and has been debated; yet when these references to Macedonian speech are considered in their context, it is not difficult for one to conclude that what is being reported is the use of a distinct, non-Greek ("barbarian") Macedonian language.

In contrast, however, other classical authors explicitly identify the Macedonians as a Greek people. Polybius, the Greek historian of the second century BC, for example, describes Macedonians and Greeks as being *homophylos* (ὁμόφυλος), "of the same race" or "akin" (*Histories* 9.37.7). For references to other, similar texts, see Katičić 1976:107–108.

An interesting case is provided by an instance in which Macedonians identify themselves as Greeks and speakers of Greek. The Roman historian Livy (first centuries BC and AD), writing of events in the war waged by Philip the Fifth of Macedon and his Arcarnanian Greek allies against Athens, with Rome as its own ally, records a meeting of the council of the Aetolian Confederacy, at which representatives from Philip, from Athens and from Rome address the council, each seeking Aetolian assistance in the war (200 BC). In his speech to the council, the Macedonian ambassador refers to the Romans as "a foreign people set apart more by *language* and customs and laws than by the space of sea and land" (31.29.12). In contrast, "Aetolians, Acarnanians and Macedonians [are] people of the *same language*... [and] with foreigners, with barbarians *all Greeks* are, and will be, at eternal war" (31.29.15). The dialect of the Aetolian Confederacy, a league of the Aetolians of northwest Greece, was the Northwest Greek Koine, a "common" dialect used throughout regions controlled by the Confederacy (see Ch. 3, §1.1.5). Is it this lingua franca to which Livy has his Macedonian diplomat self-servingly refer? One could well imagine that it would be the Macedonian's *langue de choix* on such an occasion. The Acarnanians also inhabited northwest Greece, though Acarnanian inscriptions from this period are written in the Doric Koine, only slightly different from the Aetolian dialect.

Surviving Macedonian texts have not proved helpful in identifying the native language of the Macedonians. Most of the Macedonian inscriptions are written in Attic Greek, the dialect broadly disseminated by Philip and Alexander. A fourth-century BC inscription found recently in the remains of the great Macedonian city of Pella appears to be written in a variety of Northwest Greek and has led to conjectures that this may be the previously unattested Macedonian language (see the comments of Brixhe and Panayotou 1994b:209 along with the mention of other finds in n.19).

The evidence provided by Macedonian glosses is conveniently summarized by Katičić (1976:108–112), who analyzes these as belonging to three different classes. One class consists of words that are quite close to known Greek lexemes, some, though probably not all, of which appear likely to be loanwords directly from Greek: for example, *kommárai*; compare Greek *kámmaroi* (κάμμαροι), a type of lobster (pl.). A second set is made up of Macedonian words which have no Greek counterparts, such as *alíē* "boar." The third group is similar to the first to the extent that it consists of Macedonian words apparently having Greek counterparts;

it differs from the first class, however, in that these Macedonian words are perhaps to be analyzed as cognates of the Greek lexemes, rather than borrowings. In other words, by such an analysis, the related Macedonian and Greek forms have evolved historically from words occurring in a common parent language, either Proto-Indo-European or, alternatively, some later, intermediate Balkan Indo-European language. Compare, for example, Macedonian *adê* "sky" and Greek *ait^{h}ḗr* (αἰθήρ); Macedonian *kebalá* "head" (cf. *gabalá* which the Greek lexicographer Hesychius also glosses as "head," without identifying the linguistic source of the word) and Greek *kep^{h}alḗ* (κεφαλή). If such sets are rightly analyzed as cognates, the Macedonian language departs conspicuously from Greek in showing voiced unaspirated rather than voiceless aspirated reflexes of the earlier Indo-European voiced aspirated stops (on the Greek development, see Ch. 2, §3.7.1).

7. MESSAPIC

The Messapii were a people of southeast Italy, inhabiting ancient Calabria (the Sallentine peninsula, the "heel" of the Italian "boot"). Strabo, the Greek geographer, records (*Geography* 6.3.1) that the Greeks give the name *Messapia* to that region, also called *Iapygia*, but adds that the locals of the area make a distinction between the Salentini (in the south) and the Calabri. Northward lies the country of the Peucetii and of the Daunuii (Apulia). For Polybius (*Histories* 3.88.4), however, Iapygia is the region inhabited by the Daunuii, Peucetii, and Messapii (though elsewhere he writes of "Iapyges and Messapii"; see *Histories* 2.24.11).

Messapic survives in a large number of inscriptions, recording chiefly proper names, dating from about the sixth to the first century BC (the most abundantly attested ancient language not to receive individual treatment in this volume), including many recent finds from a grotto in Lecce (see Santoro 1983–1984). This language of ancient Italy is Indo-European, but not Italic; that is, it is not a member of the subfamily to which belong Latin and Sabellian (see Chs. 4 and 5). No close genetic affiliation with any other known Indo-European language can be definitively demonstrated, though a close connection to Illyrian has been alleged. Indeed, the Messapic materials provided a major component of the evidence adduced by Krahe and others for the study of Illyrian. There do exist ancient traditions about the settling of southeast Italy by Illyrian peoples. For example, Pliny (*Natural History* 3.102) makes cursory reference to the story that the "Paediculi" of Apulia were descended from nine young men and nine young women of Illyria. A linking of the two languages, Illyrian and Messapic, must, however, remain a linguistically unverifiable hypothesis until such time as Illyrian is better attested.

In the above discussion of Macedonian vis-à-vis Greek, reference was made to *cognates* and to historical *evolution* of *attested* languages from earlier, *unattested*, parent languages. The realization that certain languages share an ancestry – that they are "sprung from some common source, which, perhaps, no longer exists" – was the fundamental genius of William Jones' remarks made to the Asiatick Society that February day in Calcutta. Cognates – individual linguistic structures (words, and structures smaller than words) having a common origin in an ancestral language – are not, of course, limited to Sanskrit, Latin, Greek, Celtic, and Gothic – the languages named by Jones in those lines with which this Introduction began.

Save Sanskrit, all of these languages – Latin, Greek, Celtic, Gothic – are treated in this volume (see Chs. 4, 2–3, 8, and 9, respectively), along with yet other languages belonging to the same language family – languages sprung from the same common source – namely, Faliscan (see Ch. 4), numerous Sabellian languages (the non-Latino-Faliscan Italic languages;

see Ch. 5), Venetic (see Ch. 6), and the language of the archaic runic inscriptions of northern Europe (see Ch. 10). Other ancient Indo-European languages – not only Sanskrit, but also Middle Indic, Hittite and other Anatolian languages, Old Persian, Avestan, Pahlavi, Phrygian, and Armenian – will be found in companion volumes. On the basis of a careful comparison of these, and still other Indo-European languages (first attested at a moment too recent in time for inclusion in these volumes), the parent language envisioned by Jones – Proto-Indo-European – has been, and continues to be, reconstructed. At the end of this volume, the reader will find an Appendix on Reconstructed Indo-European, setting out a treatment of the phonology, morphology, and syntax of this deeply archaic language – ancestor of all Indo-European languages. The remarkable method that allows such reconstruction – the comparative method of historical linguistics – which took shape in the nineteenth and twentieth centuries in the wake of Jones' observations, is described in the opening section of that Appendix and is treated more broadly and in more detail in the Appendix on "Reconstructed ancient languages" that appears at the end of the companion volume entitled *The Ancient Languages of Asia and the Americas.*

Bibliography

Bader, F. (ed.). 1994. *Langues indo-européennes.* Paris: CNRS Editions.

Brixhe, C. and A. Panayotou. 1994a. "Le thrace." In Bader 1994, pp. 179–203.

———. 1994b. "Le macédonien." In Bader 1994, pp. 205–220.

Brown, E. 1990. "Traces of Luwian dialect in Cretan text and toponym." *Studi micenei ed egeo-anatolici,* pp. 225–237.

Chadwick, J. 1990. "Linear B and related scripts." In *Reading the Past,* pp. 137–195. Introduction by J. Hooker. Los Angeles/Berkeley: University of California Press; London: British Museum.

Conway, R., J. Whatmough, and S. Johnson. 1933. *The Prae-Italic Dialects of Italy* (3 vols.). Cambridge, MA: Harvard University Press.

Cowgill, W. and M. Mayrhofer. 1986. *Indogermanische Grammatik,* vol. I. Heidelberg: Carl Winter.

Daniels, P. and W. Bright (eds.). 1996. *The World's Writing Systems.* Oxford: Oxford University Press.

Diringer, D. 1968. *The Alphabet: A Key to the History of Mankind,* vol. I. New York: Funk and Wagnalls.

Duhoux, E. 1982. *L'Etéocrétois.* Amsterdam: Gieben.

Edgerton, F. 1967. "Sir William Jones." In T. Sebeok (ed.), *Portraits of Linguists,* pp. 1–18. Bloomington: Indiana University Press.

Finkelberg, M. 1990–1991. "Minoan inscriptions on libation vessels." *Minos* 25–26:43–85.

Jackson, K. 1980. "The Pictish language." In F. Wainwright (ed.), *The Problem of the Picts,* pp. 129–160. Perth: Melven.

Katičić, R. 1976. *Ancient Languages of the Balkans,* part 1. The Hague: Mouton.

Krahe, H. 1940. "Der Anteil der Illyrier an der Indogermanisierung Europas." *Die Welt als Geschichte* 6:54–73.

———. 1955. *Die Sprache der Illyrier* (2 vols.). Wiesbaden: Otto Harrassowitz.

Mallory, J. 1989. *In Search of the Indo-Europeans.* London: Thames and Hudson.

Masson, E. 1974. *Cyprominoica.* Göteborg: Paul Åströms Forlag.

———. 1977. "Présence éventuelle de la langue hourrite sur les tablettes chypro-minoennes d'Enkomi." *Revue Roumaine de Linguistique* 22:483–488.

Masson, O. 1983. *Les inscriptions chypriotes syllabiques.* Paris: Édition E. de Boccard.

McMannus, D. 1991. *A Guide to Ogam.* Maynooth: An Sagart.

Palaima, T. 1988. "The development of the Mycenaean writing system." In J. Olivier and T. Palaima (eds.), *Texts, Tablets and Scribes,* pp. 269–342. Supplement to *Minos* 10.

———. 1989. "Cypro-Minoan scripts: Problems of historical context." In Y. Duhoux, T. Palaima, and J. Bennet (eds.), *Problems in Decipherment,* pp. 121–187. Louvain-la-Neuve: Peeters.

Palmer, L. 1968. "Linear A and the Anatolian languages." In *Atti e memorie del 1° congresso internazionale di micenologia,* vol. I, pp. 339–354. Rome: Edizioni dell'Ateneo.

Poultney, J. 1979. "The language of the Northern Picene inscriptions." *Journal of Indo-European Studies* 7:49–64.

Pulgram, E. 1978. *Italic, Latin, Italian.* Heidelberg: Carl Winter.

Santoro, C. 1983–1984. *Nuovi studi messapaci.* Galatina, Italy: Congedo.

Swiggers, P. 1996. "The Iberian Scripts." In Daniels and Bright 1996, pp. 108–112.

Untermann, J. 1975. *Monumenta Linguarum Hispanicarum* i, *Die Münzlegenden.* Wiesbaden: Dr. Ludwig Reichert.

———. 1980. *Monumenta Linguarum Hispanicarum* ii, *Die Inschriften iberischer Schrift aus Südfrankreich.* Wiesbaden: Dr. Ludwig Reichert.

———. 1990. *Monumenta Linguarum Hispanicarum* iii, *Die iberischen Inschriften aus Spanien.* Wiesbaden: Dr. Ludwig Reichert.

———. 1997. *Monumenta Linguarum Hispanicarum* iv, *Die tartessischen, keltiberischen und lusitanischen Inschriften.* Wiesbaden: Dr. Ludwig Reichert.

Wilkes, J. 1992. *The Illyrians.* Oxford: Blackwell.

Woodard, R. 1997. "Linguistic connections between Greeks and non-Greeks." In J. Coleman and C. Walz (eds.), *Greeks and Barbarians*, pp. 29–60. Bethesda, MD: CDL Press.

CHAPTER 2

Attic Greek

ROGER D. WOODARD

1. HISTORICAL AND CULTURAL CONTEXTS

Though in this introductory section, and at certain other points as well, attention is given to the ancient Greek language as a whole, the central topic of this chapter will be that dialect called Attic, the spoken dialect of the region of Attica and the principal written dialect of Classical Greek literature. The many other dialects of Greek attested in antiquity will properly be the focus of Chapter 3.

Greek is a member of the Indo-European family of languages. It resides in that major subdivision of the family called centum (see Appendix), though its closest linguistic affinities are with the Indo-Iranian and Armenian languages, both members of the satem subset. The arrival in the Balkan peninsula of those Indo-Europeans who would in time be called the Greeks is most probably to be dated to *c.* 2100 or 1900 BC. One of the three earliest attested Indo-European languages, Greek is first documented on clay tablets recovered from the ruins of various Mycenaean palaces found on the Greek mainland and on the island of Crete, dating *c.* 1400–1200 BC; already during the Mycenaean period, the language displays dialectal variation. Ancient Greek is phonologically and morphologically quite conservative and has been a cornerstone in the reconstruction of Proto-Indo-European.

The history of the language has been traditionally divided into several chronological phases. Subsequent to the Mycenaean period, the Greeks fell into a prolonged period of illiteracy (though not in Cyprus, see Ch. 3). The language which reappears at the end of this Dark Age is called Archaic Greek, represented principally by the writings of Homer and Hesiod (eighth century BC). With the advent of the fifth-century BC Greek literati, the language is labeled Classical. Though numerous dialects of Greek are attested during the first millennium BC, in both literary and nonliterary sources (enumerated in Ch. 3), the principal dialect of classical literature is Attic. With the expansion of Hellenic culture under Philip of Macedon in the middle of the fourth century BC, the Attic dialect begins to spread geographically, developing into a Hellenistic Koine. This Hellenistic period of Greek continues until the fourth century AD. The final phase of Greek in antiquity is that of the Byzantine era, stretching from the fourth to the fourteenth century AD. All of the dialects of Modern Greek are descendants of Attic, aside from the dialect of Tsaconian, which traces its ancestry to the ancient Laconian dialect.

2. WRITING SYSTEMS

The earliest preserved Greek writing systems are syllabic scripts, the Linear B syllabary of the Mycenaeans and the distinct, though clearly related, Cypriot syllabary. Both are discussed in Chapter 3, §§2.1–2.2.

The third of the ancient Greek writing systems and the longest employed is the Greek alphabet. As in the case of the two syallabic scripts which preceded it, the alphabet was founded upon a writing system that the Greeks acquired from a non-Greek people, in this instance the Phoenicians. In typical Canaanite fashion, the segmental writing system of the Phoenicians was consonantal, containing no distinct vowel characters. As the Greek adapters of this Semitic script had no phonetic need for several of the Phoenician consonantal characters (representing consonants not occurring in the Greek language), the Greeks assigned vowel values to these characters, thus creating the first fully alphabetic writing system (i.e., a segmental system containing both distinct consonant and vowel graphemes; see Table 2.1). For example, to the Phoenician character ʾaleph, representing a glottal stop, the Greeks assigned the value of a (alpha); and to the Phoenician symbol for a voiced pharyngeal fricative, ʿayin, the Greeks gave the value of o (omicron). To the end of the Phoenician script (terminating in taw (t)), additional characters were appended (not all at the same time) – symbols for vowels and for consonants, the latter showing some variation in value among the many local alphabets which arose in the Greek world. The Greek acquisition of the Phoenician script is most probably to be placed in Cyprus, likely in the ninth century BC, in the author's view, though numerous other ideas have been offered.

The numerous local or epichoric alphabets which developed as use of the script spread across the Greek-speaking world can be divided into certain fundamental alphabet-types. This classification is based chiefly, though not solely, on the presence and variety of the so-called "supplemental," non-Phoenician consonantal characters. The alphabet of Athens and the surrounding region of Attica had belonged to the category of "light blue" alphabets (the color terms which are commonly applied to ancient Greek alphabets have their origin

Table 2.1 The Greek alphabet			
Character	Phonetic value	Character	Phonetic value
A, α	a(:)	Ξ, ξ	k + s
B, β	b	O, o	o
Γ, γ	g	Π, π	p
Δ, δ	d	Ϻ	s
E, ε	e	Ϙ	k
Ϝ	w	P, ρ	r
Z, ζ	z + d	Σ, σ	s
H, η	ẹ:	T, τ	t
Θ, θ	tʰ	Υ, υ	ü(:)
I, ι	i(:)	Φ, φ	pʰ
K, κ	k	X, χ	kʰ
Λ, λ	l	Ψ, ψ	p + s
M, μ	m	Ω, ω	ǫ:
N, ν	n		

in Kirchhoff 1887; see Ch. 3, §2). In 403–402 BC, however, Athens officially adopted the east Ionian alphabet (a "dark blue" script); and it is this form of the alphabetic Greek script which is most familiar to modern readers of Greek (see Table 2.1).

3. PHONOLOGY

3.1 Consonants

The phonemic inventory of Attic Greek consonants is presented in Table 2.2.

As illustrated, Attic possesses a symmetrical system of nine oral stops: three manners of stops (voiceless unaspirated, voiceless aspirated, and voiced) produced at three distinct points of articulation (bilabial, dental, and velar; labiovelar stops /kʷ/, /kʷʰ/, and /gʷ/ are attested in the second millennium BC dialect of Mycenaean Greek, on which see Ch. 3). Filling out the set of obstruents are two voiceless fricatives – the dental /s/ and the glottal /h/. The Classical Attic sonorant system consists of two nasals, bilabial /m/ and dental /n/ (on velar [ŋ] see below), and two dental liquids, /l/ and /r/. A labiovelar glide /w/ had existed at an earlier phase of Attic and has limited attestation in Attic's sister dialect of Ionic (and various other dialects; see Ch. 3).

In addition to the bilabial and dental nasal phonemes /m/ and /n/, Attic also possessed a velar nasal [ŋ]. Velar [ŋ] is a positional variant which occurs in two contexts: the dental /n/ becomes [ŋ] when it precedes a velar stop (i.e., /n/ → [ŋ] / __ {/k/, /g/, /kʰ/}); and the velar stop /g/ becomes [ŋ] when it occurs before the bilabial nasal [m] (i.e., /g/ → [ŋ] / __ /m/) and perhaps before the dental /n/ as well. There is no distinct alphabetic symbol for the velar nasal; instead the sound is represented by the letter *gamma* (i.e., γκ, γγ, γχ, γμ). *Agma* is reported by Latin grammarians to be the name which the Greeks gave to *gamma* when used to spell [ŋ] (see Allen 1987:33–37).

In early Attic inscriptions, the alphabetic symbol *qoppa* (ϙ) was used to represent a /k/ which occurred next to a back vowel. Such spelling clearly suggests a backed allophone of the velar stop in this position.

3.2 Vowels

Figure 2.1 illustrates the vowel phonemes of Classical Attic and their approximate relative arrangement.

Table 2.2 The consonantal phonemes of Classical Attic Greek				
	Place of articulation			
Manner of articulation	Bilabial	Dental	Velar	Glottal
Stops				
Voiceless unaspirated	p	t	k	
Voiceless aspirated	pʰ	tʰ	kʰ	
Voiced	b	d	g	
Fricatives		s		h
Nasals	m	n		
Liquids				
Lateral		l		
Nonlateral		r		

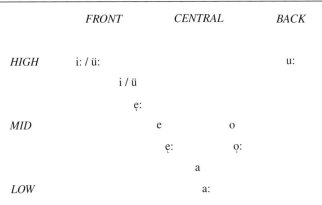

Figure 2.1 The vowel phonemes of Classical Attic Greek

As can be seen, the vowel system of Classical Attic is markedly asymmetric, with front vowels outnumbering back vowels by more than two to one. Four high-front vowels occur, /i/ (ι), /iː/ (ι), /ü/ (υ), /üː/ (υ), distinguished by vowel length and presence or absence of lip rounding. In the mid-front region there are three vowels: long tense /ẹː/ (ει), long lax /ẹ̄ː/ (η) and short /e/ (ε). Two vowels are produced in the low-central region: long /aː/ (α) and short /a/ (α). At the back of the mouth, only three vowels are articulated: long lax mid-back /ọː/ (ω), short mid-back /o/ (o), and long high-back /uː/ (ου). As indicated, long and short vowels are distinguished orthographically only in the case of the mid vowels.

In addition to the monophthongs of Figure 2.1, Classical Attic is characterized by eleven diphthongs:

(1)   <u>"Short" diphthongs</u>
    /ai/ (αι)   /au/ (αυ)
                     /eu/ (ευ)
    /oi/ (οι)
    /üi/ (υι)

      <u>"Long" diphthongs</u>
    /aːi/ (ᾱι or ᾳ)   /aːu/ (ᾱυ)
    /ẹːi/ (ηι or ῃ)   /ẹːu/ (ηυ)
    /ọːi/ (ωι or ῳ) /ọːu/ (ωυ)

At an earlier time in the history of the Attic dialect (perhaps still in the early period of Classical Attic), the vowel sounds written ει and ου had also been diphthongs, /ei/ and /ou/ respectively. However, by the fourth century BC, ει had come to be regularly used to spell both the reflex of the inherited diphthong */ei/ and that of the long vowel */ẹː/ (a long vowel which was the product of contraction and compensatory lengthening processes). Likewise, ου was utilized to represent both that sound which descended from the earlier diphthong */ou/ and that one which continued the long monophthong */ọː/ (likewise the outcome of contraction and compensatory lengthening). The orthographic merger of the two vowel sounds in each instance reveals a prior phonological merger: either the inherited diphthongs (*/ei/ and */ou/) had become monophthongs or the earlier long monophthongs (*/ẹː/ and */ọː/) had undergone diphthongization. Throughout the history of the Greek language, monophthongization is attested recurringly, leaving little doubt that */ei/ and */ou/ became /ẹː/ and /ọː/ respectively, and not vice versa. This monophthongization had probably occurred by the fifth century BC. Hence Classical Attic ει and ου are digraphic spellings of monophthongs; one often encounters the term "spurious diphthong" for these digraphs.

A second fundamental diachronic characteristic of Greek vocalic phonology is the fronting and raising of vowels, particularly long vowels, along the periphery of the vowel space. The mid-back vowel */o̞:/ (which had arisen by contraction, compensatory lengthening and monophthongization as discussed above) was raised to become high-back /u:/ (probably by the fourth century BC). This raising process appears to have followed upon an earlier fronting of inherited */u/ and */u:/ to /ü/ and /ü:/ respectively (perhaps in the sixth century BC or earlier). Fronting and raising of the low-central vowel /a:/ perhaps produced an allophone *[æ:] which occurred in all contexts except after a preceding /e/, /i/, /i:/, or /r/ and which would subsequently be further raised to merge with /e̞:/ (though it has also been argued that the raising affected all instances of /a:/ and a subsequent back-change of */æ:/ to /a:/ took place after /e/, /i/, /i:/, or /r/).

3.3 Phonotaxis

Attic Greek permits consonants to cluster freely. Word-initially, a variety of biconsonantal clusters occurs ([s + stop]; [s + nasal]; [stop + stop]; [stop + s]; [stop + nasal]; [stop + liquid]; [nasal + nasal]; and at an earlier phase [glide + liquid]) as well as two triconsonantal sequences ([s + stop + liquid]; [s + stop + nasal]). Word-internally, the juxtaposition of syllable-final and syllable-initial consonant clusters generates yet additional permutations of consonants (though many earlier word-internal clusters had been simplified prior to the fifth century). In word-final position the set of possible consonant sequences is more limited: [l + s]; [(m +) p + s]; [({ŋ, r} +) k + s]. This phonotactic restriction on possible word-final clusters reflects that one which allows only three single word-final consonants in Greek – [r], [n], and [s] (except in the case of clitics).

3.4 Syllable structure

It is generally the case that in Attic as in other Greek dialects, word-internal consonant clusters are heterosyllabic. In the case of biconsonantal clusters, a syllable boundary simply falls between the two consonants, regardless of the consonants involved. If the cluster consists of three or more consonants, the boundary falls within the cluster, with its precise location being primarily a function of the relative sonority of the particular consonants which form the cluster. Classical Attic, however, provides a notable exception to the foregoing generalization, showing a certain propensity for open syllables followed by a complex onset in the following syllable. This behavior is observed in the case of a subset of [stop + liquid] and [stop + nasal] clusters (clusters traditionally designated *muta cum liquida*); thus, metrical patterns of Classical Attic verse reveal that at times words such as [kǔpris] (Κύπρις "Cyprus") and [tékmar] (τέκμαρ "token") are syllabified [kǔ | pris] and [té | kmar].

3.5 Vowel length

As indicated in Figure 2.1, vowel length is phonemic in ancient Greek. Since the time of Gottfried Hermann, Greek vowel duration has been described in terms of morae: a short vowel is said to consist of a single mora; a long vowel or diphthong of two morae. In antiquity vowel duration was defined in terms of an essentially identical unit, the k^{h}ronós pró:tos (χρονός πρῶτος "primary measure"; see Allen 1987:99–100). By the preceding criteria, one might anticipate the so-called long diphthongs to consist of three morae; however, for purposes of accent placement, a phenomenon dependent upon the moric structure of a syllable, long diphthongs are treated like other diphthongs and long vowels, in other words as if they were bimoric. Long diphthongs, both those inherited from Proto-Indo-European and those which developed secondarily by contraction, were eliminated over time through shortening of the first vowel of the diphthong or through loss of the second. By the first century BC the spoken Greek language probably no longer possessed such sounds; though in some instances they continued as a part of Greek orthography into the Byzantine period (and hence remain part of the traditional orthography of ancient Greek), represented by the *iota*-subscript (herein transcribed by an *i* within parens).

3.6 Accent

Ancient Greek, like its Proto-Indo-European ancestor, was characterized by a pitch or tonal accent. In the traditional orthography of Attic, three different accentual markings are used: acute (´); grave (`) and circumflex (ˆ). The acute and grave diacritics are allographic variants marking high pitch and occurring in complementary distribution: the grave is used on final syllables, unless the accented word occurs at sentence end or is followed by an enclitic, or the accented word is an interrogative; in these exceptional contexts and elsewhere the acute is used. High pitch marked by the acute/grave accent can occur on syllables containing one mora (those with a short vowel) and on syllables of two morae (those with a long vowel or diphthong). In the latter case, high pitch occurs on the rightmost mora of the syllable (i.e., ... |M Ḿ|Σ ...). In contrast, the circumflex can only occur on syllables containing two morae; within such syllables high pitch occurs on the leftmost mora and falling pitch on the ensuing (rightmost) mora (i.e., ... |Ḿ M̀|Σ ...). In the case of the high pitch marked by the acute accent, falling pitch also follows, but in this instance the fall occurs across the succeeding syllable (rather than on the succeeding mora within the same syllable; Allen 1973:234).

While the pitch accent of Proto-Indo-European was free, that of Greek was fixed. The Greek accent can only occur on the final three syllables of a word: the ultima (final), penult (second to final), and antepenult (third to final). The accent of nouns tends to remain on the same syllable throughout the paradigm (subject to the aforementioned limitations), but that of verbs tends to be recessive, occurring as far from the end of the word as the limit of accentuation permits. No more than one mora is permitted to follow the pitch fall which ensues high pitch. The result is that the circumflex accent (... |Ḿ M̀|Σ ...) is limited to the ultima and penult, and can only occur on the penult when the ultima contains a short vowel (i.e., only a single mora). The acute accent (i.e., ... |(M) Ḿ|Σ ...) can then occur on the ultima (in which case it is normally marked by the grave allograph), the penult, and the antepenult, but the antepenult can only bear the acute accent (i.e., have high pitch) if the vowel of the ultima is short.

Attic accent is further characterized by particular requirements. For example, by the so-called Final Trochee Rule of Attic, the occurrence of acute and circumflex accents on the penult is a matter of complementary distribution. If the vowel of the ultima is short and that of the penult is long, high pitch occurring on the rightmost mora of the penult (i.e., acute accent) is retracted to the leftmost mora (i.e., becomes circumflex); in other words [... |M Ḿ|M̀ #] → [... |Ḿ M̀|M #], compare Doric [günaíkes] (γυναίκες "women") and Attic [günaîkes] (γυναῖκες). Thus in Attic a penult with a long vowel bears the circumflex if the ultima is short, and the acute if the ultima is long (recall that a circumflex cannot occur on the penult if the ultima is long).

3.7 Diachronic developments

3.7.1   Obstruents

Except where affected by conditioned sound changes, the stops of Proto-Indo-European (voiceless, voiced, and voiced aspirated) retain their integrity in Greek, though the voiced aspirates are devoiced: $*b^h \rightarrow$ [p^h] (φ), $*d^h \rightarrow$ [t^h] (θ), and so forth. In addition the palatal and velar stop phonemes of Proto-Indo-European merge as Greek velars; thus $*\hat{k}$ and $*k \rightarrow$ [k] (κ), $*\hat{g}$ and $*g \rightarrow$ [g] (γ), while $*g^h$ and $*\hat{g}^h \rightarrow$ [k^h] (χ). A subset of the Proto-Indo-European voiced aspirated stops will emerge in historical Greek as plain voiceless stops, without aspiration, by the operation of *Grassman's Law*: within a word, the first of two (non-contiguous) aspirated consonants loses its aspiration (a dissimilatory change also occurring in Sanskrit). Thus, Proto-Greek (PG) $*t^h rik^h os \rightarrow$ [trik^{h}ós] (τριχός "of hair"). Voiceless aspirated stops also lose their aspiration before the fricative *s*; this deaspiration occurred prior to the Grassman's Law change, thus bleeding potential instances of such change. For example, $*t^h rik^h s$, the Proto-Greek nominative of [trik^{h}ós], becomes [t^{h}ríks] (θρίξ), removing the conditioning context for aspirate dissimilation and stranding the initial aspirated stop (irregularity so introduced into many paradigms was eliminated by analogy). The Grassman's Law deaspiration also affected instances of *h* which precede an aspirated stop; for example, PG $*hek^h \bar{\varrho} \rightarrow$ [ék^{h}ǫ:] (ἔχω "I have"). Compare the future [héksǫ:] (ἕξω, in which the initial [h-] is preserved as a result of $*k^h$ having previously lost its aspiration before [-s-]).

The flagrant exception to the preservation of the integrity of Proto-Indo-European stops is provided by the reflexes of the labiovelar in Attic and other Greek dialects of the first millennium BC. Though the labiovelars are generally preserved in the second-millennium dialect of Mycenaean Greek (with loss of voicing in the case of $*g^{wh}$), they have disappeared completely by the time of the earliest attestation of Attic. Bilabial reflexes emerge as the default development of the labiovelars; in other words, PIE $*k^w$, $*g^w$, $*g^{wh} \rightarrow$ [p, b, p^h] (π, β, φ) respectively. Other developments are contextually conditioned. Before and after the high-back rounded vowel *u*, the labial element of the labiovelar is dissimilated, producing a velar reflex: $*k^w$, $*g^w$, $*g^{wh} \rightarrow$ [k, g, k^h] (κ, γ, χ). For example, PIE $*su\text{-}g^w ih_3\text{-}\bar{e}s \rightarrow$ [hügię:s] (ὑγιής "healthy"). In Attic, the labiovelars developed into dental stops when found before the mid-front vowels: PIE $*k^w$, $*g^w$, $*g^{wh} \rightarrow$ [t, d, t^h] (τ, δ, θ) respectively; for example, $*g^w elb^h\text{-}u\text{-} \rightarrow$ [delp^{h}ús] (δελφύς "womb"). Dental reflexes also arise before the high-front vowel [i], but only in the case of the voiceless labiovelar $*k^w$; voiced $*g^w$ and aspirated $*g^{wh}$ here give rise to the bilabial reflexes, [b] and [p^h] respectively. Thus, $*k^w i\text{-}nu\text{-} \rightarrow$ [tínǫ:] (τίνω "I pay"), while $*g^w ih_3\text{-}o\text{-} \rightarrow$ [bíos] (βίος "life"); compare [hügię:s] from the same root.

An almost identical course of development is displayed by the Proto-Indo-European consonantal sequence of *palatal stop* + *labiovelar glide*, except that a geminate reflex is generated word-internally. For example, PIE $*\hat{e}kwos \rightarrow$ [híppos] (ἵππος "horse"). Word-initially, the outcome is identical to the labiovelar stop development: PIE $*\hat{g}^h w\bar{e}r \rightarrow$ [t^{h}ę̄:r] (θήρ "beast").

Though involved in many particular contextual developments, the Proto-Indo-European fricative $*s$ shows, broadly speaking, three principal reflexes in Greek: [s], [h], and Ø. Word-initially, $*s$- becomes [h] when followed by either a vowel, [w], a liquid, or a nasal; for example, PIE $*septm̥ \rightarrow$ [heptá] (ἑπτά "seven"). When the ensuing consonant is [l] or a nasal, the [h] is subsequently lost (still preserved in early inscriptional Attic and in other dialects); thus, PIE $*slag^w\text{-} \rightarrow$ [lambánǫ:] (λαμβάνω "I take"). Intervocalically, $*$-s- likewise becomes

[-h-] and subsequently is lost (without attestation in the first millennium): *$\hat{g}enh_1$-es-os →
Homeric [géneos] (γένεος; and with vowel contraction) → Attic [génu:s] (γένους "of race").
The Proto-Indo-European fricative is preserved (i) word-initially when followed by a voiceless stop (e.g., *sth_2-tos → [statós] (στατός "placed")); (ii) when flanked by a voiceless stop
on one side and a vowel on the other (e.g., *$h_1$esti → [estí] (ἐστί "(s)he is")); and (iii)
word-finally (as in [génu:s]).

3.7.2   Sonorants

The Proto-Indo-European consonantal nasals, *m and *n, and liquids, *r and *l, are well
preserved in Attic as in other Greek dialects; though like *s, these consonants are affected
by a number of changes which occur in combination with other consonants (see below).
Also, Proto-Indo-European *-m regularly becomes Greek [-n] in word-final position: for
example, *sem → [hén] (ἕν "one"). On the other hand, the Proto-Indo-European syllabic
nasals, *m̥ and *n̥, and syllabic liquids, *r̥ and *l̥, are both modified in all contexts. The nasals
*m̥ and *n̥ become respectively the Greek sequences [am] and [an] before a vowel (optionally
preceded by a laryngeal, on which see below) and before a glide; elsewhere they show the
common reflex [a]. Thus, *dek̂m̥ becomes [déka] (δέκα "ten"), while the negative prefix *n̥-
shows up as [an-] in [án-üdros] (ἄν-υδρος "without water"). The syllabic liquids also show
a bifurcation of reflexes in Attic, though with somewhat different results. PIE *r̥ gives rise to
either [ar] or [ra]. There is uncertainty regarding the precise regular distribution of these
two reflexes, though [ar] may occur in approximately the same contexts as [am] and [an],
as well as in word-final position. Thus, PIE *$yēk^w r̥$ → [hę̂:par] (ἧπαρ "liver"), while PIE
*str̥-to- → [stratós] (στρατός "army"). The lateral syllabic liquid *l̥ similarly becomes Attic
[al] or [la], with perhaps the same distribution as [ar] and [ra], though without word-final
reflexes; PIE *pl̥th₂-u- → [platŭs] (πλατύς "wide, flat").

  The two remaining PIE sonorant consonants, *y and *w, are far less persistent in Greek.
A palatal glide phoneme /y/ is never attested in ancient Attic, or in any other Greek dialect
of the first millennium BC (a [y] offglide which occurs between [i] and an ensuing vowel
is sometimes spelled in the syllabic writing system of the Cypriot Greeks and presumably
existed in other dialects as well). Word-initially PIE *y in some instances becomes Greek
[h], as in [hę̂:par] (ἧπαρ "liver"), but in other, practically identical word-initial contexts,
the Greek reflex is [zd]: PIE *yes-o- → [zdéǫ:] (ζέω "I boil"). The factors conditioning this
split remain unclear. Intervocalic *y has disappeared from the Attic dialect; indirect evidence
suggests that *[h] was an intermediate reflex in this process. Thus, PIE *treyes → *[trehes] →
*[trees] → (by contraction and raising) [trê:s] (τρεῖς "three"). The palatal glide is also
involved in various changes in combination with other consonants.

  While PIE *w is preserved in many Greek dialects as late as the fourth century BC, its
disappearance from Attic-Ionic is relatively early, being attested only in a very few Central
and West Ionic inscriptions (in Attic spelling the alphabetic symbol for /w/, Ϝ, occurs at times,
used to represent a [w-] on-glide preceding the vowel /u/). Somewhat like *y, the labiovelar
glide shows a developmental bifurcation at the beginning of the word: *w becomes [h] word-
initially when followed by [r]; further erosion to φ occurs when the ensuing sound is a vowel
or [l] (though instances of an [h] reflex before a vowel do occur – perhaps conditioned by an
[s] following the vowel). Thus, PIE *$wreh_1$- → [hrę́ :tra:] (ῥήτρα "verbal agreement"), while
*$woik̂$- → [oîkos] (οἶκος "house"). Intervocalically, as with *y, *w disappears in Attic without
a trace: PIE *h_3ewi- → [óis] (ὄϊς "sheep"). When occurring in consonantal sequences, *w
experiences yet additional developments.

3.7.3 Combinatory changes

In the preceding paragraph, and repeatedly in the foregoing discussion, reference has been made to phonological reflexes which arise when consonants are in contact with one another (so-called combinatory or syntagmatic changes). The following chart summarizes some of the more significant of these phonological developments in Attic:

(2) Combinatory phonological developments of Attic

- A. PG $*p^{(h)}y \rightarrow$ [pt]
- B. PG $*t^{(h)}y \rightarrow$ [s]
- C. PG $*t^{(h)} + y \rightarrow$ [tt] (i.e., when a detectable intervening morpheme boundary occurs; on this complex matter, see Rix 1976:90–91; Lejeune 1982:103–104)
- D. PG $*k^{(w)(h)}y \rightarrow$ [t] word-initially (i.e., PG $*k$, $*k^h$, $*k^w$, $*k^{wh}$)
- E. PG $*k^{(w)(h)}y \rightarrow$ [tt] elsewhere
- F. PG $*dy \rightarrow$ [zd]
- G. PG $*g^{(w)}y \rightarrow$ [zd]
- H. PG $*tw \rightarrow$ [s] word-initially
- I. PG $*tw \rightarrow$ [tt] elsewhere
- J. PG $*\{t^{(h)}, d\}w \rightarrow \{[t^{(h)}], [d]\}$
- K. PG $*dl \rightarrow$ [ll]
- L. PG $*bn \rightarrow$ [mn]
- M. PG $*\{p^{(h)}, b\}m \rightarrow$ [mm]
- N. PG $*\{p^h, b\}s \rightarrow$ [ps]
- O. PG $*\{k^h, g\}s \rightarrow$ [ks]
- P. PG $*\{t^{(h)}, d\}s \rightarrow$ [s]
- Q. PG $*ss \rightarrow$ [s]
- R. PG $*ti \rightarrow$ [si] however, the change does not occur if $*ti$ is preceded by $*s$
- S. PG $*\{t^{(h)}, d\}t^{(h)} \rightarrow [st^{(h)}]$
- T. PG $*\{r, n\}y \rightarrow [y\{r, n\}] / [\{a, o\}]$ ___
- U. PG $*\{r, n\}y \rightarrow [\{r, n\}] / [\{e, i, u\}]$ ___ with compensatory lengthening of the preceding vowel
- V. PG $*ly \rightarrow$ [ll]
- W. PG $*ln \rightarrow$ [l] with compensatory lengthening of a preceding vowel
- X. PG $*\{r, l, n, s\}w \rightarrow [\{r, l, n\}]$ where $*s$ is of secondary origin (i.e., not inherited from Proto-Indo-European), without compensatory lengthening of a preceding vowel
- Y. PG $* N \rightarrow \alpha$ place of articulation / ___ [stop]$_{\alpha \text{ place of articulation}}$ (where $N = nasal$)
- Z. PG $*m\{y, s\} \rightarrow [n\{y, s\}]$
- AA. PG $*ns \rightarrow$ [s] word-finally; with compensatory lengthening of a preceding vowel
- BB. PG $*nsV \rightarrow$ [sV] where $*s$ is of secondary origin (i.e., not inherited from Proto-Indo-European); with compensatory lengthening of a preceding vowel
- CC. PG $*nsC \rightarrow$ [sC] without compensatory lengthening of a preceding vowel
- DD. PG $*NsV \rightarrow$ [NV] where $*s$ is inherited; with compensatory lengthening of a preceding vowel
- EE. PG $*m\{r, l\} \rightarrow [b\{r, l\}]$ and $*nr \rightarrow$ [dr] word-initially
- FF. PG $*m\{r, l\} \rightarrow [mb\{r, l\}]$ and $*nr \rightarrow$ [ndr] intervocalically
- GG. PG $*\{t^{(h)}, d\}sC \rightarrow$ [sC]
- HH. PG $*C_i sC_i \rightarrow [sC_i]$
- II. PG $*CsC \rightarrow$ [CC], in the case of most remaining PG $*CsC$ clusters
- JJ. PG $*Vsw \rightarrow$ [Vw] where $*s$ is inherited; with compensatory lengthening of the preceding vowel and subsequent loss of [w]

KK. PG *Vs{r, l, m, n} → [V{r, l, m, n}] with compensatory lengthening of the preceding vowel

LL. PG *rs → [rr] where *s does not belong to the aorist suffix

MM. PG *{r, l}s → [s] where *s belongs to the aorist suffix; with compensatory lengthening of the preceding vowel (cf. DD)

3.7.4   Laryngeals

It is the Greek language which best preserves evidence of the Proto-Indo-European consonants conventionally called *laryngeal* (*h_1, *h_2, and *h_3). When these parent laryngeal sounds are sandwiched between two consonants, each shows a distinctive vowel reflex in Greek ([e], [a], and [o] respectively): for example, PIE *$ph_2tēr$ gives Greek [paté:r] (πατήρ "father"). A laryngeal following the vowel *e results in a long vowel reflex, also distinctively colored (i.e., *eh_1 → [ẹ:]; *eh_2 → [a:] → [ẹ:] in Attic-Ionic; *eh_3 → [ọ:]); thus, PIE *deh_3- yields, with reduplication, [dí-dọ:-mi] (δί-δω-μι "I give"). If, on the other hand, the laryngeal precedes a vowel *e, it distinctively colors but does not lengthen the vowel (i.e., *h_1e → [e]; *h_2e → [a]; *h_3e → [o]): for example, PIE *dh_3-ent- produces the aorist participial stem [dont-] (δοντ- "given"). For additional laryngeal developments in Greek, see Rix 1976:68–76.

3.7.5   Vowels

As indicated above, the reduction of consonant clusters in Attic is frequently accompanied by lengthening of a short vowel which precedes the cluster. In addition, long vowels were generated by contraction of short vowels which had become contiguous through loss of intervocalic *s, *y, and *w (most commonly occurring singly, but sometimes in combination) and through morphological restructuring. Contraction is a relatively recent phenomenon in ancient Greek, as is reflected by variation in the outcome of contraction among the different first-millennium dialects. The general results of contraction in Attic are as follows:

(3)   A. Two identical short vowels contract to produce the corresponding long vowel, though the mid vowels [e] + [e] yield [ẹ:], and [o] + [o] produce *[ọ:], subsequently raised to [u:] (see §3.2)

B. A short mid-back vowel contracts with a short mid-front or a low vowel to yield a long mid-back vowel: for example, [a] + [o] gives [ọ:] and [e] + [o] gives *[ọ:], raised to [u:]

C. While [a] + [e] produces [a:], [e] + [a] yields [ẹ:]

D. The high vowels [i] and *[u] (see §3.2) form *i*- and *u*-diphthongs with a preceding vowel

Conversely, in Attic, as in all dialects, long vowels become short in certain contexts. Proto-Greek long vowels (though not those arising later) were shortened when they preceded the sequence *sonorant + consonant*; thus PG *stāntes produces Attic [stántes] (στάντες "stood") – the Greek expression of *Osthoff's Law*. As a consequence, the first vowel of the so-called long diphthongs is shortened in most word-internal contexts (the second diphthongal element serving as a glide in the operation of this change). At times, long vowels in Attic and certain other dialects also undergo shortening when followed by another vowel: compare Homeric [basiléọ:n] (βασιλήων) and Attic-Ionic [basiléo:n] (βασιλέων "of kings"). However, in the case of the sequences [ẹ:a] and [ẹ:o], concomitant with this shortening, the second vowel is sometimes lengthened (quantitative metathesis) in Ionic and, especially, Attic: thus, Homeric [basilệ:os] (βασιλῆος), but Attic [basiléọ:s] (βασιλέως "of a king").

4. MORPHOLOGY

4.1 Nominal morphology

The Greek nominal is morphologically marked for case, gender, and number. Five different grammatical cases are identified: vocative, nominative, accusative, genitive, and dative. In certain inflectional classes, each case-marker has a distinct morphological form. The functions of the Proto-Indo-European ablative have been absorbed by the Greek genitive, and the locative and instrumental by the Greek dative. Three nominal genders, feminine, masculine, and neuter, are distinguished; and nouns are inflected in three numbers: singular, dual, and plural. By the fifth century BC, however, the dual has become restricted in use, and by the Hellenistic period has disappeared except in a few frozen contexts.

4.1.1   Noun classes

Within Greek grammatical tradition, nouns are divided into three declensional classes: the principally feminine first declension; the predominantly masculine and neuter second declension; and the third declension, of mixed gender. Each of the declensions has Proto-Indo-European ancestry. Within the parent Indo-European language, nominals, as well as verbals, are characterized by a tripartite structure; each word consists of a *root*, to which is optionally attached a *suffix*, followed in turn by an *ending* (R + (S) + E). Regarding morphological typology, Greek is predominantly a fusional language. This is clearly illustrated by the paradigm of (4) below, in which endings and suffixes freely combine and lose their morphological integrity.

4.1.1.1   First declension

The majority of first declension feminine nouns of Greek are descended from Proto-Indo-European nouns formed with the suffix *-eh₂-*. As noted above, by regular sound change PIE *-eh₂-* becomes Greek [a:] (ā), which in Attic, in most contexts, is raised and fronted to [ẹ:] (η). This characteristic η vowel is obscured in the plural of the first declension by contraction and morphological restructuring. As an example of first declension nouns of this type, consider the paradigm of *tīmḗ* (τῑμή "honor").

(4)   **The Attic first declension I**

	Singular	Dual	Plural
Nominative	tīmḗ (τῑμή)	tīmá (τῑμά)	tīmaí (τῑμαί)
Vocative	tīmḗ (τῑμή)	tīmá (τῑμά)	tīmaí (τῑμαί)
Accusative	tīmḗn (τῑμήν)	tīmá (τῑμά)	tīmás (τῑμάς)
Genitive	tīmḗs (τῑμῆς)	tīmaîn (τῑμαῖν)	tīmôn (τῑμῶν)
Dative	tīmḗ(i) (τῑμῇ)	tīmaîn (τῑμαῖν)	tīmaîs (τῑμαῖς)

Early Attic attests a dative plural in which the η stem-vowel is still preserved, as in *díkēsi* (δίκησι "for penalties"). The long ā of the nominative, vocative, and accusative dual is secondary.

When the noun root ends in [e, i, i:] or [r], the [a:] reflex of the PIE *-eh₂-* suffix is preserved in Attic, thus producing a first declension singular of the type of *kʰórā* (χώρᾱ "place"):

(5) **The Attic first declension II**

	Singular
Nominative	kʰǭrā (χώρᾱ)
Vocative	kʰǭrā (χώρᾱ)
Accusative	kʰǭrān (χώρᾱν)
Genitive	kʰǭrās (χώρᾱς)
Dative	kʰǭrā(i) (χώρᾳ)

The dual and plural of this type are identical to those of the *tīmḗ* type.

Proto-Indo-European also formed nominals with an ablauting suffix *-yeh₂- (*e*-grade), *-ih₂- (ø-grade). Developing the respective Proto-Greek reflexes *-yā and *-ya, Attic [-ẹ:] (η) and [-a] (α), nouns of this type fall formally into the feminine first declension. This suffix is quite frequently attached to roots and stems ending in a consonant, which, in combination with the ensuing glide *-y, is subject to sound change. Thus, the root *ped- ("foot") provides a noun *trápezda* (τράπεζα "table"; see (2F)), *glokʰ- gives *glôtta* (γλῶττα "tongue"; see (2E)), *smor- gives *moîra* (μοῖρα "portion"; see (2S)), and so forth.

(6) **The Attic first declension III**

	Singular	
Nominative	trápezda (τράπεζα)	} with the suffix -*ih₂-
Vocative	trápezda (τράπεζα)	
Accusative	trápezdan (τράπεζαν)	
Genitive	trapézdēs (τραπέζης)	} with the suffix -*yeh₂-
Dative	trapézdē(i) (τραπέζῃ)	

The dual and plural are formed like that of *tīmḗ* and *kʰǭrā*. Thus, the so-called *ă*-feminine of the first declension differs from the other feminine nouns of this declension only in the nominative, accusative, and vocative of the singular.

Also derived from stems in *-eh₂- and placed within the Greek first declension is a group of masculine nouns having a nominative singular ending in -ḗs (-ης):

(7) **The Attic first declension IV**

	Singular
Nominative	polítēs (πολίτης)
Vocative	polîta (πολῖτα)
Accusative	polítēn (πολίτην)
Genitive	polítū (πολίτου)
Dative	polítē(i) (πολίτῃ)

The nominative and genitive singular have been influenced by the masculine nouns of the second declension. Both the dual and plural are formed like those of the feminine nouns of the first declension.

4.1.1.2 Second declension

The nouns of the Greek second declension, continuing the thematic stems of Proto-Indo-European, are characterized by a suffix terminating in the vowel *o* or *e* (sometimes obscured by sound change). The inflection of the masculine nouns is here demonstrated with *lúkos* (λύκος "wolf"):

(8)   The Attic second declension I

	Singular	Dual	Plural
Nominative	lŭkos (λύκος)	lŭkǭ (λύκω)	lŭkoi (λύκοι)
Vocative	lŭke (λύκε)	lŭkǭ (λύκω)	lŭkoi (λύκοι)
Accusative	lŭkon (λύκον)	lŭkǭ (λύκω)	lŭkūs (λύκους)
Genitive	lŭkū (λύκου)	lŭkoin (λύκοιν)	lŭkǭn (λύκων)
Dative	lŭkǭ(i) (λύκῳ)	lŭkoin (λύκοιν)	lŭkois (λύκοις)

Early Attic preserves a dative plural ending in *-oisi* (-οισι). A very few nouns following the above inflectional pattern have feminine gender.

With the exception of the nominative, vocative, and accusative case forms, both singular and plural, neuter nouns of the second declension have the same inflection as the masculine nouns. Consider the paradigm of *zdügón* (ζυγόν "yoke"):

(9)   The Attic second declension II

	Singular	Dual	Plural
Nominative	zdügón (ζυγόν)	zdügǭ (ζυγώ)	zdügá (ζυγά)
Vocative	zdügón (ζυγόν)	zdügǭ (ζυγώ)	zdügá (ζυγά)
Accusative	zdügón (ζυγόν)	zdügǭ (ζυγώ)	zdügá (ζυγά)
Genitive	zdügû (ζυγοῦ)	zdügoin (ζυγοῖν)	zdügǭ̂n (ζυγῶν)
Dative	zdügǭ(i) (ζυγῷ)	zdügoin (ζυγοῖν)	zdügois (ζυγοῖς)

Contraction of the thematic vowel with a preceding *-o-* or *-e-* gives rise to a set of second declension masculine and neuter nominals having a long vowel in the inflection of the nominative, accusative, and vocative singular: for example, nominative masculine singular *nûs* (νοῦς "mind"); accusative singular *nûn* (νοῦν); nominative, accusative neuter singular *ostûn* (ὀστοῦν "bone"). Contraction often also occurs in the nominative, accusative neuter plural, yielding a final long *-ā*, as in *ostâ* (ὀστᾶ).

Yet other sound changes, including quantitative metathesis, produce a distinctive second declension inflectional paradigm marked by the presence of the long vowel *-ǭ-* (-ω-), the so-called Attic declension. Consider the paradigm of Attic *neǭs* (νεώς "temple"; Ionic *nēós*, νηός) as an example:

(10)   The Attic second declension III

	Singular	Dual	Plural
Nominative	neǭs (νεώς)	neǭ (νεώ)	neǭ(i) (νεῴ)
Vocative	neǭs (νεώς)	neǭ (νεώ)	neǭ(i) (νεῴ)
Accusative	neǭn (νεών)	neǭ (νεώ)	neǭs (νεώς)
Genitive	neǭ (νεώ)	neǭ(i)n (νεών)	neǭn (νεών)
Dative	neǭ(i) (νεῴ)	neǭ(i)n (νεών)	neǭ(i)s (νεῴς)

4.1.1.3   Third declension

The Greek third declension is the historical, grammatical repository of a broad array of Proto-Indo-European athematic noun stems. These stems are *athematic* in that they end in a consonant or in the vowel *i* or *u* (in other words, in some sound other than the thematic vowel *o/e*). In Proto-Indo-European such stems were characterized by distinctive patterns of ablaut variation and accent placement. No fewer than four fundamental patterns have been identified for the parent language (though this is a matter on which there is not full agreement among Indo-Europeanists): acrostatic (with two subtypes), amphikinetic, proterokinetic, and hysterokinetic. The following table schematically summarizes ablaut gradation (*e*-grade/*o*-grade/*ø*-grade) and accent placement for each of these athematic noun-types of Proto-Indo-European:

Table 2.3 Ablauting noun patterns of PIE					
	Strong stem			Weak stem		
	Root	Suffix	Ending	Root	Suffix	Ending
Acrostatic I	ó	ø	ø	é	ø	ø
Acrostatic II	ḗ	ø	ø	é	ø	ø
Amphikinetic	é	o	ø	ø	ø	é
Proterokinetic	é	ø	ø	ø	é	ø
Hysterokinetic	ø	é	ø	ø	ø	é

In addition to these, Proto-Indo-European also possessed root nouns (athematic nouns having a root which serves as a stem without attachment of a suffix) displaying a distinct pattern of accent and ablaut variation between strong and weak stems. For masculine and feminine nouns, the strong stem is usually identified as that of the (a) nominative singular, dual, and plural; and (b) the accusative singular and dual. The strong stem of the neuter is that of the nominative and accusative plural. The stem of all other cases is weak.

Greek is one of the languages which best provides evidence of this Proto-Indo-European inflectional phenomenon. Even so, the ancestral patterns have often been obscured in Greek by processes of paradigm regularization; for example, within a given paradigm Greek has essentially limited ablaut variation to the suffix. Consequently, in a synchronic grammatical description of Greek, third declension noun stems are more appropriately and efficiently categorized by their final member than by their ancestral ablaut and accent pattern.

The endings which are attached to Greek nouns of the third declension are the following:

(11)   The Attic third declension endings

	Singular	*Dual*	*Plural*
Nominative	-s (-ς) or ø	-e (-ε)	-es (-ες) or -a (-α)
Vocative	-s (-ς) or ø	-e (-ε)	-es (-ες) or -a (-α)
Accusative	-a (-α) or -n (-ν)	-e (-ε)	-as (-ας), -s (-ς) or -a (-α)
Genitive	-os (-ος)	-oin (-οιν)	-ǫn (-ων)
Dative	-i (-ι)	-oin (-οιν)	-si (-σι)

The endings of the third declension and those of the first declension share a common Proto-Indo-European heritage – distinct from that set of endings utilized for inflecting thematic nouns (second declension). Sound changes will in some instances arise when the ending is attached to the stem, obscuring the phonetic shape of both ending and stem. Analogical remodeling of particular case forms also commonly occurs within third declension paradigms.

Each of the principal third declension stem-types is here illustrated using a partial paradigm (the illustration is not, however, exhaustive, as various distinct subcategories exist for most stem-types):

1. stop-stems (stems ending in a stop). (A) *pʰléb-* ("vein," fem.): *pʰlép-s* (φλέψ, nom. sg.), *pʰleb-ós* (φλεβός, gen. sg.), *pʰléb-a* (φλέβα, acc. sg.); (B) *pod-* ("foot," masc.): *pú-s* (πούς, nom. sg., the vowel is irregular, < **pod-s*); *pod-ós* (ποδός, gen. sg.); *po-sí* (ποσί, dat. pl., < **pod-si*).

2. *s*-stems. *genes-* ("race," neut.): *gén-os* (γένος, nom./acc. sg., i.e., *gén-os-ø*), *gén-ūs* (γένους, gen. sg., < **gen-e-os* < **gen-es-os*), *gén-ē̄* (γένη, nom./acc. pl., < **gen-e-a* < **gen-es-a*).

3. *n*-stems. (A) *poimen-* ("shepherd," masc.): *poi-mḗn* (ποιμήν, nom. sg., i.e., *poi-mḗn-ø*, lengthening of stem-vowel is of Proto-Indo-European date), *poi-mén-os* (ποιμένος, gen. sg.), *poi-mé-si* (ποιμέσι, dat. pl. < **poi-mn̥-si* with ø-grade of the suffix; regular phonological reflex *-ma-* analogically modified to *-me-*); (B) *sōmat-* ("body," neut.): *sō̧-ma* (σῶμα, nom./acc. sg., < **sō-mn̥-ø*), *sǫ́-mat-os* (σώματος, gen. sg., < **sō-mn̥-t-os*, the source of the *-t-* is uncertain; it occurs throughout the paradigm of the neuter *n*-stems, other than in the nom./acc. sg., and is found also in other types of third declension paradigms).

4. *r*-stems. *pater-* ("father," masc.): *pa-tḗr* (πατήρ, nom. sg., i.e., *pa-tḗr-ø*, lengthening of stem-vowel is of Proto-Indo-European date), *pa-tr-ós* (πατρός, gen. sg.), *pa-tér-as* (πατέρας, acc. pl.).

5. *r/n*-heteroclite stems (*r*-stem in the nom./acc. sg. and *n*-stem elsewhere). *hȩ̄par-* ("liver," neut.): *hȩ̂p-ar* (ἧπαρ, nom./acc. sg., i.e., *hȩ̂p-ar-ø*), *hȩ́p-at-i* (ἥπατι, dat. sg., with *-t-* as in neuter *n*-stems), *hȩ́p-a-si* (ἥπασι, dat. pl.).

6. *i*-stems. (A) *poli-* ("city," fem., ablauting suffix): *pól-i-s* (πόλις, nom. sg.), *pól-e-ō̧s* (πόλεως, gen. sg., < *pól-ȩ̄-os* by quantitative metathesis), *pól-ȩ̄s* (πόλεις, nom. pl. < **pol-ey-es*); (B) *oi-* ("sheep," masc./fem., nonablauting suffix): *oî-s* (οἶς, nom. sg.), *oi-ós* (οἰός, gen. sg.), *oî-es* (οἶες, nom. pl.); see also Ch. 3, §4.1.1.3.

7. *u*-stems. (A) *pȩ̄kʰü-* ("forearm," masc., ablauting *-ŭ-* suffix): *pȩ̄kʰ-ü-s* (πῆχυς, nom. sg.), *pȩ̄́kʰ-ȩ̄s* (πήχεις, nom. pl. < **pȩ̄kʰ-ew-es*); (B) *sü-* ("sow," fem., nonablauting *-ū-* stem): *sû-s* (σῦς, nom. sg.), *sú-es* (σύες, nom. pl. < **suw-es*).

8. diphthongal *u*-stems. *basileu-* ("king," masc., *ēu*-stem): *basil-eú-s* (βασιλεύς, nom. sg., < **basil-ēu-s*), *basil-é-ō̧s* (βασιλέως, gen. sg., < **basil-ȩ̄w-os* by quantitative metathesis), *basil-é-ās* (βασιλέᾱς, acc. pl., < **basil-ȩ̄w-as* by quantitative metathesis).

4.1.2 Adjectives

Greek adjectives are constructed by utilizing most of the nominal stem-types which were elaborated above. As adjectives agree with the nouns they modify in case, gender, and number, any single adjective, unlike most nouns, can be assigned multiple genders. The most commonly occurring adjectives are those which form the feminine, in Attic, using an *-ȩ̄-* stem (first declension) and form the masculine and neuter using a thematic stem (second declension): *agatʰ-ós* (ἀγαθ-ός "good," masc.), *agatʰ-ȩ̄́* (ἀγαθ-ή, fem.), *agatʰ-ón* (ἀγαθ-όν, neut.). Some adjectives make no *morphological* distinction between masculine and feminine gender. A subset of these are thematic adjectives with the common nonneuter gender marked by masculine inflection; such adjectives commonly contain prefixes: *á-dik-os* (ἄ-δικ-ος "unjust," masc. and fem.), *á-dik-on* (ἄ-δικ-ον, neut.). Certain adjectives of this type conform to the "Attic declension" discussed above. Similarly, consonant stem adjectives commonly have a single masculine/feminine form: for example, the *s*-stem *alȩ̄tʰȩ̄́s* (ἀληθής, "true," masc. and fem.), *alēt^{h}és* (ἀληθές, neut.). In contrast, adjectives formed from *u*-stems (stems formed with a short *-u-* suffix as opposed to the long *-ū-* of most *u*-stem nouns) distinguish the three genders morphologically, forming the feminine by utilizing the short *-a-* morphology of the first declension (i.e., the PG suffix *-ya/yā-*, PIE *-ih$_2$/yeh$_2$-): *hēdŭs* (ἡδύς, "sweet" masc.), *hēdêa* (ἡδεῖα [from PG *swād-ew-ya*], fem.), *hēdŭ*(ἡδύ, neut.). Certain *n*-stem adjectives as well as adjectives formed with a suffix terminating in *-nt-* (compare the active participle below) also make a three-way morphological distinction, utilizing the *-ya/yā-* formant for the feminine.

Comparatives and superlatives are productively generated by attaching the suffixes *-tero-* and *-tato-* respectively to the adjective stem: *glükŭs* (γλυκύς "sweet"), *glükŭ-tero-s* (γλυκύ-τερο-ς "sweeter"), *glükŭ-tato-s* (γλυκύ-τατο-ς "sweetest"). Less commonly, Greek produces the comparative with a suffix *-iŏn-* attached directly to the adjective root, in origin the ø-grade (*-is-*) of an ablauting *s*-stem suffix *-yes-* to which Greek appended a nasal formant: *hēd-ús* (ἡδ-ύς "sweet"), *hēd-íŏn* (ἡδ-ίων "sweeter"). The corresponding superlative marker is produced by attaching *-to-* to the ø-grade: *hḗd-is-to-s* (ἥδ-ισ-το-ς "sweetest").

4.1.3 Pronouns

Attic and the other dialects of ancient Greek possess a wealth of pronouns.

4.1.3.1 Personal pronouns

Personal pronouns, enclitic and accented forms, occur in the singular, dual, and plural for each of the three persons, though by the period of Classical Attic, the third-person forms, aside from the dative singular and plural, are little used, and when they are used have a reflexive function (see 4.1.3.2):

(12) Attic personal pronouns

	Singular		
	First	*Second*	*Third*
Nominative	egṓ (ἐγώ)	sŭ (σύ)	—
Genitive	emû (ἐμοῦ)	sû (σοῦ)	hû (οὗ)
Dative	emoí (ἐμοί)	soí (σοί)	hoî (οἷ)
Accusative	emé (ἐμέ)	sé (σέ)	hé (ἕ)
	Dual		
	First	*Second*	
Nom./Acc.	nṓ (νώ)	sp^{h}ṓ (σφώ)	
Gen./Dat.	nṓ(i)n (νῷν)	sp^{h}ȭ(i)n (σφῷν)	
	Plural		
	First	*Second*	*Third*
Nominative	hēmês (ἡμεῖς)	hūmês (ὑμεῖς)	sp^{h}ês (σφεῖς)
Genitive	hēmȭn (ἡμῶν)	hūmȭn (ὑμῶν)	sp^{h}ȭn (σφῶν)
Dative	hēmîn (ἡμῖν)	hūmîn (ὑμῖν)	sp^{h}ísi (σφίσι)
Accusative	hēmâs (ἡμᾶς)	hūmâs (ὑμᾶς)	sp^{h}âs (σφᾶς)

The oblique forms of the singular personal pronouns and the dative of the third-person plural also occur as enclitics, in which case the first-person pronouns lack the initial *e*- (i.e., *mū* (μου), etc.). Furthermore, the oblique cases of the first and second plural pronouns are found with accent on the initial syllable; such forms have been similarly designated as enclitic or, alternatively, as simply "unemphatic" (see Allen 1973:243).

Utilizing the stem of the personal pronouns, *possessive pronominal adjectives* were derived by attaching the thematic suffixes *-o-* and *-tero-*; feminine forms are constructed with the long *-ā-* morphology of the first declension. Nominatives of the first and second persons respectively are formed as follows: (i) *emós* (ἐμός masc.), *emḗ* (ἐμή fem.), *emón* (ἐμόν neut.); (ii) *sós* (σός masc.), *sḗ* (σή fem.), *són* (σόν neut.). Instead of the third-person possessive adjective – *hós* (ὅς masc.), *hḗ* (ἥ fem.), *hón* (ὅν neut.) – Classical Attic normally uses masculine/neuter *autû* (αὐτοῦ) and feminine *autês* (αὐτῆς), genitives of the pronoun *autós* (αὐτός, etc., see below). First and second singular possessives are at times also used reflexively. Plural possessives of the first and second persons appear in the nominative masculine singular as *hēméteros* (ἡμέτερος) and *hūméteros* (ὑμέτερος) respectively. Attic normally uses *autôn* (αὐτῶν), the genitive plural of *autós*, for third-person possession. A third-person possessive *sphéteros* (σφέτερος), etc. is reflexive in use, normally accompanied by *autôn*; the first and second plural forms are commonly used as reflexive possessives also (usually in combination with *autôn*).

4.1.3.2   *Reflexive pronouns*

The reflexive pronouns of Attic were formed from the personal pronouns used in combination with the pronoun *autós*. In the singular these have undergone univerbation (not yet having been joined in Homer) and only the second member shows inflection (occurring only in the oblique cases), with a thematic masculine/neuter and long *-ā-* feminine. The genitive singular is thus formed as follows: (i) first person *emautû* (ἐμαυτοῦ "myself," masc.), *emautês* (ἐμαυτῆς fem.); (ii) second person *s(e)autû* (σ(ε)αυτοῦ "yourself," masc.), *s(e)autês* (σ(ε)αυτῆς fem.); (iii) *h(e)autû* (ἑαυτοῦ or ἁυτοῦ "himself, itself," masc./neut.), *h(e)autês* (ἑαυτῆς or ἁυτῆς, "herself," fem.). In contrast, the two elements of the plural reflexives remain independent; consider the genitive plural (note that the genitive plural is identical for all genders): (i) first person *hēmôn autôn* (ἡμῶν αὐτῶν "ourselves"); (ii) second person *hūmôn autôn* (ὑμῶν αὐτῶν "yourselves"); (iii) third person *sphôn autôn* (σφῶν αὐτῶν "themselves"). However, at an early period in Attic, the third singular reflexive is generalized to the third plural so that *h(e)autôn* and the other case forms eventually usurp the position of *sphôn autôn*, etc. (moreover, the *h(e)aut*- morpheme will in time be completely generalized, replacing the reflexive forms of the first and second persons, singular and plural). As pointed out above, Attic also uses the third-person pronouns (*hû, hoî, hé, sphôn, sphísi, sphâs*) reflexively. These function as the so-called "indirect" or "long-distance" reflexives, appearing in subordinate clauses and having an antecedent in a higher clause (though the *h(e)aut*- third-person reflexive frequently is also so used).

4.1.3.3   *Reciprocal pronoun*

In addition to the reflexive, Greek possesses a reciprocal pronoun *allēlo-* (ἀλληλο-), meaning "each other, one another." It occurs in the oblique cases of the dual and plural. The accusative masculine, feminine, and neuter plural are offered as examples: *allḗlūs* (ἀλλήλους), *allḗlās* (ἀλλήλᾱς), *állēla* (ἀλληλα).

4.1.3.4   Definite article

Under the heading of demonstrative pronouns can be treated the Greek definite article, which had its origin as a demonstrative and still functions as such in Homer. Like the reflexive and reciprocal pronouns, the demonstratives form a thematic masculine/neuter stem and a long -*ā*- feminine; however, the declension of these pronouns is not at all points identical to that of the corresponding nouns. Such differences are to be seen in the paradigm of the Attic article; note the nominative masculine singular and the nominative/accusative neuter singular:

(13)   **Attic definite article**

	Singular		
	Masculine	*Feminine*	*Neuter*
Nominative	ho (ὁ)	hē̦ (ἡ)	tó (τό)
Genitive	tû (τοῦ)	tȇ̦s (τῆς)	tû (τοῦ)
Dative	tō̦(i) (τῷ)	tȇ̦(i) (τῇ)	tō̦(i) (τῷ)
Accusative	tón (τόν)	tȇ̦n (τήν)	tó (τό)

	Dual		
	Masculine	*Feminine*	*Neuter*
Nom./Acc.	tō̦(τώ)	tō̦(τώ)	tō̦(τώ)
Gen./Dat.	toîn (τοῖν)	toîn (τοῖν)	toîn (τοῖν)

	Plural		
	Masculine	*Feminine*	*Neuter*
Nominative	hoi (οἱ)	hai (αἱ)	tá (τά)
Genitive	tȏ̦n (τῶν)	tȏ̦n (τῶν)	tȏ̦n (τῶν)
Dative	toîs (τοῖς)	taîs (ταῖς)	toîs (τοῖς)
Accusative	tū́s (τούς)	tā́s (τάς)	tá (τά)

The nominative/accusative singular termination -*o* is from PIE *-*od* and characterizes various demonstrative pronouns.

4.1.3.5   Demonstrative pronouns

Attic has three principal demonstratives, one of which was formed from that early demonstrative which became the article, plus a particle -*de*: *hóde* (ὅδε), *hḗ̦de* (ἥδε), *tóde* (τόδε). The demonstrative *hûtos* (οὗτος masc.), *haútē̦* (αὕτη fem.), *tûto* (τοῦτο neut.) appears to trace its origin to the same source, constructed with a particle -*u*- and a formant -*to*-. Both *hóde* and *hûtos* function as near demonstratives the former is generally used to refer to some entity in nearer proximity to the speaker than the latter. The far demonstrative of Greek is *ekȇ̦nos* (ἐκεῖνος masc.), *ekȇ̦nē̦* (ἐκείνη fem.), *ekȇ̦no* (ἐκεῖνο neut.). Declined like *ekȇ̦nos* is the so-called emphatic pronoun *autós* (αὐτός masc.), *autȇ̦́* (αὐτή fem.), *autó* (αὐτό neut.). As noted above, *autós* is utilized in reflexive constructions and serves in lieu of the third-person personal pronoun in the oblique cases; in addition *autós* is used in conjunction with a noun to express emphasis or sameness.

4.1.3.6   Interrogative/indefinite pronoun

Greek inherited from Proto-Indo-European an interrogative/indefinite pronoun. The interrogative *tís*, *tí* (τίς, τί; "who, which, what") is tonic, while the segmentally identical indefinite *tis, ti* ("someone, something, etc.") is enclitic. The interrogative is illustrated in (14); the nasal which appears in most of the oblique cases has been generalized from an inherited accusative singular *tín*; as with adjectives of two endings, a gender distinction occurs only in the nominative and accusative:

(14)   **Attic interrogative pronoun**

	Singular	*Dual*	*Plural*
Nom. masc./fem.	tís (τίς)	tíne (τίνε)	tínes (τίνες)
Acc. masc./fem.	tína (τίνα)	tíne (τίνε)	tínas (τίνας)
Nom./acc. neut.	tí (τί)	tíne (τίνε)	tína (τίνα)
Genitive	tínos (τίνος)	tínoin (τίνοιν)	tínōn (τίνων)
Dative	tíni (τίνι)	tínoin (τίνοιν)	tísi (τίσι)

A thematic variant is preserved in various dialects, found in Attic in the genitive singular *tû* (τοῦ), from which a dative *tỗ* (τῷ, Homeric τέῳ) was created.

4.1.3.7   Relative pronouns

The Greek relative pronoun developed from a Proto-Indo-European stem **yo-*, **yeh₂-*; the inflection is that characteristic of *ekễnos* and *autós*: nominative *hós* (ὅς masc.), *hễ* (ἥ fem.), *hó* (ὅ neut.); genitive *hû* (οὗ masc./neut.), *hễs* (ἧς fem.), and so forth. In addition, Greek possesses an indefinite relative pronoun ("whoever, whatever, etc.") composed of the relative and indefinite pronouns in combination, with both members inflected: for example, *hóstis* (ὅστις masc.), *hễtis* (ἥτις fem.), *hóti* (ὅτι neut.); genitive *hûtinos* (οὗτινος masc./neut.), *hễstinos* (ἧστινος fem.). In Attic there also exist variant forms of the genitive and dative, singular and plural, which consist of an uninflected first member *hó-* joined to a thematized second member: for example, *hótū* (ὅτου gen. sg.), *hótǭ(i)* (ὅτῳ dat. sg., both masc./neut.).

4.2   Verbal morphology

The verbal system of ancient Greek is quite complex. Greek verbs are marked for tense, voice, mood, person, and number. The so-called tenses of Greek require some discussion and are treated in the immediately following paragraphs. Verbs are inflected for three voices (active, middle, and passive), three persons (first, second, and third) and three numbers (singular, dual, and plural). Stems are marked for four moods: indicative (the mood of declaration, factual statement), subjunctive (future-oriented, the mood of will and probability), optative (the mood of wish and potentiality), and imperative (the mood of command).

The Greek verbal system is characterized by seven inflectionally distinct tenses: present, imperfect, aorist, perfect, pluperfect, future, and future perfect. Though these verbal categories have been traditionally labeled "tenses," they possess independent temporal significance only in the indicative mood. Most fundamentally, the so-called tenses of Greek register aspectual differences.

4.2.1   Verbal aspect

At least three different verbal aspects can be identified in Greek: perfective, imperfective, and aoristic. The perfective aspect signifies action which the speaker views as complete, as a packaged whole, and the results of which continue to exist. This is the aspectual significance of the Greek perfect "tense," which Gildersleeve (1900:99) aptly and succinctly described in stating that it "looks at both ends of an action." The pluperfect (which is limited to the indicative mood and so always has temporal significance in independent clauses) denotes complete action producing a result which continued into some referential moment in the past. Similarly the future perfect represents complete action producing a result which will continue into some referential moment in the future.

While the perfective aspect signifies complete action, the imperfective aspect represents action which is continuing, ongoing (and hence not complete). The present stem denotes the imperfective aspect and provides two distinct tenses in the indicative mood: the present and the imperfect. The latter is used of action taking place in the past (and only occurs in the indicative mood), the former of non-past action. Compare imperfect indicative *égrapʰon*, "I was writing" (ἔγραφον) with perfect indicative *gégrapʰa*, "I have written" (γέγραφα).

The aoristic aspect is conveyed by the aorist "tense" stem and signifies action which is reported simply as an occurrence, an event, without suggestion as to its completeness or continuance – hence the name of the tense: aorist (ἀόριστος "undefined, unlimited"). Within the indicative mood, the aorist has temporal significance and represents past action.

The aspectual distinctions outlined above are relatively discrete in the indicative mood even though verb-stems conveying particular aspectual notions in this mood also have temporal significance (i.e., actually have tense value). However, this aspectual distinctiveness begins to blur in the case of the present and future indicative. We have seen that the present stem is a carrier of the imperfective aspect and that this is the stem of both the imperfect indicative and present indicative. While the imperfect regularly signifies imperfective aspect and the present indicative often does so, in some instances the present indicative is aspectually aoristic, being used simply to record the occurrence of an action in present time without any notion of continuation. The future indicative is sometimes analyzed as fundamentally signifying aoristic aspect, and perhaps in a majority of instances the future does simply cite the occurrence of an action, in aoristic fashion. However, in other instances the future clearly is used in an imperfective sense to signify continuous action.

4.2.2   Thematic present tense stems

In the parent Indo-European language, various means existed for forming the present tense stem, most of which survive in the grammar of Greek, at least vestigially. For the formation of thematic stems, the Attic dialect utilizes each of the following constructions:

1. The present tense stem can be formed by attaching the thematic vowel to the verb root. In Proto-Indo-European, present tense stems thus formed were of two types – those with accented *e*-grade of the root, and those with ø-grade of the root with accent on the thematic suffix (the so-called *tudáti* type). Reflexes of both types occur in Greek: *pʰérǭ* (φέρω "I bear," < **bʰér-e/o-*) is of the former type, and *grápʰǭ* (γράφω "I write," < **gr̥bʰ-é/ó-*) is of the latter. Reduplicated forms of the thematic present tense stem occur in Greek, as they did in Proto-Indo-European; the vowel used in constructing the reduplicated syllable is -*i*-, as in, for example, *tíktǭ* (τίκτω, "I bring forth," < **ti-tk-e/o-*).

2. In Greek, as in its Indo-European ancestor language, a highly productive suffix -*ye/yo*- was used to build verb-stems either by attaching the suffix directly to a verb root (primary suffix) or by adding the suffix to an already existing stem (secondary suffix), most commonly to noun stems (forming denominative verbs), but also to verb-stems (forming deverbative verbs). Primary formations are of two types – one with *e*-grade of the root, the other with ø-grade. Though a commonly utilized formant, the occurrence of -*ye/yo*- is opaque because its addition results in numerous phonological modifications to stems. These modifications give rise to three of the traditionally identified classes of present tense stems: the *tau*-class, the *iota*-class, and the contract verbs.

2A. *The τ-class*: The verbs assigned to the *tau*-class are characterized by the presence of the consonantal cluster -*pt*- (-ππ-), the reflex of an earlier sequence **bilabial + y*; for example, *sképtomai* (σκέπτομαι "I look carefully") < PG **skep-ye/o-*.

2B. *The ɪ-class*: A heterogeneous set of verbs, the *iota*-class consists of several subtypes:

(i) Verb-stems formed in -*tt*- (-ττ-) in Attic (but -*ss*- (-σσ-) in many dialects), from the earlier sequences *voiceless {dental, velar, labiovelar} stop + y*; for example, *péttǭ* (πέττω, "I cook") < PG **pekʷ-ye/o-*.

(ii) Verb-stems formed in -*zd*- (-ζ-), from the Proto-Greek sequences *voiced {dental, velar, labiovelar} stop + y*; for example, *nízdǭ* (νίζω "I wash") from **nigʷ-ye/o-*.

(iii) Verb-stems formed in -*ll*- (-λλ-) from the Proto-Greek sequence *-*ly*-; for example, *stéllǭ* (στέλλω "I set in order"), from **stel-ye/o-*.

(iv) Verb-stems in -*aín*- (-αίν-) and -*aír*- (-αίρ-), from the earlier sequences *-*any*-, *-*amy*-, *-*ary*-; for example, *baínǭ* (βαίνω, "I walk, go"), from PG **gʷm̥-ye/o-*.

(v) Verb-stems in -{*ế í, ű*} *n*- and -{*ế, í, ű*}*r*- from the Proto-Greek sequences *-{*e, i, u*}{*n, r*}*y*-; for example, *tếnǭ* (τείνω "I stretch") from **ten-ye/o-*.

(vi) Verb-stems in -*ai*- (-αι-) and *-*ei*- (*-ει-) from Proto-Greek sequences *{*a, e*}*w-ye/o*-; for example, *kaíǭ* (καίω "I light,") from **kaw-ye/o-*. In Attic and most other dialects, verbs ending in *-*eiǭ* (*-ειω) were analogically modified to -*euǭ* (-ευω), under the influence of nonpresent tenses and corresponding nouns in -*eu-s* (-ευ-ς).

2C. *The contract verbs*: A large class of verbs built with the -*ye/o*- suffix is that of the so-called contract verbs. These are predominantly denominatives, constructed by the addition of -*ye/o*- to a stem ending in a vowel (sometimes as the result of consonant loss). With the loss of intervocalic -*y*-, the resulting adjacent vowels contracted, giving this class its defining characteristic. Contract presents are of three principal types: those in -*ą̄ǭ* (-αω), -*eǭ* (-εω), and -*oǭ* (-οω).

(i) Verbs ending in -*ą̄ǭ* (-αω). These are primarily denominative verbs formed from noun stems in -*ā*- (first declension nouns); for example, *tīmą́ǭ* (τιμάω "I honor") from PG **tīm-ā-ye/o*- (cf. *tīmế* [τῑμή "honor"]).

(ii) Verbs ending in -*eǭ* (-εω). This somewhat heterogeneous class of verbs consists predominantly of denominative verbs made from thematic noun stems (second declension nouns) having *e*-grade of the thematic suffix; for example *oikéǭ* (οἰκέω "I inhabit") from PG **woik-e-ye/o*- (cf. *oíkos* [οἶκος "house"]). Among other Proto-Indo-European formations which contribute to this set are *s*-stems (e.g., *teléǭ* [τελέω, "I complete"] from PG **tel-es-ye/o*-); iterative/causatives formed with *o*-grade of the root and a suffix -*éye/o*- (e.g., *pʰobéǭ* [φοβέω "I strike with fear"] from PG **pʰogʷ-eye/o*-); and stems built with a stative formant *-*eh₁*- (e.g., *hrīgéǭ* [ῥῑγέω "I shiver with cold"] from PIE *srīg-eh₁-).

(iii) Verbs in -*oǭ* (-οω). While the preceding two types of contract verbs have Proto-Indo-European antecedents, this third type, as a productive category, is original to Greek. Contract verbs of the -*ą̄ǭ* (-αω) type furnished the pattern for analogical creation of -*oǭ* (-οω) denominatives of second declension nominals. Such verbs are commonly factitive in sense; for example *dēlóǭ* (δηλόω "I make clear") beside *dễlos* (δῆλος "clear").

In Attic, contraction of the vowels which were juxtaposed subsequent to the loss of -y- adhered to the contraction patterns outlined above, thus producing present (active indicative) paradigms such as those of *timáǭ* (τιμάω), *oikéǭ* (οἰκέω), *dēlóǭ* (δηλόω):

(15) **Attic contract verbs**

1st sg.	tīmô̄	(τῑμῶ)	oikô̄	(οἰκῶ)	dēlô̄	(δηλῶ)
2nd sg.	tīmâ(i)s	(τῑμᾷς)	oikês	(οἰκεῖς)	dēloîs	(δηλοῖς)
3rd sg.	tīmâ(i)	(τῑμᾷ)	oikê̄	(οἰκεῖ)	dēloî	(δηλοῖ)
1st pl.	tīmô̄men	(τῑμῶμεν)	oikûmen	(οἰκοῦμεν)	dēlûmen	(δηλοῦμεν)
2nd pl.	tīmâte	(τῑμᾶτε)	oikête	(οἰκεῖτε)	dēlûte	(δηλοῦτε)
3rd pl.	tīmô̄si	(τῑμῶσι)	oikûsi	(οἰκοῦσι)	dēlûsi	(δηλοῦσι)

3. The Greek thematic suffix *-ske/o-* is descended from PIE *-s(k̂)e/o-*, originally used in the formation of iteratives. Among stem formations found are those with ø-grade of the root, for example *bá-ske* (βά-σκε "go!"), in some instances with reduplication, as in *di-dá-skǭ* (δι-δά-σκω "I teach").

4. A fourth present tense formation is that of the *nu*-class, a set of verb-stems having Proto-Indo-European antecedents, built with various formants containing *n*. In the parent language, nasal presents (originally iterative or inchoative in sense) were formed by insertion of an ablauting infix *-ne/n-* before the final consonant of the root; from roots ending in *-w* and *-h* were abstracted new suffixes *-neu-/-nu-* and *-neh-/-nh-*. The parent infix *-n-* is preserved in some Greek thematic verbs, but is used in conjunction with a suffix *-ane/o-*, itself derived originally from the Proto-Indo-European nasal infix: for example, *pü-n-tʰ-áno-mai* (πυ-ν-θ-άνο-μαι "I learn"). Still other Greek nasal presents are formed with this same suffix, but without the nasal infix: for example, *auks-ánǭ* (αὐξ-άνω "I increase"). A third thematic nasal present of Greek is built with a suffix *-ne/o-*: for example, *dák-nǭ* (δάκ-νω "I bite"); certain stems display a thematicized form of the above-mentioned Proto-Indo-European suffix *-nu-*, that is PG *-nwe/o-*: for example, Attic *tí-nǭ* (τί-νω "I pay"); cf. Ionic *tí-nǭ* (τί-νω), from Proto-Attic-Ionic *ti-nwǭ (*ti-nϝω). From athematic *nu*-stems (see below) developed a thematized formant *-nuo/e-*: for example, *dēk-nǘǭ* (δεικ-νύω, "I point out").

4.2.3 Athematic present tense stems

Athematic present tense stems are of four basic types. Two of these involve Greek reflexes of the Proto-Indo-European nasal suffixes abstracted from nasal infixed roots ending in *-h* and *-w* (noted above):

1. In Attic, athematic present tense stems are formed with the suffix *-nē-* (*-nā-* outside of Attic and Ionic, from PIE *-neh₂-*) or *-na-* (from PIE *-nh₂-*). The former occurs in the active singular, the latter elsewhere: thus, active *pér-nē-mi* (πέρ-νη-μι "I sell").
2. The Attic suffixes *-nŭ* (instead of *-neu-*, an analogical formation based on *-nā-*) and *-nü-* show the same distribution as *-nē-* and *-na-*: for example, *ár-nü-mai* (ἄρ-νυ-μαι "I win," with short *ü*, being in the middle voice).
3. Root presents are formed by attaching athematic endings directly to the verb root; *e*-grade of the root occurs in the active indicative singular and in the subjunctive, elsewhere the zero-grade: for example, *pʰḗ-mí* (φη-μί "I say," from PIE *bʰeh₂-*), *pʰa-mén* (φα-μέν "we say," from PIE *bʰh₂-*).

4.   Athematic reduplicated presents are likewise formed utilizing a root stem, but with reduplication of the initial consonant of the root: for example, *dí-dǭ-mi* (δί-δω-μι "I give," from PIE *-*deh₃*-), *dí-do-men* (δί-δο-μεν "we give," from PIE *-*dh₃*-).

4.2.4   Imperfect tense

As was noted above, the Greek imperfect is built with present tense stems. The imperfect differs from the present by the use of secondary, rather than primary, verb endings (see below), and by the presence of the temporal prefix *e*-, the *augment*. Thus, beside present *pʰér-ǭ* (φέρ-ω, "I bear"), there is formed an imperfect *é-pʰer-on* (ἔ-φερ-ον, "I was bearing"). The *e*-augment is also used in the formation of the other "secondary" tenses – the aorist and pluperfect – and is also attested in Indo-Iranian, Phrygian, and Armenian. Its use is optional in early Greek, as in Vedic Sanskrit and Avestan, but in time becomes requisite.

4.2.5   Future tense stems

The future tense of Greek is formed with a suffix *-se/o*-, descended from the Proto-Indo-European desiderative suffix *-*s(y)e/o*-. Greek future stems are of two principal types, the sigmatic (or *s*-) future and the contract future. The former occurs with roots ending in a stop or -*s*, such as *dḗk-sǭ* (δείκ-σω "I will show"), and with certain roots (and stems) having a final vowel, in which case the intervocalic -*s*- of -*se/o*- (having been lost by regular sound change) has been restored analogically: *lŭ́-sǭ* (λῠ́-σω "I will loose"). Contract futures have their origin in the future stems of Proto-Indo-European roots terminating in the laryngeals *h₁ and *h₂, such as *ere -sǭ (*ερε-σω "I will speak") from PIE *werh₁-; and *ela-sǭ (*ελα-σω "I will drive") from PIE *h₁elh₂-. Regular loss of the Proto-Greek intervocalic -*s*- yields contract verbs in -*eǭ* and -*aǭ*: thus *eréǭ* (ἐρέω) and *eláǭ* (ἐλάω). The -*eǭ* contract future was then generalized to almost all Greek verb formants ending in a liquid or a nasal. In Attic this future construction was extended to yet an even wider range of verbs, resulting in the inflection dubbed the "Attic future": compare (with contraction) Attic *telô̂* (τελῶ "I will complete"; Ionic *teléǭ* (τελέω) and Homeric *teléssǭ* (τελέσσω), from the stem *teles*-.

Greek future tense verbs are not uncommonly inflected with middle endings, for example *pḗ-somai* (πεί-σομαι "I will suffer"), and in instances show reduplication as well, for example Homeric *de-dék-somai* (δεδέξομαι "I will receive"). Both of these characteristics likely have their origin in the morphology of the Proto-Indo-European desiderative. Though future middle inflection could also be used to convey passive voice, a new future passive construction was built utilizing the aorist passive suffixes (see below) -*tʰḗ*- (-θη-, the first future passive) and -*ḗ*- (-η-, the second future passive) to which was attached the future middle -*somai* (-σομαι), etc. The construction is little known in Homer but has become common by the period of Classical Attic.

4.2.6   Aorist tense stems

The morphology of the aorist tense is of three basic types: athematic, thematic (which together comprise the traditional *second aorist* category), and sigmatic (*first aorist*), each with Proto-Indo-European ancestry. The class of Greek athematic aorists consists primarily of nonablauting root verbs (though preserving traces of Proto-Indo-European ablaut): for example, *é-bȩ̄-n* (ἔ-βη-ν "I went," from PIE *$g^w eh_2$-). In the case of a small subset of three verbs, the singular athematic aorist is formed with a *-k-* extension of the root, preserving vowel gradation: for example, *é-tʰȩ̄-k-a* (ἔ-θη-κ-α "I placed," from PIE *$dʰeh_1$-; cf. Latin *fe-c-i* "I made"), displaying so-called *alpha-thematic* morphology (where *-a*, the regular reflex of the first singular ending *-m̥*, and which arose regularly in the third plural, is extended through much of the paradigm [thus second singular *é-tʰȩ̄-k-a-s* (ἔ-θη-κ-α-ς)] – a morphology also characteristic of certain other root aorists).

Thematic aorists are formed predominantly with ø-grade of the root, originally accented on the thematic suffix: for example, *é-lip-on* (ἔ-λιπ-ον "I left"). As in Sanskrit, some display reduplication: *ȩ̂p-on* (εἶπον "I spoke," from *e-we-wk^w-o-).

The Greek sigmatic aorist is clearly inherited from Proto-Indo-European, though the origin of its characteristic *-s-* marker is disputed: *é-dēk-sa* (ἔδειξα, "I showed," from *e-$deik$-s-$m̥$). The *-s-a(-)* reflex, regular in the first singular and the third plural, was analogically extended through most of the sigmatic aorist paradigm, i.e., the paradigm has become alpha-thematic.

The passive voice of the aorist could be expressed by middle inflection in early Greek, as in Sanskrit; however, a morphologically distinct aorist passive developed from intransitive aorist actives in *-ē-*, which formant is likely to be traced to a Proto-Indo-European stative suffix *-eh_1-/-h_1-: thus, *e-kʰár-ȩ̄-n* (ἐ-χάρ-η-ν, "I rejoiced; I was delighted"); with possible *o*-grade, survives only *he-ál-ō̧-n* (ἐ-ἁλ-ω-ν "I was taken"). The details of origin are uncertain, but alongside *-ē-* there developed an aorist passive marker *-tʰȩ̄-* (*second* and *first* aorist passives respectively), perhaps of greater utility for verb bases ending in a vowel, as in *e-lú̆-tʰȩ̄-n* (ἐ-λύ-θη-ν "I was released").

4.2.7 Perfect tense stems

The Greek perfect stem is formed in four principal manners and, in the active indicative, inflected with a set of *perfect endings*, continuing in part those of Proto-Indo-European. The archaic verb *oîd-a* (οἶδ-α "I know" [in origin "I have seen"], from PIE *wid-), one perfect type in and of itself, preserves the Proto-Indo-European pattern of *o*-grade of the root in the active singular, ø-grade in the plural (*ís-men* [ἴσ-μεν "we know"]), with endings attached to the root.

The so-called *first perfect* of Attic is the most commonly occurring perfect stem; its hallmark is a *-k-* formant which precedes the endings, probably to be linked to the *-k-* of the three athematic aorists mentioned above. Relatively late in origin and a uniquely Greek formation, the *k*-perfect began with verb roots ending in a long vowel, as in, for example, *bé-bȩ̄-k-a* (βέ-βη-κ-α "I have gone," from PIE *$g^w eh_2$-). The construction first appeared in the singular, spreading subsequently to the plural and to verb roots of other shapes. As in the preceding example, perfect stems normally show an initial reduplicated syllable (to be found already in the parent Indo-European language), on which see immediately below.

Lacking the *-k-* formant of the first perfect, the Attic *second perfect* is characterized by an absence of root alternation in the active voice. Both this perfect stem and that of the *k*-perfect display alpha-thematic inflection in the active indicative (extended from the first singular and third plural).

The fourth perfect type, the aspirated perfect, is primarily an Attic-Ionic development, one which had its origin in the middle voice. The perfect middle is formed by attaching endings directly to the verb root. Each of the perfect middle endings begins with a consonant except for the early third plural -*atai* (-ατaι). Through processes of assimilation, all root-final bilabial stops, whether - *p*, -*b*, or - *p^h*, are modified by the attached consonant of the ending – and all undergo identical modification, so that the original quality of the bilabial stop (voiceless, voiced, or aspirated) is obscured. Root-final velar stops (-*k*, -*g*, -*k^h*) are likewise neutralized. For example, from *trép-ǭ* (τρέπω "I turn") is generated a middle second plural *té-trap^h-t^{h}e* (τέ-τραφ-θε "you have turned"). In the case of some roots with a final bilabial or velar, the aspirated reflex of the second plural spreads to the third plural, as in *te-tráp^h-atai* (τε-τράφ-αται, rather than **te-tráp-atai*) – a stage which is preserved in Homer. From this starting point, the aspirate is then generalized through the perfect active: thus, *té-trop^h-a* (τέ-τροφ-α "I have turned") rather than **té-trop-a*.

4.2.7.1   Perfect stem reduplication

Most commonly roots beginning #C_1(C_2)V- reduplicate as #C_1e-C_1(C_2)V- (as in *bé-bę̄ -k-a*), though a good number of root-initial #CC- sequences in Attic (e.g., *ps-*, *ks-*, *gn-*) "reduplicate" synchronically by prefixing the vowel *e-* (e.g., *é-psau-k-a* (ἔ-ψαυ-κ-α "I have touched"). The latter reduplication appears to have spread from perfects of verb roots with initial #*sC*- clusters: by regular sound change **#se-sC-* yields #*he-sC-* (e.g., *hé-stę̄-k-a* (ἕ-στη-κ-α "I have stood") from **se-stę̄-k-a*). The spread of unaspirated *e-* (rather than *he-*) was likely supported by the *e-* augment of the other preterite tenses, aorist and imperfect. Moreover, in some instances of initial #*sC*- clusters, regular dissimilatory processes of deaspiration produced an *e-* reduplication: thus, *é-lēp^h-a* (εἴ-ληφ-α "I have taken") from **he-l^{h}āp^h-a*, from **se-slāp^h-a* (certain #*s* + *sonorant* clusters perhaps being particularly susceptible to this development).

Proto-Indo-European verb roots beginning with a laryngeal produce Greek perfect stems which synchronically appear to "reduplicate" by lengthening an initial vowel: for example, *ę̄g-mai* (ἦγ-μαι "I have led," perfect of *ágō* (ἄγω)), from PG **āg-*, from PIE **h₂e-h₂ĝ-*. This synchronic pattern of producing the perfect stem by lengthening an initial vowel then spread to other vowel-initial roots.

Yet a distinct type of reduplication is exhibited by verb roots which begin with a vowel followed by a sonorant consonant; such roots form a perfect stem by reduplicating the *vowel + sonorant* sequence and lengthening the vowel of the root. The exact origin of the structure is a matter of disagreement, though again is likely to lie in the presence of an initial laryngeal: thus, *el$\acute{e}$lüt^h-a* (ἐλ-ήλυθ-α "I have come"), from **h₁le-h₁ludh-*. The pattern is extended to other verb roots beginning with a vowel and becomes especially common in Attic (and Ionic), thus being dubbed *Attic reduplication*.

4.2.7.2   Pluperfect and future perfect

Before leaving perfect morphology, attention needs to be given to the pluperfect and future perfect. Both of these tenses are Greek innovations, not to be found in Proto-Indo-European. The Attic pluperfect is formed with the perfect stem, to which the augment is prefixed if the stem begins with a consonant (such is the general case at least). In the active voice, the Classical Attic pluperfect endings preserve a formant -*e-*, of uncertain origin (attested in Homer), which is followed in turn by the perfect endings in the singular and the secondary endings in the dual and plural (though the third plural appends -*san*). In the singular, Attic contracts the -*e-* and the ensuing morph: thus **e-le-lü-k-e-a* (**ἐ-λε-λύ-κ-ε-α*) yields *e-le-lǘ-k-ę̄* (ἐ-λε-λύ-κ-η "I had released"). In both Homer and later Attic, variant pluperfect active morphology occurs. The Attic middle is produced by adding the secondary middle endings to the pluperfect stem (as described above): *e-le-lǘ-mēn* (ἐ-λε-λύ-μην "I had ransomed"). Attachment of the sigmatic future *s* + *ending* complex to the perfect stem yields the future perfect.

4.2.8 Nonindicative moods

The above elaboration of the tense stems of Attic has focused upon stems as they occur in the indicative, the unmarked mood of Greek by the fifth century. A survey of the morphology of the nonindicative moods follows.

4.2.8.1 Subjunctive mood

In Proto-Indo-European the subjunctive is marked by an ablauting suffix -*e/o*- attached to the root. The Greek reflex of this construction, the so-called *short vowel subjunctive*, characterized athematic stems in early Greek and is preserved in Homer and elsewhere: for example *ḗd-o-men* (εἴδ-ο-μεν "may we know", from the *e*-grade of *wid-, perfect subjunctive). The attachment of this suffix -*e/o*- to thematic stems yielded, by contraction with the thematic vowel, the Greek *long vowel subjunctive*: *lǘ-ǭ-men* (λύ-ω-μεν "may we release," present subjunctive). Extension of this long vowel morphology to the aforementioned athematic stems results in, for example, Attic *ēd-ǭ̂-men* (εἰδ-ῶ-μεν).

4.2.8.2 Optative mood

The optative mood in the parent Indo-European language was marked by the suffix *-yeh₁/ih₁-*, originally attached to the root, with *-ih₁-* subsequently also affixed to thematic stems. The former is antecedent to the Greek athematic optative suffix, as in Attic *ḗ̄ē̄-n* (earlier *eíē̄-n* [εἴη-ν "I would be"] from *h₁s-yéh₁-*) and *ê-men* (earlier *eî-men* [εἶ-μεν "we would be"] from *h₁s-ih₁-*). In the case of thematic and alpha-thematic stems, the Attic reflex is -*oi*- and -*ai*- respectively: *pʰér-oi-mi* (φέρ-οι-μι "I would bear"), with the primary athematic ending (on primary and secondary endings see below) extended to earlier *pʰér-oi-a* (φέρ-οι-α, from *bʰér-o-ih₁-m̥*), though secondary endings are commonly preserved in the optative paradigm; *lǘ-s-ai-mi* (λύ-σ-αι-μι "I would release," aorist).

4.2.8.3 Imperative mood

A multiplicity of morphological markings characterizes the Greek imperative. As in Proto-Indo-European, the active second singular is formed with the bare stem alone (i.e., without an ending), or by attaching to the stem the particle -*tʰi* (PIE *-dʰi*); the former construction provides the most frequently occurring Greek imperative, the latter is limited to athematic stems: for example, *pʰér-e* (φέρ-ε "carry !"); *i-tʰi* (ἴ-θι, "go !"). In addition, the second singular is formed in Attic by attachment of the word-final formants -*s* (the secondary ending) and -*i* (both occurring rarely), as well as -*on*, characterizing alpha-thematic aorist inflection. Proto-Indo-European filled out portions of the imperative paradigm utilizing the injunctive mood (like the indicative in form but with secondary, rather than primary, endings and expressing "timeless truths"). Injunctive morphology is preserved in the Greek second-person plural imperative (*pʰérete* [φέρετε "carry!"]), looking like the Greek indicative (as does the second dual). The third-person singular imperative is marked by the appending of a particle -*tǭ* (-τω, PIE *-tōd*) to the verb-stem (*pʰeré-tǭ* [φερέ-τω "let him/her carry"]), from which a third dual marker -tōn (-των) was created. The third-person plural takes several forms in Attic, building with the particle -tō̜, such as *p^heró-ntōn* (φερό-ντων "let them carry"), where the bookend nasals are taken over from the primary (*-onti* > -ūsi) and secondary (-on) third plural endings. Middle imperative endings likewise continue injunctive morphology (e.g., second singular * *p^here-so* (*φερε-σο), becoming *p^hérū* (φέρου)) and display analogical reshaping (e.g., the third singular ending -st^hō̜ (-σθω), after middle second plural -st^he(-σθε) and active third singular -tō̜ (-τω)).

4.2.9   Verb endings

The verb endings of Greek are traditionally classified as *primary* and *secondary*. In broad terms, the primary endings are used with non-past tenses, the secondary endings with past tenses and the optative mood. Endings are further differentiated as thematic (attached to a thematic stem) and (otherwise) athematic. The following charts illustrate Attic verb endings. In the case of thematic verbs, division is made between the root and thematic suffix; for athematic, division is marked before the ending. In (16) primary active thematic and athematic endings are illustrated by the present active indicative of *p^hérō̜* (φέρω "I carry") and *tít^hē̜mi* (τίθημι "I place") respectively:

(16)   **Attic verb endings I: primary active**

		Thematic		Athematic	
Singular	1.	p^hér-ō̜	(φέρ-ω)	tít^hē̜ -mi	(τίθη-μι)
	2.	p^hér-ē̜s	(φέρ-εις)	tít^hē̜-s	(τίθη-ς)
	3.	p^hér-ē̜	(φέρ-ει)	tít^hē̜-si	(τίθη-σι)
Dual	2.	p^hér-eton	(φέρ-ετον)	tít^he-ton	(τίθε-τον)
	3.	p^hér-eton	(φέρ-ετον)	tít^he-ton	(τίθε-τον)
Plural	1	p^hér-omen	(φέρ-ομεν)	tít^he-men	(τίθε-μεν)
	2.	p^hér-ete	(φέρ-ετε)	tít^he-te	(τίθε-τε)
	3.	p^hér-ūsi	(φέρ-ουσι)	tit^hé-āsi	(τιθέ-ᾱσι)

Secondary active thematic and athematic endings are illustrated by the imperfect active indicative paradigms of *p^hérō̜* and *hístē̜mi* (ἵστημι "I stand") respectively:

(17)   **Attic verb endings II: secondary active**

		Thematic		Athematic	
Singular	1.	ép^her-on	(ἔφερ-ον)	hístē̜-n	(ἵστη-ν)
	2.	ép^her-es	(ἔφερ-ες)	hístē̜-s	(ἵστη-ς)
	3.	ép^her-e	(ἔφερ-ε)	hístē̜	(ἵστη)
Dual	2.	ep^hér-eton	(ἐφέρ-ετον)	hísta-ton	(ἵστα-τον)
	3.	ep^hér-étēn	(ἐφέρ-έτην)	hístá-tēn	(ἱστά-την)
Plural	1.	ep^hér-omen	(ἐφέρ-ομεν)	hísta-men	(ἵστα-μεν)
	2.	ep^hér-ete	(ἐφέρ-ετε)	hísta-te	(ἵστα-τε)
	3.	ép^her-on	(ἔφερ-ον)	hísta-san	(ἵστα-σαν)

Middle endings are used to express both middle and passive voice, as in Proto-Indo-European; though distinct passive inflection developed for particular tenses, as noted above.

In (18), the primary middle endings are illustrated with the present middle indicative paradigms of thematic *pʰérō* and athematic *títʰēmi*:

(18) Attic verb endings III: primary middle

		Thematic		*Athematic*	
Singular	1.	pʰér-omai	(φέρ-ομαι)	títʰe-mai	(τίθε-μαι)
	2.	pʰér-ẹ̄(i)	(φέρ-η)	títʰe-sai	(τίθε-σαι)
	3.	pʰér-etai	(φέρ-εται)	títʰe-tai	(τίθε-ται)
Dual	2.	pʰér-estʰon	(φέρ-εσθον)	títʰe-stʰon	(τίθε-σθον)
	3.	pʰér-estʰon	(φέρ-εσθον)	títʰe-stʰon	(τίθε-σθον)
Plural	1.	pʰer-ómetʰa	(φερ-όμεθα)	titʰé-metʰa	(τιθέ-μεθα)
	2.	pʰér-estʰe	(φέρ-εσθε)	títʰe-stʰe	(τίθε-σθε)
	3.	pʰér-ontai	(φέρ-ονται)	títʰe-ntai	(τίθε-νται)

(19) presents the secondary middle endings, utilizing the imperfect middle indicative paradigms of thematic *pʰérō* and athematic *títʰēmi*:

(19) Attic verb endings IV: secondary middle

		Thematic		*Athematic*	
Singular	1.	epʰer-ómēn	(ἐφερ-όμην)	etitʰé-mēn	(ἐτιθέ-μην)
	2.	epʰér-ū	(ἐφέρ-ου)	etítʰe-so	(ἐτίθε-σο)
	3.	epʰér-eto	(ἐφέρ-ετο)	etítʰe-to	(ἐτίθε-το)
Dual	2.	epʰér-estʰon	(ἐφέρ-εσθον)	etítʰe-stʰon	(ἐτίθε-σθον)
	3.	epʰer-éstʰēn	(ἐφερ-έσθην)	etitʰé-stʰēn	(ἐτιθέ-σθην)
Plural	1.	epʰer-ómetʰa	(ἐφερ-όμεθα)	etitʰé-metʰa	(ἐτιθέ-μεθα)
	2.	epʰér-estʰe	(ἐφέρ-εσθε)	etítʰe-stʰe	(ἐτίθε-σθε)
	3.	epʰér-onto	(ἐφέρ-οντο)	etítʰe-nto	(ἐτίθε-ντο)

In the singular active indicative, Greek preserves an inherited set of perfect endings, seen in the inflection of *oîd-a* (οἶδ-α "I know"). In the other perfect stem-types, represented below by *léloipa* (λέλοιπα "I have left"), the secondary second-person singular -*s* (-ς) has been invoked to replace inherited −*tʰa* (-θα):

(20) Attic verb endings V: perfect

Singular	1.	oîd-a	(οἶδ-α)	léloip-a	(λέλοιπ-α)
	2.	oîs-tʰa	(οἶσ-θα)	léloip-as	(λέλοιπ-ας)
	3.	oîd-e	(οἶδ-ε)	léloip-e	(λέλοιπ-ε)

4.2.10 Infinitives

Attic possesses active, middle, and passive (or middle-passive) infinitives in the present, future, aorist, and perfect tenses. While the origin of the Greek infinitives is a matter of some uncertainty, it appears likely that they developed from verbal nouns inflected for particular cases. Attic thematic stems produce an active infinitive which terminates in -*ēn* (-ειν, earlier *-ein*), apparently in origin an endingless locative of an *n*-stem (probably from *-sen*, with loss of *-s-* and contraction of the thematic vowel and the initial vowel of the remaining *-en*). Athematic verbs in Attic form the active infinitive in -*(e)nai*: thus, *titʰénai* (τιθέναι "to place," present); *dûnai* (δοῦναι "to give," aorist); *ēdénai* (εἰδέναι "to know," perfect). The origin of the formant *-(e)nai* is disputed – perhaps arising from a particle *-ai* appended to an *n*-stem, perhaps from a locative in *-eneh₂-i*. The active infinitive of sigmatic aorists terminates in *-sai* (-σαι), which perhaps preserves the particle *-ai* mentioned above, or again is perhaps to be traced to a locative. The middle infinitives – present, future, aorist, and perfect; thematic and athematic – end in *-sᵗʰai* (-σθαι), often conjectured to be related to Indo-Iranian infinitives in *-dʰyai* (as the aorist active *-sai* has been conjectured to be so related).

4.2.11   Participles

Active, middle, and passive (or middle-passive) participles occur in the present, future, aorist, and perfect tenses, and are inflected for all three genders. The active participle of the present, future, and aorist is formed with the suffix *-nt-* (-ντ-). When attached to a thematic stem, the stem bears the *o*-grade of the thematic vowel: for example, the present active participles *pʰér-o-nt-os* (φέρ-ο-ντ-ος "carrying," gen. masc./neut. sg.); *pʰér-ōn* (φέρ-ων, nom. masc. sg. from *-pʰer-o-nt-s*, with irregular lengthening of the final vowel); *pʰér-ūs-a* (φέρ-ουσ-α, nom. fem. sg. from *-pʰer-o-nt-ya*). As the preceding examples illustrate, the masculine and neuter active participles have the expected consonant-stem inflection; feminines follow the inflection of (first declension) nouns of the *-ih₂/yeh₂-* type. Sigmatic aorists form the present active participle with a formant *-ant-* rather than *-at-* (as expected by regular sound change, from *-s-ṇt-*) under the influence of thematic stems: *lú̄-s-ant-os* (λῡ́-σ-αντ-ος, "releasing," gen. masc./neut. sg.). The perfect active participle is formed with a suffix *-wos-* (prior to the disappearance of Attic *w*) in the masculine and neuter, zero-grade *-us-* in the feminine: *ēd-ṓs* (εἰδ-ώς "knowing," nom. masc. sg., from *-weid-wōs*); *ēd-uîa* (εἰδ-υῖα, nom. fem. sg., from *-wid-us-ih₂*). Middle participles are formed utilizing a thematic suffix *-meno-*.

4.2.12   Verbal adjectives

In various daughter languages, including Greek, verbal adjectives developed from the Proto-Indo-European stem formant consisting of φ-grade of the root plus the suffix *-tó-*. While the original sense was passive, the Greek verbal adjective came to express active notions as well, and lacked the root constraint of the parent language: *klü-tó-s* (κλυ-τό-ς, "heard of, famous"); *pʰilē-tó-s* (φιλη-τό-ς "to be loved"); *pis-tó-s* (πισ-τό-ς, "to be believed; believing"). This is perhaps the same suffix used in the formation of ordinals and superlatives. Adjectives indicating necessity are formed with a suffix *-téo-*, of disputed origin though frequently linked to Sanskrit *-tavya-*: *grap-téo-s* (γραπ-τέο-ς "must be written").

4.3 Adverbs

Attic, like other Greek dialects, productively forms adverbs from adjectives utilizing a formant *-ōs*: *kakós* (κακός "bad"), *kakôs* (κακῶς "ill"); *hēdús* (ἡδύς "sweet"), *hēdeōs* (ἡδεώς "sweetly"). For the comparative adverb, the accusative neuter singular of the comparative adjective is used, and for the superlative adverb, the accusative neuter plural of the superlative adjective. In addition, Greek possesses many adverbs which are simply lexicalized nouns of various case forms (some no longer productive in Attic): for example, nominative (apparently) *hápaks* (ἅπαξ "once"); accusative *tḗmeron* (τήμερον "today"); dative *koinȇ(i)* (κοινῇ "in common"); locative *oíkoi* (οἴκοι "at home"); instrumental *lát^{h}rā* (λάθρᾱ "secretly"). Similarly some adverbs are lexicalized univerbated prepositional phrases: *ek-podȏn* (ἐκποδών, "out of the way," literally "away from the feet"). Numerous suffixes, of uncertain origin, are also used for adverb formation, such as -*t^{h}en*, with ablatival sense, in, for example, *én-t^{h}en* (ἔν-θεν "thence").

4.4 Compounds

Nominal compounding is a common phenomenon in Greek as it was in the parent Indo-European language. In Greek, nominal compounds are most frequently composed of two elements, infrequently more than two, and show inflection of the last member only. While Attic displays a wide variety of compound types, these can be conveniently, if not exhaustively, classified as endocentric and exocentric, invoking categories from traditional Indo-European grammar. The former can be subdivided into copulative and determinative; the principal representative of the exocentric type is the possessive compound.

Copulative compounds coordinate two (or more) members: for example, *nük^{h}t^h-ḗmeron* (νυχθ-ήμερον "night and day"). Determinatives may be descriptive (the first member modifies the second adjectivally or adverbially) or dependent (the first member is grammatically dependent on the second, or occasionally vice versa): for example, *akró-polis* (ἀκρό-πολις "upper city") and *Diós-kūroi* (Διόσ-κουροι "sons (boys) of Zeus") respectively. Possessive compounds are similar in sense to determinatives, but are used adjectivally to indicate possession of a trait or quality: *argüró-toksos* (ἀργυρό-τοξος "having a silver bow"). At times in Greek, as commonly in Sanskrit, possessive compounds are derived from determinatives by a shift in accent.

4.5 Numerals

Of the Attic cardinals 1 through 10, only the first four are declined, as in Proto-Indo-European:

(21) **The Attic cardinals**

1	hȇs, mía, hén	εἷς, μία, ἕν	(masc. fem., neut.)
2	dúo	δύο	(declined as a dual)
3	trȇs, tría	τρεῖς, τρία	(masc./fem., neut.)
4	téttares, téttara	τέτταρες, τέτταρα	(masc./fem., neut.)
5	pénte	πέντε	
6	héks	ἕξ	
7	heptá	ἑπτά	
8	oktȏ	ὀκτώ	
9	ennéa	ἐννέα	
10	déka	δέκα	

From 11 through 199, the cardinals are indeclinable. Between 11 and 19, these are composed of compounds with *déka*: for example, *dṓ-deka* (δώ-δεκα "12"). The decads 20 to 90, composed of a form of the appropriate monad and a reflex of Proto-Indo-European **dḱṃ t-* or *o*-grade **dḱomt-* (cf. **deḱṃ(t)* "ten") are as follows:

(22) **The Attic decads**

20	ékosi	εἴκοσι
30	triákonta	τριάκοντα
40	tettarákonta	τετταράκοντα
50	pentḗkonta	πεντήκοντα
60	heksḗkonta	ἑξήκοντα
70	hebdomḗkonta	ἑβδομήκοντα
80	ogdoḗkonta	ὀγδοήκοντα
90	enenḗkonta	ἐνενήκοντα

Hundreds are expressed by *-katon* (used for 100, PIE **ḱṃtom*) and its inflected Attic derivative *-kósioi* preceded by a form of the appropriate monad; for example:

(23) **The Attic decads**

100	hekatón	ἑκατόν
200	diākósioi	διᾱκόσιοι
300	triākósioi	τριᾱκόσιοι
400	tetrakósioi	τετρακόσιοι

One thousand is *kʰī́lioi* (χίλιοι) and 10,000 is *mǖrioi* (μῡ́ριοι).

Compound numbers are expressed in various ways. Where *x* is the smaller number and *Y* the larger, the typical formulae are: (i) *x kaí Y* (where *kaí* (καί) is the conjunction "and"); (ii) *Y (kaì) x*. In the second, *kaí* is optional; compare English "three and twenty blackbirds" and "twenty-three." If the last digit of the compound is eight or nine the common practice is to express the number as the next highest decad minus two or one respectively: for example, *düoîn déontes pentḗkonta* (δυοῖν δέοντες πεντήκοντα "forty-eight," literally "fifty lacking two").

Ordinals are generally derived from the corresponding cardinals utilizing the suffix *-to-*. The ordinals "first" and "second" are exceptions regarding the cardinal base, and "seventh" and "eighth" show variation of the suffix. All ordinals are declined.

(24) **The Attic ordinals**

first	prôtos	πρῶτος
second	deúteros	δεύτερος
third	trítos	τρίτος
fourth	tétartos	τέταρτος
fifth	pémptos	πέμπτος
sixth	héktos	ἕκτος
seventh	hébdomos	ἕβδομος
eighth	ógdoos	ὄγδοος
ninth	énatos	ἔνατος
tenth	dékatos	δέκατος

5. SYNTAX

5.1 Word order

As is the case with many early Indo-European languages possessing well-developed systems
of nominal and verbal morphological marking, the word order of Greek is identified as free.
That is to say, the order of sentence constituents is highly variable, though not all possible
permutations can actually occur. Various investigators conducting statistical examinations
of Greek texts have noted a tendency in Classical Greek for the subject to precede the verb
(SV) and likewise for the object to precede the verb (OV). The result is that SV and OV have
been identified as "unmarked" orders, and variation in these and other basic constituent
orders has been commonly attributed to stylistic, pragmatic, and even prosodic factors.

5.2 Clitics

In the preceding sections allusion has been made to clitic elements; Classical Attic, like the
other dialects of ancient Greek, possessed numerous such clitics, divided into the two broad
classes of *enclitics* and *proclitics*. Traditionally these are analyzed as unaccented (atonic)
lexemes which form an accent unit with the preceding (enclitics) or following (proclitics)
tonic form. Among the enclitics are included the oblique cases of the singular personal
pronouns, the indefinite pronoun and adverbs, and various grammatical particles (of which
Greek has many, both adverbial and conjunctive). Under the heading of proclitic have been
listed monosyllabic forms of the article which begin with a vowel, and certain prepositions
and conjunctions. It should be noted that a proclitic class was not a notion treated by the
Greek grammarians and that the breadth of its membership and its prosodic nature have been
debated by modern scholars (see Devine and Stephens 1994:356–361). The occurrence of
clitics in the parent Indo-European language and their placement in Wackernagel's position
(after the first accented word of the sentence) is a well-established phenomenon, preserved
particularly clearly in Anatolian (see *WAL* Chs. 18–23).

5.3 Post- and prepositives

Classes of Greek lexemes can be further distinguished as *postpositive* and *prepositive*. Enclitics
constitute roughly a large subset of the former and proclitics of the latter (for enumeration
of class membership see Dover 1960:12–14). As formulated by Dover, postpositives (q)
are generally not permitted in clause-initial position, while prepositives (p) are normally
excluded from clause-final position. Words which are not so limited – most of the words of
the language – can be labeled *mobile* (M), again following Dover (1960:12). In early Greek,
postpositives tend to aggregate after the first mobile word of the sentence, but over time this
tendency is progressively eroded. A familiar sentence-initial syntactic pattern of Classical
Attic is $\#pq_1Mq_2$ where q_1 can only be a connecting particle, q_2 can be any other postpositive
(Dover 1960:16; Dover attributes the emergence of this pattern to an interaction of factors,
including a partial coalescence of prepositives and mobile forms).

5.4 Coordination

Greek freely allows coordination and subordination. Coordination is commonly effected
utilizing the enclitic conjunction *te* (τε) and the tonic *kaí* (καί). Both can be used to conjoin

individual words, clauses and sentences and are frequently used in combination with one another and with still other conjunctions. The conjunctive particle *dé* (δέ) is frequently used to introduce clauses and occurs in second position. Often a clause so introduced is coupled with a second clause marked by the particle *mén* (μέν), the two existing in a contrastive relationship ("on the one hand" ... "on the other hand").

5.5 Subordination

With regard to syntax, the subordinate clauses of Greek are of three basic types, distinguished by the verb form – finite, infinitival, and participial. Within each type structural variation occurs. Subordinate clauses frequently contain a finite verb and are introduced by a complementizer, of which the language possesses several. For example, the complementizers *hína* (ἵνα), *hǭs* (ὡς), and *hópǭs* (ὅπως) are used to mark subordinate clauses containing a finite verb in the subjunctive or optative mood – subordinate constructions traditionally identified as *purpose* (or *final*) *clauses*. If the verb of the matrix clause is inflected in a so-called primary tense (present, future, perfect, future perfect), the subjunctive is used in the embedded clause; if the tense of the matrix verb is "secondary" (imperfect, aorist, pluperfect), the subordinate verb appears in the optative (or subjunctive) mood.

(25) παιδεύω τὸ παιδίον ἵνα ἐκμάθῃ
      paideúǭ tò paidíon hína ekmát^{h}ę̄(i)
      "I teach (PRESENT) the child in order that he may learn (SUBJUNCTIVE)"

After a verb expressing the notion of SAYING, a complement clause commonly is introduced by *hóti* (ὅτι) or *hǭs* (ὡς); if the tense of matrix verb is primary, the mood of the subordinate verb is unaltered (i.e., the mood is retained which would have been present had the subordinate clause been independent), but may be changed to the optative if the matrix verb tense is secondary.

(26) ἔλεξεν ὅτι Σωκράτης παιδεύοι τὸ παιδίον
      éleksen hóti Sǭkrátę̄s paideúoi tò paidíon
      "(S)he said (AORIST) that Socrates was teaching (OPTATIVE) the child"

The second fundamental type of subordinate clause construction is that in which the verb is infinitival. For example, this syntax is typical of clauses embedded in matrix sentences containing a verb of THINKING or, in some cases, a verb of SAYING. If the subject of the embedded clause is identical to that of the matrix clause, it is not expressed; if the two are different, the embedded subject appears in the accusative case.

(27) νομίζει Σωκράτην παιδεύειν τὸ παιδίον
      nomízdę̄ Sǭkrátę̄n paideúę̄n tò paidíon
      "(S)he thinks that Socrates (ACCUSATIVE) is teaching (INFINITIVE) the child"

Third and less commonly, a subordinate clause may be constructed with a participial verb. Certain verbs expressing PERCEPTION and KNOWING take subordinate clauses of this construction. If both matrix and embedded clause have the same subject, the participle stands in the nominative case. If the subjects are different, the subordinate subject and participle are inflected as accusatives (or, in certain instances, some other oblique case).

(28) ἀκούω Σωκράτην παιδεύοντα τὸ παιδίον
      akoúǭ Sǭkrátę̄n paideúonta tò paidíon
      "I hear that Socrates (ACCUSATIVE) is teaching (PARTICIPLE) the child"

5.6 Conditional clauses

Attic possesses an elaborate syntactico-semantic system of conditional clauses. No fewer than eight distinct patterns can be identified, varying structurally by the verb tense and/or mood found in the protasis and in the apodosis (and the presence or absence of the particle *án* (ἄν)). The various conditional constructions differ in nuance by the partial intersection of three semantic factors: temporality (past, present, future); likelihood of fulfillment; and generality (or specificity) of the event to which reference is made. For example, the imperfect indicative in both protasis and apodosis signals a *present unreal* (or *contrary to fact*) conditional – a conditional relation which could, but does not in fact, exist:

(29) εἰ Σωκράτης ἐπαίδευε τὸ παιδίον, ἂν ἐδύνατο γράφειν
      ē̦ Sōkrátēs epaídeue tò paidíon, àn edúnato gráp^hēn
      "If Socrates taught the child, he would be able to write (but Socrates does not teach the child)"

5.7 Agreement

Agreement is expressed between: (i) subject and verb in person and number; (ii) adjective and noun in case, gender, and number; (iii) a word and its appositive in case; and (iv) a relative pronoun and its antecedent in gender and number. The case of a relative pronoun is determined by its syntactic position in the relative clause; however, the relative pronoun frequently is inflected to agree with the case of its antecedent (case attraction). A notable exception to regular subject/verb agreement is of Proto-Indo-European origin: neuter plural subjects (collectives in origin) take singular subjects.

5.8 Long-distance anaphora

In the classical Attic dialect of the fifth century BC, there exists a well-developed system of reflexive pronouns. As described above, a distinct reflexive formant occurs for each of the three persons of the singular and plural, though the third singular form has begun to be utilized in lieu of the existing third plural. A reflexive pronoun is employed when it and its antecedent occur within the same clause. In the case of the third person, however, the reflexive can also appear in a subordinate clause when its antecedent is in a dominating clause. The *h(e)aut-* third-person form is sometimes utilized in this "long-distance" fashion. As discussed earlier (see §4.1.3.2), there is a morphologically distinct, so-called "indirect" reflexive which also functions in this manner – in origin the early personal pronouns of the third person, familiar from Homer.

6. LEXICON

The lexicon of a language is a mirror of its speakers' culture and a footprint of its history. Ancient Greek is one of the grammatically most conservative of the attested Indo-European languages and not surprisingly preserves, at least within its core lexicon, many words of Proto-Indo-European pedigree (a number of which have been encountered above). These include kinship terms such as *patḗr* (πατήρ "father"), *mḗtēr* (μήτηρ "mother"), *t^hügátēr* (θυγάτηρ "daughter"); names of domesticated and wild animals, for example *híppos* (ἵππος "horse"), *taûros* (ταῦρος "bull"), *hŭs* (ὕς "pig"), *óp^his* (ὄφις "snake"), *mûs* (μῦς "mouse"); names of body parts such as *kardía* (καρδία "heart"), *hêpar* (ἧπαρ "liver"), *omp^halós* (ὀμφαλός "navel").

The reader may consult the discussion of verb morphology in §4.2 for numerous examples of inherited Proto-Indo-European verb roots.

There are a great many words of the Greek language, however, which have no clear Indo-European etymology. When the Greeks arrived in the Balkan peninsula late in the third millennium, they came to a place which had an indigenous population, and from the language or, more likely, languages of this population the Greeks certainly acquired a part of their lexicon. Some scholars have attributed a subset of these borrowings to an unattested, broadly distributed "Mediterranean" or "Aegean" substratum language, as superficially similar forms crop up in numerous of the attested languages of the ancient Mediterranean. Under this rubric have been listed words such as *erébinthos* (ἐρέβινθος "chick-pea"), *míntha* (μίνθα "mint"), *sûkon* (σῦκον "fig"), *hródon* (ῥόδον "rose"), *hüákinthos* (ὑάκινθος "hyacinth"), *mólübdos* (μόλυβδος "lead").

Some scholars have held out the possibility that one or more Indo-European languages were already spoken in the Balkan peninsula at the time the Greeks arrived and that these languages similarly provided loans to the Greek lexicon. Thus, a so-called Pelasgian element of the Greek vocabulary has been proposed, with forms cited such as *tûmbos* (τύμβος "grave") beside *táphos* (τάφος, the regular Greek reflex of PIE *$dʰmbʰos$) and *pûrgos* (πύργος "tower"), compare Germanic *burgs* ("hill-fort"). The Pelasgian hypothesis has not been widely received without reservation.

Among the attested languages of antiquity from which Greek unquestionably acquired vocabulary, Semitic occupies a prominent position. Securely identified Semitic loanwords include *déltos* (δέλτος "writing tablet"), *khitṓn* (χιτών a garment; of Sumerian origin), *khrūsós* (χρῡσός "gold"), *krókos* (κρόκος "saffron," though not of Semitic origin; perhaps originally from an Anatolian place name), *máltʰē* (μάλθη "wax"), and *sḗsamon* (σήσαμον "sesame seed"). Hittite loans include *kûanos* (κύανος "dark blue enamel"; though itself likely of non-Hittite origin). Iranian appears to provide, among other forms, *kaunákēs* (καυνάκης a woolen robe).

7. READING LIST

For a traditional grammatical treatment of classical Greek, Smyth 1956 is a standard and comprehensive work. Excellent linguistic overviews of Greek are to be found in Buck 1933 (updated and modified in Sihler 1995), Palmer 1980 and Rix 1976. Jeffery 1990 provides a valuable and detailed discussion of the Greek alphabets; on the alphabet and especially its origin, see also Woodard 1997. For phonetics and phonology, see the excellent treatments in Allen 1987, Devine and Stephens 1994 and Lejeune 1982. Chantraine 1984 provides a valuable survey of Greek morphology. Dover 1960 offers an insightful analysis of Greek word order. For the Greek lexicon, various etymological dictionaries are available; see particularly Chantraine 1968ff. An excellent overview of the development of Greek beyond the period examined herein is to be found in Browning 1983.

Bibliography

Allen, W. 1973. *Accent and Rhythm.* Cambridge: Cambridge University Press.
_____. 1987. *Vox Graeca* (3rd edition). Cambridge: Cambridge University Press.
Browning, R. 1983. *Medieval and Modern Greek* (2nd edition). Cambridge: Cambridge University Press.
Buck, C. 1933. *Comparative Grammar of Greek and Latin.* Chicago: University of Chicago Press.

Buck, C. and W. Petersen. 1945. *A Reverse Index of Greek Nouns and Adjectives*. Chicago: University of Chicago Press.

Chantraine, P. 1968ff. *Dictionnaire étymologique de la langue grecque: Histoire des mots*. Paris: Klincksieck.

_____. 1984. *Morphologie historique du grec* (2nd edition). Paris: Klincksieck.

Denniston, J. 1954. *The Greek Particles* (revised edition by K. Dover). Oxford: Oxford University Press.

Devine, A. and L. Stephens. 1994. *The Prosody of Greek Speech*. Oxford: Oxford University Press.

Dover, K. 1960. *Greek Word Order*. Cambridge: Cambridge University Press.

Gildersleeve, B. 1900. *Greek Syntax*. Amsterdam: Gieben.

Jeffery, L. 1990. *The Local Scripts of Archaic Greece* (revised edition). Supplement by A. Johnston. Oxford: Oxford University Press.

Kirchhoff, A. 1887. *Studien zur Geschichte des griechischen Alphabets*. Gütersloh: Bertelsmann.

Lejeune, M. 1982. *Phonétique historique du mycénien et du grec ancien*. Paris: Klincksieck.

Masson, O. 1983. *Les inscriptions chypriotes syllabiques*. Paris: Edition E. de Boccard.

Meier-Brügger, M. 1992. *Griechische Sprachwissenchaft* (2 vols.) Berlin: DeGruyter.

Meillet, A. 1965. *Aperçu d'une histoire de la langue grecque* (7th edition). Paris: Klincksieck.

Meillet, A. and J. Vendryes. 1979. *Traité de grammaire comparée des langues classiques* (5th edition). Paris: Champion.

Nagy, G. 1974. *Comparative Studies in Greek and Indic Meter*. Cambridge, MA: Harvard University Press.

Palmer, L. 1980. *The Greek Language*. Atlantic Highlands, NJ: Humanities Press.

Rix, H. 1976. *Historische Grammatik des Griechischen*. Darmstadt: Wissenschaftliche Buchgesellschaft.

Schwyzer, E. 1939ff. *Griechische Grammatik* (4 vols.). Munich: Beck.

Sihler, A. 1995. *New Comparative Grammar of Greek and Latin*. Oxford: Oxford University Press.

Smyth, H. 1956. *Greek Grammar* (revised edition by G. Messing). Cambridge, MA: Harvard University Press.

Threatte, L. 1980. *The Grammar of Attic Inscriptions*, vol. I. Berlin: De Gruyter.

Vendryes, J. 1916. *Traité d'accentuation grecque*. Paris: Klincksieck.

Ventris, M. and J. Chadwick. 1973. *Documents in Mycenaean Greek* (2nd edition). Cambridge: Cambridge University Press.

Woodard, R. 1997. *Greek Writing from Knossos to Homer*. Oxford: Oxford University Press.

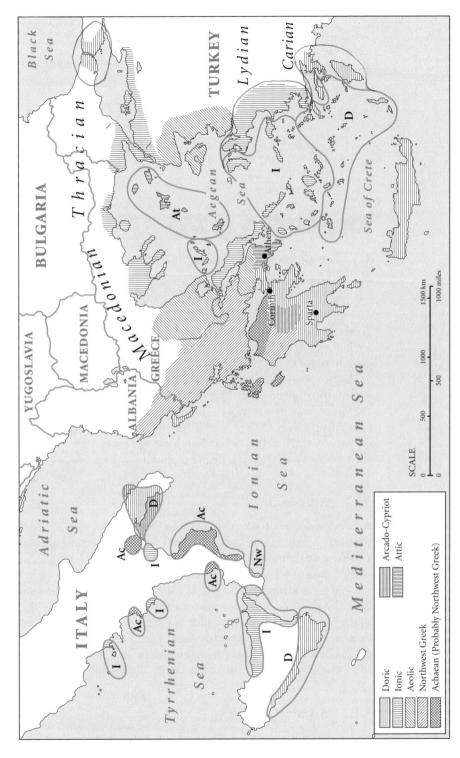

Map 1. The Greek dialects of the first millennium BC and neighboring languages

CHAPTER 3

Greek dialects

ROGER D. WOODARD

1. HISTORICAL AND CULTURAL CONTEXTS

1.1 The dialects of the first millennium BC

The ancient Greeks themselves traced their ethnic and linguistic heritage to Hellen, the eponym of both Greece (*Hellas*, Ἑλλάς) and the Greeks (*Hellenes*, Ἕλληνες). Hellen was said to be a son of Deucalion, a son of Prometheus and survivor of the great primeval flood of Greek tradition. The self-recognized diversity of Greek culture and language was attributed to descent from Hellen's three sons, Dorus, Xanthus, and Aeolus, being the alleged progenitors of the Dorian, Ionian, and Aeolian Greeks respectively.

Modern scholars recognize a dialectal distinction which fundamentally parallels this ancient tripartite division. Prior to Michael Ventris' decipherment of the Linear B tablets of the Mycenaean Greeks (see §2.1) in 1952 (see Ventris and Chadwick 1973:3–27), the ancient Greek dialects (i.e., of the first millennium BC) were broadly separated into (i) Attic-Ionic; (ii) Arcado-Cypriot; (iii) Aeolic; (iv) Doric; and (v) Northwest Greek. Each of these, in turn, shows some lesser or greater degree of internal differentiation.

1.1.1 Attic-Ionic

Attic is the dialect of Athens and the surrounding region of Attica (and is the focus of the linguistic description presented in Ch. 2). Its closely related sister dialect of Ionic is divided into three subdivisions, East, Central, and West Ionic. East Ionic is comprised of the dialects of the Ionian cities of western Anatolia (Hallicarnassus, Miletus, Smyrna, etc.) along with those of neighboring islands (such as Samos and Chios), and the Ionic of areas surrounding the Hellespont and of coastal regions along the Thracian Sea. Central Ionic is the language of the Ionian Cycladic Islands such as Naxos and Paros; while West Ionic was spoken in Euboea. The Ionic dialect contributes a significant portion to the literary language of Greek epic and is the dialect of the fifth-century historian Herodotus and the physician Hippocrates of Cos (where the native dialect was Doric), among still other Greek writers.

1.1.2 Arcado-Cypriot

Arcado-Cypriot is the dialectal subdivision to which belong the geographically far-flung but remarkably homogeneous dialects of the island of Cyprus (see §2.2) and the mountainous region of Arcadia in the Peloponnese. Their similarity is chiefly the result of the preservation of archaic features of a common ancestor dialect in two linguistically isolated areas.

Somewhat similar is the dialect of Pamphylia in southern Anatolia. Pamphylian, however, also shows similarities to West Greek, and its proper position within the network of the Greek dialects is uncertain.

1.1.3 Aeolic

The Aeolic dialect is further divided into Lesbian (Anatolian Aeolic), Thessalian, and Boeotian (Balkan Aeolic). Lesbian is the dialect of the northwest Anatolian coast (lying northward of the East Ionic regions) and associated islands, chief of which is Lesbos. The poets Sappho and Alcaeus of Lesbos composed in a literary form of their native dialect. Boeotian and Thessalian are the dialects of the regions of Boeotia and Thessaly in northeast Greece. The latter has itself two subdialects, those of Pelasgiotis (spoken in cities such as Larisa) and Thessaliotis (known from Pharsalus and elsewhere). Like Ionic, Aeolic provides linguistic components to the literary dialect of Greek epic.

1.1.4 Doric

Doric is the dialect which is attested in the greatest variety of distinct local forms. Rhodian is the dialect of the island of Rhodes and of neighboring smaller islands and coastal towns of southwest Anatolia (south of the Ionic-speaking region). A distinct Doric form is found on the islands of Cos and Calymna (northwest of Rhodes), and another on the Cycladic islands of Thera and Melos. The dialect of Crete is Doric, and itself shows internal variation. On the Balkan Peninsula, several Doric dialects are identified: Megarian, Argolic, Corinthian, Messanian, and Laconian. In literary usage, Doric figures prominently in the language of Greek choral lyric.

1.1.5 Northwest Greek

The remaining dialect group is that of Northwest Greek, being clearly a close relative of Doric. The principal Northwest Greek dialects are three. Phocian is the dialect from the area of Delphi; East and West Locrian were spoken in Locris (along the northwest coast of the Gulf of Corinth); Elean is known chiefly from the city of Olympia (in the northwest Peloponnese). In addition, a Northwest Greek Koine is known – fundamentally a hybrid dialect of Attic and certain distinctively Northwest Greek (and Doric) linguistic features. Its use is chiefly associated with the Aetolian Confederacy (Rome's Greek allies against the Macedonians; later subjugated by Rome) and dates to the second and third centuries BC.

1.2 The dialects of the second millennium BC

With the decipherment of Linear B and the translation of the documents from Pylos, Knossos, Thebes, and still other Mycenaean sites, a Greek dialect came to light – a dialect of the second millennium BC – not identical to any of those known from the later, alphabetic period (described in §1.1). Moreover, continued study of the Linear B documents led to the realization that they preserve not one, but two different dialectal forms. These distinctions were first teased apart in print by Risch (1966), who assigned to them the names *Normal Mycenaean* (*mycénien normal*; the more commonly attested type) and *Special Mycenaean* (*mycénien spécial*). Further analysis of the variation was provided by Nagy 1968 and Woodard 1986. Herein the two dialects will be referred to as *Mycenaean I* (Normal) and *Mycenaean II* (Special).

The two Mycenaean dialects are distinguished by four morphological and phonological isoglosses. On the one hand, the following features characterize Mycenaean I:

1. The athematic dative singular ending is *-ei*
2. The Proto-Indo-European syllabic nasals *$\ast\eta$* and *$\ast\eta$* develop into the mid vowel *o* in the vicinity of a labial consonant
3. The mid vowel *$\ast e$* is raised to *i* in the vicinity of a labial consonant
4. Before the high vowel *$\ast i$*, the voiceless dental stop *$\ast t$* becomes the fricative *s*

In contrast, Mycenaean II shows the following traits:

5. The athematic dative singular ending is *-i*
6. The syllabic nasals develop into the low vowel *a*
7. The mid vowel *$\ast e$* is preserved in the vicinity of a labial consonant
8. The inherited sequence *$\ast ti$* is preserved

Almost ironically, of the four isoglosses which are characteristic of the more commonly attested dialect, Mycenaean I, only a single one (4: the shift of *$\ast ti$* to *si*) is attested among the known post-Mycenaean dialects (see §3.4.3).

Of the first-millennium dialects, it is Arcado-Cypriot to which Mycenaean Greek is most closely related. The Mycenaean language as attested in the Linear B tablets does not appear, however, to be the direct precursor of Arcado-Cypriot. More than that, a comparison of the Mycenaean dialects with those of the alphabetic period suggests a linguistic heterogeneity in the second millennium which goes considerably beyond the dialectal variation preserved in the Linear B tablets (see Cowgill 1966).

1.3 Dialect interrelations

Prior to 1955, the ancient Greek dialects were conventionally divided into two major groups: *West Greek*, composed of Doric and Northwest Greek; and *East Greek*, consisting of Aeolic, Arcado-Cypriot, and Attic-Ionic. With the decipherment of the Linear B tablets, Mycenaean was folded into East Greek. A serious challenge to this analysis, however, was put forward by Ernst Risch (1955) utilizing various linguistic methodologies (such as relative chronology of language change and dialect geography) and building upon then recently published work by Walter Porzig (1954).

Risch argued that the proper bifurcation of Greek dialects is one of North versus South. A *North Greek* phylum consists of Doric, Northwest Greek, and Aeolic; *South Greek* of Mycenaean, Arcado-Cypriot, and Attic-Ionic. It is the swing position of Aeolic, obviously, which distinguishes Risch's classification from the old East versus West analysis. The Balkan Aeolic dialects, Thessalian and Boeotian, show similarities to West Greek – similarities which had been attributed to West Greek influence in the former scheme. Risch, however, contends cogently that the traits which Thessalian and Boeotian share with West Greek are archaic, while the East Greek features of Lesbian (Anatolian Aeolic) are innovations which that dialect experienced under Ionic influence.

Owing to the highly complex nature of Greek dialect geography, it can hardly be said that there presently exists a consensus regarding the proper classification of Greek dialects – East versus West or North versus South. Risch's analysis is not without its uncertainties (see the comments of Cowgill 1966:80–81; see also Coleman 1963) but offers much to commend itself.

2. WRITING SYSTEMS

2.1 Linear B

Three separate writing systems were used for recording the Greek language in antiquity. The earliest of these is the syllabic script of the Mycenaeans called Linear B (see Table 3.1). Perhaps developed in the fifteenth century BC and based upon the Minoan Linear A script, Linear B consists almost entirely of V (vowel) and CV (consonant + vowel) characters. Owing to the common occurrence of consonant clusters in the Greek language, special strategies were of necessity devised for representing consonant sequences in the Linear B script. In some instances, the initial member of a cluster is simply deleted from the orthography, as in the spelling *pe-mo* for *spérmo* (σπέρμο "seed"). Alternatively, all members of a cluster may be spelled utilizing phonetically fictitious vowel graphemes: thus, *trípos* (τρίπος "tripod") is spelled *ti-ri-po* (note that word-final consonants are not spelled). Linear B spelling does not distinguish voiced, voiceless, and voiceless aspirated consonants from one another, with the exception of the dental *d* which is distinguished from *t*[h]. Linear B script ceases to be attested after the downfall of Mycenaean society in the twelfth century BC.

2.2 The Cypriot syllabary

Consequent to the demise of Mycenaean society, large numbers of Greek émigrés settled on the island of Cyprus, where by at least the middle of the eleventh century a distinct syllabic script had been developed for writing Greek. The Cypriot syllabary appears to have been modeled graphically upon the Cypro-Minoan scripts of Cyprus, which are attested as early as the sixteenth century BC. The graphemic inventory of this the second of the Greek syllabaries was likewise composed predominantly of V and CV symbols (see Table 3.2). Fundamentally the scribal strategies utilized for spelling consonant sequences are the same as those found in Linear B practice, except that those clusters which Linear B scribes spelled with the omission strategy are now written with a phonetically fictitious vowel grapheme – one which is identical to the phonetic vowel which immediately *precedes* the cluster. Thus, *argúro* (ἀργύρω "of silver") is spelled *a-ra-ku-ro*. Cypriot spelling practice also differs from the Mycenaean in that all word-initial clusters are spelled and word-final consonants are at times written (for both practices a fictitious-vowel strategy is employed). Much like their Mycenaean predecessors, Cypriot scribes fail to distinguish orthographically between voiced, voiceless, and voiceless aspirated consonants – including dentals in Cypriot practice. The Cypriot syllabary remained in use until the late third century BC.

2.3 The epichoric alphabets

For general discussion concerning the development of the Greek alphabet from the Phoenician consonantal script, see Chapter 2, §2.

As the Greek alphabet was carried across the Greek world in the eighth century BC, numerous local or epichoric alphabets developed. While many of these differ on the basis of variation in letter-shapes, ranging from subtle to radical, the various alphabets fall grossly into four or five fundamental groups according chiefly to the absence or presence (and form and arrangement) of the so-called "supplementals," the non-Phoenician characters appended to the end of the Greek alphabet. While there is some correlation between Greek

Table 3.1   The Linear B script

Basic values

A	𐀀	E	𐀁	I	𐀂	O	𐀃	U	𐀄
DA	𐀅	DE	𐀇	DI	𐀇	DO	𐀈	DU	𐀉
JA	𐀊	JE	𐀋			JO	𐀍		
KA	𐀏	KE	𐀐	KI	𐀑	KO	𐀒	KU	𐀓
MA	𐀔	ME	𐀕	MI	𐀖	MO	𐀗	MU	𐀘
NA	𐀙	NE	𐀚	NI	𐀛	NO	𐀜	NU	𐀝
PA	𐀞	PE	𐀟	PI	𐀠	PO	𐀡	PU	𐀢
QA	𐀣	QE	𐀤	QI	𐀥	QO	𐀦		
RA	𐀨	RE	𐀩	RI	𐀪	RO	𐀫	RU	𐀬
SA	𐀭	SE	𐀮	SI	𐀯	SO	𐀰	SU	𐀱
TA	𐀲	TE	𐀳	TI	𐀴	TO	𐀵	TU	𐀶
WA	𐀷	WE	𐀸	WI	𐀹	WO	𐀺		
ZA	𐀼	ZE	𐀽			ZO	𐀿		

Special values

HA		AI		AU		DWE		DWO	
NWA		PTE		PHU		RYA		RAI	
RYO		TYA		TWE		TWO			

NUMERALS   1 | 10 — 100 O   1000 ⊕   10,000 ⊕

WEIGHTS   12 ? = 1 ♯;   4 ♯ = 1 ?;   30 ? = 1 ⚖

MEASURES   Dry   6 ◁ = 1 T; 10 T = 1 UNIT
           Wet   4 ▽ = 1 ◁;   6 ◁ = 1 ?; 3 ? = 1 UNIT

Ideograms

MAN	WOMAN	RAM	EWE	BULL/OX	COW
WOOL	LINEN	CLOTH	OXHIDE	SHEEPSKIN	WHEAT
BARLEY	OLIVES	OLIVE OIL	FIGS	WINE	
TRIPOD	JUG	AMPHORA	PAN	STIRRUP JAR	
SWORD/DAGGER	CORSLET	CHARIOT	HORSE		
GOLD	BRONZE	INGOT	FOOTSTOOL		

dialect and alphabet, such correlation is only partial. In certain cases, quite distinct dialects utilize alphabets of the same type; in others, conversely, closely related dialects are written with different alphabet-types.

Since the work of Kirchhoff 1887, the fundamental alphabet-types have been commonly referenced by color terms, following the color-coded map which Kirchhoff included at the end of the volume. Alphabets are green, blue, or red.

Table 3.2   The Cypriot syllabary

a	✳	*e*	✳	*i*	✕	*o*	⩘	*u*	Υ
ya	◊					*yo*	∿		
wa	⋈	*we*	Ι	*wi*	)(	*wo*	⌐		
ra	Ω	*re*	⋒	*ri*	⟃	*ro*	Ϙ	*ru*	)(
la	⋎	*le*	8	*li*	⋜	*lo*	+	*lu*	∩
ma	Ӿ	*me*	⋇	*mi*	⋎	*mo*	⏀	*mu*	⋇
na	⊤	*ne*	Ϣ	*ni*	ʒ	*no*	⥾	*nu*	⋊
pa	‡	*pe*	⟨	*pi*	⋎	*po*	ſ	*pu*	⥾
ta	⊦	*te*	⋇	*ti*	↑	*to*	Ϝ	*tu*	Ͱ
ka	↥	*ke*	⋨	*ki*	Υ	*ko*	∩	*ku*	✳
sa	⋁	*se*	Ⱶ	*si*	⥾	*so*	⋈	*su*	⋊
za	⋊					*zo*	⫻		
ksa	)(	*kse*	⊢						

2.3.1   Green alphabets

The green alphabets (or the "primitives") are those of Crete and the neighboring islands of Thera and Melos (and are thus used by speakers of different dialects of Doric; see §1.1.4). This alphabet-type is characterized by the absence of the supplementals as well as by the absence of a character having the sequential value [k] + [s] (the existence of which is one of the hallmark idiosyncrasies of the Greek alphabet; see Woodard 1997:147–161).

2.3.2   Blue alphabets

The blue alphabets contain the non-Phoenician supplementals – or at least a subset thereof, as this group shows internal variants, distinguished as *dark blue* versus *light blue*. Both the dark blue and light blue alphabet-types have the supplementals Φ, representing [pʰ], and X, for [kʰ]. In addition, the dark blue type has the supplemental Ψ, a biconsonantal symbol representing the sequence [p] + [s]. The light blue type, however, lacks this symbol and spells the sequence [p] + [s] componentially with the two letters Φ + Σ. Furthermore, while dark blue alphabets have the letter Ξ, spelling [k] + [s], light blue scripts lack the character and spell the sequence with two letters, X + Σ (paralleling the spelling of [p] + [s]). The blue alphabet-types (particularly the dark blue) are far more widely distributed geographically than the green. A light blue alphabet was used early in Attica and on various of the Ionian Cycladic islands, for example. Dark blue alphabets occurred, among other places, in the northeastern Peloponnese and in Ionian cities of Anatolia. The Ionian dark blue script was adopted as the official alphabet of Athens at the end of the fifth century BC.

2.3.3   Red alphabets

Like the dark blue alphabet-type, the red alphabets are marked by the presence of the non-Phoenician supplementals. However, the value assigned to these symbols only partially agrees with their blue values. Red Φ represents [pʰ] (as in the blue alphabets), but X has the sequential value [k] + [s] (and not [kʰ]), and Ψ spells [kʰ] (and not [p] + [s]; for which there is no single red-alphabet character). Red alphabets were used widely throughout the

		Local alphabets		
Letter-Name	Printed Letter	Corinthian (blue-type)	Boeotian (red-type)	Transcription
Alpha	A, α	Λ, A	Ρ, A	a
Beta	B, β	⊔⌐	B, Ƀ	b
Gamma	Γ, γ	<, C	Γ, Γ	g
Delta	Δ, δ	Δ	D, Ρ	d
Epsilon	E, ε	B, Ƀ	Ƀ, Ƀ, ⊢	e
Digamma	F	Ϝ, F	Ϝ, F, C	w
Zeta	Z, ζ	I	I	z + d
Spiritus asper	‘	⊟, H	⊟, H	h
Theta	Θ, θ	⊗, ⊕, ⊙	⊗, ⊕, ⊙	tʰ
Iota	I, ι	⪦	I	i
Kappa	K, κ	K	K	k
Lambda	Λ, λ	Γ	L	l
Mu	M, μ	⋔, M	⋔, M	m
Nu	N, ν	Ͷ, N	Ͷ, N	n
Xi	Ξ, ξ	⪥	ΥΣ, +	k + s
Omicron	O, o	O	O	o
Pi	Π, π	Γ	Γ, Γ	p
San	M	M	—	s
Qoppa	Ϙ	Ϙ	Ϙ, Ϙ	q
Rho	P, ρ	Ρ, Ρ, D	Ρ, Ρ, Ρ	r
Sigma	Σ, σ	—	Σ, Ϟ	s
Tau	T, τ	T	T	t
Upsilon	Υ, υ	Γ, Y, V	Γ, V, Y	u
Phi	Φ, φ	Φ, Φ	Φ, Φ	pʰ
Chi	X, χ	X, +	Υ, V, ↓	kʰ
Psi	Ψ, ψ	Υ, V	ΦΣ	p + s

Table 3.3 Epichoric Greek alphabets

Balkan Peninsula, thus blanketing numerous dialect boundaries. This alphabet-type was also in widespread use in Sicily and Magna Graecia (Greek Italy) and is the source of the Etruscan and Roman alphabets. On the possibility of distinguishing a "light red" from a "dark red" alphabet-type (paralleling the blue division) see Woodard 1997:215–216.

2.3.4 The Fayum alphabet

An additional Greek alphabet, one which does not fit into the preceding tripartite scheme, is known from four copper plaques, purported to have come from the Fayum in Egypt. Three of the four (two from the Schøyen collection in Oslo and one from the University of Würzburg Museum) have been examined carefully at the J. Paul Getty Museum in Los Angeles. An analysis of the physical remains reveals the plaques and the alphabets inscribed on them to be of great antiquity but does not permit an exact dating. The alphabet is epigraphically interesting in various ways, perhaps most interesting in that it ends in the letter *tau* (T), just as does the Phoenician precursor of the Greek alphabet. It is the only known Greek alphabet which matches the Semitic template in this manner, all others having the vowel letter *upsilon* (Υ) added after *tau* (on the Greek creation of vowel characters, see Ch. 2, §2), and may represent the earliest form of the Greek alphabet (see Heubeck 1986, Scott, Woodard, McCarter, *et al.* 2005, Woodard 1997).

3. PHONOLOGY

In the remaining sections of this chapter, the discussion of Greek dialectal linguistic features closely follows the format of the treatment of Attic grammar presented in Chapter 2 and is dependent upon it. For background discussion of each section, the reader should consult the corresponding section in Chapter 2. Hereafter "dialects" should be construed to refer generally to all dialects other than Classical Attic, unless stated otherwise.

3.1 Consonants

The inventory of consonant phonemes in the dialects is *grosso modo* the same as that of Attic. Variations do occur, however.

3.1.1 Obstruents

As mentioned in Chapter 2, §3.1 the Proto-Greek labiovelar stop phonemes, /kʷ/, /kʷʰ/, and /gʷ/, are preserved in Myceanean Greek. The same dialect also appears to have possessed both a voiceless and a voiced palatalized stop (or perhaps affricate), sounds which developed from earlier sequences of *[k⁽ʰ⁾y], in the case of the voiceless, and *[dy], *[gy] as well as some instances of word-initial *[y-], in the case of the voiced. Among the very few CCV characters occurring in the Linear B syllabary (see §2.1) are the symbols *twe, two, dwe, dwo, nwa, tya, rya,* and *ryo.* The existence of the signs may reveal the occurrence of palatalized and of labialized dental phonemes in the dialect at some time within the period of Mycenaean literacy and/or they may be relics of the phonological system of the non-Greek language for which the ancestor script of Linear B was designed.

The voiceless aspirated stops of Attic, /pʰ/, /tʰ/, and /kʰ/, would become the fricatives /f/, /θ/, and /x/ respectively in the post-Classical period – probably by the first or second century AD (perhaps earlier; see Allen 1987:20–23). However, there is evidence of a fricative reflex at a much earlier period among some of the dialects, such as the Doric dialect of Laconian. Thus, the later fifth-century authors Thucydides and Aristophanes, when reproducing Doric speech, use the letter σ (/s/) to spell the sound corresponding to Attic /tʰ/, suggesting an attempt to render a fricative pronunciation (i.e., /θ/). By the fourth century BC, a similar spelling practice is observed in Laconian inscriptions.

Like the voiceless aspirated stops, the voiced stops of Classical Attic have become voiced fricatives in Modern Greek: /b/, /d/, and /g/ yield /v/, /ð/, and /ɣ/ respectively. The date of the change is probably considerably later than that of the voiceless stops (as would be expected on typological grounds), though is difficult to pinpoint. In the ninth century AD, when Greek missionaries created a writing system for recording scripture translations in Old Bulgarian, the Greek letter β (Classical Attic /b/) provided a symbol for the Slavic voiced fricative /v/ (evidence from the earlier Greek-based Gothic and Armenian alphabets is inconclusive; see Allen 1987:28–30). A much earlier date (first century AD) for the shift of the voiced stops to fricatives in the Hellenistic Koine of Egypt, at least in some phonetic contexts, is suggested by spellings in nonliterary papyri (Allen 1987:154). Outside of Hellenistic Koine and its descendant, just as with voiceless stops, the fricativization of voiced stops had a dialectal head start. In Laconian inscriptions dating as early as the fourth century BC, β is used at times in lieu of Ϝ (/w/), suggesting that the sound of β was, in some instances, a continuant (or that /w/ had become a labial fricative – or both; the same spelling variation is also found in Cretan). Similarly, ζ (Attic /z/ + /d/) is at times used in place of δ (/d/) in early Elean writing, and in Boeotian (as well as in Pamphylian) inscriptions γ (Attic /g/) is at times replaced by the vowel character ι or deleted altogether.

Beyond the aforementioned early fricative reflexes of stops and the ubiquitous dental sibilant /s/, there is orthographic evidence of additional sibilant consonants occurring dialectally. In the alphabets of several Greek cities of Anatolia, there occurs a character Ͳ, used to spell the common reflex of Proto-Greek $*k^{(w)(h)}y$, $*t^{(h)} + y$ and $*tw$. The eventual reflex of the Proto-Greek consonantal sequences will be [-ss-] in the Ionic dialect of these Anatolian cities. In all likelihood the character Ͳ represents an intermediate phonological stage – a strident sound which is distinct from the /s/ represented by σ (see Lejeune 1982:89, 101; Woodard 1997:178–179). More secure is the presence of distinct sibilants in Arcadian; the evidence is again orthographic. In the Arcadian alphabet a form of the letter *san*, Ͷ, is used to spell the reflex of Proto-Greek $*k^w$ occurring before front vowels. This sibilant reflex of Arcadian (found also in Cypriot, written syllabically, however, rather than alphabetically) must be distinct from dental /s/, spelled with *sigma* (σ), and likely is to be identified as an affricate. The sound has a voiced counterpart in Arcadian (though not in Cypriot), with *zeta* (ζ) appropriated for its spelling (see Woodard 1997:178–184, 187–188).

The glottal fricative, /h/, of Attic, limited in native vocabulary to word-initial position, is shared by several other dialects. The presence or absence of this initial fricative (the *spiritus asper*, "rough breathing") has served as a major isogloss in traditional Greek grammatical studies. Dialects which lack it, East Ionic, Lesbian, Cretan, and Elean, are called *psilotic*. In a few dialects, such as Laconian and Argolic, /h/ also occurs intervocalically; Cypriot is included in this number, though the presence of /h/ in this dialect is made less transparent by the syllabic script of Cyprus. Intervocalic /h/ may have also occurred in Mycenaean Greek, though the orthographic evidence is open to alternative interpretation.

3.1.2 Sonorants

In the Doric dialect of Cretan, when the lateral liquid (Attic /l/, spelled λ) follows a vowel, the two are often spelled as a diphthong, ʋυ: thus ἀδευπιαί for Attic ἀδελφαί (*adelphaí*) "sisters." The use of *upsilon* (υ) for the liquid suggests some sort of back articulation, a velar-*l*, or perhaps a uvular approximant or fricative (see Bile 1988:120, who notes the occurrence of a velar-*l* in modern Cretan). Allen (1987:39) observes that Old Armenian transcriptions of Greek words may also suggest the presence of a velar-*l* in Asian Greek.

The use of the graphemic sequence λε for /l/ in inscriptions from the island of Cos (also attested at neighboring Cnidos and on Melos and Thasos) may be an attempt to represent a lateral alveolar fricative [ɫ] (cf. Buck 1955:64).

The Proto-Greek labial glide *w appears in Mycenaean Greek and survives later in many of the first-millennium dialects than it had in Attic. The sound first disappears word-internally; in inscriptional spellings its grapheme (Ϝ) continues word-initally until as late as the second century AD, though by this time its sound had perhaps become a fricative (see Buck 1955:46–48).

The palatal glide /y/ does not exist phonemically in any of the dialects of the first millennium BC. In Mycenaean Greek it occurs word-initially, as well as after vowels and sonorants, though in some of these contexts /y/ was perhaps in the process of evolving into /h/ during the period from which Mycenaean documents survive (see Lejeune 1982:155–156, 162, 165, 167–169, 171).

3.2 Vowels

The short and long front rounded vowel phonemes of Attic, /ü/ and /ü:/, which arose by the fronting of Proto-Greek *ŭ, are not present in all dialects. The Aeolic dialect of Boeotian, for example, preserved the high-back position, /u(:)/; this is revealed by the use of the digraph ου (= Attic /u:/) in lieu of υ (= Attic /ü(:)/) when, in the middle of the fourth century BC, Boeotian speakers adopted the Attic alphabet: for example, Boeotian ἀργούριον (*argurion*) beside Attic ἀργύριον ("money, silver"). Boeotian, however, had developed its own front rounded vowel by the third century BC, through the fronting of the earlier diphthong /oi/ (οι) – the result being perhaps /ö/, then /ü/, ultimately /i/. Similarly, Boeotian /ai/ underwent monophthongization, becoming a long lower mid-front vowel, spelled with η after the acquisition of the Attic alphabet. Proto-Greek *ei, which had given rise to the long higher mid-front vowel /ẹ:/ in Attic, probably underwent a similar development in Boeotian; but by the fifth century BC, the Boeotian vowel had moved farther upward along the front periphery of the vowel track to merge with /i:/.

Throughout the history of Greek, the language has demonstrated a tendency for vowel monophthongization and movement forward and upward. The aforementioned vowel developments that characterized Boeotian at an early period occurred later in the Attic-based Hellenistic Koine, ultimate parent of Modern Greek (see Ch. 2, §1). The change of /ẹ:/ (ει) to /i:/ was already well underway by the third century BC. The lower mid-front /ę:/ (η) in response was raised (perhaps to /ẹ:/), eventually itself becoming /i:/, in some areas, perhaps by the second century AD. By about the beginning of that century, inscriptional spellings reveal that the diphthong /ai/ was undergoing monophthongization and raising to /ę:/ – in essence filling the gap created by the upward shift of earlier /ę:/ (η). The new lower mid-front vowel /ę:/ would, prior to the Byzantine era, merge with the vowel of ε. As earlier in Boeotian, so in Hellenistic Koine, the diphthong /oi/ shifted forward, developing into a front rounded monophthong, prior to the middle of the third century AD. Both this vowel and the already existing /ü(:)/ eventually unrounded, becoming Modern Greek /i/. For detailed discussion of these and related developments, see, *inter alia*, Allen 1987:74, with further page references.

3.3 Accent

Whatever accentual idiosyncrasies might have characterized the various dialects are for the most part unknown. Aeolic is notably different than Classical Attic in that the accent of all words (except conjunctions and prepositions) – and not only verbs – is recessive: for example, [pótamos] beside Attic [potamós] (ποταμός "river"); [basíleus] beside Attic [basileús] (βασιλεύς "king"); [zdeûs] beside Attic [zdeús] (Ζεύς "Zeus"); and so forth (see Thumb-Scherer 1959:86–87; Allen 1973:238–239; 256–257). In the present work, all first-millennium dialect forms are conventionally marked with the appropriate Attic accent except in those cases in which it is known that the dialect accentuation differs from that of Attic.

The tonal accent of Classical Attic eventually gave way to a stress accent, present still in Modern Greek. Dating the shift from a pitch to a stress system is an uncertain affair, though it appears that the change was in progress in Attic by at least the first centuries AD, and perhaps much earlier. Evidence provided by Egyptian papyri suggests that among Egyptian

Greeks the change may have occurred by the last two centuries BC (see Allen 1987:119–120; Devine and Stephens 1994:215–223).

3.4 Diachronic developments

3.4.1 Obstruents

As noted earlier (see §3.1.1), the Proto-Indo-European labiovelar stops, *k^w, *g^w, and *g^{wh}, are generally preserved in Mycenaean Greek, except, of course, that voiced aspirated *g^{wh} has devoiced to k^{wh} (a Proto-Greek development), though the same set of CV graphemes is used for spelling all three types (voiceless, voiced, voiceless aspirated). The Mycenaean dialect exhibits a tendency to dissimilate one of two labiovelar consonants found within a word. Compare the spelling of the proper name *qe-re-qo-ta* (Pylos) beside *pe-re-qo-ta* (Pylos and Knossos); see Ventris and Chadwick 1973:82, 245, 399, 447).

The Aeolic dialects show labiovelar devlopments which are in part distinct from those of Classical Attic (see Ch. 2, §3.7.1) and other dialects of the first millennium BC (except Cypriot; see below). On the one hand, just as in Attic, bilabial stops constitute the unconditioned reflexes of these sounds in Aeolic: PIE *k^w, *g^w, *g^{wh} → [p, b, p^h] (π, β, φ) respectively. Aeolic also agrees with other dialects in dissimilating the labiovelars before and after the high back rounded vowel *u*: PIE *k^w, *g^w, *g^{wh} → [k, g, k^h] (κ, γ, χ). On the other hand, however, when occurring before mid-front vowels, labiovelars become bilabials in Aeolic (the default development), rather than dentals as in Attic: PIE *k^w, *g^w, *g^{wh} → Aeolic [p, b, p^h] (π, β, φ) (cf. Attic [t, d, t^h] (τ, δ, θ)). Thus, for example, while *$g^w elb^h$- gives Attic [delp^hís] (δελφίς "dolphin"), the Lesbian reflex is [bélp^his] (βέλφις); and PIE *$k^w etwr$- becomes Attic [téttares] (τέτταρες "four"), but Thessalian and Boeotian [péttares] (πέτταρες). Note, however, that in the case of the enclitic conjunction *-k^w e, the outcome is [-te] (-τε "and") in all dialects (i.e., in a clitic context, Aeolic participates in a change, a palatalization process, found regularly in non-Aeolic dialects). Aeolic also agrees with Attic in the development of a voiceless dental reflex ([t]) before the high front vowel [i], but bilabial voiced and voiceless aspirated reflexes ([b] and [p^h]) in this environment. On these labiovelar developments and their wave-like spread through dialect regions, see Stephens and Woodard 1986.

Distinct labiovelar developments also occur within Arcado-Cypriot. In part these developments constitute an isogloss distinguishing the dialectal group from all others; in part they divide the two members of the group. Within Arcado-Cypriot the palatalization of the labiovelars is carried a step beyond the [t] reflex seen elsewhere before the high front vowel. Both Arcadian and Cypriot develop a continuant reflex in this context (probably an affricate). The two sister dialects differ, however, in the extent of the development: in Arcadian the change is more pervasive, occurring before mid-front vowels also, and affecting both voiceless and voiced labiovelars (and likely the voiceless aspirated as well, though this is not yet attested). In Cypriot, the labiovelars develop bilabial reflexes before mid-front vowels, as in Aeolic. On these developments, see Woodard 1997:180–184.

3.4.2 Sonorants

The vocalization of the Proto-Indo-European syllabic liquids, *r and *l shows dialectal variation. In Aeolic the reflex of *r is either [or] or [ro], rather than the [ar] or [ra] of Attic: for example, PIE *str-*to*- → Lesbian and Boeotian [strótos] (στρότος "army") beside Attic [stratós] (στρατός). The same treatment is found in Arcado-Cypriot, as in Arcadian [storpá] (στορπά "lightning"), as well as in Mycenaean: for example, k^w etro- ("four") beside Attic [tetra-] (τετρα- "four"); compare Thessalian [petro-] (πετρο-). The Proto-Indo-European lateral syllabic liquid *$l̥$ similarly gives [ol] or [lo] (Attic [al] or [la]): for example, from PIE *$ĝ^h l̥$ - develops Lesbian [kʰólaisi] (χόλαισι "they loosen"), Attic [kʰalô:si] (χαλῶσι).

On the *o*-reflex of the Proto-Indo-European syllabic nasals in Mycenaean (Mycenaean I), see §1.2. First-millennium dialects agree with Attic and the less commonly attested form of Mycenaean (Mycenaean II) in showing the *a*-reflex.

3.4.3   Combinatory changes

The chief phonological developments which occur in Attic when two or more phonetic segments come into contact are detailed in Chapter 2, §3.7.3. Among those changes, the following dialectal developments constitute significant isoglosses (these dialectal distributions should be viewed as tendencies rather than absolutes); reconstructed sequences are presented first, followed by their reflexes in the various dialects:

1. PG *$t^{(h)}y$: (A) [tt] in Boeotian and Cretan; (B)*[ss], then becoming [s] in Attic, Ionic (though Homer has both [ss] and [s]) and Arcadian; (C) [ss] in other dialects; (D) however, following a consonant or long vowel, as well as word-initially, all dialects have [s].
2. PG *$t^{(h)}$+ y (i.e., when a detectable morpheme boundary separates the two consonants): (A) [tt] in Attic, Boeotian, and Cretan; (B) [ss] in other dialects (on this complex matter, see Rix 1976:90–91; Lejeune 1982:103–104).
3. PG *$k^{(w)(h)}y$: (A) [tt] in Attic, Boeotian, and Cretan ([t] word-initially); (B) [ss] in other dialects ([s] word-initially).
4. PG *dy and *$g^{(w)}y$: (A) [dd] in Boeotian, Thessalian, Laconian, Elean, and Cretan ([d] word-initially); (B) [zd] in other dialects.
5. PG *tw: (A) [tt] in Attic, Boeotian, and Cretan; (B) [ss] in other dialects; (C) however, all dialects have [s] word-initially.
6. PG *{$t^{(h)}$, d}s: (A) [tt] in Boeotian and Cretan; (B) *[ss], then becoming [s] in Attic, Ionic (though Homer has both [ss] and [s]) and Arcadian; (C) [ss] in other dialects; (D) however, following a long vowel, as well as word-finally, all dialects have [s].
7. PG *ss: (A) [s] in Attic, Ionic (though Homer has both [ss] and [s]) and Arcadian; (B) [ss] preserved in other dialects; (C) however, following a long vowel all dialects have [s].
8. PG *ti: (A) [si] in Attic, Ionic, Arcado-Cypriot, and Lesbian, as well as Mycenaean I (see §1.2); (B) [ti] remains in other dialects; (C) however, the change does not occur if *ti is preceded by *s; (D) and in the case of certain words [si] develops in all dialects, in the case of others [ti] is preserved in all dialects (see Buck 1955:57–58).
9. PG *{r, n}y after *{e, i, u}: (A) geminate [{rr, nn}] in Lesbian and Thessalian; (B) [{r, n}] with compensatory lengthening of the preceding vowel in other dialects.
10. PG *ln: (A) geminate [ll] in Lesbian and Thessalian; (B) [l] with compensatory lengthening of a preceding vowel in other dialects.
11. PG *{r, l, n, s}w, where *s is of secondary origin (i.e., not inherited from Proto-Indo-European): (A) [{r, l, n}] with compensatory lengthening of a preceding vowel in East and Central Ionic, and in several Doric dialects (Argolic, Cretan, Theran, and the dialects of Rhode and Cos); (B) [{r, l, n}] without compensatory lengthening of a preceding vowel in other dialects.

12. PG *ns# (word-final): (A) [ns#] preserved in Argolic and central Cretan; (B) [s#] with no effect on the preceding vowel from the loss of [n] in Arcadian, Thessalian, and Theran Doric; (C) [s#] with *i*-diphthongization of the preceding vowel in Lesbian and Elean; (D) [s#] with compensatory lengthening of a preceding vowel in most other dialects (on original conditioning by the first sound of the ensuing word and the occurrence of doublets, see Buck 1955:68; Lejeune 1982:131–132).

13. PG *nsV, where *s is of secondary origin (i.e., not inherited from Proto-Indo-European): (A) [nsV] preserved in Arcadian, Thessalian, Argolic, and central Cretan (contrast 12 [A] and [B] for dialect distribution); (B) [sV] with *i*-diphthongization of the preceding vowel in Lesbian and Cyrenaean Doric; (C) [sV] with compensatory lengthening of a preceding vowel in other dialects.

14. PG *NsV, where *s is inherited: (A) geminate [NNV] in Lesbian and Thessalian; (B) [NV] with compensatory lengthening of a preceding vowel in other dialects.

15. PG *Vsw, where *s is inherited: (A) geminate [Vww] in Lesbian and Thessalian; (B) [Vw] with compensatory lengthening of the preceding vowel and eventual loss of [w] in other dialects.

16. PG *Vs{r, l, m, n}: (A) geminate [V{rr, ll, mm, nn}] in Lesbian and Thessalian; (B) [V{r, l, m, n}] with compensatory lengthening of the preceding vowel in other dialects.

17. PG *rs, where *s does not belong to the aorist suffix: (A) geminate [rr] in Attic, West Ionic, Arcadian, Elean, and Theran Doric; (B) [rs] preserved in most other dialects.

18. PG *{r, l}s where *s belongs to the aorist suffix: (A) geminate [{rr, ll}] in Lesbian and Thessalian; (B) [{r, l}] with compensatory lengthening of the preceding vowel in other dialects (cf. 14).

19. PG *Vs# (word-final): (A) [Vr#] in Elean (especially in later inscriptions) and in late Laconian; (B) preserved in other dialects, though Plato (Cratylus 434 C) has Socrates note that Eretrian speakers have a final -r in their pronunciation of the word *sklẹrótẹs* (σκληρότης, "hardness").

20. PG *VsV: (A) [VrV] in early Eretrian, though not consistently attested; (B) [s] lost in other dialects but sometimes restored by analogy.

21. PG *sC$_{+voice}$: (A) [rC$_{+voice}$] attested in Eretrian, Thessalian, Cretan, and Laconian; (B) [zC$_{+voice}$] in most dialects.

3.4.4 Vowels

The change of [a:] to [ẹ:] which occurs in both Attic and Ionic (see Ch. 2, §3.7.4) is not identical in its distribution in these sister dialects. While the change is thoroughgoing in Ionic, it does not occur (or is reversed; see Szemerényi 1968) in Attic when [a:] is preceded by [e], [i], or [r]. The opposite change of [ẹ:] to [a:] appears to have occurred in Elean, though its attestation is inconsistent. In Northwest Greek generally, [e] is lowered to [a] when it occurs before [r]; while in Aeolic, high-front [i] is lowered to the mid vowel [e] when preceded by [r]. In Arcado-Cypriot, mid vowel [e] is raised to [i] when it occurs before the dental nasal [n]; at the back of the mouth, the same dialect raises mid vowel [o] to [u] in word-final position. In Cretan Doric [e] is raised to [i] when a vowel follows.

As in Attic-Ionic, the initial vowel in sequences of [ẹ:] + vowel commonly undergoes shortening in Doric and Northwest Greek, though without the quantitative metathesis found in Ionic and, especially, Attic (see Ch. 2, §3.7.5). In Arcado-Cypriot, Aeolic, and Elean, however, the initial vowel remains long.

The so-called spurious diphthongs of Attic, spelled ει and ου (actually long monophthongs written as digraphs; see Ch. 2, §3.2), are long vowels that arose secondarily by contraction or compensatory lengthening, and vowels that are distinct from the long *$\bar{e}$ and *$\bar{o}$ vowels inherited from Proto-Indo-European. These vowels – [ẹ:] and (*[o:] >) [u:] in Attic – are found in numerous dialects. In other dialects, however, the long vowels which develop secondarily are identical to those inherited, as in the Aeolic dialects, Arcadian, Elean, Cretan, and Laconian.

4. MORPHOLOGY

4.1 Nominal morphology

For an overview of Greek nominal morphology, see Chapter 2, §4.1

4.1.1 Noun classes

Greek nouns are traditionally divided into three declensional classes (first, second, and third); for a general discussion of these, see Chapter 2, §4.1.1.

4.1.1.1 First declension

In dialects other than Attic-Ionic, the characteristic suffix of the first declension nouns remains [-a:] (-$\bar{\alpha}$, from PIE *-eh_2), not having undergone the shift to [-ẹ:] (-η; see §3.4.4). The following Cretan (Doric) forms (see Bile 1988:188–190) exemplify the singular paradigm, where the greatest deviation from Attic-Ionic is found (cf. Ch. 2, §4.1.1.1 [4]–[5]):

(1)   *Singular*
    Nominative   gâ (γᾶ, "earth")
    Vocative   tʰeá (θεά, "O goddess")
    Accusative   stégān (στέγᾱν, "house")
    Genitive   tīmâs (τῑμᾶς, "of honor")
    Dative   stégāi (στέγᾱι, "to [the] house")

Among dialectal forms in the plural, the greatest variation occurs in the dative and, especially, the accusative (on which see below). While most dialects agree with Attic and have a dative in -*ais* (-αις), Lesbian shows -*a(:)isi* (-αισι/-αισι) and Ionic commonly has -*ẹisi* (-ηισι). Cretan and other dialects sometimes attest the infrequent -*āsi* (-ᾱσι).

Mycenaean Greek has a distinct suffix -*pi* (-φι) marking the instrumental plural (as in Linear B *a-ni-ja-pi* "with reins"). The ending is also used with place names in apparently locative or ablatival function.

The ancestral accusative plural *-*āns* is preserved in Argolic and Cretan (though -*ans* (-ανς) with vowel shortening by Osthoff's Law; see Ch. 2, §3.7.5). With loss of [n] before word-final [s], diverging dialectal reflexes emerge. Most widely occurring is the -*ās* (-ᾱς) form found in Attic; a short vowel formant -*as* (-ας) characterizes Thessalian, Arcadian, and certain Doric dialects (including Cretan, also with -*ans*, -ανς). Elean and Lesbian have -*ais* (-αις), with the former also showing a further development to -*air* (-αιρ; see §3.4.3, **19**).

Corresponding to the Attic-Ionic nominative singular -*ẹs* (-ης) of the first declension masculine nouns (see Ch. 2, §4.1.1.1 [7]), most dialects show the formant -*ās* (-ᾱς). Under the influence of the second declension, the genitive singular of the masculine is commonly formed in -*ā* (-ᾱ; from -*āo* (-ᾱο)), giving Arcado-Cypriot -*āu* (-ᾱυ; see §3.4.4).

4.1.1.2   Second declension

In the singular of the second declension (cf. Ch. 2, §4.1.1.2 (8)–(9)), both the genitive and dative show dialectal variants. Genitive *-oio* (-οιο), from PIE *-osyo*, is found, among other places, in Homer and is the source of Thessalian *-oi* (-οι). The Attic genitive formant *-ū* (-ου) is shared by Ionic and certain Doric and Northwest Greek dialects and arose by vowel contraction after the loss of the two intervening consonants. Showing a different long vowel reflex, other Doric, Northwest Greek, and Aeolic dialects, as well as Arcadian, are characterized by a genitive singular in *-ǭ* (-ω; on the dialectal distribution, see §3.4.4). Cypriot has both the expected *-ō* and an innovative *-ōn*.

As with the first declension, both the dative and accusative plural show dialectal variation. The dative formant *-oisi* (-οισι) of Early Attic also occurs, among other dialects, in Ionic, Lesbian, and Pamphylian. Most dialects agree with Classical Attic in having *-ois* (-οις).

The accusative plural distribution mirrors that of the first declension: archaic *-ons*, preserved in Argolic and Cretan (-ονς); Lesbian *-ois* (-οις; and Elean *-oir*, -οιρ; see §3.4.3, **19**); in most dialects a long vowel reflex, with the quality of the vowel showing variation, (*-ōs >*) *-ūs* (-ους) or *-ǭs* (-ως; see §3.4.4). Thessalian, Arcadian, and a subset of Doric dialects are again characterized by a short vowel form *-os* (-ος).

4.1.1.3   Third declension

Among third declension inflections, various dialectal forms occur. A widely distributed consonant stem variant is the dative plural in *-essi* (-εσσι; see Ch. 2, §4.1.1.3 (11)), found throughout the Aeolic branch and in scattered Doric dialects, as well as in Pamphylian. In Mycenaean Greek, the instrumental plural suffix *-pi* (-φι; see §4.1.1.1) also occurs on third declension nouns. Most dialects differ from Attic in preserving *s*-stem endings without contraction after loss of intervocalic *-s*-; thus, genitive *-e-os* (-εος), nominative-accusative neuter plural *-e-a* (-εα), and so forth (cf. Ch 2. §4.1.1.3, **2**). Outside of Attic (and some varieties of Ionic), *i*-stems are uniformly of the type which preserve stem-vowel *-i*-. The difference between the Attic and a typical non-Attic type (i.e., between an ablauting and non-ablauting suffix) can be illustrated by the paradigms of the *i*-stem noun *pólis* (πόλις, "city") of (2) and (3) respectively:

(2)   **Attic *i*-stem**

	Singular	Plural
Nominative	pólis (πόλις)	pólēs (πόλεις)
Vocative	póli (πόλι)	pólēs (πόλεις)
Accusative	pólin (πόλιν)	pólēs (πόλεις)
Genitive	póleǭs (πόλεως)	póleǭn (πόλεων)
Dative	pólē (πόλει)	pólesi (πόλεσι)

(3)   **Non-Attic *i*-stem**

	Singular	Plural
Nominative	pólis (πόλις)	pólies (πόλιες)
Vocative	póli (πόλι)	pólies (πόλιες)
Accusative	pólin (πόλιν)	pólīs (πόλῑς)
Genitive	pólios (πόλιος)	pólīǭn (πολίων)
Dative	pólī (πόλῑ)	pólisi (πόλισι)

With the type of (3), compare the Attic paradigm of *oîs* (οἶς, nom. sg.), *oiós* (οἰός, gen. sg.) "sheep" (see Ch. 2, §4.1.1.3, **6**)

The diphthongal *ēu*-stems in Ionic, Doric, and Northwest Greek are unlike those of Attic (see Ch. 2, §4.1.1.3, **8**) in that the initial vowel of the suffix is shortened before a vocalic ending (gen. *-eos* (-εος), etc.) rather than remaining long and triggering *quantitative metathesis* (see Ch. 2, §3.7.5). In some dialects, the second element of the diphthong is preserved intervocalically and spelled with digamma; when the second element is lost, contraction is common.

4.1.2 Pronouns

For an overview of the pronominal system of Classical Greek, see Chapter 2, §4.1.3.

4.1.2.1 Personal pronouns

Among the various dialectal differences in the personal pronouns, one of the most readily apparent is the form of the second-person stem in the singular. In some dialects the pronoun begins with *t-*, in others with *s-*; the dialectal distribution parallels that of *ti* versus *si* (see §3.4.3, **8**). These pronouns together with a few additional forms suggest a more limited assibilation of PG **t* to *s* before **u*: Proto-Greek nominative **tú* "you" gives Attic (etc.) *sú* (σύ), Doric (etc.) *tú* (τύ). Proto-Greek accusative **twé* produces Attic (etc.) *sé* (σέ; see §3.4.3, **5** – alternatively, the initial *s-* of the accusative could possibly be an analogical source for that of the nominative); the source of Doric (etc.) *té* (τέ) appears to have developed from a Proto-Greek variant **té* (see Lejeune 1982:66; Chantraine 1984:136–137). First-, second- and third-person singular pronouns from various dialects are presented in (4); compare those of Attic given in Chapter 2, §4.1.3.1:

(4)		*First*	*Second*	*Third*
	Nominative	Boeotian iṓ (ἰώ)	Boeotian toú (τού)	—
	Genitive	Ionic emeû (ἐμεῦ)	Doric teû (τεῦ)	Aeolic wét^{h}en (ϝέθεν)
	Dative	Doric emín (ἐμίν)	Doric tín (τίν)	Aeolic woi (ϝοι)
	Accusative	Ionic emé (ἐμέ)	Doric té (τέ)	Pamphylian whe (ϝhε)
				Sicilian Doric nín (νίν)

The first- and second-person plural pronouns of Attic, *hēmês* (ἡμεῖς) and *hūmês* (ὑμεῖς) in the nominative, are formed from the Proto-Greek stems **n̥sme-* and **usme-* respectively. The Thessalian and Lesbian forms of these pronouns are thus marked by their characteristic geminate reflex of the cluster **sm* (see §3.4.3, **16**). Selected dialect forms of the plural pronouns appear in (5); see, again, Chapter 2 for Attic equivalents:

(5)		*First*	*Second*
	Nominative	Lesbian ámmes (ἄμμες)	Lesbian úmmes (ὔμμες)
	Genitive	Doric hāméōn (ἁμέων)	Doric hūméōn (ὑμέων)
	Dative	Lesbian ámmi ((ἄμμι)	Lesbian úmmi (ὔμμι)
	Accusative	Thessalian hammé (ἁμμέ)	Doric hūmé (ὑμέ)

Dialect forms of the third-person plural pronoun are seen, for example, in the Doric dative *sp^{h}in* (σφιν), Lesbian dative *ásp^{h}i* (ἄσφι), Sicilian Doric *psín* (ψίν), Lesbian accusative *ásp^{h}e* (ἄσφε), and Sicilian Doric *psé* (ψέ).

The formation of possessive adjectives in the various dialects is like that in Classical Attic (see Ch. 2, §4.1.3.1). In the nominative case, the first-person possessive appears, for example, as Doric *hāmós* (ἁμός, sg.), *hāméteros* (ἁμέτερος, pl.), Lesbian *ámmos* (ἄμμος, sg.), *amméteros* (ἀμμέτερος, pl.). The second-person singular shows the same *t- ~ s-* dialect alternation that occurs in the personal pronouns: thus, Lesbian and Doric *teós* (τεός). For the second plural, Doric has *hūméteros* (ὑμέτερος), Lesbian *umméteros* (ὑμμέτερος). Among third-person forms, nominative singular appears in Cretan as *wos* (Ϝος), in Doric as *heós* (ἑός). A third plural form *sphós* (σφός) occurs in both Doric and Lesbian.

4.1.2.2   Reflexive pronouns

The dialects display a variety of constructions for the reflexive pronoun. The personal pronouns (see §4.1.2.1) alone are at times used as reflexives. Other formations involve the use of the pronoun *autós* (αὐτός) together with personal pronouns – either as a lexical pair or, as commonly in Classical Attic (see Ch. 2, §4.1.3.2), in a univerbated (compound) form. The former type is seen, for example, in the Cretan third singular dative *wìn autôi* (Ϝιν αὐτôι), the latter type in Cretan *wiautô* (Ϝιαυτô) third singular genitive. In some dialects, oblique forms of *autós* are used alone as reflexives; in some, *autós* is used in one of several reduplicated forms, such as Delphian *autosautón* (αὐτοσαυτόν), accusative singular.

4.1.2.3   Definite article

The definite article of Classical Attic (see Ch. 2, §4.1.3.4) differs most conspicuously from dialectal forms in the nominative animate plural. In Northwest Greek and all Doric dialects except Cretan, as well as in the Aeolic dialects of Boeotian and, in part, Thessalian (and in Homer), the archaic masculine *toí* (τοί) and feminine *taí* (ταί) survive, in contrast to the innovative *hoi* (οἱ) and *hai* (αἱ) found elsewhere. The definite article does not occur in Mycenaean Greek; when the aforementioned formants appear, they function as demonstrative pronouns, as they do in the Homeric dialect (see Ch. 2, §4.1.3.4).

4.1.2.4   Demonstrative pronouns

Dialectal variation occurs throughout the demonstrative pronoun paradigms (for Attic, see Ch. 2, §4.1.3.5). For example, the demonstratives *hóde* (ὅδε) and so forth of Classical Attic are formed with a particle other than *-de* in certain dialects: thus, Arcado-Cypriot has *ónu* (ὄνυ) beside Arcadian *oní* (ὀνί); Thessalian has *hóne* (ὄνε). The Attic near demonstratives *hûtos* (οὖτος) and *haútē* (αὕτη), masculine and feminine nominative singular respectively, appear in the nominative plural also with an initial *h-*; outside of the nominative (singular and plural), all members of the animate paradigm, as well as all neuter forms – including nominatives – have initial *t-*. In some Doric and Northwest Greek dialects, however, the initial *t-* of the animate nominative plural has been preserved, as in the paradigm of the article (see §4.1.2.3), thus masculine *tûtoi* (τοῦτοι) feminine *taûtai* (ταῦται). Boeotian, on the other hand, has generalized initial *h-* throughout the entire paradigm. The Attic far demonstrative, masculine *ekênos* (ἐκεῖνος) and so forth, appears in Ionic, Lesbian, and certain Doric dialects without initial *e-*. In most Doric dialects, however, the far demonstrative takes the form *tênos* (τῆνος) and so on.

4.1.2.5   Interrogative/indefinite pronoun

The interrogative *tís, tí* (τίς, τί), indefinite *tis, ti* (τις, τι) of Classical Attic (see Ch. 2, §4.1.3.6) occurs in most dialects (from PIE *$k^w i$-). Showing the advanced stage of assibilation of the labiovelars, however, Cypriot has *si-se* (the syllabic Cypriot spelling) and Arcadian Иις (see §§3.1.1, 3.4.1). The Thessalian pronoun takes the form *kís, kis* (κίς, κις).

4.1.2.6   Relative pronouns

The Classical Attic relative pronoun *hós* (ὅς masc.), *hḗ* (ἥ fem.), *hó* (ὅ neut.; see Ch. 2, §4.1.3.7) is found across the Greek dialect map. However, the definite article (see §4.1.2.3) is commonly used as a relative pronoun in Lesbian, Thessalian, and Arcado-Cypriot, and is attested in this use elsewhere as well.

4.2   Verbal morphology

The Classical Attic verb system described in Chapter 2, §4.2 is for the most part characteristic of all ancient Greek dialects. Particular differences are noted in the ensuing discussion.

4.2.1   Present tense stems

Among the various types of thematic present tense stems of Classical Attic (see Ch. 2, §4.2.2), the most notable dialect variation occurs in the so-called contract verbs. In the Aeolic dialects of Lesbian and Thessalian as well as in Arcado-Cypriot, the contract verbs are inflected as *athematic* rather than thematic constructions, in that they take the endings of the *mi*-verbs (i.e., athematic verbs; for a full presentation of the forms of the endings, see Ch. 2, §4.2.9): for example, Lesbian *pʰílēmmi* (φίλημμι) for Attic *pʰíléǭ* (φιλέω). Conversely, in Ionic (and occasionally elsewhere, even in Attic), some *mi*-verbs are inflected as thematic contract verbs, as in *titʰê̂* (τιθεῖ) beside Classical Attic *titʰę̄si* (τίθησι). Certain Attic *-aǭ* (-αω) contract verbs appear in a variety of dialects as *-eǭ* (-εω) verbs.

4.2.2   Future tense stems

In Doric and Northwest Greek, the future tense stem appears as a contract-verb construction formed in *-se-* (the so-called Doric future): thus, first singular Cretan *speusíǭ* (σπευσίω, with *e* raised to *i* before a vowel; see §3.4.4) beside Attic *speúsǭ* (σπεύσω "I will hasten"); on the Attic future, see Ch. 2, §4.2.5).

These same dialects as well as Arcado-Cypriot and Balkan Aeolic (though only partially in Boeotian) show an innovative future morphology of verbs which have a present tense stem marked by *-zd-* (ζ). In a subset of such verb-stems, the cluster [zd] had developed historically from the consonantal sequence **gy* (see §3.4.3, **4**), where the verb root ends in a velar stop to which the thematic suffix *-ye/yo-* is attached (see Ch. 2, §4.2.2, **2**). In the case of these verbs, the future stem would then be formed in *-ks-* (ξ, from a Proto-Greek velar stop followed by the *s*-formant of the future). In the aforementioned dialects, all future tense stems of *zd*-presents tend to be produced with a formant *-ks-* (rather than *-s-*), regardless of whether or not the root originally ended in a velar stop. For example, *erízdǭ* (ἐρίζω "I strive") forms a Doric future *eríksǭ* (ἐρίξω) beside Attic *erísǭ* (ἐρίσω). In the present stem of this verb, the cluster *zd* arose from the Proto-Greek sequence **dy* (see §3.4.3, **4**) rather than **gy*.

4.2.3   Aorist tense stems

The sigmatic or *s*-aorist (see Ch. 2, §4.2.6) shows a dialect variation like that of the *s*-future stems described immediately above: in Doric, Northwest Greek, Thessalian, and partially in Boeotian and Arcado-Cypriot, the *s*-aorist of present stems terminating in *-zd-* tends to be formed in *-ks-*, regardless of the historical source of *zd*. Thus, Doric shows an aorist participle *katʰíksas* (καθίξας) for the present *katʰízdǭ* (καθίζω "I set, sit"), from the root **sed-*.

4.2.4   Perfect tense stems

Among dialectal peculiarities in perfect tense morphology, notable is the occurrence of thematic inflection of the perfect indicative which is attested in Sicilian Doric and in the Doric of Rhodes and neighboring regions. For example, the Syracusan author Theocritus uses perfects such as *dedoíkō* (δεδοίκω "I fear") and *pepónt^{h}eis* (πεπόνθεις "you have suffered"). Compare – with perfect endings (see Ch. 2, §§4.2.7, 4.2.9) – the respective Attic forms *dédoika* (δέδοικα) and *pépont^{h}as* (πέπονθας). In Lesbian and some Doric and Northwest Greek dialects, the perfect infinitive is formed with the thematic formant *-ēn* (-ειν) rather than athematic *-enai* (-εναι). The Aeolic dialects form the perfect participle with thematic formants (see Ch. 2, §4.2.11).

4.2.5   Nonindicative moods

Outside of the indicative mood, several dialectal variants can be noted.

4.2.5.1   Subjunctive mood

In several dialects – such as Anatolian Ionic, Lesbian and Cretan – the *s*-aorist subjunctive is attested as a "short vowel subjunctive" (i.e., is formed with the short vowel suffix *-e/o-*; see Ch. 2, §4.2.8.1). Compare Ionic *poiḗ-se-i* (ποιήσει) and Attic *poiḗ-sē-i* (ποιήσηι "may (s)he make"), a "long vowel subjunctive."

4.2.5.2   Imperative mood

Throughout the Greek dialects, there is extensive variation in the inflection of the third-person imperative. The Attic ending *-ntǭn* (-ντων; see Ch. 2, §4.2.8.3) also occurs, among other dialects in Ionic and Cretan. Two other third plural endings are essentially substring components of the formant *-ntǭn*: *-ntǭ* (-ντω) occurs in Arcadian, Boeotian, and various Doric dialects; *-tǭn* (-των) is found in Ionic. A short vowel variant *-nton* (-ντον) is used in Lesbian and also occurs in Pamphylian.

4.2.6   Verb endings

For the verb endings of Attic, see Chapter 2, §4.2.9. In those Greek dialects which preserve **t* before *i* (see §3.4.3, **8**), the athematic active third singular ending is *-ti* (-τι), rather than *-si* (-σι). In the same way, **-ti-* is preserved in the third pural: for example, Doric thematic *p^{h}éronti* (φέροντι "they carry"), athematic *tít^{h}enti* (τίθεντι "they place").

In Doric and Northwest Greek the ending of the active first plural is *-mes* (-μες), rather than the *-men* (-μεν) of Attic and other dialects. This ending *-mes* finds cognates in Sankrit *-mas* and Latin *-mus*.

The middle third singular ending – *-tai* (-ται) in Attic and most other dialects – appears as *-toi* (-τοι) in Mycenaean and Arcadian.

4.2.7   Infinitives

The Attic thematic active infinitive formant *-ēn* (-ειν; see Ch. 2, §4.2.10) or its variant *-ēn* (-ην, see §3.4.4) occurs in many other dialects as well – such as Ionic and certain Doric dialects (*-ēn*), and Lesbian, Laconian, and Elean (*-ēn*). A short vowel form *-en* (-εν) is found in Arcadian and various Doric dialects. The athematic infinitival formant *-nai* (-ναι) of Attic is also found in Ionic and Arcado-Cypriot; Lesbian uses *-menai* (-μεναι), while Boeotian,

Thessalian, Northwest Greek, and most Doric dialects have *-men* (which Boeotian and Thessalian also use with thematic verbs). Long vowel variants of the last-named occur in Cretan and Rhodian. On the perfect infinitive, see §4.2.4.

4.3 Numerals

Most, though not all, of the dialectal variations seen in the forms of numerals, vis-à-vis their Attic counterparts (see Ch. 2, §4.5), are the result of dialect sound changes. Selected examples are presented below:

(6)

1	Cretan éns (ἕνς, masc.), Aeolic ía (ἴα, fem.)
2	Laconian dúe (δύε), West Ionic dúwo (δύϝο)
3	Cretan trées (τρέες), Heraclean trîs (τρῖς)
4	Ionic tésseres (τέσσερες), Lesbian péssures (πέσσυρες), Boeotian péttares (πέτταρες)
5	Lesbian pémpe (πέμπε), Pamphylian péde (πέδε)
6	Cretan wéks (ϝέξ)
7	Cretan ettá (ἐττά)
8	Lesbian ókto (ὄκτο), Elean optó (ὀπτό)
9	Heraclean hennéa (hεννέα)
10	Arcadian déko (δέκο)

5. SYNTAX

5.1 Dialectal syntactic features

The syntactic variation attested between dialects – to the extent that such variation can be or has been discerned – is quite minor and lexically specific. Most examples are so much so that they do not fall within the purview of the present work. A few prominent morphosyntactic isoglosses are noted below.

5.2 Coordination

In place of the pandialectal tonic conjunction *kaí* (καί), Arcado-Cypriot uses the conjunction *kás* (κάς). Thessalian utilizes a particle *má* (μά) in lieu of *dé* (δέ).

5.3 Conditional clauses

The Attic conditional particle *án* (ἄν; see Ch. 2, §5.6) also occurs in Ionic as well as in Arcadian. In Lesbian, Thessalian, and Cypriot, a particle *ke* (κε) is used instead; while a form *ka* (κα) occurs in Boeotian, Doric, and Northwest Greek.

6. LEXICON

Making allowance for dialect-specific phonological and morphological variation, a great part of ancient Greek vocabulary is common to all dialects. Yet, with even a casual perusal of a comprehensive dictionary of ancient Greek, such as Liddell and Scott's *Greek-English*

Lexicon (1996), one cannot help but be impressed by how many words appear to be limited to a particular dialect or set of dialects. The lexical distribution that such an activity suggests is to some extent illusory, of course, owing to the haphazard nature of the survival of ancient Greek documents – had a greater, more evenly distributed body of material survived, many words would certainly be found to have a broader dialectal distribution. Apt testimony of this is provided by the Mycenaean vocabulary. Prior to the decipherment of Linear B, a number of lexemes which would emerge from the Bronze-Age Mycenaean tablets were only attested in relatively late, post-Classical Greek sources (see Ventris and Chadwick 1973:91). On the other hand, chances are that more extensive documentation would also reveal yet more dialect-limited vocabulary.

The Mycenaean lexicon also contains, expectedly, both vocabulary that is not otherwise attested in ancient Greek and vocabulary preserved in the archaic poetic language of Greek epic. The agent noun *to-ko-do-mo* (*toik^hodomoi*) "builders," for example, morphologically and semantically transparent, is not found elsewhere, though a denominative verb seemingly derived from it is attested in the fourth century BC. Among words which Mycenaean shares with Homeric epic are *pa-ka-na* (pl.), *p^hásganon* (φάσγανον "sword, dagger"); *e-ke-si* (dat. pl.), *éŋk^hos* (ἔγχος "spear"); and *a-sa-mi-to*, *asáminthos* (ἀσάμινθος "bathing tub").

The Arcado-Cypriot lexicon likewise contains numerous archaic words, shared with Mycenaean Greek and the language of Homer and poetry. In Cyprus, the Mycenaean word for "king," *wanaks*, still survives as a royal title (Cypriot *wa-na-kse*), denoting the king's sons and brothers; elsewhere in the first millennium BC, *ánaks* (ἄναξ) commonly means "lord" or "master of the house." The notion "king" has come to be expressed by *basileús* (βασιλεύς), which in Mycenaean (*g^wasileus*) names, much more modestly, the "chief." Among other words which Cypriot shares with epic are *e-le-i* (dative of *élos* "meadow"), Homeric ἕλος (cf. the Mycenaean place name *e-re-e/i*, dative); *-i-ja-te-ra-ne* (accusative of *ijātēr* "healer"); Homeric ἰητήρ (Mycenaean *i-ja-te*). Arcadian shares with the epic language, *inter alia*, *kéleut^hos* (κέλευθος "path") and *âmar* (ἆμαρ "day"), Homeric ἦμαρ (cf. Armenian *awr*). Archaic words shared by Arcadian and Cypriot include, among others, *euk^hōlá* (εὐχωλά "prayer"; Cypriot spelling *e-u-ko-la*), Homeric εὐχωλή.

Interesting among dialect-specific lexemes are names of legal and religious officials. To cite but a few examples, Lesbian provides *dikáskopoi* (δικάσκοποι), the title of judges at Mytilene and Cyme ("inspectors of justice"); Thessalian has *tagós* (ταγός), the title of a magistrate at Larissa (the word more widely denotes "commander"). Among Northwest Greek dialects, Locrian shows *pentámeroi* (πεντάμεροι), officials who serve for five (*pénte*, πέντε) days (*améra*, ἀμέρα); compare the Phocian verb *pentamariteúō* (πενταμαριτεύω) "to hold office for five days" (*amára*).

In Laconian, the title of the office of overseer is *bíduoi* (βίδυοι) or *bídeoi* (βίδεοι), from the root **wid-* "to see," evidencing the Spartan fricativization of the glide **w* (see §3.1.1). The regimentation of Spartan society with its grouping of boys and young men by age for military training and common life finds expression in the Laconian lexicon, producing words such as *pratopámpais* (πρατοπάμπαις), from *prato-* (πρατο-) "first," *pân* (πᾶν) "all" and *paîs* (παῖς) "child, boy"; and *hatropámpais* (ἀτροπάμπαις), perhaps from *háteros* (ἅτερος) "another, second" – both denoting such a group of boys.

The Doric dialect of Coan preserves the title of a priest of Cos called the *gereap^hóros* (γερεαφόρος), meaning approximately the "recipient of perks," from *géras* (γέρας) "gift of honor, present." Particularly intriguing is the title of a scribe preserved in a remarkable Cretan inscription, the *poinikastás* (ποινικαστάς; see Jeffery and Morpurgo Davies 1970; Thomas 1992:69–70); he (Spensithios is his name) is the scribe who writes with *p^hoiniké̄ia* (φοινικήια) "Phoenician letters," the term the Greeks use to denote the characters of their alphabet, suggesting an awareness at the time of coining of another type of Greek character (see Burkert 1992:27). A natural further implication may be that the *poinikastás* is the scribe who wrote with Phoenician characters as opposed to a scribe using a different Greek script (see Woodard 2000) – perhaps a particularly archaic title preserved by the scribe's cultic affiliation (Spensithios is appointed to be scribe of both secular and sacred matters). Jeffery and Morpurgo Davies (1970:152) have drawn attention to the use of a similar scribal title *pʰoinikográpʰos* (φοινικογράφος) in the Aeolic dialect of Mytilene, attested alongside the common term for scribe *grammateús* (γραμματεύς), suggesting that the former may be an old title preserved because of the scribe's affiliation with the cult of Hermes.

7. READING LIST

Though rendered somewhat out of date by the absence of Mycenaean Greek data, the most helpful English treatment of the Greek dialects remains Buck's excellent 1955 volume. Helpful summaries of the Greek dialects, including Mycenaean, appear in Palmer 1980. A detailed treatment of Greek dialects is provided by the two revised volumes of Thumb: Thumb–Kieckers 1932 and Thumb–Scherer 1959. Cowgill 1966 is an excellent summary of more recent work in Greek dialectology, including a review of the seminal studies by Porzig (1954) and Risch (1955). For Mycenaean Greek, see especially Ventris and Chadwick 1973. The standard English dictionary of ancient Greek is Liddell, Scott, Stuart Jones, and McKenzie 1996. On the Mycenaean lexicon see Aura Jorro 1985–1993.

Bibliography

Allen, W. 1973. *Accent and Rhythm*. Cambridge: Cambridge University Press.

———. 1987. *Vox Graeca* (3rd edition). Cambridge: Cambridge University Press.

Aura Jorro, F. 1985–1993. *Diccionario micénico*. Madrid: Instituto Filologia.

Bile, M. 1988. *Le dialecte crétois ancien*. Athens: Ecole Française.

Browning, R. 1983. *Medieval and Modern Greek* (2nd edition). Cambridge: Cambridge University Press.

Buck, C. 1955. *The Greek Dialects*. Chicago: University of Chicago Press.

Burkert, W. 1992. *The Orientalizing Revolution*. Translated by M. Pindar and W. Burkert. Cambridge, MA: Harvard University Press.

Chadwick, J. 1956. "The Greek dialects and Greek pre-history." *Greece and Rome* NS 3:38–50.

———. 1976. "Who were the Dorians?" *Parola del passato*. 31:103–117.

Chantraine, P. 1984. *Morphologie historique du grec* (2nd edition). Paris: Klincksieck.

Coleman, R. 1963. "The dialect geography of ancient Greece." *Transactions of the Philological Society*, pp. 58–126.

Cowgill, W. 1966. "Ancient Greek dialectology in the light of Mycenaean." In H. Birnbaum and J. Puhvel (eds.), *Ancient Indo-European Dialects*, pp. 77–95. Berkeley/Los Angeles: University of California Press.

Devine, A. and L. Stephens. 1994. *The Prosody of Greek Speech*. Oxford: Oxford University Press.

Duhoux, Y. 1983. *Introduction aux dialectes grecs anciens*. Louvain-la-Neuve: Cabay.

Heubeck, A. 1986. "Die Würzburger Alphabettafel." *Würzburger Jahrbücher für die Altertumswissenschaft* NS 12:7–20.

Jeffery, L. 1990. *The Local Scripts of Archaic Greece* (revised edition). Supplement by A. Johnston. Oxford: Oxford University Press.

Jeffery, L. and A. Morpurgo Davies. 1970. "ΠΟΙΝΙΚΑΣΤΑΣ and ΠΟΙΝΙΚΑΖΕΝ: BM 1969. 4–2. 1, a new archaic inscription from Crete." *Kadmos* 9:118–156.

Kirchhoff, A. 1887. *Studien zur Geschichte des griechischen Alphabets*. Gütersloh: Bertelsmann.

Lejeune, M. 1982. *Phonétique historique du mycénien et du grec ancien.* Paris: Klincksieck.

Liddell, H. and R. Scott. 1996. *A Greek-English Lexicon with a Revised Supplement.* Revised by H. Stuart Jones and R. McKenzie. Oxford: Clarendon Press.

Masson, O. 1983. *Les inscriptions chypriotes syllabiques.* Paris: Edition E. de Boccard.

Nagy, G. 1968. "On dialectal anomalies in Pylian texts." In *Atti e memorie del 1° congresso internazionale di micenologia*, vol. II, pp. 663–679. Rome: Edizioni dell' Ateneo.

———. 1970. *Greek Dialects and the Transformation of an Indo-European Process.* Cambridge, MA: Harvard University Press.

Palmer, L. 1980. *The Greek Language.* Atlantic Highlands, NJ: Humanities Press.

Porzig, W. 1954. "Sprachgeographische Untersuchungen zu den altgriechischen Dialekten." *Indogermanische Forschungen* 61:147–169.

Risch, E. 1955. "Die Gliederung der griechischen Dialekte in neuer Sicht." *Museum Helveticum* 12:61–76.

———. 1966. "Les différences dialectales dans le mycénien." In L. Palmer and J. Chadwick (eds.), *Proceedings of the Cambridge Colloquium on Mycenaean Studies*, pp. 150–157. Cambridge: Cambridge University Press.

Rix, H. 1976. *Historische Grammatik des Griechischen.* Darmstadt: Wissenschaftliche Buchgesellschaft.

Scott, D., R. Woodard, P. McCarter, *et al.* 2005. "Greek Alphabet MS 108." In R. Pintaudi (ed.), *Papyri Graecae Schøyen*, pp. 149–160. Florence: Edizioni Gonnelli.

Stephens, L. and R. Woodard. 1986. "The palatalization of the labiovelars in Greek: a reassessment in typological perspective." *Indogermanische Forschungen* 91:129–154.

Szemerényi, O. 1968. "The Attic 'Rückverwandlung' or atomism and structuralism in action." In M. Mayrhofer (ed.), *Studien zur Sprachwissenschaft und Kulturkunde*, pp. 139–157. Innsbruck: Leopold-Franzens-Universität.

Thomas, R. 1992. *Literacy and Orality in Ancient Greece.* Cambridge: Cambridge University Press.

Threatte, L. 1980. *The Grammar of Attic Inscriptions*, vol. I. Berlin: De Gruyter.

Thumb, A. and E. Kieckers. 1932. *Handbuch der griechischen Dialekte*, part 1. Heidelberg: Carl Winter.

Thumb, A. and A. Scherer. 1959. *Handbuch der griechischen Dialekte*, part 2. Heidelberg: Carl Winter.

Ventris, M. and J. Chadwick. 1973. *Documents in Mycenaean Greek* (2nd edition). Cambridge: Cambridge University Press.

Woodard, R. 1986. "Dialectal differences at Knossos." *Kadmos* 25:49–74.

———. 1997. *Greek Writing from Knossos to Homer.* Oxford: Oxford University Press.

———. 2000. "Greek–Phoenician interaction and the origin of the alphabet." In A. Ovadiah (ed.), *Mediterranean Cultural Interaction*, pp. 33–51. Tel Aviv: Tel Aviv University Press.

CHAPTER 4

Latin

JAMES P. T. CLACKSON

1. HISTORICAL AND CULTURAL CONTEXTS

Latin – the language of Ancient Rome – takes its name from Latium, a region encompassing Rome on the west coast of Italy and bordered by the river Tiber to the northwest, the Apennines to the northeast and the Pontine marshes to the south. The Roman antiquarian Varro dated the founding of Rome to 753 BC, but there is archeological evidence for settlement much earlier than this, and it was only later, in the sixth century BC, that Rome became an organized and sophisticated city-state. Latium itself did not achieve political unity until it came under Rome's dominance in the fourth century BC, but the Latini – as the inhabitants of Latium are termed – appear to have shared cultural and religious practice, as well as their language, from well before the period of the first city-states.

The increasing control over Latium was the first stage of Rome's rise to power throughout the Italian peninsula a dominance achieved through conquest, alliance, and colonization. By the second century BC, Rome's military power was great enough to make possible the conquest and annexation of territory outside Italy, including North Africa, Spain, Southern France and Greece. Civil wars throughout much of the first century BC led to the end of the Roman Republic and the foundation of the Roman Empire under Augustus. Imperial rule continued for over four hundred years, and under Trajan (AD 98–117) and Hadrian (AD 117–138) the empire reached its maximum extent, stretching from Britain to Egypt and encompassing much of Europe and all of the area surrounding the Mediterranean.

The influence and spread of the Latin language mirrored the power and extent of the Roman Empire and, even today, Latin retains a great deal of cultural prestige. It is still widely taught and it is retained in use by many different scientific, legal, and religious institutions around the world. Moreover, over 500 million people currently speak as their first language a language derived from Latin.

Latin is one of a number of Indo-European languages which were spoken in ancient Italy. It shares several features with the Faliscan language which was spoken to the north of Latium, most importantly the existence of two thematic genitive singular morphemes -ī and -osio (the latter attested in an Early Latin inscription recently discovered in Satricum), and the formation of a future tense with a morpheme containing a reflex of Indo-European $*-b^h$-. Although we have only limited knowledge of the Faliscan language (our sources are mostly epitaphs and a few early vase-inscriptions, none of them extensive) these morphological agreements are sufficient to lead to a general consensus that Latin and Faliscan form a subgroup. More contentious is the relationship between Latin-Faliscan and the Sabellian group languages, which include Oscan and Umbrian (see Ch. 5). Many scholars have judged that the similarities between Latin and Sabellian justify the reconstruction of an Italic subgroup of Indo-European, but it has proved difficult to demonstrate conclusively that these similarities result from genetic affiliation, and have not arisen through convergence of separate branches of Indo-European over time. Our present state of knowledge of Sabellian and the early history of Latin is not sufficient to allow a definite answer to this question.

Latin has a long history. The earliest documents date from the seventh century BC, and there is a continuous literary tradition from the third century BC through to the medieval period. The following chronological stages of the language are generally recognized, although there is no clear agreement on exact dating:

1. *Early or Old Latin:* The language from the earliest times to *c.* 100 BC. A distinction is often recognized between *Pre-literary Latin*, the scantily attested language of the earliest documents, and *Pre-Classical Latin*, the language of the first extensive literary works from *c.* 240 BC to *c.* 100 BC.
2. *Classical Latin:* The language of official inscriptions and literature from *c.* 100 BC to *c.* AD 14. Following the models of the works of Cicero and the writers of the age of Augustus, Classical Latin became the standard for later canons of "Latinity," and it has remained the prestige form of written compositions right up to the present day.
3. *Post-Classical and Late Latin:* The language of writers after the Classical period. Writers of the hundred years following the death of Augustus (AD 14) have traditionally been judged harshly in comparison with their predecessors, and their language is sometimes termed *Silver Latin*, although the linguistic differences between Classical and Silver Latin are not great. The leveling effect of the standard language, and the increasing artificiality of much of the literary language makes it difficult to define exactly when the stage of *Late Latin* begins, but it is clear that by AD 400 even the standardized form of the language shows substantial differences from Classical Latin.

A further classification often encountered is *Vulgar Latin*. This is not a chronological stage per se but rather a catch-all category which is used to denote an informal register of Latin spoken by those who had received little or no literate education, as opposed to Classical Latin, the formal standard language of the elite. However, our knowledge of the spoken registers of Latin is severely limited, since the written record is always prone to influence from the standard, and the construction of a uniform "Vulgar Latin" probably oversimplifies a very complex linguistic situation. Different communities of speakers used different nonstandard varieties, and the relationship between the spoken registers and the artificial written language changed considerably over time. We should consequently bear in mind that, rather than a simple opposition between Classical Latin and Vulgar Latin, there was a much more complex relationship between an ever-evolving standard and a number of different spoken registers. In short, there is no Vulgar Latin, only "vulgar" forms present in a greater or lesser degree in individual texts.

Nowadays few scholars would recognize another distinct variety of Latin in the language used in Christian texts, although the case for *Christian Latin* was promoted enthusiastically by some Dutch scholars in the first half of the twentieth century. It is true that Christian texts show a preponderance of lexical items which do not occur as frequently elsewhere, but these words all refer to new institutions or beliefs, and in fact it can be shown that the language of the early Christian writers shows the same properties and variety as contemporary non-Christian registers.

The best evidence for dialectal varieties of Latin comes from the earlier periods of its history. Surviving inscriptions from Praeneste, an early city-state of Latium and rival to Rome, support the statements from ancient sources suggesting that Praenestine was distinct from Roman Latin. However, as Roman power and prestige grew, dialects outside Rome became stigmatized as rustic and were subsumed in the Classical period under the influence of the standard language. All later Latin is written by those who have had at least some education in the standard and it is difficult to detect any major regional differences across the empire.

2. WRITING SYSTEM

The Latin alphabet is derived, like the Faliscan alphabet, from a variety of the Etruscan script, itself an adaptation of the Western Greek Euboean alphabet. The earliest Latin script has the following letters:

(1)   ABCDEFZHIKLMNOPQRSTVX

In the use of the letters *C*, *K*, and *Q* this script shows its clear affinities with the Etruscan alphabet used in South Etruria (see Ch. 7, §2). The three letters are all used to represent both the voiceless and the voiced velar stop, but a convention loosely followed on several early inscriptions (and also found in Faliscan inscriptions) governs their distribution: *C* occurs before front vowels; *K* before /a/; and *Q* before rounded back vowels (note also the names of the letters *cē* for *C*, *kā* for *K*, and *qū* for *Q*). The very earliest Latin inscriptions use a digraph *FH* for /f/, following Etruscan practice, but this is soon replaced by the simple *F*; the Faliscan alphabet uses a new sign ↑ for /f/. The letters *B*, *D*, and *O* are not used in Etruscan texts; the Etruscan language appears to have lacked a phonemic contrast between voiced and voiceless stops, and to have had only one back vowel, written *V*. However, these letter forms are attested on Etruscan abecedaria, and so there is no need to posit a direct borrowing from Greek. The letter *X* is used for the combination /k/ + /s/. The letter *Z* is used in the Faliscan alphabet but, apart from its presence in a Latin abecedarium, it occurs in only one very fragmentary archaic Latin inscription, with uncertain value, and it dropped out of use completely by the third century BC. The position of *Z* in the Latin alphabet was taken by a new letter – *G* – invented in order to differentiate the writing of voiceless and voiced velar stops. In the first century BC the need to represent the sounds of Greek loanwords led to the adoption of the letters *Y* and *Z* directly from the Greek alphabet. The distinct writing of *V* and *J* for the consonants /w/ and /y/ as opposed to *U* and *I* for the vowels /u/ and /i/ is first made systematic only in the fifteenth century AD.

Table 4.1 The Archaic Latin alphabet			
Character	Transcription	Character	Transcription
A	a	M	m
B	b	N	n
C	c/g	O	o
D	d	P	p
E	e	Q	q
F	f	P	r
I	z	S	s
B	h	T	t
I	i	Y , V	v
K	k	+	x
L	l		

3. PHONOLOGY

3.1 Consonants

The phonemic inventory of Latin consonants is presented in Table 4.2:

Manner of articulation	Place of articulation						
	Bilabial	Labiodental	Dental	Palatal	Velar	Labiovelar	Glottal
Stop							
Voiceless	p		t		k	k^w(?)	
Voiced	b		d		g	g^w (?)	
Fricative		f	s				h
Nasal	m		n		ŋ(?)		
Liquid							
Lateral			l				
Nonlateral			r				
Glide				y		w	

Table 4.2   The consonantal phonemes of Latin

3.1.1   "Labiovelars"

The phonological status of the sounds written with the digraphs *QU* and *GU* is debated. There is no conclusive argument for favoring a realization [k^w] and [g^w] over [kw] and [gw], or indeed for supposing that *GU* must represent the voiced counterpart to *QU*, especially since the distribution of *GU* is much more restricted than *QU* (it only occurs after a nasal). Both sounds can derive from earlier unitary phonemes *k^w and *g^w, but *QU* also continues the cluster *kw. It is true that metrical texts normally require that a word such as *liquidus* "liquid" be scanned with the first syllable short, thus implying [li.k^{w}i-] (with syllable boundary represented by the dot), but there are some texts where this word is scanned with the first syllable long implying a pronunciation [lik.wi-].

3.1.2   The velar nasal

The sound [ŋ], which occurs only in syllable codas, is represented in the orthography by *N* before velars and *G* before nasal consonants. This orthographic convention may imply that [ŋ] is an allophone of both /n/ and /g/, but distinctive triplets such as *amnī* "river" (dat. sg.), *annī* "year" (gen. sg.), and *agnī* [aŋni:] "lamb" (gen. sg.) could be taken to support the existence of a separate phoneme /ŋ/.

3.1.3   Glides

In Proto-Indo-European the phonemes /i/ and /u/ have consonantal and vocalic allophones, and it is likely that this is continued into Early Latin. This is reflected in the Latin script, where a single letter, *I*, is used to represent both the vowel [i] and the glide [y], and *V* is used for [u] and [w]. Indeed, for the sake of metrical convenience, Latin poets of the Classical period occasionally interchange [i] / [y] and [u] / [w]; the word for "knees" – *genua* – is generally a trisyllable, but in verse it is found as a disyllable [gɛnwa], and the name *Iūlius* is found scanned as both a trisyllable and quadrisyllable. However, apart from this poetic license, by the Classical period [i] / [y] and [u] / [w] are no longer allophones but separate phonemes – note the minimal pairs *iambus* [ɪam-] "iambus" : *iam* [ya] "now," and *uoluit* [-luɪt] "he wanted" : *uoluit* [-lwɪt] "he rolls."

Metrical evidence from Latin poetry shows that when the glide /y/ is intervocalic it is usually pronounced as a double consonant although not normally so written – thus *maior* "greater" was pronounced [mayyor]. The glide /y/ is not usually found following a consonant, except in compounds such as *con-iungo* "join together"; hence *medius* "middle" was pronounced [mɛdɪus] not [mɛdyus]. Conversely the glide /w/ is found in clusters such as [sw] and possibly [kw] and [gw] (see §3.1.1), with the consequence that in some forms the orthography is ambiguous: for example, *sua* [sua] "one's own" (fem. nom. sg.) is written the same as *suāuis* "sweet" [swaːwɪs].

3.2 Vowels

Latin has five short vowels /i/, /e/, /a/, /o/, and /u/ and five long vowels /iː/, /eː/, /aː/, /oː/, and /uː/. Short and long vowels are paired in many areas of Latin morphology, thus one means of forming the perfect tense employs the rule that the root vowel is lengthened:

(2)   /i/ : /iː/ *uincō* "I conquer," *uīcī* "I conquered"
      /e/ : /eː/ *ueniō* "I come," *uēnī* "I came"
      /a/ : /aː/ *scabō* "I scratch," *scābī* "I scratched"
      /o/ : /oː/ *fodiō* "I dig," *fōdī* "I dug"
      /u/ : /uː/ *fugiō* "I flee," *fūgī* "I fled"

However, for the high and mid vowels, length differences also involved a change in quality; /i/ was probably realized as [ɪ] but /iː/ as [iː], and /e/ as [ɛ], but /eː/ as [eː], making /i/ actually closer in quality to /eː/ than to /iː/. This skewed phonetic realization was to have effects on the vowel system in the spoken registers from which the Romance languages originated. Vowel length was lost as a distinctive feature, becoming an automatic concomitant of the word stress, and under the stress short /i/ and long /eː/ merged as a high-mid front vowel [e]. In many areas a similar merger also took place between /u/ and /oː/, and one can suppose that there was a similar disparity between the phonetic values of long and short vowels on the back axis also.

In Classical Latin there was also a series of nasalized vowels, /ĩ/, /ẽ/, /ã/, /õ/, and /ũ/, which were restricted in occurrence to (i) word-final position, where in the standard orthography they are written *im, em, am, om, um*; or (ii) before a sequence of nasal + continuant. All nasal vowels were inherently long; they do not contrast with short nasal vowels.

In Early Latin there are a number of distinctive diphthongs: /ei/, /ai/, /oi/, /au/, /ou/, and /eu/ (the last attested only in a single inscription). These all underwent monophthongization in nonstandard varieties of Latin, but in Classical Latin /au/ was generally maintained, /ai/ was continued as a diphthong /ae/, and, in a few lexical forms, the earlier diphthong /oi/ was continued as /oe/. In a very small number of words a new diphthong /eu/ also arose as a result of contractions. The remaining diphthongs were monophthongized; the exact details are complex, but in essence (i) *ei* > *ī*; (ii) *ou* and *eu* > *ū*; and (iii) *oi* > *ū* word-internally (in most cases, although sometimes *oi* > *oe*), *oi* > *ī* word-finally and following [w].

3.3 Accent

The word accent of Early Latin was a stress accent placed on the first syllable of every word. The effects of the accent can be seen in the syncope which affected many short final vowels and a series of quality changes in vowels in noninitial syllables known collectively as "vowel weakening." One such change is the merger of non-initial, non-final short vowels in open syllables to /i/, leading to morphophonemic alternations of the type *faciō* "I make," compound form *re-ficiō* "I restore." Sometime before the beginning of the Classical period, however, the place of the word accent had changed, and the accentuation of all Latin words, bar a few special exceptions, can be predicted by the rule of the penultimate: the accent falls on the penultimate syllable, unless that syllable is metrically light (i.e., open with a short vowel nucleus) in which case the accent falls on the antepenultimate.

The nature of the word accent of Classical Latin is disputed. Ancient grammarians, who largely follow Greek models of description, uniformly use the terms applicable to the pitch accent-type of Greek to describe the Latin accent, although metrical practice and the continuing evidence for syncope throughout the Classical and post-Classical period (and in the reconstructed early development of the Romance language) strongly suggest that the word accent continued to be stress.

3.4 Syllable structure

Latin syllables can be described under the schema of (3), where O = obstruent (stop or /f/), S = sonorant, V = vocalic element (here long vowels are counted as equivalent to a double short vowel):

(3)

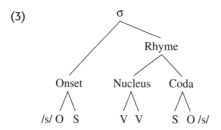

In initial or final clusters with /s/ the obstruent must be a voiceless stop; thus, the nominative singular of the word for "town" – written *urbs* in most modern editions of Latin texts – was pronounced, and sometimes written, *urps*. Some clusters are avoided: for example initial /dr-/ is rare, occurring only in loanwords and onomatopoeia; and /-ts/ is always replaced by /-s/.

Syllables with VV nucleus and an element in the coda, sometimes termed *superheavy* or *overlong*, are prone to simplification; compare the stem formations of the following verbs:

(4)   *gerō* "I manage," perfect *gessī*, supine *gestum*
        hauriō "I drain," perfect *hausī*, supine *haustum*

In both verbs the *-r-* of the present tense comes from earlier **s* which changed to *-r-* when in intervocalic position (the unchanged *-s-* is preserved in the stem of the supine, which is formed with a suffix *-tum*). The perfect stem is formed with a suffix *-s-*; the root-final *-s-* is preserved before this in *gessī* with short vowel nucleus, but in *haussī* (still so written in some early texts) the geminate is simplified. A further example of the avoidance of syllables with long nucleus and coda is the regular shortening of long vowels in final syllables before *-t, -r, -l, -nt*, and *-m* which took place in the Early Latin period; the effect of this change can be seen in some of the nominal and verbal paradigms given in the next section.

For the purposes of poetic meter, a syllable with one or more branches in the rhyme is counted as heavy (i.e., a syllable with a long vowel nucleus or final consonant). The relationship between syllables with long nucleus and syllables with coda is also evident from historical developments. When consonant clusters are simplified, preceding short vowels are often lengthened: *īdem* "the same" is a regular development from **isdem*. Such *compensatory lengthening* is, of course, paralleled in the histories of many other languages. Comparatively rare is the opposite process, whereby length is transferred from the vowel to the following consonant, but there are several examples of such a change in Latin, a standard example being the divine name *Iuppiter* < **Iūpiter* < **Dyew-pater* (the change of medial vowel reflects the process of vowel weakening discussed above). There is evidence for similar "length metatheses" throughout the period of Latin, and it is possible that this unusual change has its origin in variant pronunciations in different social registers and subsequent hypercorrection.

Latin words may be built up of one or more admissible syllables, with the following corollaries: (i) no monosyllabic word may consist of a final unchecked short vowel unless it is a clitic; (ii) word-final voiced stops are only found in nonlexicals and /st/ is also permitted as a word-final cluster.

4. MORPHOLOGY

4.1 Word formation

Latin morphology is widely used in linguistic textbooks as a standard example of the fusional or inflectional type. In Latin nominal morphology, different categories are generally expressed solely through suffixes, which encode both number and case. Thus, the suffixes -*īs* and -*bus* are used in different declensional classes as the cumulative exponents of the categories DATIVE PLURAL and ABLATIVE PLURAL, and they cannot be further analyzed into separate morphs for DATIVE or ABLATIVE and PLURAL.

Verbal morphology is also largely fusional, and person, number, and mood marking is always encoded through suffixation, although in many verbal paradigms infixation, reduplication, and ablaut of the root morpheme play a role in the formation of the tense stem.

Some verbal paradigms also approach a degree of analyticity; compare the following examples of present and future passive forms from the root *amā-* "love":

(5)   *amat* "he loves," present active indicative third singular
       amātur "he is loved," present passive indicative third singular
       amābit "he will love," future active indicative third singular
       amābitur "he will be loved," future passive indicative third singular

One possible analysis of the future passive *amābitur* would be as follows:

(6)   amā-   -bi-   -t-   -ur
       LOVE   FUTURE   3RD.SINGULAR   PASSIVE

Unfortunately, although this analysis could be made to work for the first and third persons, in the second-person forms the markers of person and voice are fused:

(7)   *amās* "you (singular) love"
       amāris "you (singular) are loved"
       amātis "you (plural) love"
       amāminī "you (plural) are loved"

Latin word structure is of the Indo-European type, the basic scheme of word formation (ignoring, for the moment, compound forms, which will be discussed further below) is as follows:

(8)   word = lexical root + (derivational suffix)^x + inflectional ending

All well-formed nominals and verbs (barring a handful of indeclinable forms) show a root and ending, and most also incorporate at least one derivational suffix. It is possible to multiply the number of derivational suffixes, and to derive verbs from nominal roots or nominals from verbal roots; thus, for example, *dictātōrius* "belonging to a dictator" can be analyzed as follows:

(9)   *dic-*   root DIC "say"   cf. *dīcere* "to say"
       -tā-   frequentative verb suffix   cf. *dictāre* "to dictate"
       -tōr-   agent noun suffix   cf. *dictātor* "dictator"
       -ius   fused adjectival suffix and inflection

A nonproductive pattern found in a few nouns and verbs attaches inflectional endings directly to the lexical root, as *dux* "leader," analyzable as lexical root (DUC-) + inflection (-s). Roots and suffixes may show alternations before further derivational suffixes. For example, from the same stem *dictātōr-* mentioned above, a feminine *dictātrīx* "female dictator" is formed, with a regular loss of the medial vowel of the agent suffix *-tōr-* before *-īc-*, the suffix denoting a female.

4.2 Nominal morphology

Latin nouns are marked for number and case, and adjectives also for gender.

4.2.1   Gender and number

There are three genders, traditionally termed masculine, feminine, and neuter, and two numbers, singular and plural. Gender for nouns denoting humans and gods, and, to a lesser extent, animals overlaps with the semantic criterion of sex, so that *mulier* "woman" is feminine, although it contains no specific feminine morpheme, and *agricola* "farmer," which belongs to the predominantly feminine declension class with nominative singular in *-a*, is nevertheless masculine. For words designating inanimates, however, all three genders are found: *nix* (feminine) "snow," *lapis* (masculine) "stone," *iecur* (neuter) "liver."

4.2.2   Case

The category of case is more complex. Classical Latin has six paradigmatic cases, traditionally labeled nominative, vocative, accusative, genitive, dative, and ablative (note that the traditional term *ablative* is potentially misleading, since this last case also serves as the instrumental and, in part, the locative). In the plural, the dative and ablative are syncretic in all declensions, and all neuter nouns have syncretic nominative, accusative, and vocative. Oscan and Umbrian have a paradigmatic seventh case, the locative; in Latin this is replaced for most nouns by the syntagm of preposition and ablative. However, proper names referring to towns and small islands retain a locative form, as do three nouns denoting place (*rūs*, "countryside," *domus* "home," and *humus* "ground"). In Classical Latin the form of the locative is always syncretic with another case (in the singular, with the genitive in declensions I and II, but with the ablative in declension III; in the plural, with the dative-ablative in all declensions).

4.2.3 Nominal declensions

Latin has five morphologically distinct declensions, which largely continue inherited types, with the exception of declension V which represents a Latin innovation. Representative paradigms are given in Table 4.3; note that the declension III has two main subtypes:

Table 4.3 Latin nominal paradigms					
I	II	IIIa	IIIb	IV	V
mēnsa	lupus	rēx	turris	manus	rēs
"table"	"wolf"	"king"	"tower"	"hand"	"thing"
Singular					
Nom. mēnsa	lupus	rēx	turris	manus	rēs
Voc. mēnsa	lupe	rēx	turris	manus	rēs
Acc. mēnsam	lupum	rēgem	turrim	manum	rem
Gen. mēnsae	lupī	rēgis	turris	manūs	reī
Dat. mēnsae	lupō	rēgī	turrī	manuī	reī
Abl. mēnsā	lupō	rēge	turrī	manū	rē
Plural					
Nom. mēnsae	lupī	rēgēs	turrēs	manūs	rēs
Voc. mēnsae	lupī	rēgēs	turrēs	manūs	rēs
Acc. mēnsās	lupōs	rēgēs	turrīs	manūs	rēs
Gen. mēnsārum	lupōrum	rēgum	turrium	manuum	rērum
Dat. mēnsīs	lupīs	rēgibus	turribus	manibus	rēbus
Abl. mēnsīs	lupīs	rēgibus	turribus	manibus	rēbus

Nouns of neuter gender only occur in declensions II, III, and IV. Their case endings are the same except in the syncretic nominative-vocative-accusative:

(10)

	II	*IIIa*	*IIIb*	*IV*
Singular	iugum	genus	rēte	genū
	"yoke"	"kind"	"net"	"knee"
Nom.-voc.-acc.	iugum	genus	rēte	genū
Gen.	iugī	generis	rētis	genūs
Plural				
Nom.-voc.-acc.	iuga	genera	rētia	genua
Gen.	iugōrum	generum	rētium	genuum

4.2.4 Comparatives and superlatives

Adjectives, as well as adverbs, have an additional category of gradation, so that alongside the unmarked "positive" degree of an adjective such as *longus* "long" there are also paradigmatic forms for the comparative *longior* "longer, too long" and a superlative *longissimus* "longest, very long"; the adverb *longē* "far off" similarly forms comparative *longius* and superlative *longissimē*.

4.3 Pronouns

The Latin pronominal system has the same categories as the nominal system. Personal pronouns are marked for number and case, and demonstrative, anaphoric, interrogative, and relative pronouns are marked for number, case, and gender. Apart from the vocative case, which is syncretic with the nominative in all pronominal declensions, the dimensions of each category are the same.

4.3.1 Personal pronouns

The declension system of personal pronouns in Latin is synchronically anomalous as the following paradigms show (note that there is no third-person pronoun other than the reflexive *sē*; oblique forms of the anaphoric pronoun *is, ea, id* are used to supply the deficiency):

(11)

	SINGULAR		PLURAL		
	First person	*Second person*	*First person*	*Second person*	*Third person*
Nom.	ego	tū	nōs	uōs	
Acc.	mē	tē	nōs	uōs	sē
Gen.	meī	tuī	nostrī	uestrī	suī
			nostrum	uestrum	
Dat.	mihi	tibi	nōbīs	uōbīs	sibi
Abl.	mē	tē	nōbīs	uōbīs	sē

Some of the irregularities of these declensions continue inherited patterns found in other Indo-European languages; others are unique to Latin. A notable development which occurred only in Latin (and, as far as we have evidence, in Faliscan) is the syncretism of accusative and ablative of *ego, tū,* and *sē*, which in Early Latin are written *mēd, tēd,* and *sēd* (*med* is found as accusative in Faliscan); no other Indo-European language shows accusative forms ending in *-d* for these pronouns. Although Latin lost the distinction between a morphologically separate set of accented and clitic forms, as found in Greek and Sanskrit, it is likely that the personal pronouns could either carry the stress accent or not, depending on context and emphasis.

4.3.2 Demonstrative pronouns

Classical Latin has a fairly rich system of demonstrative and anaphoric pronouns. There is a three-way deictic contrast between the demonstratives *hic, haec, hoc* "this" (indicating proximity to the speaker); *iste, ista, istud* "that" (indicating proximity to the hearer); and *ille, illa, illud* "that" (indicating distance from both speaker and hearer). The declension of these pronouns shows two principal peculiarities: (i) they have distinct endings for all genders in the genitive and dative singular, and for the masculine and neuter nominative; and (ii) some case forms show the amalgamation of pronominal stems with various deictic particles, which have a more independent existence in Early Latin: for example, *hic, haec, hoc* "this":

(12)

	SINGULAR			PLURAL		
	Masculine	Feminine	Neuter	Masculine	Feminine	Neuter
Nom.	hic	haec	hoc	hī	hae	haec
Acc.	hunc	hanc	hoc	hōs	hās	haec
Gen.	huius	huius	huius	hōrum	hārum	hōrum
Dat.	huīc	huīc	huīc	hīs	hīs	hīs
Abl.	hōc	hāc	hōc	hīs	hīs	hīs

The final -c, found in the neuter plural and all cases except the genitive of the singular, derives from an earlier enclitic deictic particle -ce, which in Early Latin is also found attached to other forms, as accusative plural masculine *hōsce*. For the two pronouns denoting identity, *ipse*, *ipsa, ipsum* "-self" and *īdem, eadem, idem* "the same," entirely new paradigms have been generated ultimately from the combinations of the anaphoric *is* with the particles *-pse* and *-em*.

4.3.3   Relative, interrogative, and indefinite pronouns

In Latin the same stem is used for relative, interrogative, and indefinite pronouns, which share exactly the same declension outside of the (i) nominative singular, masculine and feminine, and (ii) nominative-accusative singular neuter. The relative pronoun's declension is as follows:

(13)

	SINGULAR			PLURAL		
	Masculine	Feminine	Neuter	Masculine	Feminine	Neuter
Nom.	quī	quae	quod	quī	quae	quae
Acc.	quem	quam	quod	quōs	quās	quae
Gen.	cuius	cuius	cuius	quōrum	quārum	quōrum
Dat.	cuī	cuī	cuī	quibus	quibus	quibus
Abl.	quō	quā	quō	quibus	quibus	quibus

The distinct forms of the relative pronoun ultimately continue the Indo-European stem *k^wo-, and the distinct forms of the interrogative pronoun, *quis, quid*, continue a stem *$k^w i$-. The indefinite *quis, qua, quid*, neuter plural *qua* or *quae*, is originally an *i*-stem also, but it shows a separate feminine form. In Early Latin there is evidence for a more wide-ranging difference between the relative and the interrogative; for instance a distinct dative-ablative plural form *quīs* of the relative pronoun is widely attested. However, it appears that the declensions were confused from an early stage – witness the ubiquity of the accusative singular masculine *quem* as relative pronoun, which must continue *k^wim.

4.4 Verbal morphology

Latin finite verbs are marked for person, number, tense/aspect, mood, and voice. There are three persons and two numbers, singular and plural; three moods occur, indicative, subjunctive, and imperative.

4.4.1   Tense and mood

There are six tenses of the indicative and four of the subjunctive, built from two separate stems, here termed the *present stem* and *perfect stem*. The interrelationship between tense and mood is illustrated in (14):

(14)   The interrelationship between tense and mood in Latin

| | MOOD | | |
TENSE	*Indicative*	*Subjunctive*	*Imperative*
Present stem			
Present	Present indic.	Present subjunc.	Present imperative
Imperfect	Imperfect indic.	Imperfect subjunc.	
Future	Future indic.		Future imperative
Perfect stem			
Perfect	Perfect indic.	Perfect subjunc.	
Pluperfect	Pluperfect indic.	Pluperfect subjunc.	
Future perfect	Future perfect indic.		

The Latin verbal system does not grammaticalize aspect to the same degree as some other Indo-European languages, such as Greek and Slavic. The contrast between imperfect, used to indicate an uncompleted or ongoing event, and the perfect, indicating a finished or accomplished event, could be viewed as aspectual, but the notion of aspect is not necessary for the description of the rest of the system. Indeed, it is possible to dispense with aspect as a descriptive category of the Latin verb altogether. The present stem marks states of affairs which take place now (the present), at the same time as some past moment (the imperfect), and at the same time as some future moment (the future). In contrast, the perfect stem tenses mark states of affairs before the present (the perfect), before some specific moment in the past (pluperfect), or in the future (future perfect). The contrast between the imperfect and perfect tense is consequently a contrast between something viewed as contemporaneous with a certain moment in the past, and something viewed as anterior to a moment in the present. The imperfect, therefore, is the appropriate tense to describe ongoing events in the past, and the perfect for completed actions.

4.4.2   Voice

The array of tense and mood formations presented above applies equally to the two voices of the verb, active and passive. The active present stem and passive present stem are the same, but perfect formations of passive verbs are always periphrastic, built from the perfect passive participle and auxiliary verb *esse* "to be." Accordingly, in the perfect passive system, verbs also encode the gender of the subject, as well as the number and person.

4.4.3   Conjugation classes

The formation of the different tense and mood paradigms and personal endings is the same for all verbs conjugated in the perfect system, but in the present system there are four main conjugation classes which differ in personal endings and in the formation of the future tense and present subjunctive.

4.4.3.1   Present stem system

The conjugation of the present system is illustrated in (15)–(17) using the paradigms of the verbs *amāre* "to love" (Conjugation I); *spondēre* "to pledge" (Conjugation II); *regere* "to rule" (Conjugation III); and *uenīre* "to come" (Conjugation IV).

(15)   Latin present indicative

		Conjugation I	*Conjugation II*	*Conjugation III*	*Conjugation IV*
Singular	*1st*	amō	spondeō	regō	ueniō
	2nd	amās	spondēs	regis	uenīs
	3rd	amat	spondet	regit	uenit
Plural	*1st*	amāmus	spondēmus	regimus	uenīmus
	2nd	amātis	spondētis	regitis	uenītis
	3rd	amant	spondent	regunt	ueniunt

As can be seen, in the present indicative the four conjugations share the same set of personal endings, which are basically those of Conjugation III, but differences arise from fusion of the endings with stem-vowels in Conjugations I, II, and IV.

(16)   Latin present subjunctive

		Conjugation I	*Conjugation II*	*Conjugation III*	*Conjugation IV*
Singular	*1st*	amem	spondeam	regam	ueniam
	2nd	amēs	spondeās	regās	ueniās
	3rd	amet	spondeat	regāt	ueniat
Plural	*1st*	amēmus	spondeāmus	regāmus	ueniāmus
	2nd	amētis	spondeātis	regātis	ueniātis
	3rd	ament	spondeant	regant	ueniant

In the subjunctive, the personal endings are the same as those of the indicative (15) except for the first-person singular, which is marked by *-m* rather than *-ō*. These two endings are a survival of a much more pervasive system of differentiation of primary (= non-past, non-subjunctive) and secondary (= either + past, or + subjunctive, or both) endings, which is more widely attested in some Early Latin texts. The distribution of the *-m* and *-ō* morphemes is still largely governed by the original primary/secondary distinctions, except in the future indicative.

(17)   Latin future indicative

		Conjugation I	*Conjugation II*	*Conjugation III*	*Conjugation IV*
Singular	*1st*	amābō	spondēbō	regam	ueniam
	2nd	amābis	spondēbis	regēs	ueniēs
	3rd	amābit	spondēbit	reget	ueniet
Plural	*1st*	amābimus	spondēbimus	regēmus	ueniēmus
	2nd	amābitis	spondēbitis	regētis	ueniētis
	3rd	amābunt	spondēbunt	regent	uenient

For this future, not only is there a difference in the first-person singular morpheme in Conjugations III and IV as opposed to Conjugations I and II, but there is also a radically different stem formation. The future in *-bō* of Conjugations I and II matches a formation found in Faliscan, which has a future formed in *-fo* (inscriptional *pipafo* "I will drink" and *carefo* "I will lack"), but which does not have a clear Indo-European origin.

Note that there is also a subclass of Conjugation III of the type *facere* "to do," which forms present indicative *faciō* and *faciunt*; subjunctive *faciam faciās* and so forth; future *faciam faciēs* and so on.

The other present stem tense and mood forms of *amō* are as follows:

(18) *Imperfect indicative*   amāb-am, -ās, -at, -āmus, -ātis, -ant
      Imperfect subjunctive   amār-em, -ēs, -et, -ēmus, -ētis, ent
      Imperative I   amā, amāte
      Imperative II   amātō, amātō, amātōte, amantō

In the imperative paradigms there is no form for the first person and the forms given in (18) are respectively (i) second singular and plural for the imperative I; and (ii) second singular, third singular, second plural, and third plural for imperative II. In the second person there is consequently a difference between two different imperative forms. This is not a difference of aspect, but rather one of relative tense. Where the two forms are used in conjunction, the future imperative (imperative II) is used to refer to an event following the present imperative – note, for example, the following commands from Plautus' play *Pseudolus*:

(19) cape hās tabellās, tūte hinc narrātō tibī
      "Take these tablets and find out for yourself from them"

Cape, present imperative "take!" refers to the initial action, and *narrātō*, future imperative "tell!," refers to an action consequent on this, reading what is written on the tablets.

4.4.3.2   *Perfect stem system*

The perfect stem is generally distinguished from the present in one of four ways: (i) through the addition of a suffix (-*s*- or -*u*-), (ii) through reduplication of the initial consonant or consonant cluster of the root syllable, (iii) through change (usually lengthening) of the nucleus of the root syllable, or (iv) through suppletion. One class of perfects, however, has stems which are identical to those of the present. The perfect is further marked by a special set of personal endings in the perfect indicative. As examples of the different types of perfect formation and the endings, the perfects of the four verbs considered above are presented in (20). The perfect of *amāre* is formed with the suffix -*u*- (*amāu*-), that of *spondēre* by reduplication (*spopond*-), that of *regere* with the suffix -*s*- (*rēx*-), and that of *uenīre* by vowel lengthening (*uēn*-):

(20) **Latin perfect indicative**

		Conjugation I	*Conjugation II*	*Conjugation III*	*Conjugation IV*
Singular	*1st*	amāu-ī	spopond-ī	rēx-ī	uēn-ī
	2nd	amāu-istī	spopond-istī	rēx-istī	uēn-istī
	3rd	amāu-it	spopond-it	rēx-it	uēn-it
Plural	*1st*	amāu-imus	spopond-imus	rēx-imus	uēn-imus
	2nd	amāu-istis	spopond-istis	rēx-istis	uēn-istis
	3rd	amāu-ērunt	spopond-ērunt	rēx-ērunt	uēn-ērunt

Representative examples of perfects formed through suppletion, and the perfect with unchanged stem, can also be added: *ferō* "I carry," perfect *tulī*; *bibō* "I drink," perfect *bibī*. The third plural ending -*ērunt* of Classical Latin probably represents a conflation of two competing morphs -*ēre* and -*erunt*, both well attested in Early Latin and still used in later archaizing texts.

The remaining tenses and moods of the perfect stem take either the secondary endings found in the present system or, in the case of the future perfect, the primary endings of the present system, as sketched out in the examples from *amāre* given below:

(21) *Future perfect*   amāuer-o, -is, -it, -imus, -itis, -int
      Pluperfect   amāuer-am, -ās, -at, -āmus, -ātis, -ant
      Perfect subjunctive   amāuer-im, -is, -it, -imus, -itis, -int
      Pluperfect subjunctive amāuiss-em, -ēs, -et, -ēmus, -ētis, -ent

In Early Latin the future perfect and perfect subjunctive were better distinguished, since
the perfect subjunctive showed a long vowel in the ending, *amāuerīs, amāuerīt*, and so forth.

4.4.3.3 Passive voice marking

The Latin passive is marked against the active morphologically and semantically. For the
morphological marking, compare the third singular present indicative active *amat* with the
passive *amātur*. Semantically the prototypical use of a verb in the passive is to promote
the object of a transitive verb to subject position: active *Caesar amat Cicerōnem* "Caesar
loves Cicero"; passive *Cicerō amātur* "Cicero is loved." However, third singular forms of the
passive of intransitive verbs can also be used impersonally (the so-called *impersonal passive*):
active *Caesar it* "Caesar goes"; passive *ītur* "a journey is made" (lit. "it is gone").

A large number of verbs (termed *deponents* in traditional grammar) only show passive
morphology of finite forms but are not semantically passive. Many of these correspond to
middle or reflexive verbs in other languages: thus, *īrāscor* "I become angry," *ūtor* "I use,"
reor "I think," and *morior* "I die." Deponent verbs do not have separate active paradigms,
but they do use some nonfinite active forms (see §4.4.4), such as the present and future
participles; note also that the gerundive of deponent verbs is semantically passive.

As discussed above, the present passive system is formed using the same stem as the present
active system. Thus, for *amō* "I love" the passive present indicative, present subjunctive and
future indicative are as follows:

(22) **Latin passives of the present system**

      Present indicative   amor, amāris, amātur, amāmur, amāminī, amantur
      Present subjunctive   amer, amēris, amētur, amēmur, amēminī, amentur
      Future indicative   amābor, amāberis, amābitur, amābimur, amābiminī,
                              amābuntur

The perfect stem of the passive is different from the perfect active stem, and all moods
and tenses are formed through periphrasis with the perfect passive participle and present
stem forms of the copula verb *esse*. The perfect passive indicative and subjunctive of *amō* are
given for illustration (in all persons the forms agreeing with a masculine subject are given;
agreement for a feminine or neuter subject would be different):

(23) **Latin passives of the perfect system**

      Perfect indicative   amātus sum, amātus es, amātus est, amātī sumus, amātī estis,
                              amātī sunt
      Perfect subjunctive   amātus sim, amātus sīs, amātus sit, amātī sīmus, amātī sītis,
                              amātī sint

4.4.3.4 Diachronic developments

In the subliterary registers of Late Latin, the complex tense and mood system of Latin
undergoes many changes, and the end result of these is reflected in the modern Romance
languages. The most pervasive changes are the increasing spread of periphrastic formations
at the expense of synthetic paradigms. A striking example is the future indicative. In all

languages ways of referring to future events are prone to remarking with more direct or vivid constructions and, as we saw earlier, the formation of the Classical Latin future is anomalous, with different exponents found in different conjugations. It is therefore no surprise that the synthetic formation of the future becomes increasingly marked in Late Latin and is eventually completely replaced in Romance languages.

4.4.4   Nonfinite verbals

The nonfinite verb system is less orderly than the finite. There is a present and future participle active, and a perfect participle passive; the present participle is formed from the present stem, but the future participle is generally formed from the same stem as the perfect passive participle (which, following Aronoff, I shall call the *t*-stem), even where the verb is suppletive. A future passive participle, denoting necessity or obligation, and termed the *gerundive* in traditional grammar, is also formed from the present stem. Thus, *ferō* "I carry" has a present participle *ferēns*, and gerundive *ferendus, -a, -um*, but a future active participle *lātūrus, -a, -um* and perfect passive participle *lātus, -a, -um*.

There are six tense- and voice-marked infinitives, of which three – present active, perfect active, and present passive – are synthetic while the others are periphrastic: (i) the future active infinitive = future active participle + *esse* "to be"; (ii) the perfect passive infinitive = perfect passive participle + *esse* "to be"; and (iii) the future passive infinitive, made through the curious periphrasis of the supine (on which see below) + *īrī*, the passive infinitive of *eō* "I go."

There are also two defective verbal nouns: the first, traditionally called the *gerund*, is in form identical to the neuter singular forms of the gerundive and provides the oblique cases to the present infinitive active. The second, the *supine*, also has active meaning and is formed from the *t*-stem and has two distinct forms (originally case forms) -*um* (thus *lātum* from *ferō*) and -*ū* (*lātū*). In Classical Latin the -*um* supine is only used as an optional means of expressing purpose clauses after verbs of motion (for example, *spectātum ueniunt* "they come to watch") and the -*ū* supine is used after certain adjectives (for example, *mīrābile dictū* "amazing to describe").

4.5 Compounds

Nominal compounding is a productive process of word formation in Latin. However, at the earliest stage of the language, there was only a relatively small number of compounds. Most of these are either (i) exocentric compounds with a numeral or negative element as first member, such as *bi-dēns* "sacrificial animal" (lit. "having two teeth," formed from the prefix *bi-* "two" and *dēns* "tooth"), *in-ermis* "safe" (lit. "without weapons," formed from the negative prefix *in-* and *arma* "weapons"); or else they are (ii) verbal-governing compounds of the type of *ponti-fex* "priest" (lit. "one who makes a bridge," formed from *pōns* "bridge" and a verbal noun from the root of *faciō* "I make"), or *rēm-ex* "oarsman" (lit. "one who drives the oar," from *rēmus* "oar" and a verbal noun from the root of *agō* "I drive"). The huge influence of Greek literary texts led to a revival of compounding in Latin, and many new compounds and new types of compounding are found in works of all periods under Greek influence, many of them calques of actual Greek compounds.

Alongside "true" compounding, a number of quasi-compounds are found in Latin of all periods through juxtaposition and univerbation of adjective and noun, or noun and dependent genitive. Examples include the following: *rēs-publica* "republic" (*rēs* "affairs," *publica* "public"); *pater-familiās* "head of the household" (*pater* "father," *familiās*, continuing an archaic genitive form, "of the household"); and *aquae-ductus* "aqueduct" (*aquae* "of water," *ductus* "conveyance").

Verbal compounds are nearly all of the type preverb + verb: for example, *re-ficere* "to re-store" (*re-* "back, again" and *facere* "to make"), *inter-currere* "to run between" (*inter-* "be-tween" and *currere* "to run"). Preverbs were originally independent adverbial elements, and most preverbs have adverbial or prepositional counterparts; compare *retrō* "backwards" and *inter* "between." There are a small number of compound verbs of the type adverb + verb, noun + verb, and verb + verb. Where these occur they generally arise out of earlier juxtapositions, such as *animaduertere* "to notice" (from *animam aduertere* "to turn one's attention"), and *ne-scīre* "not to know" (from *ne* "not" and *scīre* "to know"). The analysis of a small class of verbal compounds of the type *cale-facere* "to make warm" is a long-standing problem of Latin linguistics; the second element is clearly the verb *facere* "to make," but it is disputed whether the first element derives from the verb *calēre* "to be warm."

4.6 Numerals

The only declined Latin numerals are the following: *ūnus, -a, -um* 1 (masculine and neuter genitive *ūnī* and feminine genitive *ūnae*); *duo, -ae, -o* 2 (genitive *duōrum -ārum*); *trēs, tria* 3 (genitive *trium*); and the terms for multiple hundreds, *ducentī, -ae, -a* 200 (genitive *ducentōrum -ārum*), *trecentī, -ae, -a* 300 (genitive *trecentōrum -ārum*), and so forth, which all decline like adjectives in concord with their head noun. The cardinals from 4 through 10 are as follows:

(24) *4*   quattuor   *8*   octō
      5   quīnque   *9*   novem
      6   sex   *10*   decem
      7   septem

These and all other numbers are invariable, with the exception of the word for "1,000," *mīlle,* which is indeclinable in the singular but has a declined plural *mīlia* after which the head noun is placed in the genitive plural.

The numeral system is decimal; higher numerals are formed through combination of thousands, hundreds, decads, and units. Noteworthy are the numbers 18 and 19 which are formed through a subtractive system, *duodēuīgintī* "18" (literally "2 from 20") and *undēuīgintī* "19" ("1 from 20").

Ordinals are declined as adjectives, the masculine and neuter forms having second de-clension inflection, the feminine having first declension (see §4.2.3). The ordinal numbers "first" through "tenth" are presented in (25):

(25) *First*   prīmus   *Sixth*   sextus
      Second   secundus   *Seventh*   septimus
      Third   tertius   *Eighth*   octāuus
      Fourth   quārtus   *Ninth*   nōnus
      Fifth   quīntus   *Tenth*   decimus

5. SYNTAX

5.1 Word order

Classical Latin does not have an obligatory word order, and in some Latin literary works met-rical and stylistic considerations lead to considerable variation in word order with scrambling of words belonging to separate constituent phrases. In the following line of Vergil (*Aeneid* I.109) there is an extreme example of displacement of the relative pronoun, which occurs after the subject and verb of its clause and interrupts a prepositional phrase, which is itself in a nonstandard order:

(26) saxa   vocant   Italī   mediīs quae   in fluctibus ārās

     rock   call   Italian middle which   in wave   altar

     ACC.PL.NEUT. 3RD PL.PRES. NOM.PL. ABL.PL. ACC.PL.NEUT.   ABL.PL.   ACC.PL

"Rocks in the middle of the waves which the Italians call 'The Altars' "

In this sentence the word order is clearly highly marked and artificial, but such sentences could still be understood by Roman audiences.

There is, however, a preferential ("unmarked") order of constituents observable in Classical Latin prose. In sentences the order is normally Subject–Object–Verb (SOV), but other unmarked patterns are of the "head-first" rather than "head-final" type. Thus, Latin typically has prepositions, not postpositions; and adjectives (except for subjective adjectives of the type *bonus* "good," etc.) usually follow the head noun, as do relative clauses. It appears that Latin is in a transitional phase from a "head-final" to a "head-first" language; and it is certainly true that later texts increasingly show a preponderance of SVO-type sentences, while there is evidence for an earlier unmarked pattern for adjectives preceding the noun, and postpositions (retained in some phrases such as *mē-cum,* lit. "me.ABL.-with," that is, "with me"). It is not clear, however, whether the verb-final preference of Classical prose is a wholly artificial, archaizing construct or whether it does reflect certain registers of speech.

Since Latin word order is not obligatory, emphatic positions in the sentence may be taken by any constituent which needs to be highlighted for pragmatic reasons. The position of focused elements also interacts with the word-order rule termed *Wackernagel's Law,* whereby unstressed elements occupy the second position in their clause. In Classical Latin this rule was reinterpreted with the effect that focused elements, whether initial or not, became preferential hosts for unstressed elements of different types: particles, some personal pronouns, and the copula verb *esse.* As illustration, consider the following sentence from Caesar (*Bellum Gallicum* 1.44.8; note that there is ellipsis of the main verb, for which I have supplied "he said"):

(27) prōuinciam suam   hanc   esse   Galliam,   sīcut illam

     province   his   this   to be Gaul   just as that

     ACC.SG.FEM. ACC.SG.FEM. ACC.SG.FEM. INF. ACC.SG.FEM.   ACC.SG.FEM.

     nostram

     our

     ACC.SG.FEM.

"[He said that] this Gaul was his province, just as that [Gaul was] ours"

In this clause, the clitic *esse* splits the constituent *hanc Galliam.* The placement of *esse* reflects the fact that *hanc,* standing in antithesis to *illam,* is emphasized.

5.2 Subordination

Classical Latin has a number of different subordinate clause types and subordinating procedures. It is likely that at the earliest period of Latin, subordination was a less important phenomenon; but already by the beginning of the second century BC, official Latin prose inscriptions show a highly developed system of subordination. Latin subordinate clauses can be formed with or without an explicit subordinator, but where a subordinator is present the subordinating verb must be marked as indicative or subjunctive (the imperative is sometimes found when the main verb is also imperative). Where a subordinator is not present the subordinate clause is marked either through the use of the subjunctive mood or through one of the nonfinite verb forms (infinitive, participle, gerundive, gerund, or supine; see §4.4.4).

The following sentences are given to show some of the range of subordinate types; they are all taken from Classical Latin prose works:

(28) arma   capiās   oportet
      arms   you take   it is necessary
      ACC.PL.NEUT. 2ND.SG. PRES.SUBJUNC.   3RD.SG.PRES.INDIC.
      "You ought to take up arms"

In (28) there is no subordinator; the subordinate clause is marked solely through the use of the subjunctive; this construction is largely restricted to sentences where there is a simple modal predicate.

(29) ingemescunt   nōn   quod   doleant   sed
      they groan   not   because   they are in pain   but
      3RD.PL.PRES.INDIC.   SUBORDINATOR 3RD.PL.PRES.SUBJUNC.
         quia   omne   corpus   intenditur
         because   all   body   is stretched
         SUBORDINATOR   NOM.SG.NEUT. NOM.SG.   3RD.SG.PRES.INDIC.PASS.
      "They groan, not because they are in pain, but because their whole body is stretched"

In (29) two parallel subordinate clauses show different moods (subjunctive in the first clause, indicative in the second), because the first clause describes a potential or alleged cause, and the second the actual cause.

(30) eum   hominem   occīdendum   cūrāuit
      this   man   to be killed   he arranged
      ACC.SG.MASC.   ACC.SG.   ACC.SG.MASC.GDVE 3RD.SG.PERF.INDIC.
      "He arranged for this man to be killed"

In (30) the gerundive is used to mark the embedded clause. Note that this construction with the verb *cūrō* "I arrange" is found principally with the gerundive, and never with the future active participle.

In some genres of Classical Latin prose there is a marked preference for so-called "periodic" sentences, which comprise a number of subordinate and coordinate clauses, often featuring several layers of embedding. To a large extent this is an artificial device, but it is facilitated by rules for the tense marking of subjunctives in dependent clauses. Subjunctives encode both the tense of the matrix clause and the tense of the dependent clause according to the following system, known in traditional grammar as the rules for *Sequence of Tense*:

(31) Latin sequence of tense

Tense of matrix clause	Tense of dependent clause		
	Past	*Present*	*Future*
Non-past	Perfect subjunctive	Present subjunctive	Periphrastic future (-ūrus sim, sīs, etc.)
Past	Pluperfect subjunctive	Imperfect subjunctive	Periphrastic future (-ūrus essem, essēs, etc.)

The rich array of nonfinite verbal forms discussed above (see §4.4.4) also play an important role in subordination, as we have already seen. The most important of these verbal forms is the infinitive, which not only is used after "control" verbs such as *uolō* "I want," *incipiō* "I begin," *cōnor* "I try," but which also plays a major role after other predicate types, most importantly in the construction of reported speech. The subject of the infinitive when used in this way is usually in the accusative, hence giving the traditional name of *Accusative and Infinitive* (AcI) construction. The syntactic value of the subject of the infinitive is interesting since it behaves as if it were an argument of the matrix clause. Thus if the subject of the AcI clause is also the subject of the matrix clause, the equivalence is marked through the reflexive pronoun *sē*:

(32) dīxit   sē   librōs   eōs   in   ignem
     he said   himself   books   those   in   fire
     3RD.SG. PERF.INDIC.   ACC.SG.   ACC.PL.   ACC.PL.   ACC.SG.
         coniectūrum   esse
         will be throwing   to be
     ACC.SG.MASC. FUT.ACT.PART.   PRES.INF.
     "He said that he would throw the books in the fire"

Note the formation of the future infinitive (*coniectūrum esse*) through a combination of the future participle and auxiliary, and that the participle is marked for agreement (see §5.3) with *sē*.

The subject of the infinitive can also be raised to be subject of the verb of the matrix clause, if the verb would otherwise be an impersonal passive:

(33) dīcitur   Appius   itā   precātus   esse
     is said   Appius   thus   having prayed   to be
     3RD.SG.PRES. INDIC.PASS.   NOM.SG.MASC.   NOM.SG.MASC.PERF.PART.   PRES.INF.
     "It is said that Appius prayed in this way"

In this example the subject of the infinitive is also subject of the matrix clause and consequently takes nominative case marking, as does the participle of the periphrastic infinitive; *dīcitur* consequently behaves as a "pseudo-control" verb.

5.3 Agreement

The rich nominal and verbal morphology of Latin is dependent on a strict system of agreement. Adjectives show the same number, gender, and case as their head noun and verbs agree in number and person with their subjects. When different subjects of a verb are conjoined the verb shows agreement according to the person hierarchy *first > second > third*; hence a verb with first- and second-person subjects will normally take first-person endings.

Agreement patterns in conjoined nominal phrases are more interesting: in phrases where there is a single adjective but two conjoined nouns of different genders, the adjective will either be marked for agreement with the closest noun, or will be marked masculine or neuter. The choice between masculine and neuter is governed by the animacy of the referents: if the two conjoined nouns refer to animates, adjectives take the masculine; if inanimates, adjectives are marked neuter. For example (Livy *Ab urbe conditā* 32.29.1):

(34) mūrus   et   porta   dē   caelō   tācta   erant
     wall   and   gate   from   sky   touched   had been
     NOM.SG.MASC.   NOM.SG.FEM.   ABL.SG.MASC.   NOM.PL.NEUT.   3RD PL.IMPF.
     "The wall and gate had been touched from the sky"

Here the participle *tācta* is assigned neuter gender, although the two conjoined nouns to which it refers are respectively masculine and feminine.

6. LEXICON

The Latin lexicon has long been thought to be highly conservative, and it does retain a number of roots which are only found in a few other Indo-European languages. Thus the word for "believe" *crēdō*, which developed from a periphrasis of the words for "heart" and "put," is found elsewhere only in Indo-Iranian and Celtic languages. A word for "drunk" *ēbrius* may continue a root meaning "drink" attested only in Hittite and Tocharian. The verb *spondeō* "I pledge" only has cognates in Hittite, Greek, and Tocharian. Latin *rēs* "property" is matched by forms in Umbrian and Indo-Iranian alone. The pair *hostis* "stranger, enemy" and *hospēs* "guest, host" continue forms also found in the Slavic languages and (in the case of *hostis*) Germanic.

However, the Latin vocabulary also contains a number of loanwords; some of these – for example, *ficus* "fig," *citrus* "citron-tree," *menta* "mint," and *cupressus* "cypress-tree" – almost certainly represent borrowings from lost Mediterranean languages. For others, we can identify the source language involved with more certainty. A number of Latin words were borrowed from the neighboring Faliscan and Sabellian languages, and these may be identified through their distinctive phonology or non-Latin phonological developments: *bōs* "ox, cow," *popīna* "cook-shop," *lacrima* "tear," *uafer* "wily," *rōbus* "red," and *rūfus* "red." Although these loans are often said to have come from Sabine, a Sabellian language for which we have very little direct evidence, it is possible that they represent borrowings from different languages at different times: note that the loanwords *rōbus* and *rūfus* both continue the same original formation, presumably borrowed through different Italic sources. It is also possible that some of these terms are actually derived from dialectal varieties of Latin.

A second source for the enrichment of the Latin vocabulary was Etruscan, although here too we run into problems of identification of individual words owing to lack of available evidence on the Etruscan lexicon. Some words, such as *histriō* "actor," are explicitly stated as Etruscan by ancient authorities, and Etruscan is also the most likely origin for others such as *persōna* "mask." It is often supposed that many words which derive ultimately from Greek were loaned first from Greek to Etruscan, and from there into Latin. Unfortunately, in most cases this is difficult to prove since the Etruscan evidence is lacking, but the representation of Greek voiced stops as Latin voiceless stops suggests that there was an Etruscan intermediate stage in some words, such as *catamītus* "catamite" (borrowed from the Greek name Γανυμήδης) and *sporta* "basket" (Greek σπύριδα accusative singular).

Greek civilization was the dominant cultural influence on Rome throughout much of its history, and it is no surprise that the greatest influence on the Latin lexicon was from Greek. Greek loanwords entered the language from the very earliest stages, not only denoting the material objects and professions which were associated with Greek trade – for example, *mācina* "crane," *nauta* "sailor," *ancora* "anchor" – but also reflecting the influence of Greek culture in all areas of civilized life: *balneum* "bath," *poena* "punishment," *camara* "ceiling," *poēta* "poet." In the Classical period Latin writers looked to Greek models to expand what they saw as the poverty of expression in their native tongue, and through direct borrowing and widespread calquing the Latin lexicon was enormously expanded, and new technical vocabularies were created in many fields, including grammar, rhetoric, philosophy, and medicine. The Latin Bible translations and early Christian works also incorporated many Greek terms from their exemplars, and Christian terms such as *angelus* "angel," *diabolus* "devil," and *presbyter* "priest" have entered into many Western European languages from Greek via Latin.

Bibliography

Introduction, grammars and collections of articles

Baldi, P. 1999. *The Foundations of Latin.* Berlin: Mouton de Gruyter.
Coleman, R. 1987. "Latin and the Italic languages." In B. Comrie (ed.), *The World's Major Languages*, pp. 180–202. Oxford: Oxford University Press.
Dangel, J. 1995. *Histoire de la langue latine.* Paris: Presses Universitaires de France.
Giacomelli, G. 1963. *La lingua falisca.* Florence: Leo S. Olschki.
Giacomelli, R. 1993. *Storia della lingua latina.* Roma: Jouvence.
Leumann, M. 1977. *Lateinische Laut- und Formenlehre. Lateinische Grammatik*, vol. I (7th edition). Munich: Beck.
Meiser, G. 1998. *Historische Laut- und Formenlehre der lateinischen Sprache.* Darmstadt: Wissenschaftliche Buchgesellschaft.
Palmer, L. 1954. *The Latin Language.* London: Faber and Faber.
Panagl, O. and T. Krisch (eds.). 1992. *Latein und Indogermanisch: Akten des Kolloquiums der Indogermanischen Gesellschaft, Salzburg, 23.-26. September 1986.* Innsbruck: Institut für Sprachwissenschaft der Universität Innsbruck.
Vineis, E. 1998. "Latin." In A. Ramat and P. Ramat (eds.), *The Indo-European Languages*, pp. 261–321. London/New York: Routledge.

Script

Wachter, R. 1987. *Altlateinischen Inschriften: sprachliche und epigraphische Untersuchungen zu den Dokumenten bis etwa 150 v. Chr.* Bern: Peter Lang.
Wallace, R. 1989. "The origins and development of the Latin alphabet." In W. Senner (ed.), *The Origins of Writing*, pp. 121–135. Lincoln, NE: University of Nebraska Press.

Phonology

Allen, W. 1978. *Vox Latina* (2nd edition). Cambridge: Cambridge University Press.
Cser, A. 1996. "Latin syllable structure." *Working Papers in the Theory of Grammar* 3:35–47.
Zirin, R. 1970. *The Phonological Basis of Latin Prosody.* The Hague: Mouton.

Morphology

Aronoff, M. 1994. *Morphology by Itself: Stems and Inflectional Classes.* Cambridge, MA: MIT Press.
Coleman, R. 1992. "Italic." In J. Gvozdanović (ed.), *Indo-European Numerals*, pp. 389–445. Berlin/New York: Mouton de Gruyter.
Ernout, A. 1953. *Morphologie historique du latin.* Paris: Klincksieck.
Kent, R. 1946. *The Forms of Latin.* Baltimore: Linguistic Society of America.
Neue, F. and C. Wagener. 1892–1905. *Formenlehre der lateinischen Sprache* (3rd edition, 4 vols.). Leipzig: Reisland.

Syntax

Adams, J. 1976. "A typological approach to Latin word order." *Indogermanische Forschungen* 81:70–99.
Calboli, G. (ed.). 1989. *Subordination and Other Topics in Latin: Proceedings of the Third Colloquium on Latin Linguistics, Bologna, 1–5 April 1985.* Amsterdam/Philadelphia: John Benjamins.
Hofmann, J. and A. Szantyr. 1965. *Lateinische Syntax und Stilistik. Lateinische Grammatik*, vol. II. Munich: Beck.

Kühner, R. and C. Stegmann. 1966. *Ausführliche Grammatik der lateinischen Sprache. Zweiter Teil: Satzlehre* (2 vols.). Hannover: Hahn.

Pinkster, H. 1990. *Latin Syntax and Semantics.* Translation of *Latijnse syntaxis en semantiek* by H. Mulder. London: Routledge.

Dictionaries and lexical studies

Biville, F. 1990–1995. *Les emprunts du latin au grec: approche phonétique.* Louvain: Peeters.

Glare, P. 1982. *Oxford Latin Dictionary.* Oxford: Clarendon Press.

1900–. *Thesaurus linguae Latinae.* Leipzig: Teubner.

CHAPTER 5

Sabellian languages

REX E. WALLACE

The term "Sabellian" refers to a group of genetically related languages that were spoken throughout a substantial portion of pre-Roman Italy. Oscan and Umbrian are considered the major representatives of this group because they are attested by the largest corpora of inscriptions. The former was spoken in the southern half of the Italian peninsula, in the territories of Samnium, Campania, Lucania, and Bruttium; the latter was spoken east of the Tiber River in Umbria. Other Sabellian languages include Paelignian, Marrucinian, Vestinian, Marsian, Volscian, Hernican, Aequian, and Sabine – languages which were spoken in central Italy in the hill districts lying east and southeast of Rome. Recently, South Picene, a language spoken in southern Picenum and in northern Samnium, and Pre-Samnite, the language of Sabellian peoples who inhabited southern Campania before the arrival of the Oscan-speaking Samnites, have been added to the inventory of Sabellian tongues.

Archeological evidence has not yet shed sufficient light on the dates at which or the routes by which, Sabellian speakers moved into the Italian peninsula. By the beginning of the historical period (*c.* 700 BC), however, Sabellian speakers had spread over a considerable portion of central Italy, from Umbria and Picenum in the northeast to the Sorrentine peninsula in the southwest (see Map 2). Sabellian tribes were still on the move during the fifth and fourth centuries. Roman historical sources document the invasion of Campania and the capture of Capua, Cumae, and Paestum by Oscan-speaking Samnites. By the middle of the fourth century they had pushed south into Lucania and Bruttium, and southeast into Apulian territory. At the beginning of the third century there were Oscan speakers in Sicily. The Mamertini, a band of mercenary soldiers, crossed the straits in 289 BC and wrested control of the Sicilian city of Messana from the Greeks.

The Sabellian languages did not survive Roman expansion. Those languages spoken in central Italy succumbed to Romanization earlier than did those in the north and south. Sabellian speakers in central Italy had probably shifted to Latin before the end of the Roman Republic (*c.* 30 BC). In some areas Sabellian was more tenacious. Evidence from the city of Pompeii indicates that Oscan was still being spoken there when the city was destroyed by Vesuvius in AD 79. However, it is unlikely that any Sabellian language survived much beyond the first century AD, by which time the territories of the Sabellians were securely incorporated into the Roman Empire both politically and culturally.

The Sabellian languages are documented almost exclusively by inscriptions. The texts belong to standard epigraphical types: dedications, epitaphs, proprietary inscriptions, inscriptions on public works, religious regulations, contracts, curses, trademarks, legends on coins, and so forth. A few Sabellian vocabulary items are preserved by Roman and Greek writers of the late Republic and early imperial period, but they do not add substantially to our knowledge of any Sabellian language (Vetter 1953:362–378).

Oscan owns the largest corpus of texts, approximately six hundred and fifty inscriptions. They cover a span of six hundred years, from the sixth century BC to the first century AD. Most of the inscriptions belong to the period between 300 and 89 BC, the latter being the date of the final Sabellian uprising against Rome. The nucleus of the corpus, over 30 percent of the texts, comes from the Campanian cities of Capua and Pompeii. One of the most important Oscan inscriptions was also discovered in Campania, the so-called *Cippus Abellanus*, a limestone plaque recording an agreement between the cities of Nola and Abella regarding the common use of a sanctuary of Heracles. The longest Oscan text, the *Tabula Bantina*, is from the Lucanian town of Bantia. This bronze tablet is incised with a list of statutes concerning municipal administration.

Even though the number of Umbrian inscriptions does not exceed forty, the corpus is one of the most important in ancient Italy. Umbrian was the language of the *Tabulae Iguvinae* (Iguvine Tablets), seven bronze tablets that were discovered in Gubbio (Roman Iguvium) in the fifteenth century. The tablets were incised with the ritual regulations and cultic instructions of a religious fraternity, the Atiedian brotherhood. They date from the first half of the third century (for Tablets I–Vb7) to the end of the second century (for Tablets Vb8–VII). Despite the relative lateness of these texts, it is likely that many of the ritual procedures and regulations stem from an earlier tradition (see Rix 1985).

The remaining Sabellian languages are much less well represented. For most, there are only a few short and often fragmentary inscriptions.

Examples of Sabellian inscriptions are given below (Figs. 5.1–2). According to standard epigraphical conventions, texts written in native Sabellian alphabets are transcribed in boldface type; texts written in a Republican Latin alphabet appear in italics. The *editio minor* of Sabellian inscriptions is Rix 2002. Vetter 1953 and Poccetti 1979 remain invaluable for epigraphic and linguistic commentary. An *editio maior* of the *Tabulae Iguvinae* was published by Prosdocimi in 1984. Shorter Umbrian texts are collected in Rocca 1996. Marinetti 1985 is the *editio maior* for South Picene inscriptions.

The Sabellian languages, together with Latin and Faliscan, belong to the Italic branch of the Indo-European language family. The evidence for an Italic subgroup consists of three significant morphological innovations that are shared exclusively by Sabellian and Latino-Faliscan:

(1)   Innovations shared by Sabellian and Latino-Faliscan

A.   Imperfect subjunctive suffix *-sē-, e.g., Oscan **fusíd** "should be" 3RD SG. IMPF. SUBJUNC., Latin *foret* 3RD SG. IMPF. SUBJUNC. < *fusēd*

B.   Imperfect indicative suffix *-fā-, e.g., Oscan **fufans** "they were" 3RD PL. IMPF., Latin *portābant* "they were carrying" 3RD PL. IMPF. (*-fa- > -bā- in Latin)

C.   Verbal adjective formation in *-ndo-, e.g., Oscan **úpsannam** ACC. SG. FEM. "to be built," Umbrian **pihaner** GEN. SG. MASC. "to be purified" (*-nd- > -nn- in Sabellian), Latin *operandam* ACC. SG. FEM. "to be built"

The Sabellian languages share several significant morphological innovations, among which are the spread of the *i*-stem genitive singular ending *-eis to *o*-stem and consonant-stem inflection; the spread of the *o*-stem accusative singular *-om to consonant-stems; personal and reflexive pronominal forms with accusative singular -**om**/-*om* (e.g., Umbrian *tiom* "you," **míom** "me," Oscan *siom* "himself"); and the development of a mediopassive infinitive suffix in -**fir**/-*fi* (Oscan **sakrafír** "to be consecrated," Umbrian *pihafi* "to be purified").

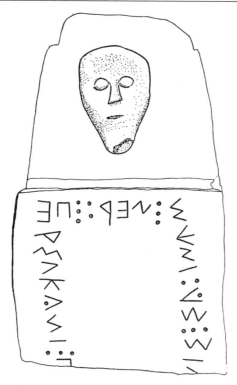

Figure 5.1 South Picene inscription. South Picene, Rix Sp TE 6, stele (fragmentary)

[–?]nis : safinúm : nerf : persukant : p[–?]

]nis-[name ?] "Sabines"-gen. pl. masc. "leaders"-acc. pl. masc. "?"-3rd pl. pres. act. "[names?] they ? the leaders of the Sabines [?]"

Prominent phonological innovations include the syncope of *o* in word-final syllables (*g^hortos* > Oscan **húrz** "enclosure"), the raising of inherited mid vowels (e.g., *ē* to *ẹ̄*, Proto-Sabellian *fēsnā* giving Oscan **fíísnú** "sanctuary," cf. Latin *fēstus* "festal"), and the change of Proto-Indo-European labiovelars to labials (*$k^w$is* > Oscan **pis** "who").

Interrelationships among the Sabellian languages are difficult to determine because there is so little evidence for the languages in central Italy. However, the split into two Sabellian subgroups, one closely aligned with Umbrian, the other with Oscan, is not supported by the evidence. Instead, the territories occupied by Sabellian speakers form a linguistic continuum with Umbrian positioned in the north, Oscan in the south, and the Sabellian languages in central Italy constituting a transitional linguistic area where the languages have both Oscoid and Umbroid features (Wallace 1985). Exactly how South Picene fits into this schema is currently under deliberation (Meiser 1987; Adiego Lajara 1990).

2. WRITING SYSTEMS

The Sabellian languages were written in a variety of different alphabets. The type of alphabet employed depended on two factors: when a Sabellian tribe became literate and from what

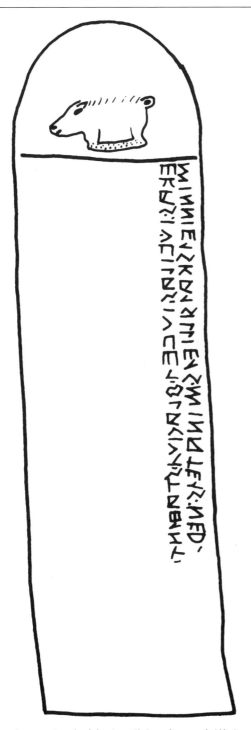

Figure 5.2 Oscan inscription. Oscan, Rix Cp25a, funerary stele (side a)

ekas : iúvilas . iuveí . flagiuí . stahínt . / minnieis kaísillieís . minateís : ner .

"these"-nom. pl. fem. "*Iovilas*"-nom. pl. fem. "Jupiter"-dat. sg. masc. "Flagius"-dat. sg. masc. "be standing"-3rd pl. pres. act. "Minis"-gen. sg. masc. "Kaisilies"-gen. sg. masc. "Minaz"-gen. sg. masc. "commander"-abbreviation for gen. sg. masc.

"These *Iovilas* are set up for Juppiter Flagius. [They belong to] Minis Kaisillies, [son of] Minas, commander."

Table 5.1	National Oscan alphabet, *c.* 250 BC		
Character	Transcription	Character	Transcription
Ͷ	a	Ϻ	m
8	b	Ͱ	n
>	g	Π	p
Я	d	ᗡ	r
Ⅎ	e	⟨	s
]	v	Τ	t
I	z	V	u
ᗑ	h	8	f
ǀ	i	⊦	í
⋋	k	V̇	ú
ꟼ	l		

source – Greek, Etruscan, or Latin – the alphabet was borrowed. Some Sabellian tribes borrowed from more than one source.

Oscan inscriptions were written in three different alphabets. Inscriptions from Campania and Samnium were composed in an alphabet that was borrowed from Etruscans who had colonized the Campanian plain in the sixth century BC. In the territories of Lucania and Bruttium, Oscan inscriptions were written in an alphabet of the East Greek type. A few inscriptions from the first century BC, including the important *Tabula Bantina*, were written in a Republican Latin alphabet.

The Oscan alphabet that developed from Campanian Etruscan sources was formed during the last half of the fifth century BC. This alphabet spread rapidly throughout Oscan-speaking Campania and into Samnium and was eventually codified as the so-called *national* Oscan script (see Table 5.1). At the beginning of the third century, two new signs were incorporated into the *abecedarium* in order to represent more accurately the phonology of Oscan mid vowels. Diacritics were added to the letters **i** and **u** to create signs for the vowels /ē/, /ẹ/ ⊦ and /o/ V. These signs are transcribed as **í** and **ú** respectively.

The Sabellian-speaking tribes in central Italy, most of whom became literate via contact with Romans, borrowed the Latin alphabet. In a few instances, there is evidence for changes in the inventory of signs. In Paelignian, for example, the sign *delta* was modified by means of a diacritic and then employed on several inscriptions to represent the outcome of the palatalization of a voiced dental stop ($^*dy$ > [ǰ]), transcribed as Đ, for example, Paelignian *petieÐu* "Petiedia" (nom. sg. fem.).

Umbrian was written in several different local versions of an Etruscan alphabet (Cristofani 1979). One of the earliest Umbrian inscriptions, that inscribed on a statue of Mars, was written in an alphabet similar to the one used in the central Etruscan city of Orvieto. The alphabet of Umbrian inscriptions from Colfiorito may also have come from this area, as is indicated by the fact that *gamma* was used for the voiceless velar /k/ rather than *kappa*. In contrast, the Iguvine Tablets I through Vb7 were inscribed in an Etruscan-based alphabet that did not have the letter *gamma*. This alphabet had a north Etruscan source, perhaps Perusia or Cortona (see Table 5.2).

The chief characteristic of the Umbrian alphabet used for the Iguvine Tablets I–Va is the absence of the signs *gamma* and *omicron*. The voiced stop /g/ was represented by *kappa*, and

Table 5.2 Umbrian alphabet, Iguvine Tablets I–Vb7, c. 250 BC			
Character	**Transcription**	**Character**	**Transcription**
Ᏽ	a	ꟽ	m
Ꮨ	b	Ꮋ	n
ꟼ	ř	ꟷ	p
Ꜫ	e	ꓷ	r
ꓶ	v	ꙅ	s
Ɪ	z	ꓕ	t
⊘	h	V	u
ꞁ	i	Ꝑ	f
ᚷ	k	d	ç
ꓥ	l		

upsilon was used for the mid vowel /o/. Interestingly, the signs *beta* and *delta* were a part of this script, although it is not clear whether they were inherited from the Etruscan alphabet that served as a model or were reborrowed from another source. *Delta* was used for a voiced fricative /z̧/ (ř) rather than for the voiced stop /d/, which was represented by *tau*. Both *pi* and *beta* shared the function of representing the voiced stop /b/, e.g., **hapinaf**, **habina** (acc. pl. fem.) 'lambs." The inherited Etruscan inventory of signs was further modified in order to represent the native Umbrian phoneme /š/. The letter d (transcribed ç), of uncertain origin, was assigned this function.

Tablets Vb8, VI, and VII and a small number of Umbrian inscriptions belonging to the second and first centuries BC were written in a Republican Latin alphabet. The inventory of signs was augmented by the addition of S′ (/š/, transcribed ś), a Latin *sigma* modified by an oblique stroke appended in the upper left quadrant of the sign space.

Sabellian inscriptions composed in an Etruscan-based alphabet were generally written sinistrograde (right to left), but some were written dextrograde and a few others were laid out in boustrophedon ("as the ox plows") style, every other line alternating in direction. Oscan inscriptions in the Greek alphabet were consistently written from left to right, as were the Sabellian inscriptions in the Latin alphabet, including Tablets Vb8, VI, and VII of the *Tabulae Iguvinae*.

Most Sabellian inscriptions in Etruscan-based alphabets use some form of punctuation to separate words, although a few of the earliest inscriptions are written *scriptio continua*. Punctuation between words is customarily a single point appearing at mid-line level, but word-dividers also take the form of double or triple puncts, the latter being particularly common on South Picene inscriptions in order to avoid confusion with the sign for /f/ : (see Figure 5.1, South Picene). In contrast, Oscan inscriptions written in the Greek alphabet rarely use punctuation for word boundaries; *scriptio continua* is the norm.

3. PHONOLOGY

Despite the genetic affiliation of the Sabellian languages, the phonological systems of each language developed distinctive characteristics. The Oscan sound system was more conservative, the Umbrian system more innovative.

Table 5.3	The consonantal phonemes of Oscan						
Manner of articulation	Place of articulation						
	Bilabial	Labiodental	Dental	Palatal	Velar	Labiovelar	Glottal
Stop							
Voiceless	p		t		k		
Voiced	b		d		g		
Fricative		f	s				h
Nasal	m		n				
Liquid							
Lateral			l				
Nonlateral			r				
Glide				y		w	

Throughout the remaining sections of this chapter, the following abbreviations are used in glossing examples: G (gentilicium); PN (praenomen); DN (name of a god or goddess).

3.1   Oscan consonants

The Oscan consonantal inventory consists of fifteen members. There are three sets of stops – labials, dentals, and velars – with each set having a contrast in voicing. The three fricatives are all voiceless, and the nasals, liquids, and semivowels voiced.

These phonemes are illustrated by the examples of (2):

(2)   Oscan consonant phonemes

> **pús** ("who") /p/, **tanginúd** ("decree") /t/, **kúmbened** ("it was agreed") /k/
> **blússii(eís)** ("Blossius" G) /b/, **deded** ("he gave") /d/, **genetaí** ("Genita" DN) /g/
> **faamat** ("he calls") /f/, **súm** ("I am") /s/, **heriiad** ("he should wish for") /h/
> **maatreís** ("mother") /m/, **niir** ("commander") /n/
> **leígúss** ("statute") /l/, **regatureí** ("the director," epithet of Jupiter) /r/
> **iúveí** ("Jupiter" DN)/y/, **veru** ("gate") /w/

The fricative /h/ was probably restricted to word-initial position. The fact that non-etymological **h** appears occasionally to mark vocalic hiatus supports this view; consider Oscan **stahínt** /stāẹnt/.

Intervocalic /s/ was phonetically voiced. The evidence is provided by inscriptions written in the Latin alphabet where the sign *z* is employed to write the sound derived from original *s, for example, *ezum* [ezum] "to be" (pres. inf.), *egmazum* [egmazum] "affairs" (gen. pl. fem.). It is possible that the fricative /f/ was also voiced intervocalically, but the writing system provides no evidence in this instance.

3.1.1   Palatalization

All geographical varieties of Oscan palatalize consonants (except for /f, s, w/) in the environment of a following /y/. Palatalization was marked in the national alphabet by gemination of the palatalized consonant: for example, **mamerttiaís** "of Mamers (name of month)"

<*-ty-, **meddikkiai** "the office of meddix" (title of political official) <*-ky-, **kúmbennieís** "assembly" <*-ny-, **vítelliú** "Italia" <*-ly-. The dialect of Bantia, which is attested by the *Tabula Bantina* (*c.* 90–80 BC), shows a more advanced stage of development. Dental and velar stops were assibilated and the glide was lost, thus, *bansae* "Bantia" (town in Apulia) <*-ty-; *meddixud* <*-ky-. Moreover, palatalized liquids were spelled without any indication of palatalization, e.g., *famelo* [-eʎo] "servant" <*-ly-; *herest* [-eŕe-] "he will wish for" <*-ry-.

3.1.2 Anaptyxis

Another feature characteristic of Oscan phonology is the anaptyxis of vowels to break up clusters consisting of sonorant (liquids, nasals) and some other consonant. Anaptyxis occurred in sonorant plus consonant clusters, for example, **aragetud** "silver" (abl. sg.) < *argentōd*, as well as in consonant plus sonorant clusters, for example, **patereí** "father" (dat. sg. masc.) < *patrei*, provided the preceding vowel was short. In the case of so-called *anterior* anaptyxis, the quality of the anaptyctic vowel was determined by the quality of the vowel preceding the sonorant, for example, **aragetud** and **herekleís** "Herakles" (gen. sg. masc.) < *herkleís. On the other hand, in *posterior* anaptyxis the quality of the anaptyctic vowel was determined by the quality of the vowel following the sonorant, as in **patereí** and **tefúrúm** "burnt offering" (acc. sg.) < *tefrom.

3.2 Oscan vowels

The Oscan vowel system is made up of eleven phonemes. There are three pairs of phonemes in the front region, each pair being distinguished by the features of height and length: /i/ and /ī/; /ẹ/ and /ẹ̄/; /e/ and /ē/. The inventory of back vowels is half that of the front region: two high vowels, /u/ and /ū/, and one mid vowel, /o/. The low vowels /a/ and /ā/ fill out the system. In the national Oscan script, long vowels in word-initial/radical syllables are distinguished from short ones (see §3.3) by double writing of the vowel sign, though this orthographic practice is by no means consistently employed, even within the same inscription.

(3) Oscan vowel phonemes

> **viíbis** (PN) /ī/, **tanginúd** ("decree") /i/ (no examples in initial syllables)
> **fiísnam** ("temple, sanctuary") /ẹ̄/, **ídík** ("it") /ẹ/
> **teer[úm]** ("territory") /ē/, **pedú** ("foot") /e/
> **fluusaí** ("Flora" DN) /ū/, **purasiaí** ("concerned with fire") /u/
> **púd** ("which") /o/ (no examples of /ō/ are attested)
> **slaagid** ("boundary") /ā/, **tanginúd** ("decree") /a/

In addition to these simple vowel phonemes Oscan also has five diphthongs, /ai/, /ei/, /oi/, /au/, and /ou/.

(4) **kvaístureí** ("quaestor") /ai/, **deívaí** ("divine") /ei/, **múinikú** ("common") /oi/
     avt ("but") /au/, **lúvkeí** ("grove") /ou/

Although the evidence is not conclusive, it is likely that the distinction in vowel length noted above was maintained only in word-initial/radical syllables (Lejeune 1970:279). It is also likely that distinctions in vowel quality were neutralized in word-final syllables. Etymological *ā in absolute final position and etymological *o, *ō, and *u in final syllables, both open and closed, are spelled either **ú** or **u** in the national Oscan alphabet, the variation in spelling being tied to the writing habits of local scribes. The use of **ú** or **u** to spell what originally were four different sounds suggests that they all developed phonetically to a mid vowel having a quality between that of [u] and [o], perhaps [ǫ] (Lejeune 1970:300–305).

At the beginning of the third century BC, the Oscan vowel system was augmented by a sound that developed from short /u/ after dental consonants. In the national alphabet this sound is spelled **iu**, for example, **tiurrí** "tower" (acc. sg.) < *turrim*, compare Latin *turrim*; this spelling probably represents a palatalized [u], in other words [tyurrẹ]. However, there is some evidence to suggest that by the end of the third century the pronunciation of this phone had developed to a front rounded vowel [ü]. For representing this sound, third- and second-century Oscan inscriptions written in the Greek alphabet use *upsilon* (υ), which had the value [ü] in Greek at the time, for example, Νιυμσδιηις /n(y)ümsdieis/ (gen. sg. masc.), Νυμψιμ/nümpsim/ (acc. sg. masc.). In order to keep the high-back vowels /u, ū/ graphically distinct from [ü], they were spelled with the digraph ου, e.g., ουπσενς /ūpsens/ "they built" (3rd pl. perf.).

3.3 Umbrian consonants

The Umbrian consonantal inventory displays several substantive differences when compared with that of Oscan. In addition to the dental fricative /s/, Umbrian has a voiceless palato-alveolar spirant that developed from the prehistoric combinations *ky, *ki, *ke, for example, **çerfie** /šerfye/ "Serfia" (epithet of deities) dat. sg. masc. Perhaps the most interesting innovation in the system was the change that introduced yet another fricative. This new sound, which was probably a voiced retroflex spirant /ẓ/, developed from intervocalic *d and also from intervocalic *l when adjacent to palatal vowels (Meiser 1986:213). In the native alphabet the sound is represented by the sign ꟼ (ř); in the Latin alphabet it is spelled with the digraph *rs*, for example, **teřa**, *dirsa* /deẓa/ "gives" (3rd sg. pres. subjunc.).

Table 5.4 **The consonantal phonemes of Umbrian**								
Manner of articulation	Bilabial	Labio-dental	Dental	Palato-alveolar	Retroflex	Palatal	Velar	Labio-velar	Glottal
Stop									
Voiceless	p		t				k		
Voiced	b		d				g		
Fricative									
Voiceless		f	s	š					h
Voiced					ẓ				
Nasal	m		n						
Liquid									
Lateral			l						
Nonlateral			r						
Glide						y		w	

These sounds can be illustrated by the following examples:

(5) Umbrian consonant phonemes

> *poplom* ("people. nation") /p/, **tuta**, *totam* ("community, state") /t/, **kumaltu**,
>   *comoltu* ("let him grind") /k/
> **krapuvi**, *grabouie* ("Grabovius," epithet of Jupiter) /b/, **teřa**, *dirsa* ("he should
>   give") /d/, *grabouie* /g/
> **fust** ("he will give") /f/, *stahu* ("stand") /s/, **çerfie**, *śerfie* ("Serfius, Serfia," epithet of
>   deities) /š/, **habia** ("he should take hold of") /h/
> *matrer* ("mother") /m/, *nerf* ("commander") /n/
> **kumaltu**, *comoltu* ("let him grind") /l/, **rufru** ("red") /r/, **teřa** ("he should give") /z̧/
> **iuviu**, *iouiu* ("of Jupiter") /y/, **verufe**, *uerir* ("gate") /w/

In Umbrian **h** is weakly articulated. The sound was lost in medial environments before the historical period, and the character **h** was frequently used to mark both vocalic hiatus and vowel length, for example, *stahu* /stāu/ "I stand" (1st sg. pres. act.), *ahatripursatu* /ā tripuẓatu/ (3rd sg. impv. II) "dance the three-step." In word-initial position **h** may also have been lost. Spellings with and without **h** are found in the earliest sections of the Tablets, for example, **eretu** "wished for" (abl. sg. neut.), as are examples of **h** appearing where unexpected on etymological grounds, for example, **ebetrafe** acc. pl. fem. + postposition versus **hebetafe** (a place name).

3.3.1 Word-final consonants

Particularly characteristic of Umbrian are changes affecting word-final consonants. In the oldest Umbrian inscriptions word-final **d** is not spelled, for example, **dede** "gave" 3rd sg. perf. Word-final **s** is spelled sporadically in Iguvine Tablets I–Vb7, indicating that it too was weakened. In those Iguvine Tablets written in the Latin alphabet, original word-final *s* was rhotacized to *r*, for example, *popler* (gen. sg. masc.) "people, nation" < *popleis* (Meiser 1986:277); furthermore, word-final *m, n, f* (<*-*ns*), and *r*, including *r* from original *s*, were in the process of being lost. The writing of word-final *f* in these Tablets is illustrative; *f* is regularly, but not always, omitted in polysyllabic words and in monosyllables ending in a consonant cluster. In other monosyllables, however, *f* is generally written. The result is a sentence such as the following, in which final *f* is spelled in two words but not in two others (*rofu, peiu*): *abrof trif fetu heriei rofu heriei peiu* (VIIa 3) "let him sacrifice three boars, either red or spotted."

3.4 Umbrian vowels

The basic inventory of Umbrian vowels is similar to that found in Oscan, though with two additional phonemes. The first is a long mid /ō/, corresponding to short /o/; the second is a short mid vowel which is phonetically lower than /o/, perhaps /ɔ/. As in Oscan, the distinction between long and short vowels is maintained in word-initial or radical syllables, etymological long vowels being shortened in medial and final syllables (Meiser 1986:150).

Umbrian has no diphthongs corresponding to those found in Oscan cognates; all diphthongs inherited from Proto-Sabellian were monophthongized before the historical period and merged with existing long or short vowel phonemes. New diphthongs subsequently arose in Umbrian as the result of phonological changes, for example, /dēytu/ **deitu** (3rd sg. impv. II) "speak," **aitu** /aytu/ (3rd sg. impv. II) "set in motion."

(6) Umbrian vowel phonemes

persnihmu ("pray") /ī/, *atiersir* ("Atiedian") /i/
sehmeniar ("of?") /ẹ̄/, **aves, avis,** *aueis* ("bird") /ẹ/
esuna, *eesona* ("religious") /ē/, **ařfertur** ("chief priest") /e/
kumnahkle ("meeting place") /ā/, **ařfertur** /a/
pihaz, *pihos* ("purified") /ɔ/
uhtur, oht ("auctor," title of political office) /ō/, *poplom,* **puplum** ("people,
     nation") /o/
struhçla ("offering") /ū/, **fust,** *fust* ("he will be") /u/

3.5 Sabellian accent

Very little is known about the word accent of any Sabellian language. Nevertheless, it is possible to make informed inferences about accentuation based on orthographic practices and on certain phonological processes that affected the Sabellian languages, in particular Oscan and Umbrian, at various stages in their development. In all Sabellian languages short vowels were lost before word-final *s. Short vowels in open medial syllables were also syncopated before the historic period. This vocalic instability suggests that Sabellian had a stress accent which was positioned on the initial syllable of words. The fact that vowel length is indicated only in initial/radical syllables in both Oscan and Umbrian (with rare exceptions) suggests that word-initial/radical accent was still in place during the historical period (Meiser 1986:150; for Oscan antepenultimate accent, see Schmid 1954).

4. MORPHOLOGY

The Sabellian languages are classified typologically as fusional, inflecting languages. All inflectional categories are signaled through endings attached to nominal and verbal stems. Several word classes, such as conjunctions, pre- and postpositions, sentential adverbs, and the cardinal numerals four and above, are uninflected.

4.1 Nominal morphology

The nominal system is composed of nouns, adjectives, and pronouns. With the exception of a handful of forms, all members inflect for the grammatical features of case, number, and gender. Sabellian has seven cases (nominative, vocative, accusative, dative, ablative, genitive, locative), two numbers (singular and plural), and three gender categories (masculine, feminine, and neuter). Nouns are generally assigned to one of the three genders on the basis of their stem-type. For example, *a*-stems are feminine, *o*-stems and *u*-stems either masculine or neuter, *men*-stems neuter, and so forth. There are, however, exceptions, particularly in the case of animate nouns, which are assigned gender based on sex, not on form. Adjectives, most pronouns, and the cardinal numerals from one to three inflect so as to agree in gender and case with the noun which they modify, for example, Umbrian **tutaper ikuvina** "for the Iguvine state" (abl. sg. fem.); Umbrian **tref sif kumiaf** "three pregnant sows" (acc. pl. fem.).

4.1.1 Nominal classes

Nouns are formally organized into subsystems – declensions – according to the formation of the stem (see Table 5.5). Sabellian has four major vocalic-stem declensions: *a*- (Oscan **aasaí**

Table 5.5 Sabellian noun stems

a-stems

	Oscan	Umbrian
NOM. SG.	víú, *touto*	muta, mutu
VOC. SG.	—	*Tursa, prestota*
ACC. SG.	víam, toutam	tuta, *totam*
DAT. SG.	deívaí	tute, *tote*
ABL. SG.	eítiuvad, toutad	tuta, *tota*
GEN. SG.	vereias	tutas, *totar*
LOC. SG.	víaí, *bansae*	tafle, *tote*
NOM. PL.	aasas, scriftas	pumpeřias, *iuengar*
ACC. PL.	víass, eituas	vitlaf, *uitla*
DAT./ABL./LOC. PL.	kerssnaís	tekuries, *dequrier*
GEN. PL.	eehiianasúm	urnasiaru, *pracatarum*

o-stems

	Oscan	Umbrian
NOM. SG.	húrz	Ikuvins
VOC. SG.	Statie, Silie	*Serfe, Tefre*
ACC. SG.	húrtúm	puplum, *poplom*
DAT. SG.	húrtúí	kumnacle, *pople*
ABL. SG.	sakaraklúd	puplu, *poplu*
GEN. SG.	sakarakleís	katles, *popler*
LOC. SG.	tereí, *comenei*	kumne, *pople*
NOM. PL.	Núvlanús	Ikuvinus, *Iouinur*
ACC. PL.	feíhúss	vitluf, *uitlu*
DAT./ABL./LOC. PL.	Núvlanúís	veskles, *uesclir*
GEN. PL.	Núvlanúm	pihaklu, *pihaclo*

i-stems

	Oscan	Umbrian
NOM. SG.	aídil	ukar
VOC. SG.	—	—
ACC. SG.	slagím	uvem, *uerfale* (NEUT.)
DAT. SG.	—	*ocre*
ABL. SG.	slagid	ocri-per
GEN. SG.	*aeteis*	*ocrer*
LOC. SG.	—	ukre, *ocre*
NOM./VOC. PL.	—	puntes, sakreu (NEUT.)
ACC. PL.	—	avif, avef, perakneu (NEUT.)
DAT./ABL./LOC. PL.	luisarifs	avis, aves
GEN. PL.	[a]íttíum	*peracrio*

consonant-stems

	Oscan	Umbrian
NOM. SG.	meddíss	ařfertur, pir (NEUT.)
VOC. SG.	—	Iupater
ACC. SG.	—	*capirso(m)*, pir (NEUT.)
DAT. SG.	medíkeí	nomne

(cont.)

Table 5.5 (*cont.*)		
	Oscan	Umbrian
ABL. SG.	—	**kapiře**
GEN. SG.	**medíkeís**	*nomner/matres*
LOC. SG.	—	—
NOM./VOC. SG.	**humuns**	**frater**/*uasor* (NEUT.)
ACC. SG.	—	**capif**, *tuderor* (NEUT.)
DAT./ABL./LOC. SG.	—	**capiřus**
GEN. SG.	**fratrúm**	**fratrum**

"altar" [loc. sg. fem.]), *o*- (Umbrian *poplom* "people" [acc. sg. masc.]), *i*- (Umbrian **uvi-kum** "with a sheep" [abl. sg. + postposition -**kum**]), and *u*-stems (Umbrian **trifu** "tribe" [acc. sg.]). In addition, four major consonant-stem declensions occur: stop- (Oscan **aitatum** "one's age" [acc. sg.]), *s*- (Umbrian **meřs** "law" [nom. sg. neut.]), *r*- (Oscan **patir** "father" [nom. sg. masc.]), and *n*-stems (Umbrian **umen** "ointment" [acc. sg. neut.]). Sabellian probably also had another vocalic-stem declension, *ē*-stems (Umbrian **re-per** "according to the ceremony" [abl. sg. fem.] + postposition -**per**). Unfortunately, the evidence is limited to a few words in Umbrian, and it is consequently impossible to determine to what extent these constituted a special inflectional class.

Within these basic inflectional categories there exist several distinct paradigmatic subclasses. For example, *o*-stems, *i*-stems, and consonant-stems split into subgroups based on the gender of the noun – neuters having inflectional endings which are distinct from masculines and feminines in the nominative and accusative singular and plural:

(7) Oscan *o*-stem masculines and neuters

	masculine	neuter
NOM. SG.	**húrz**	**tefúrúm**
ACC. SG.	**húrtúm**	**dunum**
NOM. PL.	**Núvlanús**	**veru**
ACC. PL.	**feíhúss**	**veru**

In addition, *o*-stems and *i*-stems developed subtypes as a result of sound changes that eliminated short **o* and short **i* in word-final syllables before **s* and, in the case of **o*, also in the environment **-yom*. Owing to these changes, *o*-stems that were built historically with a **yo*-suffix came to have an inflectional pattern that was distinct from other types of *o*-stems. This latter group, in turn, is distinguished depending on whether the nominative singular retained or lost its original word-final **s*. Compare, for example, the nominative and accusative singulars in (8):

(8) Subclasses of Umbrian *o*-stem nouns

	*to-stems	**ro*-stems	**lo*-stems	**yo*-stems
NOM. SG.	*taśez* /tašets/	*ager*	**katel**	**Vuvćis**
ACC. SG.	*ehiato(m)*	**kaprum**	**katlu(m)**	**graboui(m)**

4.1.2 Diachronic developments

The paradigms given in Table 5.5 also serve to illustrate the main features of the diachrony of the nominal system in the Sabellian languages, namely the formal merger of cases both within and across paradigms. The *i*-stem genitive singular ending, Oscan -**eís**/Umbrian -**e(s)**, was taken over by *o*-stems and consonant-stems. The accusative singular ending -*om*/-**úm**, originally at home in *o*-stem inflection, spread into the consonant-stems. In Oscan the similarities between these two inflectional classes are even greater because the consonant-stems also borrowed the *o*-stem ablative singular -**úd**/-**ud**, for example, Oscan **tanginúd** (abl. sg.) "decree," *ligud* (abl. sg.) "law."

Generally, however, the formal merger of cases in Umbrian is considerably more advanced than in Oscan. Sound changes in Umbrian, in particular the monophthongization of diphthongs and the loss of word-final consonants, eliminated distinctions between case endings: consider, for example, Umbrian *a*-stem **tote** (dat. sg. fem.) "state," **tote** (loc. sg. fem.) "state," compare Oscan *a*-stem **anagtiai** (dat. sg. fem.) "Angitia" (name of goddess), **aasaí** (loc. sg. fem.) "altar"; Umbrian *a*-stem **uestisia** (acc. sg. fem.) "offering cake," **uestisia** (abl. sg. fem.), compare Oscan *a*-stem **víam** (acc. sg. fem.) "road," **toutad** (abl. sg. fem.) "state."

4.1.3 Adjectives

Adjectives are organized into paradigmatic classes on the same basis as nouns, although the number of stem-types is more restricted. Adjectives are inflected as *o*-stems, *a*-stems, *i*-stems, and consonant-stems (no *u*-stems or *ē*-stems occur). Together *o*-stems and *a*-stems form one adjective declension, the masculine and neuters taking *o*-stem inflection (as in Oscan **túvtíks** "of the community, state" [nom. sg. masc.], *touticom* [acc. sg. neut.]) and the feminines taking *a*-stem inflection (Oscan *toutico* [nom. sg. fem.] with -*o* from *$\bar{a}$*). In contrast, *i*-stem and consonant-stem adjectives occur in all three gender classes (e.g., *i*-stem, Umbrian *perakri* "fit for sacrifice" [abl. sg. masc.], **perakre** [acc. sg. fem.]).

The inflectional category of degree, comparative and superlative, is marked by suffixes added to the adjective stem. The regular suffixes are -**tro**- and -**imo**- respectively, for example, Umbrian **mestru** (nom. sg. fem.) "greater," Oscan **maimas** (nom. pl. fem.) "greatest."

4.1.4 Pronouns

The Sabellian pronominal system includes personal, reflexive, demonstrative, emphatic, anaphoric, interrogative, indefinite, and relative pronouns. The pronouns for first and second persons are not marked for gender, but the rest of the forms in the pronominal system are assigned gender based on that of the noun with which they are in agreement or to which they refer, for example, Umbrian **este persklum** "this ceremony" (acc. sg. neut.).

Sabellian pronouns show significant differences in inflection when compared with nouns and adjectives. These differences are particularly strong in the personal pronouns, but are manifest also in other pronominal categories. For example, the dative singular of the first- and second-person pronouns has unique endings -**he**, -**fe**/-**fei**, for example, Umbrian **mehe** "to me," **tefe** "to you," Oscan **t(e)fei** "to you," compare Latin *tibi*. Furthermore, the dative singular and the locative singular of demonstratives and relatives are marked by distinctive endings in Umbrian, dative -**smi**, -**smei**, locative -**sme**, for example, Umbrian demonstrative **esmi-k**, *esmei* "this" (dat. sg.), relative **pusme** "who, which" (dat. sg.), demonstrative *esme* "this" (loc. sg.). The pronominal neuter nominative/accusative singular is distinguished from nominals by its case ending -**d**, Oscan **púd** "which," Umbrian **puře** "which" <*__pod-id__*.

Outside of the personal pronouns, Sabellian pronominal formations exhibit either *a-*, *o-*, or *i*-stem inflection. The relative and indefinite pronouns have the stems **po-** and **pi-**:

(9)   Oscan and Umbrian relative pronouns

	Oscan	Umbrian
NOM. SG. MASC.	—	*poi, porsi*
NOM. SG. FEM.	**paí**	—
NOM. SG. NEUT.	**púd**	*puře*
ACC. SG. FEM.	**paam**	—
DAT. SG. MASC.	**pui**	*pusme*
ABL. SG. FEM.	**pad**, *poizad*	*pora*
NOM. PL. MASC.	**pús**	*pure*
NOM./ACC. PL. NEUT.	**paí**	*porse*
ACC. PL. FEM.	—	*pafe*

Demonstrative formations typically have *a-/o-*stem inflection: for example, Paelignian *ecuc* "this" (nom. sg. fem.) < **ekā-k(e)*, Oscan **ekas** "this" (nom. pl. fem.), both with stem **eko-/ekā-*; Oscan **eíseís** "his" (gen. sg. masc.), Umbrian **erer** "this" (gen. sg. masc.), with stem **eiso-*; Umbrian *estu* "that" (acc. sg. masc.), with stem **isto-*; Oscan **eksuk** "this" (abl. sg. neut.); Umbrian *eso* "this" (nom. sg. fem.) < **eksā*, with stem **ekso-/eksā-*:

(10)   Oscan and Umbrian demonstrative pronouns (stem **i-/ei-*)

	Oscan	Umbrian
NOM. SG. MASC.	*izic*	**erek**
NOM. SG. FEM.	**iiuk**	—
NOM. SG. NEUT.	**ídík**	**eřek**
ACC. SG. MASC.	*ionc*	—
ACC. SG. FEM.	**íak**	*eam*
NOM. PL. MASC.	*iusc*	—
ACC. PL. FEM.	*iafc* (Marrucinian)	**eaf**
NOM./ACC. PL. NEUT.	*ioc*	**eu**

The Sabellian anaphoric pronoun is built with the stem **i-/ey-*, for example, Oscan *izic* "he" (nom. sg. masc.), Umbrian **erek**, *erec* "he" (nom. sg. masc.).

In the prehistory of the Sabellian languages many of these pronominal forms were augmented by means of particles. The accretion of these particles to pronominal forms had the effect of producing paradigms with inflectional endings that appear, at first glance, to have little in common with those of the nominal system. In many instances the inflectional ending of a pronominal form cannot easily be recognized until the particle has been removed, for example, Umbrian **erarunt** "the same" = **erar** (gen. sg. fem.) + particle **-unt** < **esās-ont*; Umbrian **erak** "this" = **era** (abl. sg. fem.) + particle **-k** < **esād-k(e)*; Umbrian **puře** "which" = **puř** (nom. sg. neut.) + particle **-e** < **pod-i*.

4.2 Verbal morphology

The Sabellian verb is inflected for the categories of tense, voice, mood, person, and number. There are three persons (first, second, third), two numbers (singular, plural), and two voices (active, mediopassive). The mood categories are indicative, imperative, and subjunctive. Five different tense forms are attested for Sabellian verbs: present, imperfect, future, perfect, and future perfect. The basic symmetry of the Sabellian system and the fact that it is quite similar to that of Latin suggest the occurrence of another tense form, the pluperfect, compare Latin *portauerat* "had carried."

4.2.1   Aspectual stems

The finite verb system is formally organized into subsystems based on two stem-types that mark a distinction in aspect, the *infectum* (present system) and the *perfectum* (perfect system). Present, imperfect, and future tense forms are built on the stem of the infectum, the perfect and the future perfect on that of the perfectum:

(11)

	INFECTUM	PERFECTUM
PRES.	*didet* "he gives" (Vestinian)	PERF *fefa\<c\>id* "he should do"
FUT.	*didest* "he will give"	FUT. PERF. *fefacust* "he will have done"
IMPF.	**fufans** "they were"	PLUPERF. ? —

4.2.2   Verb endings

The grammatical categories of person, number, and voice are signaled by affixes traditionally called "personal endings." These are of two basic sets, one for active and one for mediopassive voice (see Table 5.6). The active set of endings has two forms depending on the tense of the verb to which it is attached: the so-called primary endings are used for present, future, and future perfect tenses; while secondary endings are used for imperfect and perfect indicative, and for all tenses of the subjunctive. In the passive voice, only Umbrian shows a primary versus secondary distinction, for example, 3rd sg. mediopass. – primary **herter** "it is desirable" (3rd sg. pres.); secondary **emantur** "they should be accepted" (3rd sg. pres. subjunc.).

Table 5.6 Sabellian personal endings	
PRIMARY	
1ST SG. ACT.	Umbrian **suboca-u** "I invoke"
2ND SG. ACT.	Umbrian **herie-s** "you will desire"
3RD SG. ACT.	Vestinian *dide-t* "he gives"
3RD SG. MEDIOPASS.	Oscan *uinc-ter* "he is convicted"
1ST PL. ACT.	—
2ND PL.	—
3RD PL. ACT.	Umbrian *furfa-nt* "they shear"
3RD PL. MEDIOPASS.	Umbrian *ostens-endi* "they will be presented"
SECONDARY	
1ST SG. ACT.	Oscan **manaf-úm** "I entrusted"
2ND SG. ACT.	—
3RD SG. ACT.	Oscan **prúfatte-d** "he approved"
1ST PL. ACT.	South Picene **adstaeo-ms** "we have set up"
2ND PL. ACT.	Umbrian **benuso** /-us-so/ "you all will have come"
3RD PL. ACT.	Paelignian *coisat-ens* "they took care of"
3RD PL. MEDIOPASS.	Umbrian **ema-ntur** "they should be accepted"

The Sabellian languages also possess a third singular mediopassive suffix -**r** for use in impersonal constructions, for example, Umbrian **ferar** (3rd sg. pres. subjunc.). mediopass. "there is a carrying," *ier* (3rd sg. pres. mediopass.) "there is a going."

4.2.3   Verbal classes

The Sabellian verb is organized into paradigmatic classes, or conjugations, based on the form of the verb-stem found in present tense inflection. If verbs such as "to be" (Oscan **súm** "I am") and "to go" (Umbrian *est* "he will go") are excluded as "irregular," five basic conjugational patterns can be established: *a*-conjugation (Oscan **faamat** "he calls"); *e*-conjugation (Umbrian **tusetu/tusitu** "let him pursue," Oscan **fatíum** "to speak," **licitud** "let it be permitted"); *i*-conjugation (Umbrian **seritu** "let him watch out for"); *y/i*-conjugation (Umbrian **façiu** /fašyo(m)/ "to sacrifice," Oscan **fakiiad** "he should make"); and *e/ø*-conjugation (Oscan *agum* "to move," *actud* "let him move," Umbrian **aitu** "let him move"). Forms of the *y/i*- and *e/ø*-conjugations such as the Oscan imperatives *factud*, *actud* are derived from earlier forms in which medial vowels were present – short *i* for *factud* < *fakitōd*, short *e* for *actud* < *aketōd*.

4.2.4   Verb tense

Tense is typically signaled by a combination of stem-type (perfectum versus imperfectum; see §4.2.1) and suffixation. Outside of the present and perfect there are special tense-forming suffixes. The imperfect has -**fa**-, the future -**(e)s**-, and the future perfect -**us**-: for example, Oscan **fu-fa-ns** "they were" 3rd pl. impf., Oscan *deiua-s-t* "he will swear" (3rd sg. fut.), Oscan **tríbarakatt-us-et** "they will have built" (3rd pl. fut. perf.).

Sabellian perfect tense stems of active voice are formed by a number of different morphological operations: (i) reduplication (Oscan **deded** "he gave" [3rd sg. perf.], *fefacid* "he should do" [3rd sg. perf. subjunc.]; Umbrian *dede* "he gave" [3rd sg. perf.]); (ii) suffixation (-**tt**-: Oscan **prúfatted** "he approved" [3rd sg. perf.]; -**nçi**-/-*nśi*-; Umbrian *purdinśiust* "he will have presented" [3rd sg. fut. perf.]; -**f**-: Umbrian **andirsafust** "he will have made a circuit" [3rd sg. fut. perf.]); and (iii) radical vowel lengthening (Oscan **uupsens** "they built" [3rd. pl. perf.]). Some perfects are formed from the bare verb-stem, minus the suffix used to generate the present: for example, Umbrian **anpelust** "he will have slain" (3rd sg. fut. perf.) built to a present that is characterized by a suffix -**ne**, **anpentu** "let him slay" < *-pennetōd* < *-pelnetōd*. In the mediopassive, the perfect is formed by a periphrastic construction involving the past participle plus a form of the verb "to be": for example, Oscan **prúftúset** ("they have been approved" [3rd pl. perf. mediopass.]; Oscan *scriftas set* "they have been written" [3rd pl. perf. mediopass.]; Umbrian **pihaz fust** "it will have been purified" [3rd sg. fut. perf. mediopass.]). Interestingly, there is one perfect mediopassive formation that is not a periphrastic, Oscan *comparascuster* "it will have been discussed," a future perfect found in the *Tabula Bantina*. Presumably this formation is an independent (and late?) Oscan creation.

In some cases, in particular derived verbs, the stem of the perfect is built directly from the present. For example, *a*-stem presents generally form -**t(t)**-stem perfects in Oscan and in the Sabellian languages of central Italy: thus, Oscan **duunated** "he presented" (3rd sg. perf.); Paelignian *coisatens* "they took care of" (3rd pl. perf.); Marrucinian *amatens* "they seized" (3rd pl. perf.); Volscian *sistiatiens* "they set up" (3rd pl. perf.). Still, even here there are exceptions. The verb-stem **opsa**- "build" forms a perfect by lengthening the radical vowel and truncating the present stem vowel **a**, thus Oscan **uupsens** "they built" (3rd pl. perf.).

In Umbrian, *a*-stems form their perfects by means of the suffix **-f-**, *andirsafust* "he will have made the circuit" (3rd sg. fut. perf.). In many cases the type of perfect formation cannot be predicted by the paradigmatic class of the present. For example, the verb "to give" forms a reduplicated present (Vestinian *didet* "he gives" [3rd sg. pres.]) and a reduplicated perfect (Oscan *deded* "he gave" [3rd sg. perf.]), while the verb "to make" forms a *y/i-* present but a reduplicated perfect, **fakiiad** "he should make" (3rd sg. pres. subjunc.), *fefacid* "he should make" (3rd sg. perf. subjunc.).

4.2.5 Nonindicative moods

Subjunctive mood is indicated by suffixes which are attached to the verb-stem preceding the personal endings. Present subjunctive is marked by **-a** in Umbrian for all present classes except *a*-conjugation, which shows **-ia**: for example, *e*-conjugation **habi-a** "he should hold" (3rd sg. pres. subjunc.); compare *a*-conjugation *porta-ia* "he should carry" (3rd sg. pres. subjunc.). In Oscan *-i* is used for *a*-conjugation, *deiua-i-d* "he should swear" (3rd sg. pres. subjunc.), **-a** for all other conjugation classes, for example, **pútí-a-ns** "they should be able" (3rd pl. pres. subjunc.).

The imperfect subjunctive is attested only in Oscan and Paelignian. The suffix used is Oscan **-sí**, Paelignian *-se* (< *sē*): Oscan **fu-sí-d** "he should be" (3rd sg. impf. subjunc.); Paelignian *upsa-se-ter* "it was built" (3rd sg. impf. subj. mediopass.). For the perfect subjunctive active, the suffix is *-í/i*, Oscan **tríbarakatt-í-ns** "they should build" (3rd pl. perf. subjunc.).

Imperative mood forms have two special sets of person, number, and voice endings. So-called *imperative I* endings are used for commands that are to be carried out immediately following the time of speaking:

(12) Imperative I

2ND SG. ACT.	Umbrian *anserio* "observe"
3RD SG.	—
2ND PL. ACT.	Umbrian **eta-tu** "go," Paelignian *ei-te* "go"
2ND PL. MEDIOPASS.	Umbrian **katera-mu** "arrange in order"
3RD PL.	—

Imperative II endings are reserved for commands to be carried out at some undefined point in the future. This type is particularly common in the Iguvine Tablets, where sets of ritual instructions are set forth to be carried out whenever the religious observance is required:

(13) Imperative II

2ND SG. ACT.	Umbrian **ene-tu** "begin"
2ND SG. MEDIOPASS.	Umbrian *persni-mu* "pray"
3RD SG. ACT.	Oscan **liki-tud** "let it be permitted"
3RD SG. MEDIOPASS.	Oscan **censa-mur** "let him be assessed"
2ND PL. ACT.	Umbrian *ambre-tuto* "circumambulate"
2ND PL. MEDIOPASS.	Umbrian *pesni-mumo* "pray"
3RD PL. ACT.	Umbrian *habi-tuto* "let them hold"
3RD PL. MEDIOPASS.	Umbrian *pesni-mumo* "let them pray"

4.2.6   Nonfinite verbals

An important component of the Sabellian verbal system consists of a constellation of nonfinite formations. These include present infinitives, both active and mediopassive (Umbrian *erom* "to be" [pres. act.]; Umbrian *pihafi* "to be expiated" [pres. mediopass.]); present and past participles (Umbrian **zeref** "sitting" [pres. act.]; Umbrian **çersnatur** "having dined" [past. mediopass.]); supines (Umbrian **anzeriatu** "to observe"); and the so-called gerundive (Oscan **úpsannam** "to be built").

4.3   Derivational morphology

Complex Sabellian words are formed by means of the morphological processes of affixation and compounding. Affixation, in particular suffixation, appears to have been more productive than compounding.

4.3.1   Suffixation

Several suffixes are used productively to form nouns in Oscan and Umbrian. The suffix **-iuf** (nom. sg.)/**-in-** (other cases) produces nouns with abstract or concrete meanings, for example, Oscan **tríbarakkiuf** "a building," compare **tríbarakattens** "they built." The extended suffix **-tiuf/-tin-** has the same morphological function, for example, Oscan *medicatinom* "judgment," Umbrian **natine** "tribe," compare Praenestine Latin *nationu* "childbirth" (gen. sg.). The suffix **-tur** is used to form agent nouns from verb-stems, for example, Oscan **regaturei** "the director" (epithet of Jupiter) dat. sg. from **regā-* "direct," **ařfertur** "flamen, chief priest" from **ad-fer-* "to carry." The suffix **-etia**, which is added to noun stems to build abstracts, is attested in Umbrian by several formations that serve to indicate terms of elected office, for example, **kvestretie** "in the term of office as quaestor" (loc. sg.).

One productive adjective-forming suffix is **-(a)sio-** "relating to, pertaining to," used to form adjectives from nominal stems: for example, Oscan **kerssnasias** "concerned with banquets" (nom. pl. fem.), compare Oscan **kersnu** "banquet" (nom. sg. fem.); **purasiaí** "concerned with fire" (loc. sg. fem.), compare Umbrian **pir** "fire" (nom./acc. sg. neut.). The suffix **-ano-** is also used to form adjectives from nouns; most of the examples attested in inscriptions are formed from ethnic or topographical names, for example, Oscan **Abellanús** "from the city of Abella" (nom. pl. masc.), Umbrian **Treblanir** "leading to Trebula" (abl. sg. neut.).

Verbs are productively formed in all Sabellian languages by means of the suffix **-a** or by extensions of this suffix, **-ia**, **-ta**, etc. Formations in **-a**, a suffix used primarily to build verbs from nouns and adjectives, are widely attested: thus, Umbrian **kuratu** "accomplished" (acc. sg. neut. mediopass. part.); Paelignian *coisatens* "they supervised" (3rd pl. perf.) < **koisā-*, compare Latin *cūra* "concern"; Oscan *deiuaid* "he should swear" (3rd sg. pres. subjunc.) < **deiuā-*, compare Oscan **deívaí** "divine" (dat. sg. fem.); Umbrian **pihatu** "let him purify" (3rd sg. impv. II), compare Volscian *pihom* "religiously unobjectionable" (nom. sg. neut.); Oscan **teremnattens** "they set a limit on" (3rd pl. perf.) < **termnā-*, compare Oscan **teremníss** (acc. pl.), Latin *termen* "limit"; Umbrian **osatu** "let him build" (3rd sg. impv. II) < **opesā-*, compare Latin *opus* "work." This suffix, as well as variants derived from it, are also used in the formation of deverbative verbs: for example, Umbrian *andirsafust* "he will have made the circuit" (3rd sg. fut. perf.) < **am-did-ā-*; Umbrian **kumbifiatu** "deliver instructions" (2nd sg. impv. II) < **kom-bif-iā-*, compare Latin *fīdit* "he puts confidence in"; Umbrian *etaians* "they go" (3rd pl. pres. subjunc.) < **ey-tā-*.

4.3.2   Compounds

Sabellian compound formations consist in large part of words with an adverbial first constituent. In fact, the only pervasive type of verbal composition attested in Sabellian involves the use of adverbial elements: for example, Umbrian **aha-uendu** "let him turn away" (3rd sg. impv. II), **am-pendu** "let him slay" (3rd sg. impv. II), **re-vestu** "let him examine" (3rd sg. impv. II), etc. There is also a substantial number of nominals formed by means of an adverbial first constituent. The best attested are built with the privative element **a-**, **an-** "not": for example, Oscan *an-censto* "unburnt" (nom. sg. fem.); Umbrian *a-uirseto* "unseen" (nom. sg. neut.), **an-takres** "unground" (abl. pl.), **a-snata** "not wet" (acc. pl. neut.), **a-seçeta** "uncut" (abl. sg. fem.).

Nominal compounding is not well represented in Sabellian. There are a couple of good examples of possessive compounds with numerals as the first member, for example, Umbrian *petur-purs-us* (dat. pl.) "animals" (i.e., "having four feet"); *du-pursus* (dat. pl.) "having two feet." But aside from these, there are few formations that qualify as compounds from a synchronic point of view, though several forms derive historically from compounds: thus, Oscan **meddíss** "meddix" (a title of magistracy), which was originally an adjectival compound with first member **med-* "law" and second member **dik-* "speaking," compare Latin *iūdex* < **iowes-dik-* "speaking the law." The semantics of **meddíss**, the fact that it refers to a magistracy, suggests that it was no longer interpreted synchronically as a compound.

4.3.3   Locative case formation

An especially interesting morphological development is found in the Oscan and Umbrian case system. The postposition Oscan *-en* "in, upon," Umbrian **-en**, **-e**, **-em** "in, upon" governs the locative case in one of its primary functions. When this postposition was added to the locative of *o*-stem nominal forms in Oscan, or to the locative of vowel stems in Umbrian, the vowel of the case ending and initial vowel of the postposition contracted, as in Oscan **húrtín** /hortẹn/ "in the precinct" < **hortey-en*. This contracted form of ending + postposition was then reanalyzed as a new form of the locative case. That such was indeed the case is indicated by noun phrases in which this "ending" is attached to both adjectives and nouns, for example, Oscan **hurtín Kerríin** "in the precinct of Ceres" (loc. sg. masc.), Umbrian *ocrem Fisiem* "on the Fisian Mount" (loc. sg.); and by instances in which the postposition has been added to a noun already marked with the original postposition, for example, Umbrian *toteme Iouinem* "in the Iguvine community." In this instance, *toteme* can be segmented diachronically as *tote* (loc. sg. fem.) + postposition *-em* + postposition *-e*.

4.4   Numerals

Lack of evidence prevents a comprehensive treatment of numerals in Sabellian. Cardinal numbers are well represented only by "two" and "three," which inflected for gender, case, and number: Umbrian **sif trif** "three sows" (acc. pl. fem.), **triia tefra** "three pieces of burnt offering" (acc. pl. neut.). The number "four" **pettiur** is found on one Oscan inscription (Rix Sa17). Unfortunately, the inscription is fragmentary and the context in which the word occurs is no longer recoverable. The number "twelve" is attested in Umbrian in the form of a copulative compound "ten + two," *desen-duf* (acc. pl.). Other cardinals can only be pieced together from derived formations. For example, the Umbrian nominal forms **pumpeřias** "representing 5 decuriae" and **puntes** "groups of five" point to **pompe* as the form for the cardinal "five."

In addition to the cardinals, a few ordinals and multiplicative adverbs are attested. Umbrian has forms for the first three ordinals: **prumum**, *promom* "first" (acc. sg. neut.),

etre "second" (dat. sg. fem.), and **tertiam-a** "third" (acc. sg. fem.) + postposition -**a**. Multiplicatives are also attested in Umbrian: **sumel** "once," **duti** "two times," **triuper** "three times," and **nuvis** "nine times."

5. SYNTAX

5.1 Case usage

In Sabellian the role of noun phrases in a sentence is denoted by the inflectional feature case. The complements of the verb are marked by nominative case for subject, accusative case for direct object, and dative case for indirect object or beneficiary. Nominative is also used for adjectival and nominal predicates in copular sentences, and accusative case for the objects of certain prepositions and for goal of motion. Vocative is the case of direct address. The remaining oblique case forms, genitive, ablative, and locative, are used for adnominal (genitive = possession, partitive) or adverbial functions (ablative = place from which, source; locative = place where, time when).

5.2 Word order

The order of the major constituents in a Sabellian sentence is predominantly Subject–Object–Verb (SOV), but almost all possible permutations of this basic order are attested in inscriptions. Changes from basic SOV order do not affect the grammaticality of a sentence and are usually motivated by considerations of focus (topicalization), prosody (speech rhythm), or aesthetics (style).

The order of elements within a noun phrase depends on the type of modifier. Typically, adjectives occupy postnominal position (Oscan **lígatúís núvlanúís** "legates from Nola"), while genitive noun phrases are placed before the modified noun (Oscan **herekleís fíísnu** "temple of Herakles"), though adjectives can also appear in prenominal position (Oscan **múínikeí tereí** "in common territory") and genitives can follow their head noun (**sakaraklúm herekleís** "sanctuary of Herakles"). Numerals and pronominal modifiers are almost invariably placed before the noun (Umbrian **tref hapinaf** "three lambs"; Oscan **eíseí tereí** "in that territory"). Definite relative clauses usually follow the antecedent noun phrase, but there are examples in which the relative clause is preposed; sample relative clauses are given in (14):

(14) Relative clauses in Sabellian

    A. **púst.**   **feíhúís.**   **pús.**   **físnam.**
        behind walls-ABL. PL. MASC. which-NOM. PL. MASC. temple-ACC. SG. FEM.
        amfret
        surround-3RD PL. PRES.
      "Behind the walls which surround the temple" (Oscan Rix CA)

    B. *pafe.*   *trif.*   *promom.* *haburent.*
        which-ACC. PL. FEM. three-ACC. PL. FEM. first-ADV. will catch-3RD PL. FUT. PERF.
        eaf.   *acersoniem /*
        these-ACC. PL. FEM.   Acedonia-LOC. SG. FEM. + POSTPOSITION
        fetu
        sacrifice-3RD SG. IMPV. II
      "Which three [victims] they will have caught first, these he shall
        sacrifice at Acedonia" (Umbrian VIIa 52)

The Sabellian languages possess both prepositions and postpositions, Umbrian exhibiting a good selection of the latter: **-ař** "to, toward"; *-co*, **-ku** "with"; **-en, -e, -em** "into, to, upon"; **-per** "for"; *-to*, **-ta**, **-tu** "from." In the other Sabellian languages, however, postpositions are much less common (see Oscan *censtom-en* "for the census" and 4.3.3). In the case of prepositional phrases with adjective modifiers, it is common to find the preposition standing between the adjective and the noun: thus, Umbrian *nertru-co persi* (abl. sg. masc.) "at the left foot," compare Latin *magnō cum dolōre* (abl. sg. masc.) "with great sorrow."

5.3 Agreement

There are three basic rules of agreement in Sabellian:

1. Pronominal modifiers and adjectives, both attributive as well as predicative, modify their head noun in terms of the inflectional features of gender, number, and case, for example, **sif kumiaf** (fem. acc. pl.) "pregnant sows."
2. A relative pronoun agrees with the head of its antecedent noun phrase in gender and number, while case is determined by the role of the relative word within its clause (see the examples in [14] above).
3. Verbs are marked for person and number based on the person and number of their subject. So, in the Oscan sentence of (15) below, the verb form *censazet* "they will assess" (3rd pl. fut.) is marked for third-person plural in order to agree with the nominative plural subject *censtur* "censors."

(15) *pon*   *censtur*   *bansae*   *tautam*
      when-CONJ. censors-NOM. PL. MASC. Bantia-LOC. SG. FEM. people-ACC. SG. FEM.
      censazet
      "assess"-3RD PL. FUT.
      "When the censors will assess the people at Bantia" (Oscan Rix TB)

Deviations from these rules of agreement do occur and can usually be attributed to factors such as "agreement through sense." So, for example, in the following sentence from the Iguvine Tablets the main verb **prusikurent** "they will have proclaimed" (3rd pl. fut. perf.) is marked for plural based on the collective sense of the grammatically singular subject noun phrase **mestru karu** (nom. sg. fem.) "the greater portion" = "majority."

(16) **sve**   **mestru**   **karu**   **fratru**
      if-CONJ. greater-NOM. SG. FEM. portion-NOM. SG. FEM. brothers-GEN. PL. MASC.
      Atiieřiu   **pure**   **ulu**
      Atiedian-GEN. PL. MASC. who-NOM. PL. MASC. there-ADV.
      benurent   **prusikurent**   **rehte**
      come-3RD PL. FUT. PERF. proclaim-3RD PL. FUT. PERF. properly-ADV.
      kuratu eru
      has been executed-PERF. PASS. INF.
      "If a majority of the Atiedian brothers who will have come there will have proclaimed that [the ceremony] has been executed properly" (Umbrian Va 24–26)

5.4 Main clauses

The mood of a Sabellian verb in main clauses is semantically determined. Statements of fact take the indicative mood. Subjunctive mood is used for wishes (Oscan **nep pútíad** "([I hope] he is not able") and for prohibitions (*ni hipid* "let him not hold"). Commands and prescriptions appear in the imperative (Umbrian *anserio* "observe"; Oscan **factud** "let him make").

5.5 Subordinate clauses

5.5.1 Modal distribution

In dependent clauses the distribution of the subjunctive and indicative moods is a function of the type of subordination involved. In indirect commands the subjunctive mood is used as a replacement for the imperative. In Umbrian this type of subordination does not take an introductory conjunction.

(17) **kupifiatu**   **rupiname**   **erus**
     order-3RD SG. IMPV. II Rubinia-ACC. SG. FEM. + POSTPOSITION *erus*-ACC. SG. NEUT.
     tera   **ene**   **tra sahta**
     distribute-3RD SG. PRES. SUBJUNC. and-CONJ. Trans Sancta-ACC. SG. FEM.
     kupifiaia
     order-3RD SG. PRES. SUBJUNC.
     "At Rubinia he shall order him to distribute the *erus* and to give the command
      at Trans Sancta" (Umbrian Ib 35)

Indirect questions use both indicative and subjunctive depending on whether the event described in the question is considered a fact or a possibility, but there is at least one example, cited in (18), of the use of a subjunctive as a replacement for the indicative mood of the direct question.

(18) **ehvelklu**   **feia ...**   **sve**   **rehte**
     vote-ACC. SG. NEUT. take-3RD SG. PRES. SUBJUNC. if-CONJ. properly-ADV.
     kuratu si
     execute-PERF. MEDIOPASS. PART. + be-3RD SG. SUBJUNC. (= PERF. PASS.)
     "Let him take a vote on whether [the ceremony] has been properly executed"
      (Umbrian Va 23)

The spread of the subjunctive mood at the expense of the indicative appears to have been in progress during the historical period.

5.5.2 Subordinating conjunctions

Temporal clauses are introduced by a variety of conjunctions: Umbrian *arnipo* "until"; Umbrian **ape** "when"; Umbrian *ponne*, **pune**, Oscan **pun** "when"; Oscan *pruter pan*, Umbrian *prepa* "before"; Umbrian *post pane* "after." Adverbial clauses of purpose are signaled by the conjunction **puz** Oscan, *pusi* Umbrian "so that" and a subjunctive mood verb in the subordinate clause. The conjunction meaning "if," **sve** Umbrian, **svaí** Oscan, marks the protasis of a conditional clause.

5.5.3 Infinitival complements

Infinitives are used to represent the main verb of a statement that is subordinated in indirect discourse. The subject in the subordinated clause shifts from nominative to accusative case, and the tense of the infinitive is determined by the tense of the verb in direct discourse.

Thus, in the Umbrian example of (19), the perfect periphrastic infinitive is used because the tense of the verb in direct discourse was perfect:

(19) **prusikurent**   **rehte**
     proclaim-3RD PL. FUT. PERF.   properly-ADV.
       kuratu eru
     execute-PERF. MEDIOPASS. PART. ACC.SG. NEUT. + be-PRES. ACT. INF. =
       PERF. PASS. INF.
     "(A majority of the brotherhood) will have proclaimed that it [the ceremony]
       has been properly executed" (Umbrian Va 26)

Infinitives also serve as the complements of verbs that have meanings within the semantic range of "wish," "be necessary," "be fit," etc. The examples cited below are from Umbrian.

(20) A.   **pune**   **puplum**   **aferum**   **heries**
       when-CONJ.   people-ACC. SG. MASC.   purify-PRES. INF.   wish-2ND SG. FUT.
         avef   **anzeriatu**   **etu**
       birds-ACC. PL. FEM.   observe-SUPINE   go-2ND SG. IMPV. II
       "When you will wish to purify the people, go to observe the birds"
       (Umbrian Ib 10)
   B.   *perse*   *mers*   *est*   *esu*
       if-CONJ.   right-NOM. SG. NEUT.   is-3RD SG. PRES. ACT.   this-ABL. SG. MASC.
         sorsu   *persondru*
       pig-ABL. SG. MASC.   excellent-ABL. SG. MASC.
         pihaclu   *pihafi*
       victim of purification-ABL. SG. NEUT.   be purified-PRES. MEDIOPASS. INF.
       "If it is right that it be purified with this excellent pig as a victim of purification"
       (Umbrian VIb 31)

Supines are used as complements to verbs of motion; see **anzeriatu** in the first sentence of (20).

5.5.4   Sequence of tenses

In indirect commands, indirect questions, adverbial clauses of the purpose type, and subordinate clauses within indirect discourse, the tense of the subjunctive is governed by the tense of the main verb, so-called *consecutio temporum* "sequence of tenses." Present tense in the main clause requires present tense of the subjunctive in the subordinate clause; past tense in the main requires an imperfect subjunctive in the subordinate clause. In the Oscan example of (21), the verb in the subordinate clause is imperfect subjunctive because the governing verb is in the perfect tense:

(21) **kúmbened**   **thesavrúm**   **pún**
     agree-3RD SG. PERF.   treasury-ACC. SG. MASC.   when-CONJ.
       patensíns   **múiníkad**   **tanginúd**
     open-3RD PL. IMPF. SUBJUNC.   common-ABL. SG. FEM.   consent-ABL. SG. FEM.
       patensíns
     open-3RD PL. IMPF. SUBJUNC.
     "It was agreed [that] when they opened the treasury they should open it by
       joint agreement" (Oscan Rix CA)

5.5.5   Relative clause formation

There are two important Sabellian syntactic processes that concern relative clause formation – *attraction* and *incorporation*. Attraction refers to the process whereby the antecedent of a relative pronoun is attracted into the case of the relative, or the case of the relative is modified to agree with that of its antecedent (so-called *reverse* attraction). Incorporation refers to movement of the antecedent out of the main clause and into the relative clause.

In the Oscan sentence of (22), both syntactic processes are at work: (i) *ligud*, which serves as the antecedent of the relative pronoun *poizad*, is incorporated into the relative clause; and (ii) the relative pronoun *poizad*, which is the underlying direct object accusative of the verb *anget<.>uzet*, is attracted into the ablative case of the antecedent.

(22)   *censamur.*   *esuf...*   *poizad.*
       ASSESS-3RD SG. PRES. MEDIOPASS. IMPV. II   SELF-NOM. SG. MASC.   WHICH-ABL. SG. FEM.
       ligud /   *iusc.*   *censtur.*
       LAW-ABL. SG. FEM.   THIS-NOM. PL. MASC.   CENSORS-NOM. PL. MASC.
       censaum.   *anget<.>uzet*
       ASSESS-PRES. ACT. INF.   PROPOSE-3RD PL. FUT. PERF.
       "He himself shall be assessed by the law which these censors shall have proposed to take the census" (Oscan Rix TB)

6.   THE LEXICON

The basic layer of the Sabellian lexicon is made up of words inherited from Proto-Indo-European. Many of these words are attested in both branches of Italic as well as in other Indo-European languages:

(23)   **Sabellian words of Proto-Indo-European origin**

A.   "father": Oscan **pater** NOM. SG. MASC., South Picene **patereíh** DAT. SG. MASC., Latin *pater*
B.   "mother": Oscan **maatreís** GEN. SG. FEM., South Picene **matereih** DAT. SG. FEM., Latin *māter*
C.   "brother": Umbrian *frater* NOM. PL. MASC., Latin *frāter*
D.   "carries": Umbrian *ferest* 3RD SG. FUT., Volscian *ferom* PRES. INF., Marrucinian *feret* 3RD PL. PRES., Latin *fert* 3RD SG. PRES.
E.   "says": Oscan **deíkum** PRES. ACT. INF., Latin *dīcit* 3RD SG. PRES.
F.   "be": Oscan **súm**, *sim* 1ST SG. PRES., *est* 3RD SG. PRES., Umbrian *est*, Volscian *estu* 3RD SG. IMPV. II, South Picene **esum** 1ST SG. PRES., Pre-Samnite **esum**, Latin *sum, est*
G.   "foot": Umbrian **peri** ABL. SG. MASC., Oscan **pedú** GEN. PL. MASC., Latin *pēs*

Other Sabellian vocabulary items have solid etymological connections with languages in other branches of Indo-European but lack Latino-Faliscan cognates:

(24)   **Inherited Sabellian vocabulary not found in Latino-Faliscan**

A.   "son": Oscan **puklui** DAT. SG. MASC., Paelignian *puclois* DAT. PL. MASC., Marsian *pucle[s]* DAT. PL. MASC., Sanskrit *putras*, cf. Latin *filius*
B.   "daughter": Oscan **futír** NOM. SG. FEM., Greek θυγάτηρ, Sanskrit *duhitā*, cf. Latin *fīlia*
C.   "fire": Umbrian *pir* NOM./ACC. SG. NEUT., Oscan **purasíaí** "having to do with fire" LOC. SG. FEM., Greek πῦρ, English *fire*, cf. Latin *ignis*

D.   "water": Umbrian **utur** "water" NOM./ACC. SG. NEUT., Greek ὕδωρ, cf. Latin *aqua* but note also Oscan **aapa** "water"

E.   "community": Oscan *touto* NOM. SG. FEM., Umbrian **totam** ACC. SG. FEM., Marrucinian *toutai* DAT. SG. FEM., cf. Venetic **teuta[m]** ACC. SG. FEM., Lithuanian *tauta* "people," Gothic *piuda* "people," Old Irish *tuath* "people"

A small set of vocabulary items are restricted to Italic. A substantial number of these shared vocabulary items are associated with religion and ritual practices: for example, Latin *sacer* "sacred," Oscan **sakrím** "victim" (acc. sg.); Latin *sanctum* "consecrated," Oscan **saahtúm** (acc. sg. neut.); Latin *pius* "obedient," *piat* "he propitiates," Volscian *pihom* "religiously unobjectionable" (nom. sg. neut.), Umbrian **pihatu** "let him purify" (3rd sg. impv. II); Latin *feriae* "days of religious observance," Oscan **fíísíaís** (dat pl. fem.). A few items in this category, however, belong to "secular" levels of the lexicon: thus, Latin *cēna* "dinner," Oscan **kersnu** (nom. sg. fem.); Latin *habet* "he has, holds," Oscan **hafiest** (3rd sg. fut.); Latin *ūtī* "to use," Oscan **úíttiuf** "use" (nom. sg.); Latin *familia* "family," Oscan *famelo* "household" (nom. sg. fem.); Latin *cūrat* "he superintends," Paelignian *coisatens* (3rd pl. perf.), Umbrian **kuraia** (3rd sg. pres. subjunc.).

Loanwords entered the Sabellian languages from three main sources: Greek, Etruscan, and Latin. The earliest layer of loanwords in Oscan resulted from contact with Greeks and Etruscans in southern Italy. A considerable portion of these loans are the names of deities or their divine epithets: for example, **Herekleís** "Herakles" (gen. sg.), compare Etruscan **hercle**, Greek Ἡρακλῆς; **Herukinaí** (dat. sg.), compare Greek Ἐρυκίνη, epithet of Aphrodite; Αππελλουνηι "Apollo" (dat. sg.), **Appelluneís** (gen. sg.), compare Doric Greek Ἀπέλλων. Outside of *nomina sacra*, there is a handful of cultural borrowings: for example, Oscan **kúíníks** "quarts" (nom. pl.), compare Greek χοῖνιξ "quart (dry measure)"; Oscan **thesavrúm** "storehouse" (acc. sg.), compare Greek θησαυρός. Other words, ultimately of Greek origin, made their way into Sabellian via Etruscan intermediation, for example, Oscan **culchna** (nom. sg.) "kylix," cf. Etruscan **culíχna**, Greek κυλίχνα.

Greek loans, particularly the names of divinities, penetrated also into the Sabellian languages of central Italy. A late second-century Paelignian inscription (Ve 213) reveals the names of two Greek divinities: *Uranias* "Urania" (gen. sg.), *Perseponas* "Persephone" (gen. sg.).

Etruscan may be the source for one of the most important sacred terms in Sabellian. The word for "god" that is attested in the central Sabellian languages (Marrucinian *aisos* "gods" [nom. pl. masc.], Marsian *esos* [nom. pl. masc.], Paelignian *aisis* [dat. pl. masc.]) and in Oscan (**aisu(s)is** dat. pl. masc.) is based on the root **ais-**, which is the uninflected form of the word in Etruscan, *ais* "god."

In the third and second centuries BC, as the influence of Roman Latin became progressively more pervasive, Latin loanwords began to appear in all levels of the Sabellian lexicon, but most importantly in the spheres of politics and the law. Oscan and Umbrian public officials appear in inscriptions with the titles of magistracies borrowed from Rome: Latin *quaestor* gives Umbrian **kvestur** (nom. sg.), Oscan **kvaísstur** (nom. sg.); Latin *cēnsor* provides Oscan **keenzstur** (nom. sg.); and Latin *aedilis* is taken over as Oscan **aídil** (nom. sg.). The Oscan word for assembly is replaced by Latin *senātus*, thus Oscan *senateis* (gen. sg.). Oscan *ceus* "citizen" is based on Latin *cīuis*. The Oscan *Tabula Bantina*, inscribed at the beginning of the first century BC, attests a formidable array of borrowings and calques based on Latin legal and political terminology. The borrowings in this text are a barometer of Rome's growing cultural, political, and linguistic supremacy in first-century Italy and of the Sabellian languages' declining linguistic fortunes.

Bibliography

Adiego Lajara, I. J. 1990. "Der Archaismus des Sudpikenischen." *Historische Sprachforschung* 103:69–79.

Benediktsson, H. 1960. "The vowel syncope in Oscan-Umbrian." *Norsk Tidsskrift for Sprogvidenskap* 19:157–295.

Briquel, Dominique. 1972. "Sur des faits d'écriture en Sabine et dans l'ager Capenas. Mélanges de l'Ecole française de Rome." *Antiquité* 84:789–845.

Buck, C. Darling. 1928. *A Grammar of Oscan and Umbrian* (2nd edition). Boston: Ginn.

Colonna, G. 1974. "Nuovi dati epigrafici sulla protostoria della Campania." *Atti della riunione scientifica*, pp. 151–169.

Cowgill, W. 1970. "Italic and Celtic superlatives and the dialects of Indo-European." In G. Cardona, H. Hoenigswald, and A. Senn (eds.), *Indoeuropean and Indoeuropeans*, pp. 113–153. Philadelphia, PA: University of Pennsylvania Press.

———. 1973. "The source of Latin *stāre*, with notes on comparable forms elsewhere in Indo-European." *Journal of Indo-European Studies* 1:271–303.

———. 1976. "The second plural of the Umbrian verb." In G. Cardona and N. H. Zide (eds.), *Festschrift for Henry Hoenigswald*, pp. 81–90. Tübingen: Narr.

Cristofani, M. 1979. "Recent advances in Etruscan epigraphy and language." In D. and F. R. Ridgway (eds.), *Italy before the Romans: The Iron Age, Orientalizing and Etruscan Periods*, pp. 373–412. London/New York/San Francisco: Academic Press.

Durante, M. 1978. "I dialetti medio-italici." In A. L. Prosdocimi (ed.), *Lingue e dialetti dell'Italia antica*, pp. 789–823. Popoli e civiltà dell'Italia antica VI. Roma: Biblioteca di Storia Patria.

García-Ramon, J. L. 1993. "Zur Morphosyntax der passivischen Infinitive im Oskisch-Umbrisch." In H. Rix (ed.), *Oskisch-Umbrisch. Texte und Grammatik. Arbeitstagung der Indogermanischen Gesellschaft und der Società Italiana di Glottologia vom 25. bis 28. September 1991 in Freiburg*, pp. 106–124. Wiesbaden: Dr. Ludwig Reichert.

Gusmani, R. 1966. "Umbrisch *pihafi* und Verwandtes." *Indogermanische Forschungen* 71:64–80.

———. 1970. "Osco sipus." *Archivio glottologico italiano* 55:145–149.

Jeffers, R. 1973. "Problems with the reconstruction of Proto-Italic." *Journal of Indo-European Studies* 1:330–344.

Jones, D. M. 1950. "The relation of Latin to Osco-Umbrian." *Transactions of the Philological Society*, pp. 60–87.

———. 1962. "Imperative and jussive subjunctive in Umbrian." *Glotta* 40:210–219.

Joseph, B. D. and R. E. Wallace. 1987. "Latin *sum* and Oscan **súm**, *sim*, **esum**." *American Journal of Philology* 108:675–93.

Lejeune, M. 1949. "Sur le traitement osque de *-ā final." *Bulletin de la Société Linguistique de Paris* 45:104–110.

———. 1970. "Phonologie osque et graphie grecque." *Revue des Études Anciennes* 72:271–316.

———. 1975. "Réflexions sur la phonologie du vocalism osque." *Bulletin de la Société Linguistique de Paris* 70:233–251.

Marinetti, A. 1981. "Il sudpiceno come italico (e come 'sabino'?): nota preliminare." *Studi etruschi* 49:113–158.

———. 1985. *Le iscrizioni sudpicene. I: Testi*. Lingue e iscrizioni dell'Italia antica 5. Firenze: Leo S. Olschki.

Meiser, G. 1986. *Lautgeschichte der umbrischen Sprache*. Innsbruck: Institut für Sprachwissenschaft der Universität Innsbruck (IBS 51).

———. 1987. "Pälignisch, Latein und Südpikenisch." *Glotta* 65:104–125.

———. 1993. "Uritalisches Modussyntax: zur Genese des Konjunktiv Imperfekt." In H. Rix (ed.), *Oskisch-Umbrisch. Texte und Grammatik. Arbeitstagung der Indogermanischen Gesellschaft und der Società Italiana di Glottologia vom 25. bis 28. September 1991 in Freiburg*, pp. 167–195. Wiesbaden: Dr. Ludwig Reichert.

Negri, M. 1976. "I perfetti oscoumbri in -f-." *Rendiconti dell'Istituto Lombardo di Scienze e Lettere, classe di lettere e scienze morali e storiche* 110:3–10.

Nussbaum, A. 1973. "*Benuso, couortuso,* and the archetype of Tab. IG. I and VI–VIIa." *Journal of Indo-European Studies* 1:356–369.

_____. 1976. "Umbrian 'pisher." *Glotta* 54:241–253.

Olzscha, K. 1958. "Das umbrische Perfekt auf -*nki*-." *Glotta* 36:300–304.

_____. 1963. "Das f-Perfektum im Oskisch-Umbrischen." *Glotta* 41:290–299.

Poccetti, P. 1979. *Nuovi documenti italici a complemento del Manuale di E. Vetter.* Pisa: Giardini.

Porzio Gernia, M. L. 1970. "Aspetti dell'influsso latino sul lessico e sulla sintassi osca." *Archivio glottologico italiano* 55:94–144.

Poultney, J. W. 1959. *The Bronze Tables of Iguvium.* Baltimore: American Philological Association.

Prosdocimi, A. L. 1978a. "L'Osco." In A. L. Prosdocimi (ed.), *Lingue e dialetti dell'Italia antica,* pp. 825–911. Popoli e civiltà dell'Italia antica VI. Roma: Biblioteca di Storia Patria.

_____. 1978b. "L'Umbro." In A. L. Prosdocimi (ed.), *Lingue e dialetti dell'Italia antica,* pp. 587–787. Popoli e civiltà dell'Italia antica VI. Roma: Biblioteca di Storia Patria.

_____. 1984. *Le tavole iguvine, I.* Firenze: Leo S. Olschki.

Rix, H. 1976a. "Die umbrischen Infinitive auf -fi und die urindogermanische Infinitivendung *-dhiōi.* In A. Morpurgo Davies and W. Meid (eds.), *Studies in Greek, Italic, and Indo-European Linguistics offered to Leonard Palmer,* pp. 319–331. Innsbruck: Institut für Sprachwissenschaft der Universität Innsbruck.

_____. 1976b. "Subjonctif et infinitif dans les complétives de l'ombrien." *Bulletin de la Société Linguistique de Paris* 71:221–220.

_____. 1976c. "Umbrisch **ene...kupifiaia**." *Münchener Studien zur Sprachwissenschaft* 34:151–164.

_____. 1983. "Umbro e Proto-Osco-Umbro." In E. Vineis (ed.), *Le lingue indoeuropee di frammentaria attestazione. Atti del Convegno della Società Italiana di Glottologia e della Indogermanische Gesellschaft, Udine, 22–24 settembre 1981,* pp. 91–107. Pisa: Giardini.

_____. 1985. "Descrizioni di rituali in Etrusco e in Italico. L'Etrusco e le lingue dell'Italia antica." In A. Moreschini (ed.), *Atti del Convegno della Società Italiana di Glottologia, Pisa, 8 e 9 dicembre 1984,* pp. 21–37. Pisa: Giardini.

_____. 1986. "Die Endung des Akkusativ Plural commune im Oskischen." In A. Etter (ed.), *o-o-pe-ro-si, Festschrift für Ernst Risch zum 75. Geburtstag,* pp. 583–597. Berlin/New York: de Gruyter.

_____. 1992a. "La lingua dei Volsci. Testi e parentela." *I Volsci.* Quaderni di archeologia etrusco-italica 20:37–49.

_____. 1992b. "Una firma paleo-umbra." *Archivio glottologico italiano* 77:243–252.

Rix, H. 2002. *Sabellische Texte. Die Texte des Oskischen, Umbrischen und Südpikenishen.* Heidelberg: C. Winter.

Rocca, G. 1996. *Iscrizioni* **umbre** *minori.* Firenze: Olschki.

Schmid, W. 1954. "Anaptyze, Doppelschreibung und Akzent im Oskischen." *Zeitschrift für vergleichende Sprachforschung* 72:30–46.

Untermann, J. 1973. "The Osco-Umbrian preverbs a-, ad-, and an-." *Journal of Indo-European Studies* 1:387–393.

Untermann, J. 2000. *Wörterbuch des Oskisch-Umbrischen.* Heidelberg: Carl Winter.

Wallace, R. E. 1985. "Volscian sistiatiens." *Glotta* 63:93–101.

Vetter, E. 1953. *Handbuch der italischen Dialekte. I. Texte mit Erklärung, Glossen, Wörterverzeichnis.* Heidelberg: Carl Winter.

Von Planta, R. 1892–1897. *Grammatik der oskisch-umbrischen Dialekte* (2 vols.). Strasburg: Trübner.

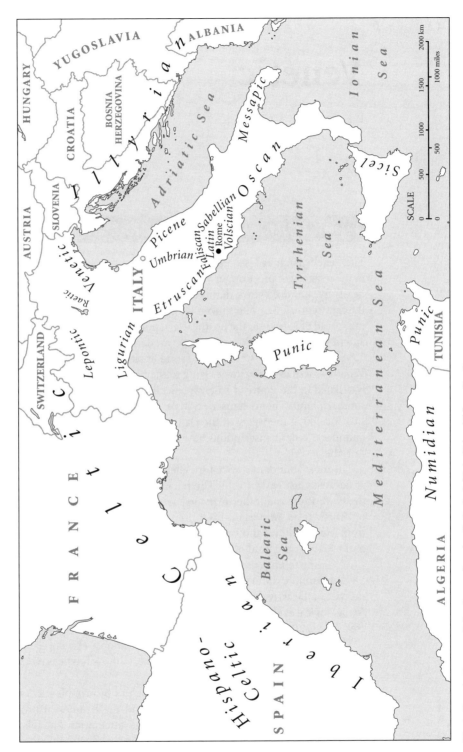

Map 2. The ancient languages of Italy and surrounding regions (for the Greek dialects of Italy and Sicily, see Map 1)

CHAPTER 6

Venetic

REX E. WALLACE

1. HISTORICAL AND CULTURAL CONTEXTS

The Venetic language is attested by approximately 350 inscriptions that have come to light in the territory of pre-Roman Venetia in northeastern Italy. The inscriptions cover a span of nearly five hundred years, dating from the final quarter of the sixth century to the middle of the first century BC. The spoken language did not survive Roman colonial expansion and the spread of Latin into the northeastern portions of the Italian peninsula during the second and first centuries BC. Venetic has no modern descendants.

Venetic inscriptions have been found at sites scattered throughout most of pre-Roman Venetia as well as in territories lying to the north and east. The community of Adria, which is situated in the Po River valley a few kilometers inland from the Adriatic Sea, marks the southern limit. The rock inscriptions at Würmlach and the votive texts from Gurina, both sites located in the valley of the Gail River in Austrian Carinthia, mark the northernmost boundary. Venetic inscriptions have been uncovered as far east as Trieste at the head of the Adriatic.

The most abundant source for Venetic inscriptions is the sanctuary of the goddess Reitia at Baratella just east of Este. The religious sanctuary at Làgole di Calalzo in the valley of the Piave River is another principal source, yielding nearly a quarter of the total number of Venetic texts. Important inscriptions come also from Padova and Vicenza in the south, from Montebelluna and Belluno located along the Piave River, from Oderzo, situated east of the Piave at the head of the Adriatic Sea, and from Gurina in the valley of the Gail River.

According to Livy, the Veneti arrived in northeastern Italy as exiles from the Trojan War. Livy's account of the arrival of the Veneti is fictitious (he was a native of Venetic Padua), but the date of the arrival of Venetic-speaking peoples implied by his tale is likely to be accurate. Archeological evidence points to the development of an independent Iron Age culture in this area shortly after the beginning of the first millennium BC (Fogolari 1988; Ridgway 1979).

The corpus of Venetic inscriptions consists almost exclusively of two epigraphic types, votive inscriptions and funerary inscriptions, with each type accounting for approximately one-half of the total number of inscriptions.

Votive texts were inscribed on objects such as bronze plaques, small replicas of alphabetic tablets, bronze writing implements, and the handles of bronze pails, all of which were commissioned for dedication at religious sanctuaries. The following are typical votive inscriptions (see Fig. 6.1). Inscriptions in the native Venetic alphabet are printed in boldface type; those in the Latin alphabet are in italics. Inscriptions are cited from Pellegrini and Prosdocimi 1967 = PP; Prosdocimi 1978 = P*.

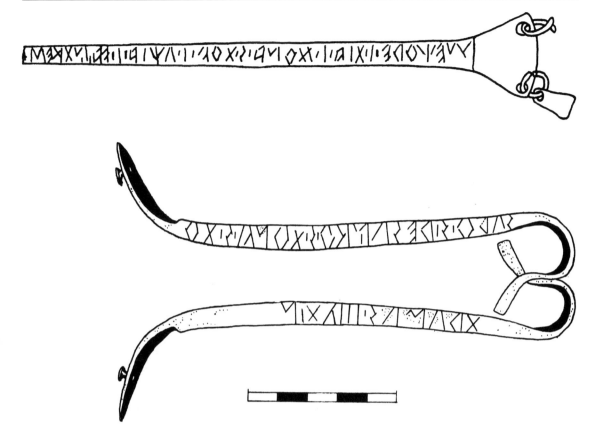

Figure 6.1 Venetic votive inscriptions

A, Este, PP Es 57, bronze stylus

mego re.i.tiia.i. dona.s.to vhugia.i. va.n.tkeni [a]

"me"-acc. sg. "Reitia"-dat. sg. fem. "gave"-3rd sg. past "Fugia"-dat. sg. fem.

"Vantkenia"-nom. sg. fem. "Vantkenia gave me [as a gift]

   to Reitia on behalf of Fugia"

B, Lagole, PP Ca 7, bronze handle

suro.s. resun.k.o.s. tona.s.to trumus.iiatin

"Suros"-nom. sg. masc. "Resunkos"-nom. sg. masc. "gave"-3rd sg. past "Trumusiats"-acc. sg. fem "Suros Resunkos gave [me as a gift]

   to Trumusiats"

The oldest Venetic funerary inscriptions from Este are incised on stone cippi in the shape of obelisks (see Fig. 6.2A). Inscribed funerary stelae with figures sculpted in relief are characteristic of Padova (see Figure 6.2B). Less impressive, but more numerous, are the funerary inscriptions scratched on the bodies or on the covers of terracotta vases that served as repositories for the ashes of the deceased (see Fig. 6.2C).

In addition to the aforementioned epigraphic types, a few inscriptions have been found, less than ten in number, that belong to other epigraphical categories. For example, PP Pa 19 is a manufacturer's advertisement stamped on a large storage container (dolium), **keutini**/*ceutini* "[from the workshop] of Keutinos."

Dating Venetic inscriptions is often problematic because the archeological contexts in which they were discovered were not adequately recorded. In lieu of dating by archeological criteria, most Venetic texts are dated, albeit very roughly, on the basis of a few key

characteristics of the writing system. Venetic texts from Este are divided into four chronological periods based on these orthographic/paleographic features:

(1)   Archaic, *c.* 525–475 BC (no syllabic punctuation)
        Ancient, *c.* 475–300 BC (syllabic punctuation, /h/ = 日, 日)
        Recent, *c.* 300–150 BC (innovative /h/ = ·|·)
        Latino-Venetic, *c.* 150–50 BC (use of Latin alphabet)

Venetic is a member of the Indo-European language family, but its often-mentioned
affiliation with the languages of the Italic branch, in particular with Latin, is difficult to
determine. On the basis of existing evidence the precise position of Venetic within Indo-
European remains an open question (see Beeler 1981; Carruba 1976; Euler 1993; Lejeune
1974:173; Polomé 1966:71–76; Untermann 1980:315–316).

Venetic shows the "centum"-style treatment of the Proto-Indo-European (PIE) dorsal
stops. The Proto-Indo-European palatals and velars merge as velars (Venetic **ke** "and" from
PIE *$\hat{k}e$; Venetic **lo.u.ki** "grove" from PIE *$lowkos$); but there is a distinctive reflex for Proto-
Indo-European labiovelars (Venetic **-kve** "and" from PIE *-k^we).

A third-person singular mediopassive ending in **-r** may also be attested, but the verb forms
that have this suffix appear to be functionally active (transitive) rather than mediopassive,
for example, **tuler donom** "brings/brought (?) a gift [as an offering]."

Several features that are common to the Indo-European languages of the west are found
in Venetic. The Proto-Indo-European laryngeal consonants appear as **a** in Venetic in the
environment between consonants, as in Italic and Celtic: for example, Venetic **vha.g.s.to** "set
up [as an offering]," Latin *facit*, Oscan **fakiiad**, all from the zero-grade of the Proto-Indo-
European root *d^heh_1- with *k- extension (< *$d^h h_1$-k-). Venetic probably also shares with

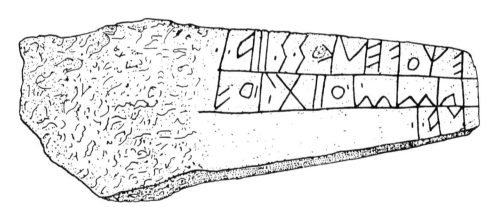

Figure 6.2 Venetic epitaphs
A. Este, PP Es 2, cippus
ego vhu.k.s.siia.i. vo.l.tiio.m.mnina.i.
"I"-nom. sg. "Fugsya"-dat. sg. fem. "Voltiomnina"-dat. sg. fem. "I [belong] to Fugsia Voltiomnina"
B, Padova, PP Pa 2, stele
plede.i. ve.i.gno.i. kara.n.mniio.i. e.kupetari.s. e.go
"Pledes"-dat. sg. masc. "Veignos"-dat. sg. masc. "Karanmnis"-dat. sg. masc.
"funerary monument?"-nom. sg. "I"-nom. sg. "I [am] the *ekupetaris* (funerary monument ?)
    belonging to Pledes Veignos Karanmnis"
C, Este, PP Es 77, terracotta vase
va.n.t.s..a.froi
"Vants"-nom. sg. masc. "Afros"-dat. sg. masc. "Vants, for Afros"

Figure 6.2 (cont.)

Latin and with Celtic an *o*-stem genitive singular ending -ī, for example, **keutini** "[from the workshop] of Keutinos," **lo.u.ki** "of grove," but the diagnostic importance of this isogloss is not securely established (see §4.1.1).

Linguistically, Venetic inscriptions are relatively homogeneous over the whole of the Venetic-speaking world. Very little evidence points to regional dialect differences. There is, however, one phonological isogloss that can be extracted from extant documents, namely the treatment of the nasals **n** and **m** in word-final position.

In prehistoric Venetic, *m and *n merged as **n** in word-final position throughout most of Venetia, for example, **.e.kvo[.]n[.]** "horse" < *ék̂wom. However, in the valley of the Piave River near Cadore the spelling of word-final nasals is in a state of flux. The bilabial **m** appears regularly in word-final position in inscriptions incised in the local writing system, for example, **dono.m.** "gift." However, a few inscriptions written in a system strongly influenced by the one used at Este show **n** in this position, thus, **donon.**. Regardless of how the **m** versus **n** variation is to be explained diachronically (preservation of original **m** with **n** introduced via dialect borrowing or reintroduction of **m** through contact with Latin speakers), this is a phonological feature that serves to set off the region of Cadore from the rest of Venetia during the Recent Venetic period.

2. WRITING SYSTEMS

2.1 The Venetic alphabet

Venetic texts prior to the Latino-Venetic period were written in an alphabetic script that was introduced into southern Venetia from Etruria during the first half of the sixth century BC (Cristofani 1979:388–389; Pandolfini and Prosdocimi 1990:244–289). The source of the Venetic alphabet was a northern Etruscan script of the "reformed" type, namely one that had eliminated the letters *beta, gamma, delta,* and *omicron* from the canonical list of letters forming the teaching alphabet. The fact that the Etruscan alphabet introduced into Venetia lacked these letters forced those responsible for adaptation to use the letters *phi, khi,* and *theta* with a new function, namely as signs for the voiced stops /b/, /g/, and /d/ respectively. At some point during the formative stages, the letter *omicron* was "reborrowed," most likely from a Greek source, and added to the very end of the alphabetic series, thus yielding the earliest form of the native Venetic alphabet, the so-called *alphabet princeps* (see Table 6.1).

Local differences in the spelling of the dental stop phonemes /t/ and /d/ developed during the latter half of the sixth century and the first decades of the fifth century as the *alphabet princeps* spread throughout Venetia. Other communities altered the spelling of the *alphabet princeps* in diverse ways, thus giving rise to the local writing traditions attested by Venetic inscriptions (see Table 6.2).

During the Recent Venetic period (*c.* 300–150 BC) orthographic changes and stylistic developments that altered the shapes of certain letters introduced greater geographical diversity into Venetic orthography.

One interesting diachronic change concerns the spelling of the labiodental phoneme /f/. In the northern Etruscan writing system of the sixth century, /f/ was spelled by

Table 6.1 Venetic *alphabet princeps* (c. 550 BC)	
A	a
Ǝ	e
ꓯ	v
Ӿ	z
ᛒ	h
⊠	d
I	i
Ж	k
ꓶ	l
ᛘ	m
ꓩ	n
ꓶ	p
M	s
ꓷ	r
?	s
T	t
V	u
Φ	b
Ψ	g
O	o
ꓭꓩ	spelling for /f/

Table 6.2 Spelling of Venetic dental stops		
	/t/	/d/
Este, Làgole	✕	⋇
Padova	⊙, ◇	⊤
Vicenza	✕	⊤
Cadore	✕	⋎

means of a digraph **vh** 𐌇𐌚. Venetic inherited and maintained this digraphic spelling in most local writing traditions. However, at Cadore, after the sound /h/ was lost, the digraphic spelling of /f/ was simplified to *heta* 𐌇 = /f/, for example, 𐌚𐌋𐌗𐌗𐌏𐌔 = /futtos/ (PP Ca 15).

Inscriptions from Este dating to the period before 300 BC typically show the letter *heta* in its older shapes 𐌇, 𐌇. Near the end of the fourth century **h** is stylistically streamlined to a form without horizontal strokes ·|·, a form that is all but identical to *iota* with syllabic punctuation (see §2.2). For example, the personal name **vhaba.i.tonia** shows both **.i.** (*iota* with syllabic punctuation) and **h** with precisely the same form ·|·. The motivation for this stylistic change is not clear, but the innovative form of **h** spread rapidly from Este throughout most of Venetia during the first decades of the Recent Venetic period. Interestingly, this innovation failed to gain a foothold at Làgole and at Idria in the Julian Alps. Even more remarkable is the fact that at Idria the letter **h** 𐌇 was used with the same functions that the letter ·|· had in other local writing systems: it represented the second part of *i*-diphthongs and the second part of the digraphic spelling of the sound /f/, for example, **la.i.v.na.i.** = 𐌋𐌇𐌉𐌇𐌅𐌍𐌇𐌋 (PP Is 1).

Venetic inscriptions were written *scriptio continua*, without spaces separating words, though in modern copies of the texts word breaks are generally indicated. The most common direction of writing was sinistrograde, but dextrograde writing was not unusual. A few Venetic inscriptions were written in boustrophedon style ("as the ox plows"), with every other line alternating in direction. The precise layout and arrangement of inscriptions on obelisks, stelae, and bronze plaques depended to some extent on the aesthetic considerations of the sponsor or of the craftsman responsible for the work (see Fig. 6.2a and b).

2.2 Syllabic punctuation

The most striking feature of the Venetic orthography was "syllabic punctuation." This was a form of punctuation (indicated in transliteration by a period) in which all syllable-initial vowels (word-initial vowels and vowels in hiatus), with the usual exception of **i**, and all syllable-final consonants, including the final element of diphthongs, received a mark in the form of a short vertical stroke or, less often, a point, for example, 𐌌, 𐌍. Punctuation was generally placed both in front of and behind the letter, as noted above, but at Làgole inscriptions are found in which punctuation is marked with a single point, usually placed after the letter.

Syllabic punctuation is not found on the earliest Venetic inscriptions and thus must be a secondary development postdating the borrowing of the alphabet from Etruscans. It appears first on Venetic inscriptions from the fifth century and is an obligatory feature of the writing system from this period onward. The probable source of syllabic punctuation is the scribal school affiliated with the religious sanctuary of Apollo in the southern Etruscan city of Veii (Wachter 1986). Syllabic punctuation is used on votive inscriptions at this sanctuary from *c.* 600 to *c.* 500 BC and it is likely that this orthographic feature was introduced into Venetia by

Figure 6.3 Latino-Venetic inscription
Frema..l.vantina..Ktulistoi vesces
"Frema"-nom. sg. fem. "luvantina"-nom. sg. fem. Ktulistoi-dat. sg. masc. "*vesces?*"-nom. sg. fem.(?) "Frema luvantina, for Ktulistos, *vesces?*"

means of contacts between the scribes of the Etruscan sanctuary at Veii and scribes affiliated with Venetic religious communities. One scenario suggests that syllabic punctuation was first adopted by scribes at the sanctuary of Reitia at Este and then, because of this sanctuary's prominence, spread throughout Venetia via other important religious sanctuaries.

2.3 The Latin alphabet

During the final period of the Venetic language, inscriptions ceased to be written in the native Venetic alphabet and were written instead in a Latin alphabet characteristic of the late Roman Republic. These late Venetic inscriptions composed in the Latin script employed the usual features of Republican orthography: dextrograde ductus, punctuation between words, and letter-forms typical of "cursive" Latin orthography (see Fig. 6.3).

3. PHONOLOGY

3.1 Consonants

The inventory of Venetic consonants consisted of sixteen, possibly seventeen, phonemes. There were two sets of stop consonants with four distinctive points of articulation – labial, dental, velar, and labiovelar. The labials, dentals, and velars had a contrast in voicing. The fricatives in the system were voiceless. The nasals, liquids, and semivowels were voiced. Table 6.3 summarizes the Venetic consonant system:

Table 6.3 The consonantal phonemes of Venetic							
	Place of articulation						
Manner of articulation	Bilabial	Labiodental	Dental	Palatal	Velar	Labiovelar	Glottal
Stop							
Voiceless	p		t		k	k^w	
Voiced	b		d		g		
Fricative		f	s				h
Nasal	m		n				
Liquid							
Lateral			l				
Nonlateral			r				
Glide				y		w	

The consonantal phonemes are illustrated by the examples of (2). Here and throughout the remaining sections of this chapter, the following abbreviations are used in glossing examples: ID (personal name); PT (patronymic); DN (name of a god or goddess).

(2) **Venetic consonantal phonemes**

> **per.** ("by, through"?) /p/, **te.r.monio.s.** ("of the boundaries") /t/, **ke** ("and")
> /k/, **.e.kvo[.]n[.]** ("horse") /kʷ/
> **bu.k.ka** ("Bukka" ID) /b/, **de.i.vo.s.** ("god") /d/, **.e.go** ('I') /g/
> **vha.g.s.to** ("he made") /f/, **donasan** ("they gave") /s/, **ho.s.tihavo.s.** ("Hostihavos"
> ID) /h/
> **murtuvoi** ("dead") /m/, **dono.m.** ("gift") /n/
> **lo.u.derobo.s.** ("children") /l/, **re.i.tiia.n.** ("Reitia" DN) /r/
> **iorobo.s.** ("?") /y/, **vo.l.tiiomno.i.** ("Voltiomnos" ID) /w/

In addition to these sounds, the letter *san* M (transcribed by ś) probably represented a phoneme distinct from /s/, most likely a palatal fricative /š/ or a dental affricate /tˢ/ (Lejeune 1974:152–157). Unfortunately, neither the status nor the quality of the sound represented by ś can be securely determined.

3.2 Vowels

There were at least five vowels in the Venetic phonemic inventory, all differing in quality. The writing system did not distinguish vowel quantity but it is possible that Venetic maintained the distinction in length that it inherited from Proto-Indo-European. If so, the Venetic vowel system had a five-way distinction in quality accompanied by a distinction in quantity at each position.

(3) **Venetic vowel phonemes**

> **vivoi** ("living") /ī/, **tribus.iiate.i.** ("Tribusiatis" epithet of Reitia) /i/
> *pater* ("father") /ē/, **te.r.monio.s.** ("of the boundaries") /e/
> **vhratere.i.** ("brother") /ā/, **vha.g.s.to** ("he made") /a/
> **dono.n.** ("gift") /ō/, **hostihavo.s** ("Hostihavos" ID) /o/
> **.u.** ("on behalf of") /ū/, **klutiiari.s.** ("Klutiaris" PT) /u/

The simple vowel phonemes listed above were complemented by six diphthongs:

(4) **de.i.vo.s.** ("gods") /ei/, **te[.]u[.]ta** ("community, nation") /eu/
  bro.i.joko.s. ("Broijokos" ID) /oi/, **vhouge** ("Fougonta" ID) /ou/
  .a..i.su.n. ("god") /ai/, **augar** ("?") /au/

Of these the diphthong **eu** was subject to both geographical and chronological restrictions, found in a handful of words from Làgole and also attested once at Padova. All of the examples date to the Recent Venetic period or later, which makes interference via contact with non-Venetic (Celtic?) speakers a likely culprit (see Lejeune 1974:110–111), though a sound change **ou** > **eu** (geographically restricted?) cannot be ruled out of the picture.

3.3 Diachronic developments

The inventory of vowels remained relatively stable throughout the history of the language. However, in the Latino-Venetic period, particularly in Venetic inscriptions written in the Latin alphabet, there is evidence for sporadic monophthongization: **ou** > *o* /ō/, *Toticinai* (dat. sg. fem.), and **ei** > *e* /ē/, *Trumusiate* (dat. sg. fem.). Since **ou** and **ei** develop to /o/ and /e/ in nonurban Latin inscriptions, it is possible that these changes were contact-induced.

The major features of the diachronic phonology of Venetic vowels are the changes affecting the suffix *-yo-*. In the prehistoric period *$*o$* was lost before word-final *$*s$* in the environment *$*C$-yos*; thus, *$*Cyos$* > *$*Cis$*. Onomastic formations in *$*-yo-$*, for example, **ve.n.noni.s.** (nom. sg. masc.) < *$*-nyos$* and **klutiiari.s.** (nom. sg. masc.) < *$*-ryos$* illustrate this development. In the historic period, the **i** resulting from loss of *$*o$* in this suffix was also lost before word-final -**s**, for example, **.e.ge.s.t.s.** (nom. sg. masc.) < *$*egestis$* < *$*egestyos$*, compare **.e.ge.s.tiio.i.** (dat. sg. masc.). This change is characteristic of the Recent Venetic and Latino-Venetic periods, though it seems to have affected different areas of the Venetic-speaking world at different times and with varying degrees of intensity (Lejeune 1974:111–125).

The inventory of consonantal phonemes was subject to reorganization as a result of several phonological changes. The earliest documented change involved the loss of the glottal fricative **h**. The sound disappeared in all Venetic-speaking areas between *c*. 350 and 300 BC.

By the beginning of the Latino-Venetic period the distinction between **s** and **ś** also seems to have been eliminated. In Venetic inscriptions written in the Latin alphabet, both sounds are represented by means of Latin *sigma*, though it should be kept in mind that the lack of an orthographic distinction here could be attributed to underdifferentiation on the part of the Latin spelling system, Latin having a single sibilant sound in its phonemic inventory.

3.4 Accent

No direct evidence is available to determine the accentual system of Venetic. It is possible to infer, however, from the syncope of short vowels in noninitial syllables, that Venetic had a stress accent system with stress positioned on or near the initial syllable (Lejeune 1974:125; Prosdocimi 1978:318).

4. MORPHOLOGY

Venetic was, like all ancient Indo-European languages, an inflecting language. Inflectional categories were specified by means of suffixes attached to nominal and verbal stems.

4.1 Nominal morphology

The Venetic nominal system, comprising nouns, adjectives, and pronominal forms possesses the inflectional features of case, number, and grammatical gender. There are three genders (masculine, feminine, and neuter) and two numbers (singular and plural). The total sum of cases in the nominal system cannot be securely determined because the extant inscriptions are so few, and because the inscriptions that are attested belong to such restricted epigraphic types. As a result, there are serious gaps in all nominal paradigms. From the evidence at hand, however, it is possible to recognize five cases: nominative, dative, accusative, genitive, and ablative.

4.1.1 Nominal classes

Venetic adjectives and nouns are organized into inflectional classes based on the sound characterizing the stem. There are five vocalic-stem classes: *o*-stems (**ke.l.lo.s.** nom. sg. masc.); *a*-stems (**vhugiia** fem. sg. masc.); *u*-stems (**.a..i.su.n.** "god" acc. sg.); *i*-stems (**trumusijatin** acc. sg. fem.); and *e*-stems (**.e.nogene.s.** nom. sg. masc. vs. **.e.nogene.i.** dat. sg.). The *o*-stems split into subtypes: stems in *-yo-* had the vowel(s) of the nominative singular syncopated, for example, *yo*-stem **.a.kut.s.** (nom. sg. masc.) < ***akutis* < **akutyos*, compare **.a.kutiio.i.** (dat. sg. masc.). Consonant-stems had three inflectional types: stop-stems (**va.n.t.s.** nom. sg. masc.); r-stems (**lemetore**<**.i.**> dat. sg. masc.); and n-stems (**mo.l.do** nom. sg. masc. with loss of final **-n**, compare **pupone.i.** dat. sg. masc.).

(5) Venetic o-, yo-, and a-stems

	o-stems	*yo*-stems	*a*-stems
NOM. SG.	**vo.l.tiiomno.s.**	**.a.kut.s.**	**vhrema**
ACC. SG.	**.e.kvo[.]n[.]**	—	**re.i.tia.n.**
DAT. SG.	**vo.l.tiiomno.i.**	**.a.kutiio.i.**	**vhu.k.s.siia.i.**
ABL. SG.	**leno**	**vo.l.tio**	—
GEN. SG.	**keutini**	—	—
NOM. PL.	—	—	—
ACC. PL.	**de.i.vo.s.**	**te.r.monio.s.**	—
DAT./ABL. PL.	*andeticobos*	—	—

(6) Venetic r-, n-, and stop-stems

	r-stems	*n*-stems	stop-stems
NOM. SG.	**lemetor**	**molo**	**va.n.t.s.**
ACC. SG.	—	—	—
DAT. SG.	**lemetore.i.**	**pupone.i.**	**va.n.te.i.**
ABL. SG.	—	—	—
GEN. SG.	—	—	—
NOM. PL.	**.a.nsores**	—	—
ACC. PL.	—	—	—
DAT./ABL. PL.	—	—	—

The evidence for the *o*-stem genitive singular **-i** rests on a small number of forms, almost all of which are problematic in one way or another (see Untermann 1960, 1980). The least controversial example of this case ending is stamped, along with a version in Latin, on the body of a large storage container (PP Pa 19), namely **keutini**, Latin *ceutini*, "[from the workshop] of Keutinos." But since this inscription belongs to the latest Venetic period, it may not be possible to rule out Latin influence here, even though the name appears to be of local origin (Prosdocimi 1978:303). The only other reasonably good example of this **i**-ending is **lo.u.ki**, which is found on an inscription from Padova (PP Pa 14; Prosdocimi 1979) as the object in a prepositional phrase **.e.n.to.l.lo.u.ki** "within the grove" (/entol/ for **entos* via assimilation ?). Unfortunately, this text and its interpretation are not at all clear and so the analysis of **lo.u.ki** as a genitive must be viewed with some caution.

The publication of an inscription discovered near Oderzo (Prosdocimi 1984 *Od 7) offers a more interesting entry in the discussion of *o*-stem genitives in Venetic. The text, which is cited below, is incised on an oval-shaped funerary stone. Side (b) has a bipartite onomastic phrase in the nominative case; side (a) is inscribed with a single word.

(7) Oderzo, P *Od 7, oval-shaped funerary stone
  (b) **padros . pompeteguaios.**
  (a) **kaialoiso**

Side (a) has been interpreted as the genitive singular of an *o*-stem idionym **kaialo-** (Gambiari and Colonna 1988:138; Lejeune 1989). This interpretation may prove to be correct but it is not without difficulties because the Proto-Indo-European form of the *o*-stem geni-tive singular is *-*osyo*, not **-oiso** (cf. the Latin *o*-stem genitive singulars *ualesiosio popliosio*). A satisfactory explanation for the change in this putative Venetic ending *-*osyo* > **-oiso** has not yet been offered (for suggestions, see Gambiari and Colonna 1988:138; Lejeune 1989:64; Eska 1995:42–43). Interestingly, forms with what appear to be the same ending **-oiso** are attested on Lepontic inscriptions (for which, see Gambiari and Colonna 1988; Eska 1995), so that a final determination concerning Venetic **kaialoiso** must be made with due consid-eration of the Celtic evidence (see now Eska and Wallace 1999).

4.1.2   Pronouns

Venetic inscriptions have thus far yielded only three pronominal forms. Two forms belong to the first-person pronoun: **ego** (nom. sg.) and **mego** (acc. sg.). The third form is a pronominal adjective *sselboisselboi* "himself" (dat. sg.), which is interesting not only because of its double spelling of the sibilant and its reduplicative structure, but also because of its etymological connection to forms found in Gothic *silba* and Old High German *selbselbo*.

4.2   Verbal morphology

Venetic verbs are inflected for tense (present, past), mood (indicative, imperative, and pos-sibly subjunctive), voice (active, mediopassive), person (first, second, third), and number (singular, plural).

4.2.1   Verbal classes

The number of inflectional classes for present tense verbs cannot be determined. The past tense forms **dona.s.to** "gave," **donasan**, presuppose *a*-stem inflection in the present (**dona-**). **atisteit** "sets up" is customarily analyzed as a present tense form built from the zero-grade of the PIE root *steh₂- "stand" + prefix **ati-**, but exactly how and with what morphemes the stem **-stei-** has been formed is not at all clear (Lejeune 1974; Prosdocimi 1978; Untermann 1980).

   Dona.s.to, **donasan**, and **vha.g.s.to** "offered" form their past tense stems by means of a suffix **-s-**, and so may be parsed as **dona-s-to**, **dona-s-an**, **vhag-s-to**. For etymological reasons **doto** "gave" probably also qualifies as a past tense form. In most Proto-Indo-European languages the past tense (aorist) of the verb "give" is a root formation and Venetic **doto** appears to have a similar structure (**do-to**), compare Greek *édōke* (3rd sg. act.), *édoto* (3rd sg. mediopass.) "he gave" and Vedic *adāt* (3rd sg. act.), *adita* (3rd sg. mediopass.) "he gave."

   The tense of the verb forms **tole.r.**, **tule.r.**, **tola.r.** "brought" (?) is more difficult to gauge because the suffixes **-e/a-r** and their functions are not clear. The fact that the verbs **tole.r.**, **tule.r.**, **tola.r.** are used in votive texts, contexts in which past tense forms are preferred to presents by a significantly large margin, points to a past tense formation. However, neither the suffixes **-e/a-**, nor the bare mediopassive ending (?) **-r**, are characteristic of past tense formations.

4.2.2   Verb endings

The inflectional features of person, number, and voice are marked by "personal endings." The ending for active voice is attested by the third singular **-t** (**atisteit**). It is also likely that the endings were split into sets based on tense stems, a set of primary endings for present and a set of secondary endings for past (sg. pres. **-t**, sg. past **-to**, pl. past **-an**).

The third singular past ending **-to** looks like the secondary mediopassive ending found in Greek *-to* and Sanskrit *-ta*. The Venetic ending may share with these a common etymological source, but it is not clear that it has middle force in Venetic, and it seems to correspond functionally to the active third plural ending **-an**.

(8) Venetic verb forms: summary

present	**atisteit** ("sets up")
past	**dona.s.to** ("gave"), **donasan**
	vha.g.s.to ("made"), **doto** ("gave")
	tole.r. (?), **tola.r.**
	tule.r.

4.2.3   Nonfinite verbals

The nonfinite forms of the verb system are even less well represented than the finite forms. There is one possible example of a present participle in **-nt-**, **horvionte**, but its root form, meaning, and case are not readily apparent. Other participle forms in **-nt-** appear in onomastic formations, for example, **vho.u.go.n.ta.i.** (dat. sg. fem.), **vho.u.go.n.te[.i.]** (dat. sg. masc.), both from the root **vhoug-** "flee," compare Greek *p^h eúgont-* "flees," Latin *fugient-* (3rd-*iō*). A Latino-Venetic inscription from the first century (PP Es 113) contains the only possible example in Venetic of a deverbal adjective in *-to-*, *poltos* "distressed."

4.3 Naming constructions

The basic form for personal names, of both women and men, is the individual name or idionym (**va.n.t.s.** masc.; **vhugia** fem.). Additional names were commonly added to the idionym to create two- or three-part onomastic phrases (**suro.s. resu.n.ko.s.** masc.; **va.n.t.s. mo.l.do.n.ke.o. kara.n.mn.s.** masc.).

Some idionyms were originally substantives, and their derivational history is clear. For example, the idionym **vho.u.go.n.t-** is in origin a participial formation in **-ont-** built to the verb root **vhoug-** "flee" (see §4.2.3). **domator-*, an idionym presupposed by the derived name **tomatoriio.i.** dat. sg. masc. (initial **t** by distant assimilation?), is built from the stem **doma-* by means of an agent noun suffix **-tor**, compare Latin *domitor* "tamer" (< PIE **domh₂-* "tame").

Feminine idionyms are generally secondary formations. Most are derived from masculine *o*-stem idionyms by replacing the stem-vowel **-o** with **-a**, for example, masculine **vhugiio-** gives feminine **vhugiia**. Feminines built to consonant-stems generally add **-a** to the final consonant of the masculine stem, thus, masculine **vhougont-** provides feminine **vho.u.go.n.ta**.

The forms making up the second and third members of Venetic personal names are derived from idionyms by means of a limited set of suffixes belonging to either *o*-stem (for masculine) or *a*-stem (for feminine) inflection: for example, **-io: vho.u.go.n.tio.i.** (dat. sg. masc.); **-ia: vhu.k.s.siia.i.** (dat. sg. fem.); **-ko: ossoko.s.** (nom. sg. masc.); **-ka: vho.u.go.n.tiiaka** (nom. sg. fem.); **-(V)nko: .a.r.bo.n.ko.s.** (nom. sg. masc.); **-na: vho.u.go.n.tna** (nom. sg. fem.); and **-kno: bo.i.kno.s.** (nom. sg. masc.).

The familial relationships specified by the second and third members of personal name constructions are the subject of serious disagreement. One of the interpretations currently under debate regards the formations built with **-io/-ia**, **-ko/-ka**, **-kno**, etc. as patronymics

(Lejeune 1974:53–57). Thus, in bipartite constructions the second member of the phrase specified the patronymic of the idionym, for example, **va.n.t.s. mo.l.donke.o.** "Vants, (son) of Moldo," while in tripartite constructions the third member referred to the grandfather of the idionym, for example, **ka.n.te.s. vo.t.te.i.iio.s. a.kut.s.** "Kantes, (son) of Vottos, (the son) of Akutos" (for a dissenting view, see Untermann 1980).

Feminine constructions having derived forms in **-na** as the second or third member indicate a different type of relationship. The **na**-suffix is specialized to designate the gamonymic (Lejeune 1974:60–63). Thus, in the phrase **ne.r.ka lemeto.r.na**, the second member specifies the "wife of Lemetor." Three-member constructions, such as **vhugiia.i. a.n.detina.i. vhuginiia.i.**, indicate both gamonymic and patronymic, thus "Fugia, (wife) of Andetos, (daughter) of Fugs."

4.4 Compounds

Several nominal compounds are attested in the Venetic onomastic system. There are native formations such as **ho.s.ti-havo.s.**, **volti-genei**, **vo.l.to-pariko.s.**, and **eno-kleves**, as well as formations of Celtic origin, for example **ve.r.ko.n.darna** < *Wer-kon-daros*. Outside of the anthroponymic formations, however, the inscriptions give us only a single example of a nominal compound, **.ekvopetari[.]s.** plus variants **.e.kupetari.s.**, **.e.p.petari.s.**, *ecupetaris*, and *equpetars*.

This compound undoubtedly refers to a funerary monument of some type, perhaps for members of an equestrian social class, suggested, of course, by the fact that the first element is the stem **.ekvo-** "horse." Nevertheless, this compound continues to generate considerable discussion, not only because the second constituent **pet-** has yet to be given a convincing etymological explanation, but also because it is not clear how the variants **.ekvo-, e.p.-,** etc. are to be connected to one another, if at all (see Brewer 1985; Lejeune 1971a; Prosdocimi 1978:297–301; Pulgram 1976).

5. SYNTAX

5.1 Case usage

In typical Indo-European fashion, the role of Venetic noun phrases (NPs) is denoted by the inflectional feature case. The complements of the verb are marked by nominative case for subject, accusative case for direct object, and dative case for indirect object and for beneficiary. The genitive case is used to indicate possession. Accusative and ablative serve as the cases to mark NPs as the objects of prepositions, the case of the object being determined by the preposition: **per** "by, through (?)" and **.u.** "on behalf of" governed the accusative case; **.o.p** "because of (?)" took the ablative.

5.2 Word order

Nothing definitive can be said about the underlying order of the major constituents (subject, direct object, verb) in a Venetic sentence. Only votive inscriptions have finite verb forms, and the order of the constituents attested for this sentential type may be the result of syntactic processes such as topicalization.

At Este, *iscrizioni parlanti* ("speaking inscriptions") are found with SVO (Subject–Verb–Object), OVS, and OSV orders:

(9)   Este, PP Es 48, stylus
      SVO: **vhu.g.siia vo.l.tiio.n.mnin.(a) dona.s.to r(e).i.tiia.i. mego**
      "Fugsia"-NOM. SG. FEM. "Voltionmnina"-NOM. SG. FEM. "give"-3RD SG. PAST
         "Reitia"-DAT. SG. FEM. "me"-1ST PRO. ACC. SG.
      "Fugsia, wife of Voltiomnos, gave me to Reitia"

      Este, PP Es 54, stylus
      OSV: **mego (v)hugia dona.s.to re.i.tia.i.**
      "me"-1ST PRO. ACC. SG. "Fugia"-NOM. SG. FEM. "give"-3RD SG. PAST "Reitia"-DAT.
         SG. FEM.
      "Fugia gave me to Reitia"

      Este, PP Es 53, stylus
      OVS: **mego dona.s.to re.i.tiia.i. ner(.)ka lemeto.r.na**
      "me"-1ST PRO. ACC. SG. "give"-3RD SG. PAST "Reitia"-DAT. SG. FEM. "Ner(i)ka"-NOM.
         SG. FEM. "Lemetorna"-NOM. SG. FEM.
      "Nerka, wife of Lemetor, gave me to Reitia"

Numerically, OVS is the most prominent, followed by OSV. These orders could be the result of the movement of the direct object pronoun **mego** "me" into sentence-initial position, which is a common position for the first-person pronoun in votive inscriptions of this type in all of the languages of ancient Italy. As a result, it is quite possible that the basic order at Este was SVO, which has the smallest actual number of attestations, and that the various permutations of this basic order are the result of syntactic movement rules: SVO becomes OSV by fronting the direct object, OVS by subject–verb inversion. This would bring the basic order of the major constituents at Este in line with what is attested for votive inscriptions at Lagolè (Berman 1973).

The order of elements within a noun phrase depends upon the type of modifier present. As far as can be determined, adjectives are generally positioned before the head noun (**te.r.mon.io.s. de.i.vo.s.** "gods of the boundary"?). In onomastic noun phrases, however, the patronymic and gamonymic modifiers followed the idionym (**vhugiia.i. a.n.detina.i. vhuginiia.i.** "Fugia, (wife) of Andetos, (daughter) of Fugs").

5.3 Agreement

The Venetic verb is marked with an inflectional ending which agrees with its subject in number and person (third person unless a pronominal non-third-person subject is used); thus, below, the verb **doto** takes the third singular ending **-to**, having the singular subject **vhrema.i.s.tina**.

(10) Este, PP Es 41, stylus
      vhrema.i.s.tina doto re.i.tiia.i.
         "Fremaistina"-NOM. SG. FEM. "gave"-3RD SG. PAST ACT. "Reitia"-DAT. SG. FEM.
         (a divinity)
      "Fremaistina gave [me] to Reitia"

Agreement is also found in Venetic noun phrases. An attributive adjective agrees with its head noun in case, number, and gender, for example, **te.r.mon.io.s. de.i.vo.s.** (masc. acc. pl.) "gods of the boundary" (?). In onomastic phrases the modifiers of the idionym similarly show agreement (see §5.2).

5.4 Coordination

Unfortunately, Venetic inscriptions do not attest any examples of sentential subordination. There is, however, some evidence for coordination. Coordinate noun phrases and coordinate sentences were linked by one of two conjunctions, **kve** or **ke**. The two forms appear to be functionally similar but differ in terms of their syntax. **kve** is judged to be enclitic on etymological grounds (**vivoi oliialekve murtuvoi** "for [him] living and **oliiale** (?) dead"); **ke** may have been proclitic (**.<a>.i.mo.i. ke lo.u.derobo.s.** "for Aimos and [her] children").

6. LEXICON

Apart from personal names and theonyms the number of vocabulary items in the known Venetic lexicon amounts to approximately fifty words. So few lexemes cannot provide an adequate picture of the lexicon; this condition is only exacerbated by the fact that the vocabulary is drawn basically from two text-types.

The "core" element of the Venetic lexicon consists of those words which have etymological connections to lexemes in other Indo-European languages. The words listed in (11) have solid Indo-European comparanda.

(11)   Venetic words with cognates in Indo-European

> **dono.m./dono.n.** ACC. SG. NEUT. "gift," cf. Latin *dōnum*, Oscan **dúnum** "gift"
> **doto** "gave," cf. Greek *dídōsi* "gives," *édoto* "gave"
> **dona.s.to** "presented (as a gift)," Latin *dōnat* "presents (as a gift)," Oscan **duunated** "presented (as a gift)"
> **vha.g.s.to** "offered," cf. Latin *facit* "makes," Oscan **fakiiad** "makes"
> **<v>hratere.i.** DAT. SG. MASC. "brother," cf. Latin *frāter* "brother," Umbrian **frater** NOM. PL. MASC. "brothers," Greek *pʰrétēr* "brotherhood"
> **hostei** DAT. SG. MASC. "host," cf. Latin *hostis* "guest"
> **vivoi** DAT. SG. MASC. "living," cf. Latin *uīuus* "alive," Oscan **bivus** NOM. PL. MASC. "alive"
> **murtuvoi** DAT. SG. MASC. "dead," cf. Latin *mortuus* "dead"
> **kve** "and," cf. Latin *que* "and," Greek *te* "and"

In addition to vocabulary with sound Indo-European pedigrees, there is a handful of words with probable etymological connections within Indo-European. For example, the root **vol-**, found in the ablative form **vo.l.tiio**, is most likely connected with the Proto-Indo-European root **wel-* "wish, desire." **vo.l.tiio** is probably an adjective built from a *nomen actionis* **wl̥-ti-* (Lejeune 1974:88). Similarly, the root **mag-**, which forms the base of the Venetic noun **magetlon**, **mag-** plus instrumental suffix **-(e)tlo-**, referring in all likelihood to an offering of some type, may be etymologically connected with the root attested in Latin *mactus* "honored, adored."

Venetic also has a small cache of vocabulary items that are without Indo-European etymologies. An interesting example is the nominal form *vesces* (nom. sg.), **ve.s.ke.ś.** (nom. sg.), **ve.s.ketei** (dat. sg.), which is used as either an attribute of, or an appositional noun phrase referring to, masculine and feminine names. The meaning of this form remains unclear, at least in part because it lacks an etymological connection within Indo-European (for an attempt, see Lejeune 1973; contra, see Untermann 1980). The Venetic noun **.a..i.su.n.** (acc. sg.), **.a..i.su.s.** (acc. pl.), which is assigned the meaning "god(s)" on the basis of comparison with forms found in the Sabellian languages, e.g., Paelignian *aisis* "gods," Marrucinian *aisos*, etc., could be a western Indo-European formation. However, it is worth noting that the stem **ais-** is also found in Etruscan (*ais*, *eis* "god") and may well have been borrowed into Venetic and Sabellian through contact with Etruscan speakers.

During the second and first centuries BC, Roman presence in territories beyond the Po Valley intensified. One result of contact between Romans and the Veneti was the introduction of Latin loanwords into Venetic. The best examples are *miles* "soldier" and **liber.tos.** "freedman." It is also worth mentioning that the kinship term *filia* "daughter," which is often assumed to be a native Venetic word (Lejeune 1967), may actually be a loan from Latin. The inscription on which this word appears is incised in a Latin alphabet and can thus be dated to *c.* 150–50 BC. Admittedly, the status of this word in the Venetic lexicon cannot be securely determined on the basis of this inscription alone, but the fact that a loan from Latin cannot be ruled out serves as a reminder that the shift from Venetic to Latin as the language of choice in this area was well underway at this time.

Bibliography

Beeler, M. S. 1981. "Venetic revisited." In Y. Arbeitman and A. Bomhard (eds.), *Bono Homini Donum. Essays in Historical Linguistics in Memory of J. Alexander Kerns*, part I, pp. 65–71. Amsterdam: John Benjamins.

Berman, H. 1973. "Word order in Venetic." *Journal of Indo-European Studies* 1:252–256.

Brewer, W. A. 1985. "Notes on Venetic *.e.kvopetari.s.*" *Zeitschrift für vergleichende Sprachforschung* 98:54–58.

Carruba, O. 1976. "La posizione linguistica del venetico." *Athenaeum, fascicolo speciale*, pp. 110–121.

Cristofani, M. 1979. "Recent advances in Etruscan epigraphy and language." In D. and F. R. Ridgway (eds.), *Italy before the Romans: The Iron Age, Orientalizing and Etruscan Periods*, pp. 373–412. London/New York/San Francisco: Academic Press.

Eska, J. F. 1995. "Observations on the thematic genitive singular in Lepontic and Hispano-Celtic." In J. R. Eska, R. Geraint Gruffydd, and N. Jacobs (eds.), *Hispano-Gallo-Brittonica. Essays in Honour of Professor D. Ellis Evans on the Occasion of his Sixty-fifth Birthday*, pp. 33–46. Cardiff: University of Wales Press.

Eska, J. F. and R. Wallace. 1999. "The linguistic milieu of *Oderzo 7." *Historische Sprachforschung* 109:122–136.

Euler, W. 1993. "Oskisch-Umbrisch, Venetisch und Lateinisch." In H. Rix (ed.), *Oskisch-Umbrisch. Texte und Grammatik. Arbeitstagung der Indogermanischen Gesellschaft und der Società Italiana di Glottologia vom 25. bis 28. September 1991 in Freiburg*, pp. 96–105. Wiesbaden: Dr. Ludwig Reichert.

Fogolari, G. 1988. "La cultura." In G. Fogolari and A. L. Prosdocimi (eds.), *I Veneti antichi. Lingua e cultura*, pp. 15–195. Padova: Studio Editoriale Programma.

Gambiari, F. G. and G. Colonna. 1988. "Il bicchiere con iscrizione arcaica da Castelletto ticino e l'adozione della scrittura nell'Italia nord-occidentale." *Studi etruschi* 54:119–164.

Lejeune, M. 1966. "Le verbe vénète." *Bulletin de la Société Linguistique de Paris* 61:191–208.

———. 1967. "Fils et Filles dans les langues de l'Italie ancienne." *Bulletin de la Société de Linguistique de Paris* 62:67–86.

———. 1971a. "Problèmes de philologie vénète. XIV: Les épitaphes *ekupetaris*." *Revue Philologie* 45:7–26.

———. 1971b. "Sur l'enseignement de l'écriture et de l'orthographe vénète à Este." *Bulletin de la Société Linguistique de Paris* 66:267–298.

———. 1973. "The Venetic vocabulary of relations between persons." *Journal of Indo-European Studies* 1:345–351.

———. 1974. *Manuel de la langue vénète*. Heidelberg: Carl Winter.

———. 1989. "Notes de linguistique italique. XXXVIII. Notes sur la dédicace de Satricum; XXXIX. Génitifs en -osio et génitifs en -i." *Revue des Études Latines* 67:60–77.

Pandolfini, M. and A. L. Prosdocimi. 1990. *Alfabetari e insegnamento della scrittura in Etruria e nell'Italia antica*. Biblioteca di "Studi etruschi" 20. Firenze: Leo S. Olschki.

Pellegrini, G. B. and A. L. Prosdocimi. 1967. *La lingua venetica I. Le iscrizioni*. Firenze: Istituto di glottologia dell'Università di Padova – Circolo Linguistico Fiorentino.

Polomé, E. 1966. "The position of Illyrian and Venetic." In H. Birnbaum and J. Puhvel (eds.), *Ancient Indo-European Dialects*, pp. 59–76. Berkeley/Los Angeles: University of California Press.

Prosdocimi, A. L. 1972. "Venetico." *Studi etruschi* 40:193–245.

———. 1978. "Il venetico." In A. L. Prosdocimi (ed.), *Lingue e dialetti dell'Italia antica*, pp. 257–389. Popoli e civiltà dell'Italia antica VI. Roma: Biblioteca di Storia Patria.

———. 1979. "Venetico. L'altra faccia di Pa 14, il senso dell'iscrizione e un nuovo verbo." In *Studi in onore di Carlo Battisti*, pp. 279–307. Firenze: Leo S. Olschki.

———. 1984. "Una nuova iscrizione venetica da Oderzo (*Od 7) con elementi celtici." In *Studi di antichità in onore di Guglielmo Maetzke, volume secondo*, pp. 423–442. Roma: Giorgio Bretschneider.

———. 1988. "La lingua". In G. Fogolari and A. L. Prosdocimi (eds.), *I Veneti antichi. Lingua e cultura*, pp. 225–420. Padova: Studio Editoriale Programma.

Pulgram, E. 1976. "Venetic. *e.kupethari. s.*" In A. Morpurgo Davies and W. Meid (eds.), *Studies in Greek, Italic, and Indo-European Linguistics: Offered to Leonard R. Palmer on the Occasion of his Seventieth Birthday, June 5, 1976*, pp. 299–304. Innsbruck: Institut für Sprachwissenschaft der Universität Innsbruck.

Ridgway, F. R. 1979. "The Este and Golasecca cultures: a chronological guide." In D. and F. R. Ridgway (eds.), *Italy before the Romans: The Iron Age, Orientalizing and Etruscan Periods*, pp. 419–487. London/New York/San Francisco: Academic Press.

Schmidt, K. H. 1963. "Venetische Medialformen." *Indogermanische Forschungen* 68:160–169.

Untermann, J. 1960 "Zur venetischen Nominalflexion." *Indogermanische Forschungen* 65:140–160.

———. 1961a. *Die venetischen Personennamen*. Wiesbaden: Otto Harrassowitz.

———. 1961b. "Zur venetischen Nominalflexion." *Indogermanische Forschungen* 66:105–124.

———. 1980. "Die venetische Sprache." *Glotta* 58:281–317.

Wachter, R. 1986. "Die etruskische und venetische Silbenpunktierung." *Museum Helveticum* 43:111–126.

CHAPTER 7

Etruscan

HELMUT RIX

1. HISTORICAL AND CULTURAL CONTEXTS

Etruscan, the language of the Etruscans, is attested between 700 BC and AD 50 in the area of northwest central Italy between the Arno, the Tiber, and the Tyrrhenian Sea. A few Etruscan texts come from other areas of Italy (especially from Campania and Emilia) and from Corsica, and isolated examples are known from Provence, Tunisia, Greece, and Egypt.

The most important source of Etruscan is the *c.* nine thousand inscriptions. The majority are funerary inscriptions, which often consist of no more than the name of the deceased. The second largest group is formed by the likewise mostly short texts on objects of daily life which indicate the owner or the manufacturer, or the object as a present or a dedication. Readily comprehensible are the labels inscribed next to figures in pictorial representations. The longer inscriptions are legal or ritual in character. The quasi-bilingual from Pyrgi (with a parallel text in Phoenician) reports the dedication of a cult building; the Perugine cippus records a contract about a piece of land; the clay tablet of Capua (which, with 300 preserved words, is the longest Etruscan inscription) preserves a ritual calendar; and the recently published (Agostiniani and Nicosia 2000) bronze tablet of Cortona seems to contain, as I think, a record of the treatment of tenant farmers after the sale of an estate rented by them. A calendar of rituals is also described in the one noninscriptional, and at the same time longest (1,500 words), Etruscan text – a linen book, which was torn up and used as wrappings on a mummy in Egypt and of which a good half is preserved (often called the Zagreb mummy after its present location). Interesting secondary sources for the lexicon and for textual interpretation are glosses (meanings of Etruscan words given by Latin and Greek authors; e.g., *aesar . . . etrusca lingua deus*, ["*aesar . . .* the Etruscan word for god"] Suetonius, *The Life of Augustus* 97) and loanwords in Latin (*satelles* "body guard" < Etr. *zat[i]laθ* "striker").

The prehistory of the Etruscans has been disputed for two thousand years. Historians of the fifth century BC (Herodotus 1.94, Hellanicus in Dionysius of Halicarnassus 1.28.3–4) had claimed immigration from the Aegean; the orator Dionysius of Halicarnassus (first century BC) argued from the lack of related languages (but see below) for the autochthony of the Etruscans in Italy. Until now archeological arguments (Pallottino 1988:77–101) have been as poorly conclusive as linguistic.

In the course of their history (seventh to first centuries BC) the Etruscans never formed a centrally governed state. Rather they lived in separate city-states, which were first ruled by monarchs and which later, from around 500 BC, became oligarchies, and were tied to each other through common cult festivals. The Etruscans who possessed citizenship, the Ῥάσεννα (Dionysius of Halicarnassus 1.30.3; < Etr. *rasna* "army, people"; see Rix 1984b), clearly made up only a part of the population. Beside these there was a rural population (Πενέσται, Dionysius of Halicarnassus 9.5.4), with personal freedom and economic independence, but without political rights and at least in part of Italic origin. Only in the third to second centuries was this section of the population incorporated into the Etruscan citizenry (Rix 1963:372–376).

Until the beginning of the fifth century BC the Etruscans were the dominating power in upper and central Italy. The defeat at Cumae by the Greeks in 474 BC marks the beginning of the Etruscan decline, which was accelerated by the invasion of the Celts in the fourth century BC. Politically the Etruscans became dependent allies of Rome at the beginning of the third century and two hundred years later Roman citizens. Shortly after the turn of the millennium, Etruscan ceased to be written; around which time the language would also have ceased to be spoken.

The syncope of unaccented internal vowels (see §3.5.2.4) – which around 480 BC changed the structure of many words and may well be connected with the social and political changes of the time – marks the break between *Archaic Etruscan* and *Late Etruscan*. Since the third century, and intensely in the first century, Latin influence is perceptible (orthography, morphology); incorrect texts appear. In spite of changes in the development of the sound system (both some regional changes [see §3.5.1] and fewer affecting the whole of the Etruscan area [see §3.5.2]), there is no evidence that distinct Etruscan dialects developed. This correlates with the political structure of Etruria and speaks for a relatively late spread of the language from a limited area.

To the same language family as Etruscan there belong only two poorly attested languages: Lemnian in the Northeast of the Aegean (sixth century BC; Agostiniani 1986) and Rhaetic in the Alps (fifth to first centuries BC; Schumacher 1992:246–248; Rix 1998). Lemnian and Rhaetic are so close to Etruscan that Etruscan can be used to understand them. The date of the common source language, *Proto-Tyrsenic*, can probably be fixed to the last quarter of the second millennium BC. The location of its homeland is disputed, however; possibilities include: (i) the northern Aegean, whence Proto-Etruscan and Proto-Rhaetic speakers would have come in the course of the Aegean migration westwards at the end of the second millennium (similarly Herodotus [1.94] identifies Lydia as the Etruscan homeland); (ii) central Italy, from which Proto-Lemnian speakers would have migrated eastwards and Proto-Rhaetic speakers northwards. A decisive judgment is not currently possible.

The lack of well-known related languages limits the comparative method's access to Etruscan to the area of loanwords (see §6). Moreover, in reading an Etruscan text, one must first attempt to determine a text's message from its context, and then to correlate the elements of content in the message with the structural elements in the text. Hereby glosses, loanwords, and above all texts in the better-known languages of the same cultural area (Latin, Greek, and so on) can help. From the results, a grammar and a lexicon can be constructed tentatively; these serve to test hypotheses and require continual amendment.

In this way a significant number of elements and rules have been identified more or less securely for the grammar and lexicon of Etruscan, and the meaning of a considerable number of texts and text fragments has been made clear. We are, of course, still far from a complete understanding of the Etruscan language, so that much of what is presented below still needs to be stated more precisely, amended, and corrected.

Table 7.1 The Etruscan alphabet of archaic inscriptions			
Character	Transcription	Character	Transcription
A	a	↑	p
Ɔ	c	M	σ
∃	e	Ọ	q
٦	v	٩	r
I	z	ξ	s
⊟	h	T	t
⊗	θ	Y	u
I	i	X	ś
Ͷ	k	Φ	Φ
ل	l	Ψ	X
ᛉ	m	8	f
И	n		

2. WRITING SYSTEMS

The Etruscan writing system is an alphabet, which was created at the end of the eighth century BC, in several local variants, from an alphabet of West Greek origin; it was taught in scribal schools and is attested in inscriptions (see Table 7.1). The West Greek alphabet contained twenty-two letters derived from Phoenician characters plus four additional signs of Greek origin. This form of the Greek alphabet used X for the sequence /k/ + /s/ and Ψ for /kʰ/. A few letters, for which Etruscan had no use, were not used in texts ("lettres mortes"): ß, ▷, ○ and Phoenician *samekh* (∓) = East Greek ∓).

The southern variant of the "working" alphabet used three different letters for the three phonetic variants of /k/: (i) *q* (Ọ; Greek *koppa*) before following /u/; (ii) *k* (Ͷ; Greek *kappa*) before /a/; and (iii) *c* (Ɔ; Greek *gamma*) before /i/ or /e/. This distribution, which continued and generalized an early Greek practice (*koppa* before or after /u/), was possible because Etruscan did not have voiced obstruents and so had no other use for Greek *gamma* (spelling /g/ in Greek). Of the two sibilant phonemes (see §3.1.1), the southern Etruscan script chiefly represents alveolar /s/ with a three-stroke *sigma* (ξ) (in the far south X [= East Greek ∓] is also used) and the less common palato-alveolar /š/ with Greek *san* (M = Phoenician *ṣade*; details in Cristofani 1972:469–473; see also Woodard 1997:161–188).

In the northern writing area of Etruria /k/ is at first written simply as *k*. *Sigma* and *san* were used in a way quite the reverse of that in the south – *sigma* represents palato-alveolar /š/, *san* represents alveolar /s/. Since in the north, alveolar /s/ before consonants had developed prehistorically to palato-alveolar /š/, this reversal may have arisen by the creator of the northern alphabetic variants beginning with words which he himself pronounced with /š/ but which in his southern model he found written with *sigma* (for instance *spura* "community"; Rix 1998). In the north in the later period, alveolar-/s/ was occasionally written with *sigma* as a result of Latin influence. Otherwise the north–south opposition with regard to the writing of the sibilants was maintained up to the end of the Etruscan writing tradition.

In contrast to traditional transliteration based on graphemes, sibilant signs are herein transcribed phonemically (as in Rix and Meiser 1991): /s/ as *s*, if *sigma* is written, and as *ś*, if *san* is written; and /š/ with σ, if *san*, and as ό, if *sigma* is written; likewise northern /s/ (which in certain contexts became [š]) is *phonemically* transcribed with *s*.

By 300 BC the inventory of the Etruscan alphabets had decreased significantly. In the sixth century the south gave up X, *q*, and *k*. In the north, in the fourth century, *c* won out for representing /k/, as it also did in the northeast by the middle of the third century. By around 250 BC only nineteen of the twenty-six letters of the "school" or teaching alphabet survived uniformly throughout Etruria.

Beside this loss of signs, there was only one addition to the alphabet. The labiodental fricative /f/ was initially represented by the grapheme cluster *vh* (Greek FH) or *hv* (HF) (out of which Latin F was simplified). Towards 600 BC in the north, where there are no local attestations of *vh*/*hv*, there occurs a sign 8 for *f* (Vn 1.1), which from around 500 BC was in general use in the south too. The origin of this sign, which is also used in sixth- to fourth-century Lydian, has not found a satisfactory explanation; the oldest attestation comes from a Sabellic inscription that dates from the end of the seventh century (Poggio Sommavilla; Rix 1996).

The oldest and latest sequences of the alphabet are contrasted in (1):

(1) *Archaic school alphabet:* a b c d e v z h θ i k l m n š o p σ q r s t u φ š χ
    Late "working" alphabet: a   c   e v z h θ i   l m n   p σ   r s t u φ   χ f

Note that in the northeast in the fourth to third centuries BC, instead of M for /m/ a simpler sign was used that looks like the numeral character for "5" Λ; it was certainly chosen, because *maχ*, the word for "5," begins with /m/.

Of the early archaic texts some are written from left to right and some from right to left. Around 600 BC the direction from right to left became standard and was only reversed occasionally in the first century under Latin influence.

Most archaic texts employ *scriptio continua*; only towards 500 BC does word division become more common. This was normally achieved by the use of dots (one dot or two to three dots in a vertical arrangement); spaces alone occur infrequently. The syllabic punctuation used from 600 to 470 BC in the south, in which letters for vowels at the beginning of a syllable and for consonants at the end of a syllable are furnished with dots, is clearly a school rule borrowed from a syllabic writing system (see Rix 1968) and has limited functional value (see Wachter 1986).

The Etruscan numeral characters have the same shape as the Roman ones derived from them: I "1"; X "10"; ∧ (Roman V) "5"; ↑ (Roman L) "50"; and Ӿ/⊕ (Roman C) "100". The principle of "subtraction numerals" is also known from Latin: for example, *XIX* "19," to which Etruscan *θun-em zaθrum-s* "-1 20" corresponds. The numeral *X* is at one and the same time a symbol for the outstretched fingers of two hands and a letter (*š*) for the initial sound of Etruscan *sar* "10." In the latter it is possible to see an echo of the acrophonic numeral system of Greek (Π for πέντε "5" and so on). The system as a whole, however, is autonomous.

3. PHONOLOGY

Texts and forms cited in the following discussions can be found via the index in Rix and Meiser 1991. A meaning given in brackets (*zusle* [sacrificial animal]) indicates the semantic class of a lexeme, but this cannot be defined further.

Statements about Etruscan phonetics and phonology are based on the sound values of Etruscan letters in other languages: Greek, Phoenician (the source of Etruscan letters); and Latin, Sabellic, Venetic (for which, conversely, Etruscan letters are the source). Amendments and corrections are supplied by the spelling and spelling variations of Etruscan words; in addition, typology is sometimes helpful. In a poorly accessible, small-corpus language such as Etruscan, however, many questions, especially concerning phonetics, cannot be answered or at least not explicitly so.

In the following discussion, the Archaic Period of the seventh to sixth centuries BC is described first; where appropriate, phenomena first attested in the Late Period, and occasionally prehistoric phenomena, will be included. Subsequently, general changes in the transition to and within the Late Period are described. Context-sensitive developments of little consequence are only treated (and then on an ad hoc basis) where they have relevance for morphology.

3.1 Consonants

3.1.1 Obstruents

The obstruents of Etruscan are phonemically voiceless. In word-initial position they were realised as fortes ([+ tense]) and internally as lenes ([− tense, −/+ son]). Latin transcriptions with *p, t, c, f* at the beginning of a word and *b, d, g* internally lead to this reconstruction (*Pabassa, Tidi, Pergomsna, Fraunal, Noborsinia* for *Papaθa, Titi, Percumsna, Fraucnal, Nufrznei* [personal names]).

The *communis opinio* classifies the Etruscan obstruent phonemes essentially on the basis of the sound values of the corresponding Greek characters:

(2)

	Graphemes			*Phonemes*		
Voiceless stops	<p>	<t>	<c/k/q>	/p/	/t/	/k/
Voiceless aspirated stops	<φ>	<θ>	<χ>	/pʰ/	/tʰ/	/kʰ/
Fricatives	<f>	<s><(ś)>	<σ><(ǵ)>	/f/	/s/	/š/

This model (2) leaves unconsidered <h> for the aspirate /h/ and <z> for the affricate /tˢ/ (which is clarified by spellings such as *rutzs*). Nor does it account for the spelling variants <Ki>/<K> and the complementary distribution of <h> (word-initially) and <χ> (word-internally and word-finally).

The alternative model (3) overcomes these shortcomings, but suffers from meager typological support (see Rix 1984a; Boisson 1991):

(3)

	Graphemes			*Phonemes*		
Unmarked stops	<p>	<t>	<c/k/q>	/p/	/t/	/k/
Fricatives	<f>	<θ><s>	<σ> <χ/h>	/f/	/θ//s/	/š/ /x/
Palatalized stops	<φ>	<θ>	<z>	/pʸ/	/tʸ/	/tˢ/(<*/kʸ/)

The assumption of palatalized rather than aspirated stops allows the morphologically inexplicable alternation *Larθia* : *Larθa* (Late Etruscan *Larθial* : *Larθal*) in the genitive of the praenomen *Larθ* to be understood as orthographic variation. And under the simple assumption of a (prehistoric) development **/kʸ/ > /tˢ/*, this affricate then fits into the system pattern. The phonetic similarity of aspirated and palatalized sounds makes the use of Greek aspirated stop symbols for palatalized stops understandable.

Beside the undisputed fricatives /f/ (labiodental), /s/ (alveolar) and /š/ (palato-alveolar; spelling variants *huśiur* : *huθur*, orthographic *Larθaliσa* for [-alša]), two further fricatives are herein identified: a velar /x/ and an interdental /θ/, written <χ> and <θ>. The fricatival nature of /x/ is suggested by the word-initial variant [h]; and by the palatalization /xwa/ > [jwa] (<va>) of the plural suffix -χva (see §4.2.3.2) following a palatal. Evidence may also be provided by the spelling <χσ> in loanwords which contained [k⁽ʰ⁾s] originally (Greek

Ἀλέξανδρος > *Aliχsantre,* Proto-Italic *louksnā > Umbrian *lōxsnā > Etruscan *lusχnei* "moon"; Meiser 1986:170f.). There are two arguments for the letter θ also representing a fricative: (i) the letter occurs too frequently to be only the spelling of a palatalized stop (<φ> for [pʸ] and <z> for /tˢ/ < */kʸ/ are much less common); and (ii) the fricative dissimilation /xʷa/ > /kʷa/ following /s/ in the plural ending (§4.2.3.2). That two phonemes can be represented by a single letter is not unparalleled.

3.1.2   Sonorants

Etruscan has two nasal and two liquid phonemes; glides occur as allophonic variants of high vowels (see §3.2):

(4)   *Nasals*   m   n
       Liquids   r
                        l

Within a syllable, the nasals /m/ and /n/ sometimes join with a preceding vowel to create a nasalized vowel and are consequently no longer written (e.g., *Araθ* = *Aranθ*). In loanwords /-n/ is replaced by Etruscan /-m/: thus, *pruχum* from the Greek accusative προχοῦν "a vessel for pouring."

Following the vowel /a/, the liquid /l/ shows a velar variant [ɫ], which is not written in archaic texts: *Larϑia* Late Etruscan *Larϑial.*

The palatalized sonorants /lʸ/, /rʸ/, /nʸ/, written <l(i)> <r(i)> <n(i)>, which occur infrequently and developed in part from geminates, should perhaps be reconstructed. Such an analysis would account for several disparate phenomena: (i) the umlaut in genitive *clens* and the spelling *cliniiaras* (gen. pl.), from *clan* "son"; (ii) the variants *tina/tinia* ([tinʸa]), "Jupiter" (as if from **tin-na,* derived from *tin "day"; Cristofani 1997, 212); (iii) Late Etruscan *rasnea* "public" from **rasn(a)-na,* derived from *rasna* "people"; and (iv) *Melakre* and *Araθa* as the Etruscan renderings of the Greek names Μελέαγρος and Ἀριάδνα.

3.2   Vowels

The Etruscan vowel system contains four phonemes:

(5)   /i/   /u/
          /e/
             /a/

In Archaic Etruscan, a rounded phonetic realization of /a/ as [å] is suggested by the orthographic omission of [ɫ] after /a/ (see §3.1.2) in word-final position: for example, *Larϑia* (/lartʸal/, see §4.2.2.2; Agostiniani 1997).

Etruscan shows the diphthongs /ei/, /ai/, /ui/, and /au/, as seen, for example, in *zuslei* "with (a sacrificial animal)," *Hamaiθi* "at Hamae," *papui* "in [name of a month]," *lavtun* "family." The diphthong /eu/ appears in Late Etruscan.

Before another vowel, the high vowels /i/ and /u/ are phonetically realized as consonantal allophones – the glides of, for example, *vacil* "then," *avil* "year," *ilucve* "on the (festival day)," *iane* "?," *Hirminaia* [a family name].

No phonemic distinction of vowel length occurs in Etruscan (but see §3.5.2.5); vowels are lengthened phonetically when accented and in word-final position. The realization of nonaccented vowels shows some variation: for example, *mulvanice/mulvenece/mulvunuke* "gave as a present" (for detailed discussion, see de Simone 1970a:66–70).

3.3 Syllable structure

In the Archaic Period the syllabic nucleus was always a vowel. After unaccented vowels underwent syncope (see §3.5.2.4), however, both liquids and nasals could also serve as syllabic nuclei (e.g., *Vestrcna* < *Vestiricina*), as could sibilants in pronouns (e.g., *cs*, *pσl*). An Etruscan syllable can begin with a vowel or with one, two, or three consonants; a syllable can end in a vowel or in one or two consonants. Prehistoric apocope (see §3.5.2.1) and late archaic syncope (see §3.5.2.4) caused many previously open syllables to become closed.

3.4 Accent

The Etruscan word accent, not represented orthographically, was in the Archaic Period characterized by strong expiration, which led in the end to the loss of unaccented internal vowels (see §3.5.2.4). In native Etruscan words the accent falls on the initial syllable; however, from their use as enclitics, demonstrative pronouns acquire a generalized final accent (see §4.3.2). Foreign words which were borrowed from languages having phonemic vowel length appear to have carried the accent on the last word-internal long vowel: for example, *Zimite* < *Ziumite* (by syncope) < Greek Διομήδης; Greek γρῡμεῖα > Etruscan **crumí-na* > Latin *crŭmína* "money bag." In other words, Etruscan speakers interpreted word-internal length as an indicator of accent.

3.5 Diachronic developments

3.5.1 Consonants

Changes in consonant quality are without exception limited by context or by region. Two such changes may be mentioned here: (i) the the change of /f/ to /p/ before liquids or nasals (e.g., *θafna* > *θapna* "cup"; *Θuflθa* > *Θuplθa* [a theonym]); and (ii) the depalatalization of word-final /tʸ/ (deaspiration of /tʰ/?) in an area of the northeast (e.g., *Larθ*, *zilaθ* > *Lart*, *zilat*; see Rix 1989b:1300–1302). There is also an occasional alternation of the letters used to spell fricatives (aspirates?) and stops (e.g., *zamθic* ~ *zamtic*, *Preχu* ~ *Precu*), though there is no justification for proposing a free alternation or a suspension of a phonemic opposition next to continuants (*pace* de Simone 1970a:175).

3.5.2 Vowels

Several distinct vowel changes can be identified.

3.5.2.1 Apocope

Inflectional phenomena, also attested for Lemnian and Rhaetic, allow the supposition that in the Proto-Tyrsenic period (see §1) word-final vowels were apocopated due to a penultimate accent (see Prosdocimi 1986:608–616): for example, nominative **seχi* > *seχ*, beside genitive *seχi-s* (see §3.5.2). Compare the later apocope of the final vowel of the enclitic: Archaic Etruscan *-ca* > Late Etruscan *-c* "and" (see §4.3.2).

3.5.2.2 Vowel lowering

From the beginning of the Late Period, the phonetic realization of vowels is lowered: (i) /u/ as [o]; cf. the Latin name of the Etruscan King *Porsenna* (500 BC) and Etruscan *Purze*; and (ii) /i/ as [e] before /a/ or /e/ in the following syllable, except when occurring after /tˢ/ <z>: *ica* > *eca* "this," *Θihvarie* > *Θefarie* "Tiberius," *ci* "3," *firin* "?", *zilaθ* "praetor." Note also a change which occurs in the quality of /a/: thus, *Luvcie* instead of *Laucie* for Italic *Loukios*. See Agostiniani 1986:27–28.

Beyond the aforementioned lowering of /i/ to [e], intervocalic /i/ is lost (cf. §3.5.2.4), except in the northwest, as in the genitive of female names: Archaic Etruscan *Apucuial*, Volterran *Felmuial*, but otherwise *Velual*.

3.5.2.3 Vowel raising

Around 400 BC /ai/ becomes /ei/, and in the fourth century /ei/, whatever its origin, becomes /e/ before /u/ and word-finally: for example, *Kaikna* (fifth/fourth century) > *Ceicna* (third century; a family name); *Aivas* (fifth/fourth century) > *Eivas* (fourth/third century) > *Evas* (third century), from Greek Αἴας; Archaic Etruscan *Nuzarnai*, Late Etruscan *Peθnei*, *Peθne* (female family names); in final position /ei/ is for the most part restored by analogy.

3.5.2.4 Syncope

Unaccented word-internal vowels disappear between 500 and 470 BC, even in closed and word-final syllables: for example, *turuce* "sacrificed" > *turce*; *Larecena* > *Larcna* (family name); *Scanesna Scanasna* > *Scansna* (family name); *Aranθ* > *Arnθ* (praenomen). As a result of this syncope, consonantal sonorants become syllabic between consonants: for example, *Spuriena* ([spuryena]) > *Spurina* (family name), *muluvene* > *mulune* "gives as a gift"; *Leθamsul* > *Leθnsl* (theonym); *vacil vacal* > *vacl* "then." Syncope is not simply a graphic phenomenon (*pace* Pfiffig 1969:53–63), but a phonetic one. The proof is provided by cases in which an anaptyctic vowel later appears as a secondary consequence of syncope; for example, *Hercele* for *Hercle* < Ἡρακλῆς.

Morphologically relevant vowels are preserved analogically or restored: for example, genitive *Aules* instead of *Auls by analogy to the nominative *Aule*; preterite *lupuce* after perfect *lupu* "has died." A vowel before final -/n/ is not syncopated (e.g., *Turan* "Venus"), because it was nasalized and thereby phonetically lengthened (see §3.1.2). In some cases in which the expected syncope has not occurred, no compelling reason can be given for its absence – as in the /a/ preserved in *zilaθ* "praetor."

3.5.2.5 *ê* of Cortona

The new text of Cortona (see §1; about 200 BC) has shown that the inverted Ǝ <*ê*>, used only at Cortona, represented a phoneme different from the one written with normal <e>. This /ê/ seems to be recent: some examples go back to diphthongs (clitic -σνê < *-σναι), others to compensatory lengthening (prenoun *Vêl* < *Vell < *Venl, syncopated from *Venel*); for some there is no motivation. The rest of Etruria ignored this phenomenon at least in the script (Agostiniani[-Nicosia] 2000: 47–52).

4. MORPHOLOGY

4.1 Word formation

The usual process of word formation in Etruscan is suffixation. Less commonly, word formation may also be accomplished by, in essence, a phonological modification of morphemes. Less productive still is prefixation. Suffixes can be added both to the *root*, a formant that cannot be analyzed further, and to the *base*, a formant that is already suffixed.

Word-building via apparent phonological modification is commonly the result of phonological processes occurring at morpheme junctures, obscuring the boundaries. For example,

the joining of morphemes may create diphthongs which then undergo monophthongization, as in the locative *zusleve* < *zusleva-i*; compare the nominative *zusleva* (see §4.2.2.3).
Less common is distant vowel assimilation, or *umlaut*, as in, for example, genitive *clens*
< *klanias; by analogy the ablative is *clen* rather than the expected *clan < *klania, beside
nominative *clan* < *klania (cf. gen. pl. *cliniiaras*).

A possible Etruscan prefix is *e-* in *eprθnevc* (title of an official) beside *purθne, purθ* "first"
(?); also in **etrs-* (Latin *Etrus-ci*) beside **turs-* (Greek Τυρσ-ηνοί, Umbrian *Turs-com*, Latin
Tusci). As the precise meanings of these words are not clear, it is impossible to determine the
function of the prefix. The prothetic vowel *e-* in *esl-z* "twice" and *eslem* ("−2" = "8" in
numerals), from *zal* "two," is phonetically motivated.

Typologically, Etruscan is not uniform. Many of its morphological processes are agglutinative. In the noun, for instance, number and case are each marked by their own suffixes:
clan "son," genitive *clen-s*, plural *clen-ar*, genitive plural *clinii-ar-as*. Certain cases are not
formed from the *base*, but from the genitive, as with the "pertinentive" *clen-ar-as-i* or the
ablative *Arnθ -al-s* (see §4.2.2.4); here the genitive is treated like an adjective.

Other morphological processes, however, are more fusional in nature. These generally
result from sound changes which have obscured an agglutinative structure. Thus, locative
plural *zusleve* beside nominative plural *zusleva* (from *zusle* [a sacrificial animal]) can be traced
to a form *zusle-va-i*, in which the locative suffix *-i* has been added to the plural suffix -(χ)*va-*.
The allomorphy *-s/ -as/ -es/ -is/ -us/ -ls* in the genitive I arose as a consequence of the apocope
of final vowels (see §3.5.2.1); earlier this genitive was uniformly characterized by **-s* (< **-si*?).

The *-s/ -l* genitive allomorphy (see §4.2.2.2), in contrast, cannot be a consequence of sound
change, but is a morphophonemic phenomenon. *Praenomina* (first names in the Etruscan
naming system), in which *-s* and *-l* are distributed according to the final phoneme of the base
form, reveal the nature of this allomorphy: following dental obstruents (/s/, /θ/) *-l* occurs,
otherwise *-s*: thus, *Laris–Larisal, Larθ –Larθal: Aule–Aules, Vel– Velus*. As for appellative pairs
such as *cilθ-ś : cilθ -l* [locality], συθi-ó: συθi-l "grave," no functional difference has yet been
distinguished. The distribution seen in family names – such as genitive *Velimna-ś* for men :
Velimna-l for women – is a relatively late development that came into being around 700 BC
with the appearance of the Etruscan system of family nomenclature. The *-s/ -l* allomorphy can
only have arisen as a result of syncretism, perhaps through the merging of a genitive in *-l(a)*
with an ablative in *-s* (see §4.2.2.4), and does not argue against an agglutinative morphology.

4.2 Nominal morphology

Both nouns and adjectives are here treated under the rubric of nominal morphology.

4.2.1 Gender

Unlike the Indo-European languages with which it was in contact, Etruscan has no grammatical gender (see Fiesel 1922). The female sex is indicated by a suffix, either *-θa, -θu*, or *-i*: for
example, *lautni* "freedman": *lautni-θa* "freedwoman"; *Racvu* [man's name] : *Racu-θu, Rakv-i*
[women's names]. The suffix *-i* (< Italic -$\bar{i}$ < **-ih_2*-) was borrowed from Italic and was used
under Italic influence with family names that were in origin adjectives: for example, *Tarna-i*.

4.2.2 Case

Etruscan nouns and adjectives are marked for case and number (singular and plural; see
§4.2.3). The following cases have been identified: nominative-accusative, genitive, locative,
ablative, and "pertinentive."

4.2.2.1 Nominative-accusative

The nominative-accusative is the base form of the nominal paradigm and indicates the subject (*mini zinace Aranθ* "Aranth produced me"); the predicate (*ca σuθi* "this [is] the grave"); the direct object (*cn σuθi ceriχunce* "he erected this grave"); and the *nominativus pendens*. It is governed by the infrequent postposition *-pi* "?": for example, *Aritimi-pi* "? Artemis."

4.2.2.2 Genitive

The *genitive I* is formed with one of the allomorphic suffixes *-s, -as, -es, -is, -us, -ls* (see Rix 1989a). After vowels *-s* occurs; after consonants no morphophonemic rule is apparent. Following prehistoric apocope (see §3.5.2.1) the original word-final vowel of the base was interpreted as part of the ending and was generalized in a number of semantic groups: *-as* in the *-r*-plurals (see §4.2.3.1); *-us* in individual names (*Velθur-us, Θanacvil-us*); *-ls* in the south for multiples of ten and *-uś* in the north (*cealχ-ls* : *cealχ-uś* "30," syncopated from *-χvis*; Lemnian *σialχv-is*). Not belonging to any such semantic groups are, for example, *clen-s* "son," *meθlum-es* "city," *seχ-is* "daughter."

The suffix of the *genitive II* (see Nucciarelli 1975) is *-l* < *-la* (see §4.2.2.4), as seen in, for example, *spura-l* "community," *pui-l* < **puia-l* "wife," *murσ-l* "urn," *culs-l* "gate." In proper names velar [ł] is mostly written *al* (Archaic Etruscan *a*): for example, *Larθi-al, Larθi-a, Velu-al* < **Velui-al*.

The genitive is used to indicate (i) nominal dependency (chiefly possession); (ii) the addressee in dedications (*itun turuce Venel Atelinas Tina-s cliniiar-as* "Venel Atelinas dedicated this to the sons of Zeus") and ordinals (*huθ-iś zaθrum-iś* "the 26th").

4.2.2.3 Locative

The suffix of the locative is *-i*: Archaic Etruscan *zusle-i* > Late Etruscan *zusle*, plural *zusleve* (< *-e-χva-i*) "with [sacrificial animal]"; *zilc-i* "in the praetorship." When occurring after a vowel, this *-i* suffix escaped the prehistoric apocope (see §3.5.2.1) and was later extended to base forms ending in a consonant.

The locative indicates (i) sojourn in place and time (e.g., *spure* < *-a-i* "in the community"; *uσl-i* "during the day": *uσil*); (ii) motion to a place (e.g., *celi* < *-le-i* "to the earth"); and (iii) instrument (e.g., *turza-i* "with [tool of sacrifice]").

For the purpose of clarifying syntactic-semantic functions, enclitic postpositions are utilized: *-ri*, indicating a benefactive notion (*meθlumeri* < *-e-i-ri* "for the city"); and *-θi*, *-θ, -te, -ti*, indicating location (e.g., Archaic Etruscan *Hama-i-θi* "at Hamae"; Late Etruscan *spure-θi* < *-a-i-θi* "in the community"; *velθite* < *-a-i-te* "to the earth"; *lauχumneti* < *-na-i-ti* "in the royal house"). These postpositions can also substitute the locative suffix *-i*: for example, *cela-ti* "in the burial chamber."

4.2.2.4 Ablative

The ablative occurs in three forms (see Rix 1984a:226–227). The *ablative I* is formed with the suffix *-s* and palatalization of the preceding vowel: for example, Archaic Etruscan *lavtunu-is* "family," *turza-is* (a sacrificial offering); Late Etruscan *faśe-iś* "porridge," *Apatru-is, Tarnes* < *-na-is, Tetnis* < *-nie-is* (family names). The *ablative II* is formed with the suffix *-las* > *-ls*: for example, Archaic Etruscan *Veleθna-las*; Late Etruscan *Visna{ia}-ls* (family name), *Arnθ-als* (praenomen).

It is possible that originally the ablative was formed by the addition of a suffix *-s* to the genitive suffix. In the case of the ablative II, it would have been attached to the ending *-l* of the genitive II, which, prior to the prehistoric apocope, must have been *-la* (cf. §4.2.2.5). In the case of the ablative I, the suffix would have been added to the *-s* of the genitive I, whereupon /ss/# was shortened with palatalization of the preceding vowel.

The rare *ablative III* has no ending and its morphology is therefore identical with that of the nominative-accusative: for example, *faśe* "porridge," *Ravnθu* (praenomen) (an exception is *clen*, nom.-acc. *clan*; see §4.1). This homomorphy arose through a sound change that we are not able to reconstruct. The combination of the endless ablative III forms with the ablative II suffixed forms (in *-als; Tute Arnθals*) has led to the suffix of the latter being incorrectly interpreted as a group inflection.

The ablative expresses (i) the agent in passive constructions (e.g., *anc farθnaχe Tute Arnθ-als Haθli-als Ravnθu* "which was -?-ed by Arnth Tute and Ravnthu Hathli"), (ii) origin (e.g., *paci-als* "[stemming] from Paci"); and (iii) the shared whole (partitive: *śin aiser faśe-iś* "take, O gods, from the porridge"). The ablative is governed by the postposition *ceχa* "because of": for example, *clen ceχa* "because of a son."

4.2.2.5 Pertinentive

The two constructions of the so-called pertinentive case are likewise based on genitive forms. The *pertinentive I* ends in *-(V)si*, the *pertinentive II* in *-(a)le*. An originally uniform morphology can be hypothesized by proposing that the locative suffix in *-i* (see §4.2.2.3) was added to forms of the two genitives. An original structure *-(a)la* (see §§4.2.2.2; 4.2.2.4) is proposed for the suffix of the genitive II; the diphthong in *-(a)la-i* developed prehistorically to *-(al)e*. At times the local postposition *-ti/-θi* (see §4.2.2.3) substituted for the locative suffix *-i*: thus, Archaic Etruscan *Misala-la-ti* "in the [area] of Misala" (with genitive II in *-la!*); *Uni-al-θi*, Late Etruscan *Uni-al-ti* "in the [temple] of Juno."

The pertinentive often functions simply as a genitival locative: for example, *spureθi apa-s-i* "in the community, in [that] of the father"; *zilci Ceisinie-s-i V(elu-s-i)* "in the praetorship of V. Ceisinie"; *Uni-al-θi* "in the [temple] of Juno." In several syntactic constructions, however, this use is not obvious. For instance, in *mini Spuriaza [Teiθu]rnas mulvanice Alsaiana-s-i* "Spuriaza Teithurna gave me as a present (into the sphere of =) to Alsaiana," the pertinentive signifies the addressee (that is, functions as a dative); on the stamp marked *Serturie-s-i* "in [the workshop] of Serturie," it denotes manufacturer (the agent, that is, it functions as an ablative). Expressions of the type *mi mulu Kavie-s-i* "I [am] a present for/from Gavie" are ambiguous.

4.2.3 Number

Etruscan nominals are marked for two numbers, singular and plural; *Tinas cliniiaras* "Zeus' sons" (gen.) does not demonstrate a dual (*pace* Agostiniani 1985; *-ia-* belongs to the stem).

Etruscan has two suffixes for forming the plural: (i) *-r* with the variants *-ar, -er, -ir, -ur*; and (ii) *-χva* with the variants *-cva* and *-va/-ua*. The variants *-ar, -er, -ir, -ur*, like the corresponding variants of the genitive (see §4.1), arose as a consequence of the stem-final vowel, apocopated in the suffixless base form, being preserved (or transferred by analogy) before the suffix. The word endings *-ras* and *-rasi* in the genitive and pertinentive demonstrate that *-ra-* was the original form of the plural suffix. The variants of *-χva* ([x^{w}a]) are phonetically conditioned.

The *-r*-plural is predominantly, though not exclusively, used with nominals denoting human referents ([+ hum]). The *-χva*-plural occurs solely with nonhuman referents ([− hum]; see Agostiniani 1993:34–38).

By the side of numerals (Agostiniani 1993:38) the -χva-plural is first used in the Late Period, and its use is not consistent: for example, *zusle-va-c mac* "and five *zusle*-sacrificial animals," but *avils σas* "of six (σa) years." Otherwise the nominative-accusative or the genitive singular is used: Archaic Etruscan *ci zusle* "three *zusle*-sacrificial animals"; Late Etruscan *muró-l* XX "20 urns." The use of the -r-plural does not show this sort of optionality: thus, Archaic Etruscan *ki aiser* "three gods," Late Etruscan *ci clenar* "three sons."

4.2.3.1   The -r-plural

This plural suffix, having the semantic characteristic [+ hum], is used with nouns such as the following (i): *ais-er*, genitive *ais-er-as*; from *ais* "god"; (ii) *clen-ar*, genitive *clinii-ar-as*, pertinentive *clen-ar-asi*; from *clan* "son"; *papals-er*; from *papals* "grandchild," *θanó-ur*; from *θanó* "merciful" (referring to gods). Worthy of note is *tuśurθi-r* "married couple," literally "those on the two cushions," formed from the locative plural *tuś-ur-θi* "on the cushions." Among -r-plural substantives having the semantic characteristics [− hum, − anim] are the following: (i) genitive *tiv-r-s/ tiu-r-as*; from *tiu* "month" (gen. *tiv-s* "moon"), (ii) locative *tuś-ur-θi*; locative singular *tuś-θi*; from *tuś-θi* "cushion"; (iii) locative *ramu-r-θi*; locative singular *ramu-e(θ)* [a vessel].

Distributive numerals are formed like -r-plurals, although they do not necessarily accompany substantives which are [+ hum]: for example, *θu* (stem *θun-*) "one," in *tun-ur clutiva* "a *cluti*-vessel each" (Pe 5.2); further consider *zel-ur*, from *zal* "two"; *ci-ar*, from *ci* "three."

In family names and in the formation of collectives *-(V)r* is replaced by *-θur* (having the original meaning "descendant"?): for example, *heva Marcniθur Pupeinal* "all Marcni [children] of Pupeinei"; *maru paχaθur-as* "priest of the Bacchantes."

4.2.3.2   -χva-plurals

Plurals made with this formant having the semantic characteristics [− hum, − anim] include the following: *caper-χva*, from *caper*, a vessel; *θesn-χva*, from *θesan* "morning, day"; locative *sren-χve*, from *sren* "picture"; *culś-cva*, genitive singular *culs-l* "gate"; *luθ-cva*, from *luθ* "altar"; *hupniva*, from *hupni* "burial couch"; *zuθeva*, from *zuθe*, a cult vessel; *murzua*, from *muró* "urn."

Two such plurals show the semantic qualification [− hum, + anim]: (i) *fler-χva* (locative *flerχve*); from *fler* "victim," which is introduced in a sacrificial prayer as *zivas* "living" and is then *θezine* "to be slaughtered"; and (ii) *zusleva* (locative *zusleve*, ablative *zuśleveś*), from *zusle*, a kind of sacrificial animal. The use of the -r-plural suffix was consequently not (or no longer) determined by the feature [+ anim], but by [+ hum]. There is no valid example of a -χva-plural with the qualification [+ hum]: *marunuχva* is derived from *marunuχ* "office of a *maru* (a cult official)," not from *marunu* "being *maru*" (Agostiniani 1997:4–9, Maggiani 1998:109–113).

4.3 Pronouns

The pronominal paradigm is identical to that of the noun except that the accusative is a separate category, distinct in form from the nominative. The accusative suffix -*ni* is only (after /i/?) preserved in Archaic Etruscan *mi-ni* "me," and before enclitic -*m* in the archaic adverb *ita-ni-m* "just as" (< "*but this"). Otherwise, as a consequence of the prehistoric apocope (see §3.5.2.1), the suffix became -*n*. Plural forms are rare; only "articulated" forms are certain: nom. *sani-óva* ([saŋniśwa]), built from *sa(c)ni-óa* (see §5.2) with the plural suffix -χva, gen. *Larisali-óvla* (Cortona, see 1), "pert." *Larθiali-óvle*.

4.3.1 Personal pronouns

The following pronominal lexemes are known:

(6)   *First person*   *Second person*
    Nominative   mi   *una
    Accusative   mi-ni   un < *una-n
    Locative   une < *una-i

4.3.2 Demonstrative pronouns

There are three demonstrative pronouns in Etruscan, among which *ϑa* only occurs in enclitic position (see §5.2)

The demonstrative pronouns *ica, ita* > *eca, eta* (see §3.5.2.2) > *ca, ta* are at times used as independent words, usually positioned before those words they determine, and at times as enclitics, fusing with the words they determine (serving as "articles"; see §5.2). The following forms are known (those marked with superscript *ⁱ* are only attested as an "article"):

(7)

	Archaic	*Late*		*Archaic*	*Late*	
Nominative	ica, ika-	eca	ca	ita	eta	ta
Accusative	ican, ikan	ecn	cn	itan	etan	tn
Genitive I	-ⁱcas	ecs	cś	-ⁱtas	etas	tś
Genitive II			cla	-ⁱtala, -ⁱtula		-ⁱtla
Locative			cei	(tei?)		tei
Ablative			ceś (cś?)			teiś (?)
Pertinentive				-ⁱtale		-ⁱtle
with		[ecl]θ, eclθi clθ, clθi		-ⁱtalte, -ⁱtultei		
postposition						

The final-syllable accent (see §3.4) reveals itself in the preservation of final *-a* in the genitive II, in the syncope of unaccented /a/ in the penultimate syllable (e.g., -ⁱ *tala* > -ⁱ *tla*), and in the potential disappearance of the word-initial vowels.

The pertinentive demonstrative is used to designate place and time: for example, *clθ ϑuθiθ* "in this grave"; Archaic Etruscan *iove-itule*, Late Etruscan *eóv-itle*, place or time of a ritual. The locative forms are, it seems, only instrumental in sense: e.g., *tesne rasne cei* "according to this state regulation" (?).

Archaic Etruscan *itunia* (< **ita-n(i)-na*), *itu-na, eta-na-l*, Late Etruscan *ca-n-l, c-n-l* are accusative and genitive II adjectives which are derived from an accusative pronoun by means of a formant *-na*; the meaning seems to be the same as that of the pronoun itself.

4.3.3 Relative/interrogative pronoun

A pronoun attested by the forms of (8) functions as an interrogative (*ipas ika-m* "but whose is this?") and as a relative (see §5.5).

(8) *Nominative*   ipa
     Accusative   inpa
     Genitive I   ipa-s   Archaic Etruscan
     Genitive II   ipal   Archaic Etruscan
     Genitive II   epl   Late Etruscan
     Locative   ipei, ipe
     Locative   inpein   Archaic Etruscan
        with postposition ipe-ri

This could be a derivative of the relative pronoun *in* (see §4.3.4). On the basis of *in-pa*, interpreted as accusative, a stem *i-pa* could have been abstracted and inflected nominally.

4.3.4 Relative pronouns

The relative pronouns *an* and *in* (also *anc, inc* with *-c* "and") are only attested in nominative and accusative function. Their use is conditioned by the quality of the antecedent: [+hum] requires *an*, [-hum] *in* (Agostiniani and Nicosia 2000:100). The contexts in which the reduplicated *ananc, ininc* occur, which (like Latin *quisquis*) could be generalizing, are unclear.

4.3.5 Indefinite pronoun

A pronoun expressing an indefinite quantity (cf. Latin *aliquantus*) is seen in nominative *heva*, accusative *hevn*, genitive *hevl, heul* (Steinbauer 1999: 95. 427).

The recently published archaic text *ein θui ara enan* "*not here do/put anything" contains the accusative *ena-n* of an indefinite pronoun. Its genitive *ena-ś* 'of anything' in formulas like *spureri meθlumeric enaś* of the Zagreb mummy text (see §1) declares the authorities *spura* 'community' and *meθlum* 'town' as not specified for a certain community (Benelli 2001:221).

4.4 Verbal morphology

There are fewer attestations of verbal than nominal forms. Thus far, study in this area has been almost exclusively focused on interpreting texts and not on clarification of points of morphology and syntax (but see now Wylin 2000). The following section must therefore be considered highly provisional in nature.

The verb paradigm is of simple structure, characterized by only a single dimension. Verbal categories are not combined with one another, but are each formed directly to the root or the base. Speakers are not designated (i.e., there is no category of person), nor is there a number distinction. The absence of person and number distinction is revealed, for example, by the following pairs:

(9) A. Turis mi une *ame*
        "Doris *I am* (= I belong) to you," beside
        [t]eurat tanna la rezus *ame*
        "(The) judge thereby *is* Larth Rezu";
     B. mi Araθiale *ziχuχe*
        "I am *written* from/for Aranth," beside
        iχ ca ceχa *ziχuχe*
        "As this is *written* above";
     C. Araθ Spuriana σ[uθ]il *hecece* (see 4.4.1.2)
        "Aranth Spuriana *set up* the burial construction," beside
        Arnθ Larθ Velimnaś Arzneal huśiur śuθi acil *hece* (see 4.4.1.2)
        "Arnth [and] Larth Velimna, children of Arznei, *set up* grave [and] furnishings"

Thus far, the following verbal categories have been identified: (i) present and preterite tenses, with the latter showing a distinction of active and passive voice; (ii) imperative, subjunctive, and necessitative moods, aside from the indicative. Various verbal nouns are also identified.

Formation of denominative verbs is quite productive. Moreover, many nouns serving as *base forms* (see §4.1) can be analyzed as verbal nouns, derived from simpler verbal forms by the attachment of various suffixes: for example, (i) *-u* (see §4.4.3.1), giving *lup-u* "died," *mul-u* "gift," *ziχ-u* "writer, writing"; and (ii) *-θ* (see §4.4.3.2), providing *trin-θ* "speaking, speaker," *sval-θ** "who has lived" (not yet analyzable as verbal nouns are *zilaχ** > *zilχ* "praetorship," *acas*, "a sacrifice"). There thus arise whole chains of alternately nominal and verbal derivatives.

The most important denominative suffix is *-ane* (the quality of the vowels is uncertain): thus, *mulu-ane** "to make a present of," *ziχu-ane** "to write," *acilu-ane** "to manage, get done," *acna-ane** "to make into a possession, get." The suffix *-ie* (Late Etruscan *-i*), which is frequent in verbal bases, may also be denominative: for example, *vat-ie** "wish", *θez-ie** "slaughtering."

As there are no personal endings, it is not always easy to distinguish nominal from verbal forms. Roots, that is, monosyllabic segments that (unlike bases) cannot undergo further analysis (e.g., *ziχ* "scratch, write"; *mul** "give as a gift"; *am* "be"; *men* "make"; *trau* "keep" (?); for additional examples see §4.4.2.1), can be inflected both verbally and nominally. Roots used verbally and their derivatives can only be identified as such (when they can be identified) via the syntax. Nouns can be recognized by the occurrence of case suffixes; yet it appears – unless in the few apparent examples there is chance homonymy – as though case suffixes can also be attached to some typically verbal suffixes, such as the preterite suffixes *-ce* and *-χe*: for example, genitive *tlena-ce-s*, ablative *tlena-χe-is*.

4.4.1 Tense and voice

4.4.1.1 *Present*

Forms of the present, which are rare and not easy to identify, are marked with the suffix *-e*. They express the actual or contextualized present: for example, *ame* "I am," "he is" (see the examples of [9]); *ale* "gives as a present, places." With bisyllabic bases, no *-e*-suffix occurs, so that the present is then identical in form with the imperative (see §4.4.2.1): *nunθen* "I call" (as in *un mlaχ nunθen* "you, you good one, I call"). The denominative suffix *-ane*, on the other hand, retains final *-e*: for example, Archaic Etruscan *muluvene* > Late Etruscan *mulune* "makes a present of"; Late Etruscan *acilune* "gets done."

4.4.1.2 *Preterite active*

The preterite active, reporting past events, is formed with the suffix *-ce*, which in the Archaic Period was preceded by a vowel, of unpredictable quality, which was later syncopated. At present there is insufficient evidence to determine whether this vowel (*a*, *e*, *i*, or *u*) was originally the root-final vowel which was prehistorically apocopated (see §3.5.2.1) or belonged to the suffix. The following are examples of the preterite active: *amuce/amake* > *amce* "was"; *turuce/turice* > *turce* "sacrificed"; *zinace/zineke* > *zince* "produced"; *hecece* > *hecce/hece* "erected"; *farice* > *farce* "prepared"; denominative *acasce* > *akśke* "sacrificed"; and with a nasal suffix *amavunice* > *amavence* "produced" (lit. "brought into being"); *ziχ(v)anace* > *ziχunce* "had written" (lit. "brought to writing"); Archaic Etruscan *muluvanice* "gave as a present"; Late Etruscan *ceriχunce* (< **cer-ie-χ(e)-u-ana-ce*) "built"; *θezince* (< **θez-ie-ana-ce*) "slaughtered"; *zilaχnuce* (< **zilaχ -an(a)-u-ce*) "was praetor."

4.4.1.3 *Preterite passive*

The suffix of the only recently identified preterite passive is *-χe*. Here too, between roots ending in a consonant and the suffix there occurs one of the four Etruscan vowels, but these vowels are nowhere syncopated (to maximize the distinction between the two phonetically similar suffixes *-ce and -χe*?). As with the preterite active, it is impossible to determine whether this vowel originally belonged to the root or to the suffix. Examples of the preterite passive are the following: Archaic Etruscan *zinaχe* "was produced"; *vatieχe* "was wished for"; Late Etruscan *ziχuχe* "was written"; *menaχe* "was prepared"; denominative *farθnaχe* "was prayed for" (?); and with nasal suffix, *muluaniχ(e)* "was given as a present."

The passive character of these forms follows from: (i) the number of participants (in each instance only one in a direct case); (ii) passages in which a pronominal subject in the nominative denotes the patient (the agent is in the ablative; see §4.2.2.4):

(10) A. mi titasi cver *menaχe*
          "I *was created* for/by Tita as a present"
      B. inpein . . . mlaχuta *ziχuχe*
          "Which . . . as good (the articulated nominative) *was carved*"

4.4.2 Mood

In addition to the indicative, Etruscan has an imperative, subjunctive, and necessitative mood.

4.4.2.1 Imperative

The imperative, the mood of strict command, occurring frequently in ritual texts, is identical with the verbal base. Monosyllabic roots provide most of the attested imperatives: for example, *ar* "make," *al* "give," *tur* "sacrifice," *trin* "speak," *óuθ* "lay," *heχz* "pour." The remaining imperatives belong to denominative bases formed with *-en* or *-ie* (Late Etruscan *-i*) or, with "reverse" nasalization (see §3.1.2), *-in*: for example, *nunθen* "invoke"; *θezi, θezin* "slaughter"; *uói, mutin, firin* "?"

4.4.2.2 Subjunctive

The subjunctive mood, expressing wish, obligation, and futurity, is marked by the suffix *-a*. Consider the following examples:

(11) A. *mula* "he/you should give as a present"
      B. *scuna* "he should/will put at (somebody's) disposal"
      C. *acasa* "you/he should sacrifice" (denominative)

The subjunctive is also used in subordinate clauses with the conjunction *ipa* "that" (see §5.5). In ritual prescriptions of the Zagreb mummy (see §1), subjunctives alternate with imperative forms: *raχθ tura/tur* "you should sacrifice/sacrifice in fire."

The subjunctive is also used to express prohibition (see Colonna 1989:345):

(12) A. *ei . . . ara* "he should not make"
      B. *ei truta* "he should not injure [by means of an evil look]"

4.4.2.3 Necessitative

In the necessitative, which indicates that an action must be carried out, a suffix *-ri* is added to the base; base-final *-ie* appears in Archaic as *i* (*fani-ri*) and Late *e* (*fane-ri, θeze-ri*). The nasal *n* is assimilated to the *r* of this suffix as in, for example, *nunθeri* < **nunθen-ri* (cf. the assimilation in the *preaenomen Venel* > *Venl-is* > Late Etruscan *Vel*). Examples of necessitatives appear in (13):

(13) A. *acasri* "X is to be sacrificed" (denominative)
      B. *perpri* "?"
      C. *ziχri* "is to be written, carved," Late Etruscan

D. *nunθeri* "is to be sacrificed (by invocation)"

E. *θezeri* "is to be sacrificed (by slaughter)"

As these examples illustrate, the necessitative has a passive sense. Identification of its voice as passive follows from the same phenomena noted for the preterite passive (see §4.4.1.3): *esvita . . . spetri* "the *esvita* (articulated nominative; see §5.2) is to be expiated."

4.4.3   Verbal nouns

Without an accompanying auxiliary, verbal nouns were used as predicates; these are formed with the suffixes *-u*, *-θ*, and *-as*. Locative verbal nouns in *-e* were used as infinitives.

4.4.3.1   *Verbal nouns in -u*

These function as nouns for results of actions and agent nouns (see §4.4), and they are indifferent to voice. With transitive verbs they can be used both passively (*mul-u* "given as a gift, gift") and actively (*zic-u* "writer"). They serve as predicates of matrix sentences and designate a state which began in the past and continued over a long period of time, often right up to the present (in this respect, they are reminiscent of the Ancient Greek perfect):

(14) A. mi *mul-u* kaviiesi

"*I (am) presented / a present* for/from [see §4.2.2.5] Gavius"

B. eθ *fan-u* lavtn precuś ipa

"Thus (?) *has decided* the Precu family that . . . "

The difference between this formation, with its stative sense, and the preterite, which records past events, is revealed by sentences such as the following:

(15) *lupu-ce* (PRETERITE) munisuleθ . . . avils LXX *lup-u* (VERBAL NOUN)

"*He died* while holding the . . . -office; *dead* at the age of 70"

Enlarged verbal stems can also provide the base of verbal nouns in *-u*, the final vowel of these enlarged stems disappearing before the *-u*-suffix: **zina-ce +-u > zinaku* "produced, product"; **cerie-χe* (cf. *vatieχe*) + *-u > ceriχu* "having erected," **zilaχ-ane + -u > zilaχnu* "been praetor."

There is no explanation for the locatives *ten-v-e* and *zilaχn-v-e* which are attested once in the context in which the nominatives *tenu* and *zilaχnu* otherwise occur.

4.4.3.2   *Verbal nouns in -θ*

As predicates, the verbal nouns in *-θ* designate an action that is both current and contemporaneous with another action. They are thus comparable with the present active participles of the Indo-European languages:

(16) A. celi śuθ *heχś-θ* vin(u)m

"Lay on the ground, *pouring* wine"

B. racθ śuθ *nunθen-θ*

"Lay on the fire, *invoking*"

Other examples include: *ar-θ* "making," *trin-θ* "speaking," and *zarfne-θ* "?" These verbal nouns constitute a special case of the agent nouns in *-θ* such as *zil-aθ* "praetor"; *tevara-θ > [t]eurat* "judge"; *tesin-θ* [a servant]. The alternative suggestion that the above predicates are imperatives II (so Pfiffig 1969:137) explains neither the distribution (why imperative II in particular?) nor the relationship to the agent nouns.

4.4.3.3 *Verbal nouns in -as*

Verbal nouns formed with the suffix *-as*, occasionally also appearing as *-asa* (without there being any distinguishable difference in function), usually occur as the predicates of embedded sentences, denoting a state completed in the past, and hence correspond to a preterite participle. These are formed directly on the root in rare instances. On occasion, the predicate of the matrix sentence is connected with this verbal noun via a coordinating conjunction (*-c, -um*; see §5.4):

(17) A. raχ … *menaś* … mula-χ huślna vinum
          "*Having prepared* fire, you/he ought also to give young wine"
      B. *araś* θui uśeti cepen faθin-um
          "*having made* a ? here in the ?, but then ? (imperative)"

More frequently, this verbal noun is formed from a base having the denominative suffix *-ane* (see §4.4) or the suffix *-θ* of the present participle (see §4.4.3.2); examples of the type *-ane + -as > -anas* follow:

(18) A. zelarven-as (< *zal-ur-u-ane-as)
          "Having doubled" (cf. zelur "every two," see §4.2.3.1)
      B. raχθ   śut-anas   celi   śuθ
          in the fire   having placed   on the earth   place
          "Having placed in the fire, place on the earth"
      C. husur   maχ   acn-anas   arce   manim
          children   five   having had   he made   manim
          "Having had five children, he made manim" (a taboo expression for "he died")
      D. papalser   acn-anasa   VI manim   arce
          grandchildren   having had   6   manim   he made
          "Having had six grandchildren, he died"

As examples of verbal nouns formed from bases ending in *-θ*, consider *sval-θas* "having lived"; *trin-θasa* "having spoken" and the following:

(19) A. eslz   zilaχn-θas   avils   θunem muvalχls   lupu
          twice   having held the praetorship   of year minus one fifty   dead
          "Having twice held the praetorship, he died at the age of forty-nine"
      B. arce …   zilc   marunuχva   ten-θas
          he made …   presidency   marunuχva   having held
          "He [died], having held the presidency of the maru"

The verbal noun in-*as* also expresses contemporaneous action in the instance of *sval-as* "living" (*sval-ce* "lived"), the only such verbal noun formed from a stative verb:

(20) zilaχnce   spureθi   apasi   sval-as
      he held the praetorship   in the community   in that of his father   living
      "He held the praetorship, [while] living in the community of his father"

The locative in *-as-i* serves as a predicate in an embedded locative absolute clause:

(21) clensi   muleθ   svalasi   zilaχnce
      in the sons   in the mula   living   he held the praetorship
      "While the son lived in the mula, he held the praetorship"

4.4.3.4 Verbal nouns in -e

Verbal noun forms ending in -e, all of them late and therefore open to interpretation as locatives of stems in -e or in -a, function as predicates of embedded sentences with two characteristics: (i) the subjects of matrix and embedded sentences are not identical; and (ii) the verbal nouns lack congruence with another constituent of the embedded sentence (as is the case with the locative absolute). The verbal nouns thus function as infinitives. On the wrappings of the Zagreb mummy, ritual acts are sometimes expressed by a combination of these forms with *acil* (*ame*) "one ought" (Olzscha 1961:155–173): for example, *ture acil* "one ought to sacrifice"; *neχσe acil ame* (VII 14) "one ought to?" Other examples of matrix predicates include *nunθene* "to call," *ziχne* "to write, scratch." Consider also the following:

(22)   une... puθs... zivaś   fler   θezine... zati   zatlχne
       for you   placed   the living   victim   to kill   with the axe   to strike dead
       "For you... [is] placed... the still living sacrificial animal to kill, to strike dead with
           the ax"

4.5 Numerals

The following cardinal numerals are attested: *θu* (1); *zal* (2); *ci* (3); *σa* (4); *maχ* (5); *huθ* (6); *semφ* (7?); *cezp* (8?); *nurφ* (9?); *śar* (10); *zaθrum* (20); *cialχ / cealχ* (30); *σealχ* (40); *muvalχ* (50); *semφalχ* (70); and *cezpalχ* (80). Ordinals identified are as follows: *θunśna* (1st); *cis* (3rd); *huθiś* (6th); *śariś* (10th); and *zaθrumiś / zaθrumsna* (20th).

5. SYNTAX

5.1 Word order

The word order phenomena of Etruscan have not yet been extensively studied (see Pfiffig 1969:207–211; Agostiniani 1982:278–280; Schulze-Thulin 1993). Departure from the unmarked word order occurs often, without any discernible reason. That unmarked word order for phrases with a verbal nucleus is Subject–Object–Verb (SOV):

(23)   A. Laris   Avle...   cn   σuθi   ceriχunce
          Laris   Aule   this   grave   they set up
          "Laris [and] Aule... set up this grave"
       B. Velχinei   Śelvanśl   turce
          Velchinei   to Silvanus   she dedicated
          "Velchinei dedicated [the statue] to Silvanus"
       C. ita   tmia...   vatieχe   Unialastres
          this   cult space   was wished for   by Juno herself
          "This cult space... was wished for by Juno herself"
       D. ipa   murzua...   ein   heczri
          that   the urns   not   are to be sprinkled
          "That the urns... are not to be sprinkled [with libation]"

Not infrequently, however, Object and Verb reverse positions (SVO):

(24)   Vipia...   turce   Verσenas   cana
       Vibia   dedicated   to Versena   the statue
       "Vibia... dedicated the statue to Versena"

Objects which consist of or contain a deictic pronoun regularly appear at the beginning of the sentence (topicalization) and draw the verb after them creating the order Object–Verb–Subject:

(25)   mini   mulvanice   Mamarce   Quθaniies
        me   gave   Mamarce   Kutanie
        "Mamarce Kutanie gave me [as a present]"

Typical of a language having basic SOV-structure, Etruscan has postpositions: -*pi* "?" (see §4.2.2.1); -*ri* "for"; *θi*, -*θ*, -*te*, *ti* "in" (see §4.2.2.3); *ceχa* "because of" (see §4.2.2.4).

In nominal phrases, evolutionary developments occur between the Archaic and Late Periods which are consistent with a typological shift from SOV to SVO; this is seen most clearly with modifying numerals. In the Archaic Period the numeral is always placed before the substantive it modifies (e.g., *zal rapa* "two *rapa*-offerings," *ci avil* "three years," *huθ zusle* "six victims"); in the Late Period, however, the order is almost always reversed (e.g., *halχza θu* "one little *halχ*-vessel," *clenar zal* "two sons," *naper ci* "three *naper* (square measure)," although isolated examples of the earlier order still occur (e.g., *hut naper* and *ci avil*). The attributive genitive (as far as it can be identified) behaves similarly: Archaic Etruscan shows the order Genitive–Noun, as in *Marhies acel* "Marhie's production"; but Late Etruscan has the order Noun–Genitive, *flerχvetr[-] Neθunśl*, "in the rite of Neptunus," *luθcva Caθaś* "the altars of Catha." The same is true of the attributive adjective, for which, however, there are no clear Archaic examples; thus Late Etruscan, with the order Noun–Adjective, provides examples such as: *ziχ neθśrac* "text concerning the inspection of the liver," *aiseraś śeuś* "of the ? gods." Compare, however, Late Etruscan *huślna vinum* "young wine" (Adjective–Noun).

In deictic function, the demonstrative pronoun is always placed before the noun it modifies: Archaic Etruscan *ica tmia* "this cult space," *etula natinusnal* "of this ?"; Late Etruscan *cn σuθi* "this grave," *clθi mutnaiθi* "in this sarcophagus."

5.2 Clitics

Demonstrative pronouns can also be used enclitically; they are attached to adjectives and genitival forms, merging with these phonetically, and function essentially as "articles." The enclitic use of the demonstrative is frequently observed in theonyms such as *Selvans Sanχuneta* "Silvanus, the one belonging to Sancus." If the modified word ends in a vowel, the resulting diphthong is monophthongized in Late Etruscan (e.g., /e-i/ > /i/). Consider the following examples: Archaic Etruscan *riθna-ita* "the ?" (nom.), *riθna-itula* (gen.), *riθna-itul-te* (pert. with postposition); Late Etruscan *eśvita* (< *iσve-ita*) "the ?" (indicating locality), *eśvitle* (< Archaic *iσve-itule*, pert.). Following final -*s* the initial *i*- of the pronoun disappears with palatalization of the vowel before -*s*: for example, Archaic Etruscan *tameresca* < (-*a*^{i}*s-ka* < -*as-ika*) "the master of the house"; *aθeme-i-s-cas* "?" > Late Etruscan *aθumi(s)cś* (gen.); *θapneśtś* (< -*nas-ites*, abl.) "from [the contents of] the goblet."

In addition to -*ita* and -*ica*, -*σa* is also used as an article, being added to the genitives of personal names and to a few adjectives that refer to persons (e.g., *sacni-σa* "the one dedicated," that is, a member of a *śacni-ca* "cult brotherhood"). After the word-final velar-*l* of the genitive II, a phonetically motivated *i* appears: for example, *Larθial-i-σa* (gen. *Larθal-i-σla*; pert. pl. *Larθial-i-σvle*) "the [son] of Larth"; *Alfnal-i-σa* "the [son] of Alfnei." The word-final -*s* of the genitive I and the initial fricative of -*σa* form a geminate cluster, only revealed in Latin transcriptions: for example, *Veluσa* < -*s-σa* (gen. *Veluσla*) "the [son] of

Vel"; *Hanuóa*, Latin *Hanossa* (gen. *Hanuóla*) "the [son] of Hanu," "articulated" again as *Hanuólióa* "the [son] of Hanossa." The double genitives of the type *Larθalióla*, *Veluóla* are not an absurdness of Etruscan, but quite regular forms.

Apart from these demonstrative pronouns, only the copulative conjunctions *-c* and *-m* (see §5.4) are enclitic.

5.3 Agreement

Since neither grammatical gender nor personal endings are found in Etruscan, agreement occurs only in case and number in nominal phrases. Adjectives and pronouns carry no plural marking when they occur immediately next to the substantive which they modify and there is no chance of misconstruing their relationship: for example, *ais-er-aś śeu-ś* "of the ? gods," *clen-ar sval* "sons, living (= in their lifetime)," *icac heramaσ-va* "and these statues." But if the phonetic distance is greater or there is some possibility of ambiguity, the plural is marked on the adjective: thus, *ais-er śic śeuc*... [9 words intervening] ...*θanó-ur* "gods, ? and ?... graceful"; *apac atic saniσ-va* "father and mother, members of the cult association" (i.e., both, not just the mother).

Case agreement is marked on both adjectives and pronouns: for example, genitive *aiser-aś śeu-ś* "of the ? gods"; locative *tesne raśne* "with regulation, of the state"; locative + pertinentive (functioning as a locative; see §4.2.2.5) *θaure lautneścle* "on the area, that of the family"; *cl-θi mutna-i-θi* "in this sarcophagus"; ablative III *meχ θuta* "with one's own means."

5.4 Coordination

The coordination of words and sentences can be accomplished using the semantically un-marked conjunction *-c* < *-ca/ka* (see §3.5.2.1) and the weakly adversative conjunction *-m*. The conjunction *-c* can be attached to each member of a coordinated phrase (e.g., *apa-c ati-c* "both father and mother") or only to the final member (e.g., Archaic Etruscan *hecece farice-ca* "set up and prepared"; Late Etruscan *śacnicleri*... *śpureri meθlumeri-c* "for the cult association, the community and the city").

Asyndetic construction is also not uncommon: *Laris Avle Larisal clenar* "Laris [and] Aule, the sons (pl.) of Laris"; *acilune turune ścune* "gets done, makes over (to someone), puts at (someone's) disposal."

The coordinating comparative particle is *iχ* "as": *etnam iχ matam* "just as earlier"; *eisna iχ flereś crapśti* "a sacrifice as for Flere Crapsti."

5.5 Subordination

Clause embedding is accomplished utilizing (i) verbal noun constructions (verbal nouns, participles, and infinitives; for examples see §§4.4.3.1–4.4.3.4); and (ii) subordinate clauses introduced by pronouns and conjunctions. Embedded clauses can function as subjects, objects, adverbials, or attributives.

The only subordinate clauses introduced by a pronoun which are thus far attested are relative clauses; these function attributively, in part with a pronominal antecedent. Such clauses are introduced with *ipa*, *an*, or *in* (also *anc* and *inc*), all of which appear to function in the same way. In shortened relative clauses without a predicate, only *in* occurs:

(26) A. Vete...   ipa   amake   apa...
          Vete   who   was   father...
          "Vete..., who was the father..."

      B. śuluśi θuni   śerφue   acil   ipei...   χaśri
          LOCATIVE   INFINITIVE   is necessary   where   NECESSITATIVE

      C. Vel...   an   cn   σuθi   ceriχunce
          Vel   who   this   grave   set up
          "Vel..., who set up this grave"

      D. flere   in   crapsti
          divinity   which   in *crap*
          "divinity, which [is] in *crap*"

      E. Tins   in   marle
          of Jupiter   who   in *marle*
          "of Juppiter, who [is] in *marle*"

The relative pronoun can be omitted, as in *flereś crapśti* "of the divinity in the *crap*."

The following subordinating conjunctions have been identified: (i) *ipa* "that" (used with a verb in the subjunctive or necessitative mood) and *iχnac* "as" in object sentences; (ii) *iχ*, *iχnac* in comparative sentences; and (iii) *iχ*, *iχnac*, *nac* ("then" >) "as" in adverbial temporal sentences. Consider the following examples:

(27) A. tezan   fusleri...   ipa   ama...   naper   XII
          ruling   to be made   that   there are   *naper*   12
          "A ruling is to be made, that there are 12 *naper* (unit of square measure)"
              (contract about a plot of land)

      B. eθ   fanu   lautn   precuś   ipa   murzua...   ein   heczri
          thus   established   the family   of Precu   that   the urns   not   to be sprinkled
          "Thus the family Precu established, that the urns ... are not to be sprinkled
              [with a libation]"

      C. eca   sren   tva   iχnac   Hercle   Unial   clan   θrasce
          this   picture   shows   how   Heracles   of Juno   the son   became
          "This picture (shows?), how Hercules (became?) the son of Juno"

      D. iχ   ca   ceχa   ziχuχe
          as   this   above   was written
          "As this was written above"

6. LEXICON

The major part of the Etruscan lexicon is native. Some words are also attested in Lemnian or Rhaetic, revealing their origin in Proto-Tyrsenic; for example *zal*, Rhaetic *zal* "2," *maχ*, *σealχls* (gen.), Lemnian *mav*, *σialχvis* "5," "40"; *zinace*, Rhaetic *t'inaχe* "he made"; *avils* (gen.) = Lemnian *avis* "of years."

Within the sphere of trade and crafts, Etruscan borrowed some words from Greek (de Simone 1968), such as the names of vessels (often in the accusative) like *aska* from ἀσκός; *pruχum* from προχοῦν (acc.). Also from Greek come *spurta* from σπυρίδα (acc.) "basket"; *elaiva-* from ἐλαίϝα "oil"; and probably also *φersu* "[demon with] mask" (*φersu-na* > Latin *persōna*) from πρόσωπα "mask." From Greek there also come several slave names, such as *Tinusi* from Διονύσιος; a few theonyms, for example, *Aplu* from Ἀπόλλων; and many mythic names, like *Aχle* from Ἀχιλλεύς and *Castur* from Κάστωρ.

The existence of only a few Latin loanwords has been demonstrated, such as *cela* from *cella* "small room" or *macstr-* from *magister* "master." Etruscan *cletram* is from Umbrian *kletram* (acc.) "litter." Numerous Etruscan personal names, however, come from the Italic languages: for example, *Marce* from *Marcus*, *Crespe* from *Crispus*, *Vuvzies* from Umbrian *Vuvçis* "Lucius." A good number of theonyms are also of Italic origin: *Menerva* from Latin *Minerva*, *Neθuns* from Umbrian **Nehtuns* "Neptune."

The transmission of loanwords from Etruscan into Italic conforms to a similar picture: there are many onomastic borrowings (such as Latin *Aulus* from *Avile, Aule*), but few borrowings can be demonstrated in the realm of common nouns (Latin *satelles* "body guard" from *zat[i]laθ*). The sociological and cultic contacts between Etruscans and the Italic peoples seem clearly to have been more intimate than their linguistic contacts.

Bibliography

Agostiniani, L. 1982. *Le iscrizioni parlanti dell'Italia antica*. Florence: Leo S. Olschki.

———. 1985. "La sequenza tinas cliniiaras e la categoria del numero in etrusco." In *Studi linguistici e filologici per Carlo Alberto Mastrelli*, pp. 13–19. Pisa: Pacini.

———. 1986. "Sull'etrusco della stele di Lemno e su alcuni aspetti del consonantismo etrusco." *Archivio glottologico italiano* 71:15–46.

———. 1993. "La considerazione tipologica nello studio dell'etrusco." *Incontri linguistici* 16:23–44.

———. 1997. "Considerazioni linguistiche su alcuni aspetti della terminologia magistrale etrusca." In R. Ambrosini (ed.), *Scríbthair a ainm n-ogaim: Scritti in memoria di Enrico Campanile*, pp. 1–16. Pisa: Pacini.

Agostiniani, L. and F. Nicosia. 2000. *Tabula Cortonensis*. Rome: Bretschneider.

Beekes, R. and L. van der Meer. 1991. *De etrusken spreken*. Muiderberg: Coutinho.

Benelli, E. 2001. "Quattro nuove iscrizioni etrusche arcaiche dall'agro chiusino." *Studi etruschi* 64:213–234.

Boisson, C. 1991. "Note typologique sur le système des occlusives en etrusque." *Studi etruschi* 56:175–187.

Bonfante, G. and L. Bonfante. 1983. *The Etruscan Language. An Introduction*. New York: New York University Press.

Caffarello, N. 1975. *Avviamento allo studio della lingua etrusca*. Florence: Leo S. Olschki.

Colonna, G. 1975. "Al proposito del morfema etrusco -si." In *Archaeologia: Scritti in onore di Aldo Neppi Modona*, pp. 156–171. Florence: Leo S. Olschki.

———. 1989. Contribution to "Rivista di epigrafia etrusca." *Studi etruschi* 55:273–353.

Cristofani, M. 1971. "Sul morfema etrusco -als." *Archivio glottologico italiano* 56:38–42.

———. 1972. "Sull'origine e la diffusione dell'alfabeto etrusco." In H. Temporini (ed.), *Aufstieg und Niedergang der römischen Welt*, vol. I, part 2, pp. 466–489.

———. 1991. *Introduzione allo studio dell'etrusco*. Nuova edizione interamente aggiornata. Florence: Leo S. Olschki.

De Simone, C. 1968. *Die griechischen Entlehnungen im Etruskischen*, vol. I. Wiesbaden: Otto Harrassowitz.

———. 1970a. *Die griechischen Entlehnungen im Etruskischen*, vol. II. Wiesbaden: Otto Harrassowitz.

———. 1970b. "I morfemi etruschi -ce (-ke) e -χe." *Studi etruschi* 38:115–139.

———. 1997. "Masculin/féminin dans la théonymie étrusque," In F. Gautier and D. Briquel (eds.), *Les Étrusques les plus religieux des hommes*. Paris: La documentation française.

Fiesel, E. 1922. *Das grammatische Geschlecht im Etruskischen*. Göttingen: Vandenhoeck and Ruprecht.

Maggiani, A. 1998. "Appunti sulle magistrature etrusche." *Studi etruschi* 62:95–138.

Meiser, G. 1986. *Lautgeschichte der umbrischen Sprache*. Innsbruck: Institut für Sprachwissenschaft der Universität.

Nucciarelli, F. 1975. "I genitivi etruschi in -l, -us." *Annali della Facoltà di lettere e di filosofia della Università degli Studi di Perugia* 12:1–26.

Olzscha, K. 1961. "Etruskisch *acil*." *Studi etruschi* 29:155–173.

Pallottino, M. 1978. *La langue étrusque. Problèmes et perspectives*. Translated by J. Heurgon. Paris: Société d'Edition Les Belles Lettres.

————. 1988. Etruskologie: *Geschichte und Kultur der Etrusker*. Translated by S. Steingräber. Basle/ Boston/Berlin: Birkhäuser.

Pfiffig, A. 1969. *Die etruskische Sprache*. *Versuch einer Gesamtdarstellung*. Graz: Akademische Druck- und Verlagsanstalt.

Prosdocimi, A. 1986. "Sull'accento latino e italico." In A. Etter (ed.), *o-o-pe-ro-si*. *Festschrift für Ernst Risch zum 75. Geburtstag*, pp. 601–618. Berlin/New York: Walter de Gruyter.

Rix, H. 1963. *Das etruskische Cognomen*. Wiesbaden: Otto Harrassowitz.

————. 1968. "Zur etruskischen Silbenpunktierung." *Münchener Studien zur Sprachwissenschaft* 23:85–104.

————. 1975. Review of Pfiffig 1969. *Göttingische Gelehrte Anzeigen* 227:117–143.

————. 1983. "Norme e variazioni nell'ortografia etrusca." *ΑΙΩΝ, sezione linguistica* 5:127–140.

————. 1984a. "La scrittura e la lingua." In M. Cristofani (ed.), *Gli etruschi. Una nuova immagine*, pp. 210–238. Florence: Giunti Martello.

————. 1984b. "Etr. meχ rasnal = lat. res publica." In *Studi di antichità in onore di Guglielmo Maetzke*, pp. 455–468. Roma: Bretschneider.

————. 1989a. "Zur Morphostruktur des etruskischen s-Genetivs." *Studi etruschi* 55:169–193.

————. 1989b. "Per una grammatica storica dell'etrusco." In *Secondo Congresso Internazionale Etrusco, Firenze 26 Maggio–2 Giugno 1985*, vol. 3, pp. 1293–1306. Roma: Bretschneider.

————. 1996. "Il testo paleoumbro di Poggio Sommavilla." *Studi etruschi* 61:233–246.

————. 1998. *Rätisch und Etruskisch*. Innsbruck: Institut für Sprachwissenschaft der Universität.

Rix, H. and G. Meiser. 1991. *Etruskische Texte. Editio minor*. Vol. I, *Einleitung, Konkordanz, Indices*; vol. II, *Texte*. Tübingen: Narr.

Schulze-Thulin, B. 1993. "Zur Wortstellung im Etruskischen." *Studi etruschi* 58:177–195.

Schumacher, S. 1992. *Die rätischen Inschriften. Geschichte und heutiger Stand der Forschung*. Innsbruck: Institut für Sprachwissenschaft der Universität.

Steinbauer, D. 1999. *Neues Handbuch des Etruskischen*. St. Katharinen: Scripta Mercaturae Verlag [appeared after completion of the manuscript].

Wachter, R. 1986. "Die etruskische und venetische Silbenpunktierung." *Museum Helveticum* 43:111–126.

Woodard, R. 1997. *Greek Writing from Knossos to Homer*. Oxford: Oxford University Press.

Wylin, K. 2000. *Il verbo etrusco. Ricerca morfosintattica delle forme usate in funzione verbale*. Roma: Bretschneider. [appeared after completion of the manuscript]

CHAPTER 8

Continental Celtic

JOSEPH F. ESKA

1. HISTORICAL AND CULTURAL CONTEXTS

The term *Continental Celtic* does not refer to a single linguistic entity – it is not a synonym for Gaulish – but to the entirety of the Celtic linguistic documentation from the ancient European continent. At the present time we can distinguish a discrete language called *Hispano-Celtic* (also known as *Celtiberian*), spoken in the north central meseta of the Iberian peninsula, from *Gaulish*, varieties of which were spoken from Asia Minor in the east through central Europe southward into the northern Italian peninsula and extending to the English Channel and eventually, with the Belgic migrations, over it into Britain. The variety of Gaulish spoken around the northern Italian lake district, usually called *Lepontic*, and that spoken in Asia Minor, usually called *Galatian*, are viewed by some as separate languages, though this view has weakened in recent years (Eska 1998b; cf. Uhlich, forthcoming). It is now commonly believed that Hispano-Celtic first separated from the Proto-Celtic speech area in central Europe sometime in the early first millennium BC, and developed henceforth on its own. The remainder of the Proto-Celtic speech area then developed as a dialect continuum as speakers spread across Europe and into Asia Minor. The traditional view is that this continuum subsequently divided into a *Goidelic* branch and a *Gallo-Brittonic* branch, but an increasing number of scholars have begun to stress the prehistoric unity of Insular Celtic as opposed to Gaulish. Galatian and British, the ancestor of the Brittonic languages, are very poorly attested and will not be discussed further herein.

It is often very difficult to date Continental Celtic inscriptions precisely. While there is some evidence for morphological innovations within the periods of attestation of the various languages, individual inscriptions usually can be identified only as earlier or later on the basis of the script employed (earlier inscriptions being engraved in non-Roman scripts), or on other epigraphic or extra-linguistic grounds. The earliest records are found in Lepontic, which is attested from *c.* 600 BC to the end of the millennium. Cisalpine Gaulish, probably differentiated from Lepontic only chronologically, is attested in eight inscriptions from the last two centuries of the first millennium BC. Transalpine Gaulish, first attested in the third century BC, was engraved in Greek characters until it gave way after the Roman conquest to Roman characters. The language probably ceased to be spoken in the second half of the first millennium AD. Though the last to be attested, from *c.* 200 BC to the second century AD, Hispano-Celtic is, by and large, the most conservative variety of Continental Celtic. As with Gaulish, earlier and later periods are distinguished through the employment of non-Roman or Roman scripts and other extra-linguistic means.

The various corpora of Continental Celtic are fragmentary and primarily epigraphic. Inscriptions and graffiti are engraved on stone buildings and monuments, metal plaques (usually lead in Gaul and bronze in Iberia), domestic implements, ceramic ware, and coins. The longest inscriptions are legal or magical-religious in substance. Shorter inscriptions include dedications, funeral monuments, proprietary statements, and expressions of various human sentiments and activities concerning, for example, affection, sex, and drinking. Secondary sources for Continental Celtic are individual lexical items or formulae recorded by classical or medieval writers and lexical items borrowed into ancient languages or surviving as substrate forms, especially in the Romance languages, but also in Basque. It is clear from the subject matter of the surviving records that the languages/dialects were in use at all levels of society. Occasionally, marked surface clausal configurations provide some evidence of a higher, poetic or more formal, register.

As mentioned above, it is probable that Lepontic and Galatian are not discrete languages, but regional dialects of Gaulish. Otherwise there is only sporadic evidence that is indicative of dialectal differentiation. Some scholars, in view of the existence of a few forms that have resisted the Gaulish labialization of Proto-Indo-European (PIE) $*k^w$ to p, believe that an archaic dialect of the language may have been preserved. However, since these forms are all month or (ultimately) divine names, it is more likely that they resisted the sound change because of their sacred character, as is not uncommon cross-linguistically.

2. WRITING SYSTEMS

As alluded to above, the Continental Celtic languages were recorded in the earlier periods of their attestation, and sometimes entirely, in various local indigenous scripts before the employment of Roman characters was adopted (see Campanile 1983).

2.1 Hispano-Celtic

The large majority of the Hispano-Celtic corpus was engraved in an adaptation of the semi-moraic, semi-segmental Iberian script. Stops are noted with moraic characters that do not indicate voicing and include an inherent vocalism neutral to quantity; thus, there are five characters to write, for example, the dental stops *t/d* plus each of the five vowels: (transcribed) *Ta, Te, Ti, To, Tu*. The remaining consonants – nasals, liquids, semivowels, and sibilants – are noted with segmental characters, as are the vowels, which do not indicate quantity. The forms of the characters attested at Botorrita are given in Table 8.1.

In (1) are listed some alternative characters. The transcription is the traditional one. See further Tovar (1975), Untermann (1975:71–74), and Lejeune (1993).

Table 8.1	The Celtic adaptation of the Iberian script				
a	Ca	Pa	Ta	m	n
e	Ce	Pe	Te	l	ŕ
i	Ci	Pi	Ti	s	ś
o	Co	Po	To		
u	Cu	Pu	Tu		

(1)   The alternative nasal and rhotic sets

ṁ 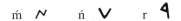   ń V   r 𐌒

There are a number of points to be noted about the mechanics of the script. There were two geographic zones which employed differing sets of characters to write the nasals. Broadly speaking, <ṁ> and <ń> were employed in the west, <m> and <n> in the east. Nasals are sometimes not written before stops; it is probable that this represents the transference of nasality to a preceding vowel (see Eska 2002a). The character <r> is attested only in some late coin legends; it does not contrast with <ŕ>. It now seems clear that <ś> represents PIE *s unchanged whereas <s> represents *s in voiced environments and *d in certain medial environments and in final position. Some scholars, therefore, elect to transcribe Ś as <z> or <đ> (and hence then elect to transcribe M as <s> instead of traditional <ś>). It is not yet clear whether this character represents more than one sound (or phoneme). Geminate consonants are written as single. The sequence <ei> is employed to write the inherited diphthong *ei*, and sometimes *e* from unstressed *i* (perhaps phonetically a raised [e]), as well as the phoneme which continues PIE *ē* in final syllables, which eventually became *ī* (perhaps phonetically a lowered [i:]).

Owing to the moraic quality of the stop characters, stop + liquid groups are difficult to represent. A variety of solutions are found, as listed in (2):

(2)   A. An empty vowel (having no phonetic reality) may be written which copies the quality of the following phonemic vowel: e.g., *enTaŕa* /entra:/
       B. The liquid and following phonemic vowel may be metathesized orthographically: e.g., *ConTeŕPia* /kontrebia:/
       C. The liquid may be elided orthographically: e.g., *ConPouTo* /konblowto/

The moraic quality of the stop characters also makes it difficult to determine the manner in which final stops were written; for example, it is unclear whether the third singular primary ending *-ti* is continued intact or with the vowel apocopated in the verbal form *aśeCaTi*. Owing to the influence of the segmental character of the Roman script, but prior to its adoption, syllabic characters came to be followed by a separate character denoting the inherent vowel: for example, in *moñiTuuCooś*. On the use of empty vowels in the Celtic adaptation of the script, see De Bernardo Stempel (1996).

The origin of the Iberian script, which was deciphered by Gómez-Moreno (1922), remains a subject of debate (see de Hoz 1983). While it is agreed that there are Phoenician and Greek elements underlying the script, it is uncertain whether they were integrated simultaneously or whether an original script based upon one was renewed with elements of the other.

2.2   Lepontic

The entirety of the Lepontic and Cisalpine Gaulish corpora are engraved in variants of the north Etruscan script. The script is segmental, but shares various features of the Iberian script. Neither the voicing of stops nor the quantity of vowels is noted. Nasals are rarely noted before stops; as with this feature in Hispano-Celtic, in which it is sporadic, it is probable that this represents the transference of nasality to a preceding vowel (see Uhlich 1999:280 and 293 and Eska 2002b: 263–269). Table 35.2, adapted after De Marinis (1991:94), records the Lugano script, in which the corpus is engraved. See further Lejeune (1971:8–27; 1988:3–8).

The infrequently attested characters <χ> and <θ> were inserted into the script in order to introduce a voicing distinction for the dental and velar stops. Whether the new character

Table 8.2 The Lugano script

6–5 Centuries	Transcription	3–2 Centuries
A A	a	*A ꓨ*
ꓯ	e	*ꓯ ꓮ*
ꓯ ꓯ	v	—
ǂ	z	*⵰*
ꓩ	h	—
⊙	θ	—
I	i	*I*
ꓘ	K	*ꓘ ꓫ*
ꓶ ✓	l	*ꓶ*
ꟽ	m	*ꟽ M*
ꓬ	n	*ꓬ ꓥ*
ꟼ	P	*ꟼ*
ꟷ ꟷ	ś	*ꟷ ꟷ ꟷ*
ꓷ ꓷ	r	*ꓷ ◁ ꓷ*
⟨ ⟨ ⟩ ⟩	s	*⟨ ⟩*
X +	T	*X*
V ꓵ	u	*V*
↓	X	*ꓦ*
ꝗ O	o	*O ◇ ꝗ*

represents the voiceless or voiced stop varies among inscriptions. The phonetic value of the character <v> has been much disputed, but may well represent /ɸ/ from PIE *p; see Eska (1998a). The character <ś> and the twice attested <z> represent a sound (or two acoustically similar sounds) known as the *tau Gallicum* (see §3.3.1.1).

2.3 Gaulish in Greek characters

Prior to the Roman conquest of Transalpine Gaul, the Massiliote Greek script was employed to write in Gaulish. Noteworthy orthographic features of Greek-character Gaulish are the use of the digraph <ου> for Roman <u> and <v>, and the occasional use of <ει> for <ι>, <η> for <ε>, and <ω> for <o> (i.e., long-vowel graphemes for short vowels). The *tau Gallicum* sound (see §3.3.1.1) is variously written: <θ, θθ, σ, σσ, τ, ττ, σθ>. See further Lejeune (1985:427–434, 441–446).

2.4 Gaulish in Roman characters

Gaulish was engraved in Roman characters in both capitals and cursive script with the expected values. The *i-longa* is frequently attested, but it does not seem to be differentiated in value from <i>; it is now conventionally transcribed as <j>. The *tau Gallicum* sound (see §3.3.1.1) is written with a wide variety of mono-, di-, and trigraphs: <t, tt, th, tth, d, dd, đ, đđ, ts, ds, s, ss, ss, sc, sd, st>. In some later Gaulish inscriptions, the appearance of final <-m> has been attributed to Roman influence (i.e., perhaps the engraver was principally a Latin speaker).

3. PHONOLOGY

Since the Continental Celtic languages are not only fragmentarily attested, but also often engraved in scripts which are phonologically ill-suited to them, it is difficult to establish complete phonemic inventories. It is often necessary to rely upon Indo-European and Insular Celtic etymologies to determine the expected phonology of a form. Readers should keep in mind that the descriptions presented in this and subsequent sections may be incomplete.

3.1 Hispano-Celtic

3.1.1 Consonants

The consonantal phonemic inventory of Hispano-Celtic is as follows:

(3) Hispano-Celtic consonantal phonemes

$$
\begin{array}{llll}
 & t & k & k^w \\
b & d & g & g^w \\
m & n & & \\
 & s & & \\
 & l & & \\
 & r & & \\
 & & y & w
\end{array}
$$

The sound represented by the character <s> (NB that /s/ is represented by <ś>), whose status as a phoneme remains to be determined, is not included in (3). Phonetic values for it that have been suggested include the fricatives [z] or [ð] (Villar 1995a:65–82) and affricates [tˢ] or [dᶻ] (Ballester 1993–1995).

3.1.2 Vowels

The monophthongs and diphthongs of Hispano-Celtic are listed in (4):

(4) Hispano-Celtic vocalic phonemes

Monophthongs			*Diphthongs*	
i ī		u ū	ai	au
e ē	o		ei	eu
a ā			oi	ou

It is possible, but uncertain, that PIE $*\bar{e}$ is preserved in unstressed syllables; the element -*réś*, which is normally assumed to continue $*h_3r\bar{e}\hat{g}s$ "king," occurs several times as the second member of compound forms. Elsewhere, PIE $*\bar{e}$ has been raised to merge, at least phonemically, with ī. In some later inscriptions, PIE $*ei$ has been monophthongized to $\bar{e}$. A gap in the vowel system was caused by the raising of PIE $*\bar{o}$ to ū in mono- and final syllables and its lowering to ā elsewhere. Unstressed $*i$ has a tendency to be lowered to *e*: for example, *aŕe*- "fore-" from $*pr̥h_xí$-.

3.1.3 Consonant clusters

Groups of stop + *s* are routinely written as <ś>, which suggests that such groups assimilated to -*ss*-. The group *ks* appears to have sometimes been preserved, however, at least to judge from Roman character spellings which employ the character <x>. The inherited group *ln* also assimilates to *ll*. Other groups are generally preserved. Noteworthy is the fact that nasals do not always assimilate to the place of following stops, for example *TinPiTus* from *dě-en-b-*. The form *ConPouTo* is peculiar since the basic form of the prefix is *kom-* (but see now Eska 2002a: passim).

3.2 Lepontic

3.2.1 Consonants

The consonantal inventory of Lepontic is set out in (5):

(5) **Lepontic consonantal phonemes**

(ɸ/)p	t	k	(kʷ)
b		d	g	(gʷ)
m		n	
		s	
		l	
		r	
	y	w	

The sound(s) spelled by the characters <ś> and <z>, usually called the *tau Gallicum*, is not listed in (5), but is discussed at some length below (see §3.3.1.1). Though it is ordinarily considered to continue the sequence *ts* immediately, <ś> is apparently also used to spell the outcome of the group *-ksy-* in the accusative singular *naśom*, the Lepontic adaptation of the Greek neuter nominative-accusative adjective Νάξιον (Náksion). It is possible that early Lepontic continued PIE *p* as the bilabial fricative [ɸ] and preserved PIE *kʷ* in forms such as *Kuaśoni*; the latter might, however, contain *gʷ* from PIE *gʷʰ*.

3.2.2 Vowels

The inventory of Lepontic monophthongs and diphthongs is identical to that of Hispano-Celtic; see (4). The gap in the vowel system is as with Hispano-Celtic (see §3.1.2). PIE *ei* is preserved in final position, but elsewhere has been monophthongized to *ē*.

3.2.3 Consonant clusters

Consonant groups do not assimilate, save for *-nd-* > -*nn*- and the predecessors of the *tau Gallicum*.

3.3 Gaulish

Since the Gaulish corpus is the largest of the Continental Celtic languages and is attested over the longest chronological period, it is difficult to ascertain a synchronic phonemic inventory. Readers should be aware that the phonemic inventory presented in (6) and (7) is a composite.

3.3.1   Consonants

The consonantal phonemes of Gaulish appear to be as follows:

(6)   Gaulish consonantal phonemes

$$
\begin{array}{lll}
\text{p} & \text{t} & \text{k} \quad (\text{k}^{\text{w}}) \\
\text{b} & \text{d} & \text{g} \\
\text{m} & \text{n} & \\
 & \text{s} & \\
 & \text{l} & \\
 & \text{r} & \\
 & \quad \text{y} & \text{w}
\end{array}
$$

The labiovelar k^w is preserved only in a few archaic forms.

3.3.1.1   Tau Gallicum

The *tau Gallicum* is not included in (6). Based upon the diversity of graphemes with which it is written, it is usually assumed to have been a dental affricate, fricative, or sibilant. This is supported by etymological considerations, as the *tau Gallicum* often immediately continues *ts* and **ds*, and ultimately **st* (including **st* < **tst* < **-t-t-* and **-d-t-*). It is commonly believed that the most likely phonetic value for it is [tˢ], but other suggestions include [tᶿ], [θ] (or retracted [θ̱]), [θs], and [tʰ]. It is usually assumed that the *tau Gallicum*, even when written as a di- or trigraph, was a single segment, but in view of the fact that it is cognate with Insular Celtic *-ss-*, it is probable that it often was a geminate. The most complete discussion of the *tau Gallicum* is that of Evans (1967:410–420), but see also Eska (1998c).

3.3.2   Vowels

The monophthongs and diphthongs of Gaulish are listed in (7):

(7)   Gaulish vocalic phonemes

	Monophthongs		*Diphthongs*	
i ī		u ū	ai	au
e ē	o ō		ei	eu
a ā			oi	ou

The diphthongs *ai* and *eu* appear only in older forms; in later forms, *ai* is contracted to *ī* and *eu* merges with *ou*, which subsequently contracts to *ō*. The diphthong *oi* is attested early, then is contracted to *ī*; it reemerges later, as does *ei* (PIE **ei* having become *ē* in Gaulish), as the result of the loss of intervocalic **p* and **w*. There is a tendency for long diphthongs to shorten: for example, *ā*-stem dative singular **-āi* > *-ai* > *ī*; and *u*-stem dative singular (from the locative) **-oū* > *-ou*. Unstressed *i* frequently is lowered to *e*: for example, **pr̥h$_x$í-* "fore-" > *are-*; and dative or instrumental plural *-bi* > *-be*.

3.4   Allophonic variation

Though the Continental Celtic languages – as far as the scripts employed will allow – are usually written phonemically, occasional quasi-phonetic orthographies occur which provide some evidence for allophonic variation in Hispano-Celtic and Gaulish.

In Hispano-Celtic, there is a strong tendency towards labialization of *o* to *u* when adjacent to a nonfinal labial: for example, the *o*-stem dative plural is often written <-uPós> and the first plural present ending is written <-mu(s)>. That *-o-* occurs at all may be the product of phonemic or conservative orthography; but the *o*-stem accusative singular *-om*, for example, is always written with <-o->.

In Gaulish, the velar stop /k/ becomes the fricative [x] before *s* and *t*. Mid vowels in hiatus with non-high vowels tend to be raised: for example, *to = me = declaï* < **lā-* + **-e*; compare *coetic* and *cuet[ic]*, both with prevocalic /ko/-; and Λουερνιος /luernios/ < **lo-erno-* < **h₂lop-erno-*.

Hispano-Celtic and Gaulish share a tendency for *e* to raise to *i* before nasal + stop clusters (Gaulish more so). It is presumed that in all of Continental Celtic nasals were realized as [ŋ] before velars. This view is supported by Gaulish inscriptions engraved in Greek characters which employ <γγ> (the Greek grapheme for [ŋg]), for example, εσκιγγορειξ for [eskiŋgori:ks].

There is substantial evidence for phonetic lenition in both Hispano-Celtic and Gaulish. In Hispano-Celtic, /s/ = <ś> is normally spelled as <s> in voiced environments (perhaps here being [z]). The clearest evidence for phonetic lenition is provided by genitive singular *TuaTeŕoś* and nominative plural *Tua[Te]ŕés* < **dugater-* < **dʰugh₂ter-* "daughter," which exhibit the change of [g] > [γ] > ø. The absence of indication for voicing or manner of articulation in the Iberian script and the rarity of quasi-phonetic orthography in Roman character inscriptions conceal any further evidence.

In Gaulish, there are two forms which provide evidence for [s] > ø / V __ V: dative or instrumental plural *suiorebe* < **swesor-* "sister"; and *sioxt* < 3rd sg. preterite **sesog-* + *-t* (base **seg-* "add"; see Eska 1994c). In later Gaulish, [g] also is often deleted intervocalically. Gaulish is also well known for orthographic variation between <c> and <g> (similar variation between other homorganic stops is much less common); it remains uncertain whether this represents phonetic or orthographic variation, though, since the large majority of tokens involve the substitution of a voiceless for a voiced stop, Gray (1944:227) may be correct in suspecting that the voiced stop phonemes of Gaulish were phonetically voiceless. This orthographic variation would then be another type of quasi-phonetic orthography. There are also several examples in which /t/ in lenited position is engraved with one of the graphemes employed to write the *tau Gallicum* (see §3.3.1.1): for example, *eđđic* (cf. *etic*) "and"; *gnatha* (cf. *nata*) "daughter"; and *bueđ* (cf. *buet*) "be" – suggesting that the lenited allophone of /t/ was either identical, or acoustically similar, to the *tau Gallicum* consonant.

3.5   Accent

There is little, if any, direct evidence for the placement of stress in any of the Continental Celtic languages. In Hispano-Celtic, the failure of final *-m* to labialize a preceding *-o-* indicates that it was very weakly articulated, which suggests that the stress may have been fixed towards the beginning of the word. Likewise, in later Gaulish there was a tendency for final *-s* and *-n* to be dropped. However, French toponyms suggest that stress could be variably placed; there are numerous examples in which two different French toponyms are descended from a single, but variably stressed, Gaulish ancestor, for example, *Nemours* from *Nemáusus*, but *Nîmes* from *Némausus*. Falc'hun (1981:294–313) has suggested that penultimate stress was more archaic and that antepenultimate stress was an innovation which spread from the Mediterranean. The placement of stress in Gaulish has also been discussed recently by De Bernardo Stempel (1994; 1995) and Schrijver (1995:20–21).

4. MORPHOLOGY

4.1 Word formation

Like other ancient languages of the Indo-European family, the Continental Celtic languages are fusional. Words are composed of a basic morpheme to which derivational prefixes and suffixes may be affixed. There is some evidence that multiple prefixation, as is common in the Insular Celtic languages, was productive. A stem-vowel could be added to the end of this complex, after which the inflectional ending, if any, was attached.

4.2 Nominal morphology

Nominals, which include nouns, adjectives, and pronouns, are inflected for case, gender, and number. There is evidence for all eight classical Indo-European cases – nominative, accusative, genitive, dative, locative, instrumental, ablative, and vocative – but not in all numbers and declensions, and not in all languages. The familiar three genders – masculine, feminine, and neuter – of the Indo-European family are well documented, as are the singular and plural numbers. There is some slight evidence that the dual also existed.

4.2.1 Nominal stem-classes

4.2.1.1 Hispano-Celtic

The nominal inflection of Hispano-Celtic as presently attested is given in Table 8.3. Uncertain identifications are followed by a question mark.

The *o*-stem genitive singular in *-o* is an innovation via a proportional analogy with the pronominal paradigm. Compare the Proto-Celtic *ā*-stem genitive singular syntagm *sosyās bnās* "this woman" with *o*-stem *sosyo wirī* "this man". In order to extrapolate the nominal

Table 8.3 Hispano-Celtic nominal inflection

	ā-stem	o-stem	i-stem	u-stem	n-stem[1]	n-stem[2]	r-stem	nt-stem	C-stem
Singular									
Nom.	-a	-oś	-iś		-u	-i			-ś
Acc.	-am	-om	-im					-nTam	
Nom.-acc. neut.		-om							
Gen.	-aś	-o	-eś?		-unoś	-inoś	-eŕoś	-nToś	-oś
Dat.	-ai	-ui	-e/-ei?	-uei	-unei	-inei			-ei
Loc.		-ei							
Instr.		-u?			-unu?				
Abl.	-as	-us	-is	-ues?	-unes				-es
Plural									
Nom.	-aś?	-oi?	-iś					-eŕeś	-eś
Acc.	-aś	-uś?		-uś?					
Nom.-acc. neut.		-a							
Gen.	-aum	-um							
Dat.		-o/uPoś							

Table 8.4	Lepontic nominal inflection				
	ā-stem	o-stem	i-stem	n-stem	C-stem
Singular					
Nom.	-a	-os	-is	-u	
Acc.	-am	-om			
Nom.-acc. neut.		-om			
Gen.		-oiso, -i			
Dat.	-ai	-ui	-ei?	-onei/-oni	
Plural					
Nom.		-oi		-ones	
Acc.					-eś
Dat.		-oPos		-onePos	

genitive singular in -o one need only notice that in the ā-stem inflection the pronominal and nominal endings are identical after the -y- in the demonstrative (see Prosdocimi 1991: 158–159; Eska 1995:41–42). The identification of o- and n-stem forms in -u as instrumental singulars has been proposed by Villar (1993–1995). The o-stem nominative plural in -oi is perhaps attested once (or twice) in a single inscription. A single accusative plural form in -uś could be either an o- or u-stem. In the animate n[1]-stems, the lengthened-grade suffix *-ō(n)-, proper only to the nominative singular, has been extended throughout the paradigm.

4.2.1.2   Lepontic

The nominal inflection of Lepontic as attested is given in Table 8.4. Uncertain identifications are followed by a question mark.

The o-stem genitive singular in -oiso is attested only in very early forms. It appears to continue Indo-European pronominal *-osyo; Colonna (in Gambari and Colonna 1986:138) and Lejeune (1989:64) treat the Lepontic ending, which is also attested once in Venetic (see Ch. 34, §4.1.1 [7]) (but see now Eska and Wallace 1999), as a metathesized variant. Eska (1995:42) suggests that it is the result of a crossing with the Lepontic descendant of the Proto-Indo-European pronominal genitive plural *-oisōm (cf. Hisp.-Celt. śoiśum). De Hoz (1990) suggests that, in addition to earlier -oiso and later-ī, Lepontic also had an o-stem genitive singular in -ū from ablative singular *-ōd. These forms have traditionally been interpreted as animate n-stem nominative singulars (see Eska 1995, especially pp. 34–37 for a critique of de Hoz's proposal). Attested once, the n-stem dative singular -oni seems to represent an early instance of the locative in dative function (see now Eska and Wallace 2001). The consonant-stem accusative plural ending -eś (attested once) presumably has been remade by analogy with the vocalism of the nominative plural ending, since inherited *-ns would have yielded Proto-Celtic *-ans > *-ās. The spelling of the sibilant with <ś> perhaps indicates that an epenthetic *-t- was inserted into the inherited *-ns group (perhaps *-ens > *-ents > <-éś> = /-ēts/), as is attested elsewhere in the accusative plural ending of Luwian (so also in Cis. Gaul. acc. pl. arTuaś).

4.2.1.3   Gaulish

The nominal inflection of Gaulish as attested is given in Table 8.5. Multiple exponents of a single ending are given in chronological order of attestation. The inflectional morphemes

Table 8.5 Gaulish nominal inflection

	ā-stem	o-stem	i-stem	u-stem	n-stem	r-stem	C-stem
Singular							
Nom.	-a	-os, -o	-is	-us	-u	-ir	-s
Acc.	-an,-em	-om, -on	-in			-erem	
	-en, -im						
Nom.-acc. neut.		-on	-e?	-u	-an		
Gen.	-as, -ias	-i	-ios?				-os
Dat.	-ai, -i	-ui, -u	-e	-ou			-i
Loc.		-e					
Instr.	-ia	-u					
Voc.	-a	-e					
Dual							
Nom.-acc.		-o					
Plural							
Nom.	-as	-oi, -i	-is	-oues			-es
Acc.	-as	-os, -us					
Nom.-acc. neut.		-a					
Gen.	-anom	-on	-iom			-ron	
Dat.	-abo, -abi?	-obo, -obe?				-rebo, -rebe?	-bi
Instr.	-abi?	-obe?				-rebe?	

attested only in north Etruscan or Greek characters are here transcribed into Roman characters. Uncertain identifications are followed by a question mark.

The ā-stem inflection in later Gaulish has been deeply affected by the inherited ī-stem inflection. Accusative singular forms with *e*-vocalism in the ā- and *r*-stems appear to be the result of the raising of /a/ before the final nasal, as is also indicated for Old Irish. The final -*m* of ā-stem accusative singular -*em* is usually taken to be archaic. The ā-stem dative singular in -*ī* is the result of contraction of -*ai* < *-āi. The ā-stem genitive plural in -*anom* is attested in only one inscription and could, therefore, represent a local innovation. Owing to the difficulty of interpreting the documents, it is unclear whether ā-, *o*-, and *r*-stem forms in -*bi*, -*be* are dative or instrumental plural. The *o*-stem dative singular in -*ū* could represent either the apocope of -*i* from earlier -*ūi* or syncretism of the dative, instrumental (and ablative?) singular. The neuter nominative-accusative singular *n*-stem in -*an* regularly continues *-m̥. The consonant-stem dative singular in -*i* continues the inherited locative singular ending.

4.2.2 Pronouns

Partial paradigms of a variety of pronominals are attested in Continental Celtic. The demonstrative stem *so/ā-* is attested in Hispano-Celtic and Gaulish, with the initial *s*-, originally only in the masculine and feminine nominative singular, extended throughout the paradigm. It seems to have been fully stressed in Hispano-Celtic; it is unclear whether it ever was stressed in Gaulish. Gaulish also had a reduplicated formation attested in nominative-accusative neuter singular *sosin* and *sosio*. This -*sin* element also seems to be found in several forms which appear to be ancestors of the Insular Celtic article, namely, *in=sinde, indas* (with early loss of initial *s*-; the sign = represents a clitic boundary), and *o='nda* (contracted in composition with a preposition).

The relative pronominal stem **yo-* appears as a stressed and inflected form in Hispano-Celtic. In Gaulish, it has been reduced to an uninflected subordinating clitic particle *=yo*.

The anaphoric pronominal stem **ei-* appears to continue its inherited function in two Gaulish forms, namely, *eianom* and *eiabi*. It also can function as a clitic object pronoun. Many scholars believe that the nominative can also be attached as a clitic to a verb for emphasis, for example, neuter singular *buet=id*, though some would segment the sequence otherwise.

Seemingly related to the anaphoric stem is a series of forms which may ultimately be related to the Latin pronoun *iste*. These are Hisp.-Celt. *iśTe* and *śTaṁ* and *śTena* (with aphaeresis?), Lep. *iśos*, and Gaul. *ison* and *isoc* (with attached deitic **=k̂e?*).

Hispano-Celtic also has a pronominal stem *o*- attested in the the forms *osiaś* (fem. gen. sg.?) and *osaś* (fem. acc. pl.?) which perhaps displays a different ablaut grade of the anaphoric stem.

There are very few personal pronouns attested. The only ones which have been securely identified are the clitic accusatives, Gaulish first singular *=me*, first plural *=snj* and first singular dative *=mi < *moi̯*. The attested possessive pronouns are first singular *imon* and *mon* and second singular *to*. It also seems probable that the first singular nominative form *=mi* (< acc. **mē*) and second singular *= tu* are attested as emphasizing pronouns, though they have been otherwise interpreted (see §4.3.6).

Finally, the deictic stem **k̂ei-* is attested in the Gaulish syntagm *du=ci*, literally "to here," employed as a connective "and."

4.3 Verbal morphology

In typical Indo-European fashion, the Continental Celtic verb is marked for tense, voice, and mood.

4.3.1 Tense

In the verbal system, there is good evidence for the present, preterite, and future tenses; Meid (1994:392–393) suggests that Hispano-Celtic also continued the Indo-European imperfect, but this is uncertain. The present tense is attested in a number of common Indo-European formations.

The preterite is composed of forms which continue Indo-European perfects, *s*-aorists, and renewed imperfects. There is also at least one example of suppletion (see Schmidt 1986 and Eska 1990). Owing to phonological reductions, the Continental Celtic *s*-preterite has in some cases been augmented with a thematic (i.e., *o*-stem) ending; compare unaugmented Gaul. 3rd sg. *prinas* "he sold" < **kʷri-n-h₂-s-t* (which would have been homophonous with the second singular), and augmented Gaul. 3rd sg. *legasit* "he placed" < **legʰ-eh₂-s-t + *-et*. The Continental Celtic *t*-preterite is of multiple origin. Like the Insular Celtic *t*-preterite, it continues the Indo-European *s*-aorist in certain forms: for example, Gaul. 3rd sg. *toberte* < **to-bʰer-s-t +* 3rd sg. perf. *-e*, which was affixed to characterize the form as third singular overtly once the *-t* was regrammaticalized as the exponent of tense. A perfect ending was also affixed to inherited imperfect forms in order to recharacterize them as preterites: for example, Lep. 3rd sg. *KariTe* "he placed" < **k-r̥-ye-t + -e* after the apocope of primary **-i* (at least after voiceless consonants) caused the present and imperfect to fall together.

The attested Continental Celtic future forms all continue the Indo-European desiderative in *-(h₁)sye/o-: for example, Gaul. 1st sg. *marcosior* (a derivative of *marc* "horse," of uncertain meaning) and 3rd sg. *bissjet*. A reduplicated formation appears to be attested in Gaul. 1st sg. *siaxsiou* < ⁺*si-sag-si̯ū*. (Pierre-Yves Lambert has proposed that Gaul. *lilous* is a third singular reduplicated perfect, but this is very uncertain.)

4.3.2 Aspect

There is a small amount of evidence for perfective aspect in Hispano-Celtic and Gaulish. In Hispano-Celtic, the perfectivizer *Con-* is prefixed in the verbal adjective *ConśCiliTom* "cut up." It is attested in the Gaul. 3rd sg. perf. *To=śo=KoTe* "he offered it." The prefix *ek-* likewise is a perfectivizer in the Gaul. 3rd sg. perf. *to=me=declai* "she set me up" < *de-ek-*. The prefix *ro-*, the most common perfectivizer in Insular Celtic, may occur in reduced form in Gaul. 3rd sg. perf. *readdas* "he dedicated (it)." These prefixes are all attested in this function in Insular Celtic.

4.3.3 Voice

The large majority of verbs presently attested in the Continental Celtic corpus, if not all, are active in voice. There are not a few forms which terminate in *-r*, but the majority of these are deponents, and hence active in voice. Two forms which have been claimed to be passive in voice are Gaul. 3rd pl. *diligentir* and Hisp.-Celt. 3rd pl. *PinToŕ*.

4.3.4 Mood

There is good evidence for the indicative, subjunctive, and imperative moods in Continental Celtic. Subjunctives are characterized by the suffixes *-se/o-* (e.g., Hisp.-Celt. 3rd sg. pres. *CaPiseTi*) or *-ā-* (e.g., Gaul. 2nd sg. pres. *lubijas* "you enjoy/love"). The subjunctive mood can also be characterized by the thematic vowel (e.g., Gaul. 3rd sg. *buet* /bwet/ "he may be").

Imperatives are attested in both the simple and so-called future type. The former, which are certainly attested in only the second singular, take the form of the bare present stem, for example, Gaul. *gabi* "take!" < *gʰabʰ-ye-ø* or continue the imperative in *-si*, for example, *jexs*. The latter, which was characterized by the affixation of *-tōd* to the simple imperative in Proto-Indo-European, appears in Hispano-Celtic in the third singular with the ending *-Tus*. This ending has also been claimed to underlie Gaulish third singular and plural forms in *-tutu* and *-ntutu*, respectively, with an iterated ending as attested in Umbrian.

Lambert (1994:63) suggests that the optative mood is also attested in Gaulish, indicated by the exponent *-si-* in the form *ni=tixsintor*.

4.3.5 Verbal stem-classes

Owing to the fragmentary nature of the corpus, there is insufficient material available to try to attempt to reconstruct the verbal conjugations of Continental Celtic.

4.3.6 Verb endings

The endings of the verb are also far from complete. Those attested for the present tense are given in Table 8.6, those of the preterite in Table 8.7.

In the Gaulish first singular, both thematic *-u* and athematic *-mi* are attested. Some first-person verbs terminate with the sequence *-umi*, which some have taken to represent a fusion of the two endings (cf. Sanskrit *-āmi*). It is also possible, however, that the segment *-mi* in

Table 8.6 Present endings of Continental Celtic

		Hispano-Celtic	Gaulish
Singular	1.		-u, -mi
	2.		-s
	3.	-Ti, -t	-t
Singular deponent	1.		-or
	3.		-toi?
Plural	1.	-mus, -mu	
	2.		-tes, -tis
	3.	-nTi	-nt
Plural deponent	3.		-ntor
Plural passive	3.	-nTof?	-ntir?

Table 8.7 Preterite endings of Continental Celtic

		Hispano-Celtic	Lepontic	Gaulish
Singular	3.	-es?	-e, -u	-s, -t, -e, -u, -ai?, -i?
Plural	3.			-us
Plural deponent	3.	-nTo?		

such endings is a clitic emphasizing pronoun. This seems likely since first singular verbs can terminate with both *-u* and *-umi* in the same text.

Villar (1995a:31–33 = 1995b:17–19) has proposed that some Hispano-Celtic forms in *-es* may continue third singular perfects to which secondary *-t* was affixed, as in Old Latin, which then was voiced to *-d* and subsequently developed into the phone(me) represented by -<s>. The Gaulish ending *-ai*, later contracted to *-ī*, apparently is third singular to judge by context. Forms in *-us* have traditionally been interpreted as third plural, made by the affixation of a pluralizing *-s* to third singular *-u*, but this has recently been challenged by de Hoz (1995).

4.3.7 Nonfinite verbals

Like the Insular Celtic languages, Continental Celtic did not have true infinitives, but employed nominalized verbs. There are three attested in Hispano-Celtic, all formed with the exponent *-un-* and inflected for the dative case (it is not clear whether this suffix continues *-w(e)r/n-* or *-mn-*).

There is a variety of participial forms attested. A single Gaulish inscription has four examples of the present active participle in *-nt-*, all of which terminate in *-ontias* (*ā*-stem gen. sg. or nom. or acc. pl.). The same inscription contains a single example of a form in *-mno-* which has been interpreted as a mediopassive participle (though this would require syncope in *-mano- < *-mh₁no-*). More widely attested is the passive participle in *-to/ā-*. It is attested in Hispano-Celtic as a verbal adjective and often in Gaulish in anthroponyms.

4.4 Derivational morphology

The principal method of derivation in all of the Continental Celtic languages is affixation. Prefixation is as common as suffixation. Compounding is also very frequent, especially in the formation of anthroponyms (Schmidt 1957; Evans 1967). There is one particularly interesting example of a *dvandva* compound (see *WAL* Ch. 26, §4.4.2.1) in Gaulish, genitive plural *Teuoχ̑Tonịọn* "of gods and men" < *$deiwo$- + *d^hg^honyo-.

4.5 Numerals

There is a little evidence for numerals in Continental Celtic. In Hispano-Celtic, the attested cardinals are *Tiṛiś* "three" (masc. acc.), *śueś* "six," and *CanTom* "one hundred." A single ordinal, "tenth," is attested as acc. sg. *TeCameTam*. For some forms which arise in onomastics, see Tovar (1954).

There are only two cardinals attested in Gaulish: *tiďres* "three" (fem. acc.) and possibly *trịcontis* "thirty." Compositional forms include *cintu-* "first," *tri-* "third," *petru-* "four" and *pompe-*"five." We are fortunate that a nearly complete set of ordinals for 1–10 have been preserved; these are listed in (8):

(8) | | | | |
|---|---|---|---|
| *1st* | cintuxo[s] | *6th* | suexos |
| *2nd* | allos | *7th* | sextametos |
| *3rd* | tr[itios] | *8th* | oxtumetos |
| *4th* | petuar[ios] | *9th* | namet[os] |
| *5th* | pinpetos | *10th* | decametos |

A further ordinal, Latinized dative-ablative singular *petrudecameto* "fourteenth," indicates that the tens were formed by compounding. One final form, probably the fraction "one-third," which appears to be calqued on Latin acc. pl. *trientēs*, is *trianis*.

5. SYNTAX

Owing to the fragmentary nature of the Continental Celtic corpus, we have a much less complete picture of syntax than of phonology or morphology. This section, then, does no more than present a selection of the principal constructions that are attested. We are, however, in the fortunate position, owing to the varying degrees of conservatism of the individual languages, of being able to observe the evolution of Celtic clausal configuration in fieri (see Eska 1994b). The languages are addressed in order of increasing innovation. In the examples, translations are provided only when fairly secure.

5.1 Hispano-Celtic

5.1.1 Word order

Hispano-Celtic is an SOV (Subject–Object–Verb) language, exhibiting "*pro*-drop" (i.e., the subject can be expressed merely by verb inflection), as is usually reconstructed for Proto-Indo-European:

(9) uTa   ośCues   śTena   ueŕsoniTi
     CONN.   PRO.NOM.SG.   NP.ACC.PL.   V.3RD SG.
     "whoever carries out these things"

It is noteworthy that imperative verbs are also clause-final, for example:

(10) TeCameTam   TaTus
      NP.ACC.SG.   V.3RD SG. IMPV.
      "let him offer a tithe"

Verbs are not bound to clause-final position, however; they may be raised to clause-initial position for various pragmatic purposes, for example:

(11) iom   aśeCaTi   amPiTinCounei   śTena
      CONN.   V.3RD SG.   NP.DAT.SG.   NP.ACC.PL.

It is possible for a non-core argument to appear to the right of the verb. In the following example, the noun phrase (NP) to the right of the verb is in a disjunctive relationship (see §5.1.2) with a core argument:

(12) ioś   uŕanTiom = ue   auseTi   aŕaTim = ue
      PRO.NOM.SG.   NP.ACC.SG. = DISJ.   V.3RD SG.   NP.ACC.SG. = DISJ.

Though it is an SOV language, Hispano-Celtic is not rigorously head-final. While attributive genitives do precede their head nouns, for example,

(13) A. ologas   togias
         NP.GEN.SG.   NP.ACC.PL.
     B. tiaso   togias
         NP.GEN.SG.   NP.ACC.PL.

subordinate clauses usually follow matrix clauses (see [17]), and adjectives follow their head nouns, for example,

(14) A TiŕiCanTam   PeŕCuneTaCam
       N.ACC.SG.   ADJ.ACC.SG.
     B śleiTom   ConśCiliTom
       N.ACC.SG.   ADJ.ACC.SG.

In prepositional phrases, both prepositions and postpositions are attested. Individual pre- and postpositions are consistent in their placement:

(15) A. eś   ueŕTai
        from   NP.DAT.SG.
     B. TiŕiCanTam   eni
        NP.ACC.SG.   in/at

5.1.2 Clitics

The corpus does not provide any examples of pronominal clitics. The only clitics attested to date are the connective =*Cue*, =*que* < *=$k^w e$ and the disjunctive =*ue* < *=*we*. In the earlier language, they are attached to each member of a serial correlation, as in (16A), but in the later language are attached only to the final member, as in (16B):

(16) A PouśTom = ue   Córuinom = ue   maCási[.]m = ue   ailam = ue
       NP.ACC.SG. = DISJ.   NP.ACC.SG. = DISJ.   NP.ACC.SG. = DISJ.   NP.ACC.SG. = DISJ.
     B eniorosei   equeisui = que
       NP.DAT.SG.   NP.DAT.SG. = CONN.

5.1.3 Coordination

The attested corpus exhibits a variety of connectives with which clauses can be coordinated, *uTa* (cf. Sanskrit *utá*), *to* (cf. Old Hittite *ta*), and *iom*. Asyndeton is also common.

5.1.4 Subordination

Subordinate clauses generally, but not always, follow main clauses. In the following example, the subject of the subordinate clause (17B) is a stressed relative pronoun which agrees with the NP in the main clause (17A) to which it is bound:

(17) A. iom   CuśTaiCoś   aŕsnaś   CuaTi
          CONN.   NP.NOM.SG.   NP.FEM.ACC.PL.   V.3RD SG.
      B. iaś   osiaś   ueŕTaToś = ue   Temei = ue   ŕoPiśeTi
          REL.PRO.FEM.ACC.PL.   PRO.GEN.SG?   ADV. = DISJ.   ADV. = DISJ.   V.3RD SG

The attested corpus also contains an interesting example of the Proto-Indo-European correlative construction (cf. Sanskrit *yá-…sá-…*):

(18) A. iomui   liśTaś   TiTaś   sisonTi
          REL.PRO.DAT.SG.   NP   NP   V.3RD PL
      B. śomui   iom   aŕsnaś   PionTi
          DEM.PRO.DAT.SG.   CONN.   NP   V.3RD PL

5.1.5 Agreement

Presently, all evidence points to subject–verb agreement for person and number, and noun–adjective agreement for case, number, and gender.

5.2 Lepontic

5.2.1 Word order

The Lepontic corpus presently contains only three verbal sequences. One of them is archetypally SOV in structure:

(19) uvamoKozis Plialeθu   uvl TiauioPos ariuonePos   siTeś   TeTu
      NP.NOM.SG.   NP.DAT.PL.   NP.ACC.PL.   V.3RD SG
      "U. B. offered s. to the U. A."

The underlying configuration of the remaining two verbal sequences, which both occur in the same inscription, is unclear owing to movement:

(20) A. PelKui   Pruiam   Teu   KariTe
          NP.DAT.SG.   NP.ACC.SG.   NP.NOM.SG.   V.3RD SG.
          "D. set up the b. for B."
      B. iśos   KaliTe   Palam
          PRO.NOM.SG.   V.3RD SG.   NP.ACC.SG.
          "he (likewise) erected the memorial stone"

It is, of course, necessary to analyze both clauses together. It is unclear whether they are SOV underlyingly, with postposition of the accusative argument in (20B), or SVO, with raising of both the dative and accusative arguments in (20A). What can be said with certainty, however, is that, unlike Hispano-Celtic, a core argument can appear to the right of the verb at the surface, as in (20B).

Lepontic adjectives follow the nouns they determine, for example:

(21) uinom   naśom
      N.NOM-ACC.SG.   ADJ.NOM-ACC.SG.
      "Naxian wine"

5.2.2 Clitics

There are no clitic pronominals attested in the Lepontic corpus. The connective $=$Pe $< * = k^w e$ is attested; it attaches to the final member of a serial correlation, for example:

(22) laTumarui   saPsuTai $=$ Pe
      NP.DAT.SG.   NP.DAT.SG. $=$ CONN.
      "for L. and S."

5.2.3 Agreement

Lepontic shows subject–verb agreement for person and number and noun–adjective agreement for case, number, and gender.

5.3 Gaulish

5.3.1 Word order

It is difficult to be sure about the underlying configuration of the Gaulish clause owing to the wide diversity of surface configurations attested; verb-initial, verb-medial, and verb-final are all found. Some of this variation could be due to dialectal or chronological differences, and much, no doubt, is the result of movement for pragmatic purposes and syntactic rules (see now Eska, forthcoming). There are only a handful of verb-final clauses attested, and the majority of verb-initial clauses contain imperative verbs. Those which are not imperative, for example,

(23) regu $=$ c   cambion
      V.1ST SG. $=$ CONN?   NP.ACC.SG.
      "I straighten the bent thing"

cannot be diagnosed as underlyingly verb-initial clauses, however, since they can also be analyzed as SVO clauses with *pro*-drop. It is clear, however, that Gaulish was not a verb-second language, as the following inscription, with two NPs preceding the verb, demonstrates (the bracketed character is superfluous):

(24) ratin briuatiom   frontu tarbetis[o]nios   ie{i}uru
      NP.ACC.SG.   NP.NOM.SG.   V.3RD SG.
      "F. T. dedicated the r. of the b."

The large majority of Gaulish clauses are verb-internal at the surface, for example:

(25) martialis dannotali   ieuru   ucuete   sosin celicnon
      NP.NOM.SG.   V.3RD SG.   NP.DAT.SG.   NP.ACC.SG.
      "M. D. dedicated this edifice to U."

A very important feature to take notice of is that, whenever a clitic pronominal object (see §5.3.3) is present in the clause, it must be syntactically hosted (i.e., adjacent) to the verb; this constraint on second-position clitics is known as *Vendryes' Restriction*. Since *Wackernagel's Law* was strongly grammaticalized in Celtic (at least by this time), this had the effect of ensuring that the verb occupied clause-initial position. In such cases, the verb either occupies absolute initial position in the clause, for example,

(26) sioxt = i   albanos   panna(s)   extra tuđ(on)   ccc
      V. = PRO.NEUT.   NP.NOM.SG.   NP.FEM.ACC.PL. PP   NUM.
      NOM.-ACC.PL.
      "A. added them, vessels beyond the allotment (in the amount of) 300"

or is preceded only by a null-position, semantically empty, sentential connective, the original purpose of which was to host the clitic phonologically (as familiar from Anatolian; see Ch. 18, §5.1), for example,

(27) to = me = declai   obalda natina
      CONN. = PRO.1ST SG.ACC.=V.3RD SG.   NP.NOM.SG.
      "O., (their) dear daughter, set me up"

It is commonly agreed that Vendryes' Restriction had a large role to play in the development of the VSO configuration of the Insular Celtic languages.

As one would expect in a language which is – predominately, at least – not verb-final, other syntactic configurations strongly tend to be head-initial. Genitives follow their head nouns, for example:

(28) A. ratin   briuatiom
          N.ACC.SG.   N.GEN.PL.
          "the fort of the b."
      B. aТоṃ   TeuoχTonioṇ
          N.ACC.SG.   N.GEN.PL.
          "the border of gods and men"

Likewise, the unmarked position for adjectives appears to be after their head nouns,

(29) A. τοουτιο{υ}ς   ναμαυσατις
          N.NOM.SG.   ADJ.NOM.SG.
          "citizen of Nîmes"
      B. ματρεβο   ναμαυσικαβο
          N.DAT.PL.   ADJ.DAT.PL.
          "to the Matres of Nîmes"

and PPs are always prepositional:

(30) A. in   alixie
          in   NP.LOC.SG.
          "in Alisia"
      B. extra   tuđ(on)
          beyond   NP.ACC.SG.
          "beyond the allotment"

A good example of a passive clause, though verbless, has been identified by Prosdocimi (1989):

(31) ουατιοουνουι   σο νεμετος   κομμου εσκεγγιλου
      NP.DAT.SG.   NP.NOM.SG.   NP.INSTR.SG.
      "to U. this n. [was dedicated] by C. E."

5.3.2 Subordination

Subordinate clauses generally follow their head and are characterized by the presence of an uninflected subordinating particle $=yo$ which is attached to the initial verb of the subordinate clause, for example:

(32) gobedbi   dugijonti = jo   ucuetin   in alisija
      NP.DAT.-INSTR.PL.   V.3RD PL. = PCL.   NP.ACC.SG.   PP
      "to the smiths who serve U. in Alisia"

This particle is used not only in relative clauses, but also to construct the equivalent of *that*-clauses, as in this charm to remove a blockage in the throat recorded by Marcellus of Bordeaux:

(33) scrisu = mi = [j]o   uelor
      V.1ST SG = PRO.1ST SG = PCL.   V.1ST SG.
      "I wish to spit" (lit. "I wish that I spit")

5.3.3 Clitics

There are a number of clitic pronominals attested in Gaulish. Those which are commonly agreed upon are the object pronominals as exemplified in (26) and (27), to which may be added the following example:

(34) To = ṡo = Ko-Te
      CONN. = PRO.3RD SG.ACC = PERFVZ-V.3RD SG
      "he gave it"

Other forms are less certain. The forms first singular $= mi$, second singular $=tu$, and third singular neuter $=id$ are often interpreted as subject pronominals which function like the emphasizing particles known as *notae augentes* in the Insular Celtic languages, for example:

(35) A. dessu = mj = js
          V.1ST SG. = EMPH.-PCL.1ST SG.NOM. = PRO.3RD PL.ACC.
          "I prepare them"
      B. buet = id
          V.3RD SG.PRES.SUBJUNC. = EMPH.-PCL. 3RD SG.NOM.NEUT.
          "it should be"

These forms have been interpreted otherwise by some, however, as discussed in §§4.2.2; 4.3.6.

Finally, it may be mentioned that several examples of clitic doubling are attested. One example is illustrated in (26), in which a neuter pronominal doubles an intrinsically inanimate but grammatically animate nominal, a construction which is also attested in Old Irish. A further example of a clause with clitic doubling (and left dislocation) is:

(36) aKisios arKaToKo{K}maTereKos   To = ṡo = Ko-Te
      NP.NOM.SG.   CONN. = PRO.3RD SG.MASC.ACC. =
        aToṃ TeuoχTonioṇ   PERFVZ.-V.3RD SG.
        NP.ACC.SG.
      "A. A., he gave it, a border of gods and men"

5.3.4 Agreement

Noun–adjective agreement is marked for case, number, and gender. Subject–verb agreement is normally marked for person and number, but there is a single example in which agreement for number may be lacking:

(37) eluontiu   ieru   aneuno oclicno   lugurix aneunicno
      NP.DAT.SG.   V.3RD SG?   NP.NOM.SG.   NP.NOM.SG.
      "To E., A. O. and L. A. dedicated [this stele]"

In this inscription, a compound subject appears not to agree with an apparently third singular verb. However, it has been noted that final postvocalic *-s* apparently has been lost in the language of this text, the addition of which to the verb would make it third plural. The lack of subject–verb agreement might, therefore, be illusory. It should also be borne in mind that, cross-linguistically, it is not uncommon for a singular verb to be used with conjoined subjects.

6. LEXICON

With the exception of onomastic material, there have been remarkably few etyma of foreign origin identified in the Continental Celtic lexicon. These Celtic languages appear to have much more frequently been loaning than borrowing languages. Within the onomastic material of foreign origin, Latin, Iberian, and Greek elements (in descending order of frequency) are found in the Hispano-Celtic speech area. As one would expect, Latin elements are common among the Gauls, especially in the later period, and some Greek influence is also felt (see Meid 1980). Greek elements are not uncommon in the Galatian speech area. A so-called Mediterranean substratum has been alleged to be the source of some borrowings into Gaulish and Lepontic.

The most noteworthy borrowing into Continental Celtic is the Lepontic patronymic suffix *-alo/ā-*, which is otherwise unknown in Celtic. It has been connected to the Raetic or Etruscan genitive singular in *-al* (otherwise Prosdocimi 1991:163–176). One further surprising borrowing is Hispano-Celtic *śilaPuŕ*, apparently "silver," which is attested twice beside native *aŕCaTo-*. The etymon is found elsewhere in Indo-European, in Germanic and Balto-Slavonic, and also in Basque. It has been maintained to be of ultimate Semitic origin.

7. READING LIST

The individual corpora of the Continental Celtic languages are in the process of publication. The Hispano-Celtic corpus is to be part of Jürgen Untermann's *Monumenta Linguarum Hispanicarum*; vol. I (1975) contains the Celtic coin legends, and vol. II (1980) contains one Celtic inscription (B.3.1). The remainder of the Celtic corpus appears in vol. IV (1997). For subsequently published inscriptions, see Jordán Cólera (2001). Wodtko (2000) provides a Hispano-Cettic lexicon. The Lepontic corpus as known in 1970 is treated by Lejeune (1971); Tibiletti Bruno (1981) may also be consulted, but is inferior to Lejeune's work. The most recent collection, which focuses upon all of Cisalpine Celtic, is Solinas (1995); it concentrates almost exclusively on epigraphic matters. The most recent discussion of the Lepontic corpus is Motta (2000). The Gaulish corpus is published as the *Receuil des Inscriptions Gauloises*; the volumes treat the inscriptions in Greek characters (Lejeune 1985; supplemented by Lejeune 1988–1995), north Etruscan characters and Roman characters on stone (both in Lejeune 1988), the calendrical inscriptions (Duval and Pinault 1986), the coin legends (Colbert de Beanlieu and Fischer 1998), and the inscriptions on movable objects, which are largely engraved in Roman cursive (Lambert 2002b). In addition, Marichal (1988) has collected the graffiti from La Graufesenque in similar format. Delamarre (2003) provides a useful dictionary. Billy (1993) is useful for locating Gaulish lexical items embedded in non-Celtic texts. The sparse Galatian materials have been treated by Weisgerber (1931) and more recently by Schmidt 1994. A new collection has been prepared by Phillip Freeman (2001). The language of the British coin legends has been discussed by De Bernardo Stempel (1991). Tomlin (1987) prints two possible British defixio texts.

Eska and Evans (1993) discusses the various categories of inscriptions in the Continental Celtic corpus and interesting features of the individual languages, but is somewhat dated due to recent discoveries. Schmidt (1983) also surveys some of the important features of Continental Celtic. Particularly important now for Hispano-Celtic grammar are Villar (1995a; 1995b). Jordán Cólera (1998) provides a general introduction. Lambert (2002a) treats Gaulish grammar and provides an excellent selection of the various categories of inscriptions in the corpus, though usually only his own interpretations.

For an alternative treatment of Continental Celtic phonology to that presented herein, see McCone (1996). Certain pronominal forms are discussed in Schrijver (1997). The features of Continental Celtic clausal configuration are treated by Eska (1994b). Eska (1994a) is an exploratory treatment of Vendryes' Restriction.

I should like to thank Joshua Katz and Peter Schrijver for their substantial comments on a preliminary version of this chapter.

Bibliography

Ballester, X. 1993–1995. "Sobre el valor fonético de Ś en celtibérico." *Kalathos* 13–14:319–323.

Billy, P.-H. 1993. *Thesaurus linguae Gallicae.* Hildesheim: Olms; Zürich: Weidmann.

Campanile, E. 1983. "Considerazioni sugli alfabeti dei Celti continentali." *Annali del seminario di studi del mondo classico. Sezione linguistica* 5:63–74.

Colbert de Beaulieu, J.-P. and B. Fischer. 1998. *Recueil des inscriptions gauloises iv, légendes monétaices* Paris: CNRS Editions.

De Bernardo Stempel, P. 1991. "Die Sprache altbritannischer Münzlegenden." *Zeitschrift für celtische Philologie* 44:36–55.

_____. 1994. "Zum gallischen Akzent. Eine sprachinterne Betrachtung." *Zeitschrift für celtische Philologie* 46:14–35.

_____. 1995. "Gaulish accentuation. Results and outlook." In Eska *et al.* 1995, pp. 16–32.

_____. 1996. "Die Stummvokale. Eine Bilanz für das Keltiberische." In W. Meid and P. Anreiter (eds.), *Die grösseren altkeltischen Sprachdenkmäler,* pp. 212–226. Innsbruck: Institut für Sprachwissenschaft der Universität Innsbruck.

De Hoz, J. 1983. "Origine ed evoluzione delle scritture ispaniche." *Annali del seminario di studi del mondo classico. Sezione linguistica* 5:27–62.

_____. 1990. "El genitivo céltico de los temas en -*o*-. El testimonio lepóntico." In F. Villar (ed.), *Studia Indogermanica et palaeohispanica in honorem A. Tovar et L. Michelena,* pp. 315–329. Vitoria-Gasteiz: Universidad del País Vasco/Salamanca: Universidad de Salamanca.

_____. 1995. "Is -*s* the mark of the plural of the puterite in the Gaulish verb?" In Eska *et al.* 1995, 58–67.

Delamarre, X. 2003. *Dictionnaire de la langue gauloise,* second edition. Paris: Errance.

De Marinis, R. C. 1991. "Golasecca culture and its links with the Celts beyond the Alps." In V. Kruta, O. Hermann, B. Raferty, *et al.* (eds.), *The Celts,* pp. 93–102. London: Thames and Hudson.

Duval, P.-M. and G. Pinault. 1986. *Recueil des inscriptions gauloises iii, Les calendriers (Coligny, Villards d'Heria).* Paris: CNRS Editions.

Eska, J. F. 1990. "The so-called weak or dental preterite in Continental Celtic, Watkins' Law, and related matters." *Historische Sprachforschung* 103:81–91.

_____. 1994a. "On the crossroads of phonology and syntax. Remarks on the origin of Vendryes' Restriction and related matters." *Studia Celtica* 28:39–62.

_____. 1994b. "Rethinking the evolution of Celtic constituent configuration." *Münchener Studien zur Sprachwissenschaft* 55:7–39.

_____. 1994c. "More on Gaul. siöxt = i." *Études Celtiques* 30:205–210.

_____. 1995. "Observations on the thematic genitive singular in Lepontic and Hispano-Celtic." In Eska *et al.* 1995, pp. 33–46.

_____. 1998a. "PIE *p ≯ ø in Proto-Celtic." *Münchener Studien zur Sprachwissenschaft* 58: 63–80.

_____. 1998b. "The linguistic position of Lepontic." *Proceedings of the Berkeley Linguistics Society* 24S:2–11.

_____. 1998c. "Tau Gallicum." *Studia Celtica* 32:115–127.

_____. 2002a. "Symptoms of nasal effacement in Hispano-Celtic." *Palaeohispanica* 2:141–158.

_____. 2002b, "Aspects of nasal phonology in Cisalpine Celtic." In *Studia linguarum 3. Memoriae A. A. Korolev dicata*, A. S. Kassian and A. V. Sidel'tsev (eds.), 253–275. Moscow: Languages of Slavonic Culture.

_____. Forthcoming. "On basic configuration and movement in the Gaulish clause." In P.-Y. Lambert and and G.-J. Pinault (eds.), *Actes du colloque international "Gaulois et celtique continental"*. Paris: EPHE.

Eska, J. F. and D. Ellis Evans. 1993. "Continental Celtic." In M. J. Ball with J. Fife (eds.), *The Celtic Languages*, pp. 26–63. London: Routledge.

Eska, J. F., R. Geraint Gruffydd, and N. Jacobs (eds.). 1995. *Hispano-Gallo-Brittonica. Essays in Honour of Professor D. Ellis Evans on the Occasion of his Sixty-Fifth Birthday.* Cardiff: University of Wales Press.

Eska, J. F. and R. E. Wallace. 1999.. "The linguistic milieu of *Oderzo 7." *Historische Sprachforschung* 112: 122–136.

Evans, D. Ellis. 1967. *Gaulish Personal Names. A Study of Some Continental Celtic Formations.* Oxford: Clarendon Press.

Falc'hun, F. 1981. *Perspectives nouvelles sur l'histoire de la langue bretonne.* Paris: Union Générale d'Editions.

Freeman, P. 2001. *The Galatian language.* Lewiston: Edwin Mellen.

Gambari, F. G., and G. Colonna. 1986. "Il bicchiere con iscrizione arcaica da Castelletto Ticino e l'adozione della scrittura nell'Italia nord-occidentale." *Studi etruschi* 54:119–164.

Gómez-Moreno, M. 1922. "De epigrafía ibérica. El plomo de Alcoy." *Revista de filología Española* 9:341–366.

Gray, L. H. 1944. "Mutation in Gaulish." *Language* 20:223–230.

Jordán Cólera, C. 1998. *Introduction al celtibérico.* Zaragoza: Universidad de Zaragoza.

_____. 2001. "Chronica Epigraphica Celtiberica I." *Novedades en epigraphía celtibérica. Palaeohispanica* 1:369–391.

Lambert, P.-Y. 2002a. *La langue gauloise. Description linguistique, commentaire d'inscriptions choisies,* second edition. Paris: Errance.

_____. 2002b. *Recueil des inscriptions gauloises ii/2, Textes gallo-latins sur instrumentum.* Paris: CNRS Editions.

Lejeune, M. 1971. *Lepontica.* Paris: Société d'Editions "Les Belles Lettres."

_____. 1985. *Recueil des inscriptions gauloises i, Textes gallo-grecs.* Paris: CNRS Editions.

_____. 1988. *Recueil des inscriptions gauloises ii/1, Textes gallo-étrusques, textes gallo-latins sur pierre.* Paris: CNRS Editions.

_____. 1988–1995. "Compléments gallo-grecs." *Etudes celtiques* 25:79–106, 27:175–177, 30:181–189, 31:99-113.

_____. 1989. "Notes de linguistique italique. xxxix. Génitifs en -*osio* et génitifs en -*i.*" *Revue des études latines* 67:63–77.

_____. 1993. "D'Alcoy à Espanca. Réflexions sur les écritures paléohispaniques." In *Michel Lejeune. Notice biographique et bibliographique*, pp. 53–86. Leuven: Centre International de Dialectologie Général.

Marichal, R. 1988. *Les graffites de la Graufesenque.* Paris: CNRS Editions.

McCone, K. 1996. *Towards a Relative Chronology of Ancient and Medieval Celtic Sound Change.* Maynooth: Dept. of Old Irish, National University of Ireland.

Meid, W. 1980. *Gallisch oder Lateinisch? Soziolinguistische und andere Bemerkungen zu populären gallo-lateinischen Inschriften.* Innsbruck: Institut für Sprachwissenschaft der Universität Innsbruck.

——. 1994. "Die 'grosse' Felsinschrift von Peñalba de Villastar." In R. Bielmeier and R. Stempel with R. Lanszweert (eds.). In *Indogermanica et Caucasica. Festschrift für Karl Horst Schmidt zum 65. Geburtstag,* pp. 385–394. Berlin: Walter de Gruyter.

Motta, F. 2000. "La documentazione epigrafica e linguistica." In R. C. de Marinis and S. Biaggo Simona (eds.), *I leponti tra mito e realtà,* 2, pp. 181–222. Locarno: Armando Dadò.

Prosdocimi, A. L. 1989. "Gaulish σονεμετος and σοσιν νεμητον. À propos of *RIG* i 154." *Zeitschrift für celtische Philologie* 43:199–206.

——. 1991. "Note sul celtico in Italia." *Studi etruschi* 57:139–177.

Schmidt, K. H. 1957. "Die Komposition in gallischen Personennamen." *Zeitschrift für celtische Philologie* 26:33–301.

——. 1983. "Grundlagen einer festlandkeltischen Grammatik." In E. Vineis (ed.), *Le lingue indoeuropee di frammentaria attestazione. Die Indogermanischen Restsprachen,* pp. 65–90. Pisa: Giardini.

——. 1986. "Zur Rekonstruktion des Keltischen. Festlandkeltisches und inselkeltisches Verbum." *Zeitschrift für celtische Philologie* 41:159–179.

——. 1994. "Galatische Sprachreste." In E. Schwertheim (ed.), *Forschungen in Galatien,* pp. 15–28. Bonn: Dr. Rudolf Habelt.

Schrijver, P. 1995. *Studies in British Celtic Historical Phonology.* Amsterdam: Rodopi.

——. 1997. *Studies in the History of Celtic Pronouns and Particles.* Maynooth: Dept. of Old Irish, National University of Ireland.

Solinas, P. 1995. "Il Celtico in Italia." *Studi etruschi* 60:311–408.

Tibiletti Bruno, M. G. 1981. "Le iscrizioni celtiche d'Italia." In E. Campanile (ed.), *I Celti d'Italia,* pp. 157–207. Pisa: Giardini.

Tomlin, R. S. O. 1987. "Was ancient British Celtic ever a written language? Two texts from Roman Bath." *Bulletin of the Board of Celtic Studies* 34:18–25.

Tovar, A. 1954. "Numerales indoeuropeos en Hispania." *Zephyrus* 5:17–22.

——. 1975. "Les écritures de l'ancienne Hispania." In *Le déchiffrement des écritures et des langues,* pp. 15–23. Paris: L'Asiathèque.

Uhlich, J. 1999. "Zur sprachlichen Einordnung des Lepontischen." In S. Zimmer, R. Ködderitzsch, and A. Wigge (eds.), *Akten des zweiten deutschen Keltologen-Symposiums,* pp. 277–304. Tübingen: Max Niemeyer.

——. Forthcoming. "On the linguistic classification of Lepontic." In G.-J. Pinault and P.-Y. Lambert (eds.), *Actes du colloque international "gaulois et celtique Continental."* Paris: Ecole Practique des Hautes Etudes.

Untermann, J. 1975. *Monumenta Linguarum Hispanicarum i, Die Münzlegenden.* Wiesbaden: Dr. Ludwig Reichert.

——. 1980. *Monumenta Linguarum Hispanicarum ii, Die Inschriften iberischer Schrift aus Südfrankreich.* Wiesbaden: Dr. Ludwig Reichert.

——. 1997. *Monumenta Linguarum Hispanicarum iv, Die tartessischen, keltiberischen und lusitanischen Inschriften.* Wiesbaden: Dr. Ludwig Reichert.

Villar, F. 1993–1995. "El instrumental en celtibérico." *Kalathos* 13–14:325–338.

——. 1995a. *Estudios de Celtibérico y de Toponimia Prerromana.* Salamanca: Universidad de Salamanca.

——. 1995b. *A New Interpretation of Celtiberian Grammar.* Innsbruck: Institut für Sprachwissenschaft der Universität.

Weisgerber, L. 1931. "Galatische Sprachreste." In R. Helm (ed.), *Natalicium Johannes Geffcken zum 70. Geburtstag 2. Mai 1931 gewidmet von Freunden, Kollegen und Schülern,* pp. 151–175. Heidelberg: Carl Winter.

Wodtko, D. S. 2000. *Monumenta Linguarum Hispanicarum v, Wörterbuch der keltiberischen Inschriften.* Wiesbaden: Dr. Ludwig Reichert.

CHAPTER 9

Gothic

JAY H. JASANOFF

1. HISTORICAL AND CULTURAL CONTEXTS

Gothic, mainly known from a Bible translation of the fourth century AD, is the only Germanic language that has come down to us from antiquity in a reasonably complete state of preservation. Lacking direct descendants itself, it is closely related to the early medieval dialects ancestral to Modern English, German, Dutch, and the Scandinavian languages (Danish, Swedish, Norwegian, Icelandic, Faroese). The family tree of the Germanic languages can be drawn as follows:

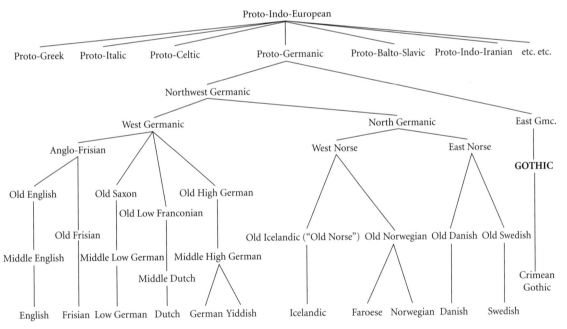

Figure 9.1 The Germanic languages

As can be seen from this figure, Gothic is the sole representative of the East Germanic branch of the family. The more numerous North and West Germanic languages are much later: Old English and Old High German are first substantially attested in the eighth century, while Old Saxon and Old Low Franconian date from the ninth and tenth centuries,

189

respectively. The remaining "Old" Germanic languages – Old Frisian and the early Scandinavian dialects – are essentially languages of the High Middle Ages, contemporary with Middle English and Middle High German. It is thus not surprising that Gothic presents a significantly more conservative appearance than its Germanic sister dialects. The only comparably archaic remains of an early Germanic language are the Early Northwest Germanic inscriptions of the third, fourth, and fifth centuries, mostly from Denmark and written in the indigenous runic alphabet (see Ch. 10). These, however, are only tantalizing fragments, often deliberately obscure and topheavy with personal names.

Like other East Germanic tribes such as the Vandals, Burgundians, Gepids, and Heruls, the Goths originally lived in the area of present-day Poland and eastern Germany; their own traditions placed their earliest home in southern Sweden. Moving toward the mouth of the Danube and the Black Sea shortly before 200 AD, they first began to make serious raids into Roman territory in the middle of the third century. A hundred years later they had expanded significantly eastwards and split into two sub-peoples: the *Ostrogoths* ("East Goths"), located beyond the Dniester, who controlled most of the modern eastern Ukraine; and the *Visigoths* (meaning unclear; *not* "West Goths"), who remained centered in the southwest of the Ukraine and adjacent parts of Moldova and Rumania. It was in the latter area, toward the middle of the fourth century, that the Arian Christian Wulfila (Ulfilas, Ulphilas) began his ultimately successful effort to convert the Goths to Christianity. Wulfila (Gothic for "Little Wolf") was himself a native speaker of Gothic, and like many missionaries then and now, recognized the value of translating the Christian scriptures into the language of his intended converts. For this purpose he devised a Greek-based alphabet which remained in use for as long as Gothic continued to be written (see §2). The surviving remains of Wulfila's translation, amounting to somewhat less than half of the New Testament, constitute the great bulk of the Gothic corpus that has come down to us. Although the Christian Gothic community over which Wulfila presided as bishop was still small at the time of his death (*c*. 382), he laid the groundwork for future missionary work so effectively that Arian Christianity soon became something like a national religion among the Germanic tribes of eastern and central Europe. Yet, interestingly, the Bible seems never to have been translated into Vandal, or Burgundian, or Herulian; evidently these East Germanic languages were close enough to Gothic to make such endeavors unnecessary.

The career of the Goths in the upheavals that accompanied the end of the Western Roman Empire was short but spectacular. The Visigoths, after sacking Rome in 410, established themselves in southern Gaul and subsequently in Spain; here their kingdom lasted until the Moorish conquest of 711, although all our documents from Visigothic Spain are in Latin. The Ostrogoths, in the meantime, established a short-lived kingdom in Italy under their great ruler Theodoric (492–526). Unlike their Spanish cousins, the "Italian" Goths appear to have cultivated their fledgling literary tradition during their half-century of independence. It is to sixth-century Italy, and not to Spain, that we owe our surviving manuscripts of the Gothic Bible, including the famous 188-page Codex Argenteus now housed in Uppsala, Sweden. Also of Italian origin are the few surviving non-Biblical Gothic monuments, which include a fragmentary commentary on the Gospel of John (the so-called *Skeireins* or "explanation"), a calendar, and two very short legal documents. Following the Byzantine reconquest of Italy in 552, the Ostrogoths – and with them the Gothic language – disappear from history.

Or nearly disappear. By chance, a ninth- or tenth-century parchment (the Salzburg–Vienna Alcuin Ms.) has come down to us containing two incomplete versions of the Gothic alphabet and a few verses from the Gothic Bible, the latter accompanied by a mixed transcription/ translation into Old High German. A curious feature of this document is that the Gothic letters bear names, which closely resemble the names of the corresponding runes in Old English and Old Norse. We can only guess at the specific circumstances under which

this information came to be recorded, but one thing seems certain: the descendants of the
Ostrogoths who withdrew over the Alps in the middle of the sixth century somehow man-
aged to retain a shadow of their linguistic and religious identity, albeit tenuously, for a period
of three or four hundred years.

Another Gothic "survival" turns up much later in a very different corner of Europe. In
the middle of the sixteenth century AD, Ogier van Busbecq, the ambassador of the emperor
Charles V to the court of the Turkish sultan Suleiman the Magnificent, recorded eighty-six
words of a language spoken in the sultan's Crimean dominions that reminded him of his
native Flemish. Most of the lexical items written down by Busbecq are, in fact, obviously
Germanic, and one, *ada* "egg," appears to show the distinctively East Germanic sound change
of *-jj-* to *-ddj-* (see §3.6.4). It is usually held, therefore, that the Crimean Goths were the
last remnants of the Gothic population that once occupied the northern shore of the Black
Sea, and that their language was a direct descendant of the Gothic of the fourth century.
Unfortunately, by the time anyone thought to extend Busbecq's vocabulary, Crimean Gothic
had disappeared.

2. WRITING SYSTEMS

Apart from Busbecq's word list and two or three problematic runic inscriptions, the entire
surviving Gothic corpus is written in Wulfila's alphabet. Table 9.1 shows the letters as they
appear in our most important Gothic manuscript, the Codex Argenteus:

Table 9.1 Wulfila's alphabet			
	Transcription	Numerical value	Name
Λ	a	1	aza
ᚱ	b	2	bercna
Γ	g	3	geuua
Λ	d	4	daaz
Є	e	5	eyz
U	q	6	quertra
Z	z	7	ezec
h	h	8	haal
Ψ	p	9	thyth
ï	i, ï	10	iiz
K	k	20	chozma
Λ	l	30	laaz
M	m	40	manna
N	n	50	noicz
G	j	60	gaar
Π	u	70	uraz
Π	p	80	pertra
Ц	–	90	—
K	r	100	reda
S	s	200	sugil
T	t	300	tyz
Y	w	400	uuinne
F	f	500	fe
X	x	600	enguz
Θ	ƕ	700	uuaer
Ω	o	800	utal
↑	—	900	—

The essentially Greek inspiration of this alphabet is shown by a number of features, including:

1.   The form of the letters, about two-thirds of which closely resemble their uncial Greek counterparts;
2.   The order of the letters and their associated numerical values;
3.   Greek orthographic practices, such as the (late) use of *ai* to stand for the monophthong [ɛ], and the use of *g* to stand for the the velar nasal [ŋ] before velar consonants.

Wulfila did not, however, adhere slavishly to his Greek model. In several instances he assigned altogether new values to Greek letters which would otherwise have been useless in Gothic. This was the case with Greek **F** ([w]), which became Gothic *q* ([kʷ]), and with **Ψ** (psi), which was probably the source of the Gothic character *ƕ*([hʷ]). Curiously, Wulfila chose not to use the letters **Φ** (phi) and **Θ** (theta) to write the Gothic voiceless fricatives [f] and [ð], respectively, despite the fact that **Φ** and **Θ** had precisely these values in fourth-century Greek. Instead, he employed **Φ** to write Gothic [ð] and borrowed the Latin letter **F** to write Gothic [f]. The new phonetic value of **Φ** led to its being moved to the alphabetic position formerly occupied by **Θ**, while the new Latin-derived *f* took over the place vacated by **Φ**. Other Latin letters that found their way into the Gothic alphabet were *r* and *h*, as well as the variant of the *s*-character used in the Codex Argenteus (other Gothic manuscripts show an *s* that is decidedly more Greek-looking). In addition, several Gothic letters have been claimed to come from the runic alphabet – *u*, for example, which Wulfila used in place of the Greek digraph **OY**. But the extent to which runic writing played a role in the creation of the Gothic alphabet is highly controversial, not least because many of the characters in the runic alphabet are very similar to their Latin counterparts.

3. PHONOLOGY

3.1 Consonants

The most highly structured part of the Gothic consonant system consists of a symmetrically organized subsystem of twelve stops and fricatives (the term *coronal* is used here to denote the dental, alveolar, and palatal regions):

(1)

	Labial	Coronal	Velar	Labiovelar
Voiceless stops	/p/	/t/	/k/	/kʷ/ <q>
Voiceless fricatives	/f/	/þ/	/h/	/hʷ/ <ƕ>
Voiced stops/Fricatives	/b/	/d/	/g/	/gʷ/ <gw>

Of the voiceless stops, the labial /p/ is infrequent outside obvious Greek and Latin loanwords (e.g., *praufetus* "prophet," *pund* "pound"). The labiovelar /kʷ/, which Wulfila's native-speaker intuition led him to write with a single character (*q*), patterns phonotactically as a single consonant (cf. *qrammiþa* "moistness," with initial *qr*-) and is best analyzed as a unitary phoneme. The voiceless fricatives include /h/ and /hʷ/ (likewise a unitary phoneme), which, phonetically, were probably indistinguishable from the English sounds spelled *h* and *wh* – in other words, simple glottal fricatives with no significant velar occlusion. (This was doubtless also the case in syllable-final position, as, e.g., in *saƕ* "saw" [1st, 3rd sg.], *nahts* "night" and *saƕt* "saw" [2nd sg.]; the development of [h] to velar [x] in this position in German [cf. *Nacht*, etc.] had no parallel in Gothic). Historically, however, they arose from older **x* and

x^w, and structurally their place is still clearly with the oral fricatives /f/ and /þ/, with which they share important distributional properties.

The sounds denoted by the letters *b*, *d*, *g(w)* were voiced stops in some environments and voiced fricatives in others. The stop reading is certain after consonants (e.g., *windan* [windan] "wind," *siggwan* [siŋgʷan] "sing," *þaurban* "need" [þɔrban]), and probable, at least for *b* and *d*, in word-initial position (*barn* [b-] "child," *dags* [d-] "day"). After vowels, single *b*, *d*, and *g* are fricatives (e.g., *sibun* [siƀun] "seven," *bidjan* [biđjan] "ask," *ligan* [liǥan] "lie." The stop /gʷ/ is found only after nasals (in words like *siggwan*) and in the geminate combination -*ggw*- (e.g., *bliggwan* [-ggʷ-] "strike"); there is thus no fricative allophone [gʷ].

The remaining Gothic consonants include two sibilants and a standard complement of nasals, liquids, and glides:

(2)

	Labial	Coronal	Velar
Nasals	/m/	/n/	([ŋ] <g>)
Voiceless sibilant		/s/	
Voiced sibilant		/z/	
Liquids		/r/, /l/	
Glides	/w/	/y/	

The voiced sibilant /z/ is not found in word-initial position. The velar nasal [ŋ], spelled <g> in imitation of Greek practice, is the automatic realization of /n/ before velar and labiovelar stops. The graphic sequence -*ggw*- is thus ambiguous, representing both [-ggʷ-] and [-ŋgʷ-].

3.2 Vowels

Gothic has five short and seven long vowels, along with a single diphthong:

(3)

	Short		Long	
	Front	*Back*	*Front*	*Back*
High	/i/ <i>	/u/ <u>	/i:/ <ei>	/u:/ <u>
High-mid			/e:/ <e>	/o:/ <o>
Low-mid	/ɛ/ <ai>	/ɔ/ <au>	/ɛ:/ <ai>	/ɔ:/ <au>
Low	/a/ <a>		/a:/ <a>	
Diphthong	/iu/			

3.2.1 Short vowels

Among the short vowels, /ɛ/ and /ɔ/ are only marginally phonemic, being in most cases mere positional variants of underlying /i/ and /u/ before -*r*, -*h*, and -*ƕ* (*breaking*; see §3.4.2). But both have a general distribution in foreign (i.e., Greek and Biblical Semitic) words (e.g., *aikklesjo* [ɛkkle:sjo:] "church," Greek ἐκκλησία; *apaustaulus* [apɔstɔlus] "apostle," Greek ἀπόστολος), and /ɛ/ serves as the normal reduplication vowel in native Gothic preterites of the type *letan – lailot* [lɛlo:t] "let," *aukan – aiauk* [ɛɔ:k] "increase." The use of the graphic diphthong <ai> to stand for a front monophthong is based directly on late Greek practice; the parallel use of <au> for [ɔ] is an innovation of Wulfila's system.

3.2.2   Long vowels

The long vowels include the high-mid vowels /eː/ and /oː/, which lack short counterparts and are unambiguously indicated by the letters *e* and *o*. The Gothic alphabet, however, does not mark length as such. The long versions of [a], [ɛ], [ɔ], and [u] are not written differently from their short equivalents; orthography alone gives no indication that *þahta* "(s)he thought," *air* "early," *hauhs* "high," and *bruþs* "young woman" represent [þaːhta], [ɛːr], [hɔːhs], and [bruːþs], respectively, with distinctive length (note that the modern editorial practice of writing *þâhta*, *aír*, *haúhs*, and *brûþs* to indicate length, and writing *ái* and *áu* for short /ɛ/ and /ɔ/, has no basis in ancient usage). The case of /i/ and /iː/, which are orthographically distinguished as <i> and <ei> (cf. *bitan* "bitten" [nom. sg. neut.] vs. *beitan* "to bite" [inf.]), is exceptional. Wulfila's practice probably reflects a qualitative difference between the two *i*-vowels, perhaps comparable to that between the relatively low [-ɪ-] and the relatively high [-iː-] of German *bitten* "ask" versus *bieten* "offer."

The seven long vowels show considerable differences of patterning and distribution. Low central /aː/ is rare, being confined in the native Gothic lexicon to etymological sequences of **-anh-*, which yielded [-ãh-] in Proto-Germanic and subsequently lost its nasalization in Gothic (cf. 3.4.4). The lower-mid vowels /ɛː/ and /ɔː/, on the other hand, are relatively common; they represent the Proto-Germanic diphthongs *ai and *au and pattern as the *o*-grade counterparts of /i/ and /u/. There is little basis for the view, rooted in a coincidence of Germanic etymology and Greek orthography, that "long" *ai* and *au* actually represent synchronic diphthongs in Wulfila's Gothic. The only true Gothic diphthong is /iu/.

3.3 Accent

The position of the word accent is not overtly indicated. To judge from the other Germanic languages, ordinary words were stressed on their first syllable. But in verbal compounds consisting of a prefix and a lexical verb, the prefix was proclitic, so that the accent probably remained on the initial syllable of the verbal root (cf. *af-niman* [af-níman] "take away" and *and-niman* [and-níman] "receive," with the accentuation of the simplex *niman* [níman] "take"). The accent pattern of the corresponding nominal compounds (e.g., *anda-numts* "reception," *anda-numja* "receiver") is uncertain.

3.4 Synchronic phonological processes

A number of automatic phonological rules, reflecting historical sound changes, affect the surface form of Gothic words.

3.4.1   Word-final devoicing

This rule applies exclusively to fricatives, converting [ƀ], [đ], [g], and [z] to [f], [þ], [x], and [s] in absolute-final position: for example, *gaf* < *gab, third singular preterite of *giban* "give"; *baþ* < *bad, third singular preterite of *bidjan* "ask"; *maujos* < *maujoz, genitive singular of *mawi* "girl." The devoicing of [g] to [x] is not noted orthographically (cf. *mag* [max] "is able"), presumably because the [g] : [x] contrast was not phonemic and there was no letter in ordinary use to denote the voiceless velar fricative (Wulfila's use of the letter *x* is virtually confined to the divine name *Xristus* "Christ"). No devoicing is found in forms of the type *band* "bound" and *waurd* "word," showing that the final consonant was a stop in these environments.

3.4.2   Breaking

This is the traditional name (German *Brechung*) for the regular lowering of synchronically underlying **i* and **u* to *ai* [ɛ] and *au* [ɔ] before *-r*, *-h*, and *-ƕ*, for example, *wairþan* "become," first singular preterite *warþ*, first plural preterite *waurþum*, participle *waurþans*, paralleling the regular pattern seen in *hilpan* "help" *halp*, *hulpum*, *hulpans*.

3.4.3   Hiatus lowering

This is the regular but comparatively rare process by which long high and high-mid vowels were replaced by their low-mid counterparts when immediately followed by another vowel: as in *saian* [sɛːan] < **sean* [seːan] "sow"; *stauida* [stɔːiđa] < **stoida* [stoːiđa], third singular preterite of *stojan* "judge."

3.4.4   Loss of *-n-* before *-h-* with compensatory lengthening

This process is found not only after *-a-* (cf. *þahta* < **þanhta*; see §3.2.2), but also after *-u-* (cf. *þuhta* < **þunhta*, third singular preterite of *þugkjan* "seem") and *-i-* (cf. *þeihan* < **þinhan* "prosper"). The nasalized vowels that originally resulted from **-Vnh-* sequences fell together with non-nasal /aː/, /uː/, and /iː/ in Wulfila's language.

3.5   Morphophonemic processes

Phonological processes that have been *morphologized*, i.e., restricted to specific morphemes and/or morphological categories, include the following:

3.5.1   Grammatical change

Grammatical change (German *grammatischer Wechsel*) is the traditional name for the alternation of word-internal voiceless and voiced fricatives (or stops derived from fricatives) under conditions originally governed by Verner's Law (see §3.6.2): for example, *hafjan* "lift" versus *uf-haban* "lift up"; *fra-wairþan* "perish" versus *fra-wardjan* "destroy"; third singular *aih* [ɛːh] "has" versus third plural *aigun* [ɛːɡun]. Voiced : voiceless pairs of this type are much rarer in Gothic than in the other early Germanic languages. But Gothic has a number of derivational suffixes which vary according to *Thurneysen's Law*: a voiced fricative appears when the preceding syllable begins with a voiceless consonant, and vice versa: for example *auþida* "desert" versus *diupiþa* "depth"; *wulþags* "glorious" versus *stainahs* "stony"; *fraistubni* "temptation" versus *waldufni* "power".

3.5.2   Ablaut

Ablaut, or apophony, is the system of morphologically governed vowel alternations inherited by Gothic and the other Germanic languages from Proto-Indo-European (PIE). The clearest examples are seen in the formation of the principal parts of strong verbs, as in *wairþan* (< PIE **wert-*; "e-grade"), *warþ* (< PIE **wort-*; "o-grade"), *waurþum* (< PIE **wṛt-*; "zero-grade"), *waurþans* (likewise < PIE **wṛt-*). But ablaut changes are also associated with other derivational and inflectional processes, ranging from the inflection of *n*-stem nouns (e.g., acc. sg. *auhsan* "ox" < pre-Germanic **ukson-*; dat. sg. *auhsin* < **uksen-*; gen. pl. *auhsne* < **uksn̥-*) to the formation of causatives from underlying strong verbs (e.g., *frawairþan* → *frawardjan*, *sitan* "sit" → *satjan* "set").

3.5.3   Sievers' Law

Sievers' Law describes the regulated distribution – observable in both *ja*-stem nouns and adjectives, and in verbs with infinitives in *-jan* – of *-ji-* after "light" sequences (i.e., sequences of the form *-V̆C-) and *-ei-* [i:] after "heavy" sequences (i.e., sequences of the form *-V̄C- and *-VCC-): e.g., *harjis* "army" versus *hairdeis* "shepherd"; third singular *satjiþ* "sets" versus *frawardeiþ* "destroys." In its Proto-Indo-European form, Sievers' Law mandated the realization of underlying *-y- as *-iy- after heavy sequences; the *-ei-* of *hairdeis* and *frawardeiþ* is the contraction product of pre-Germanic *-iji-*.

3.5.4   **Dental substitution**

Suffix-initial *-d-* is replaced by *-s-* after an immediately preceding root-final *-t-* or *-d-*, or by *-t-* after any other root-final obstruent. In the former case the root-final *-t-* or *-d-* itself becomes *-s-*; in the latter case the root-final obstruent is represented by the corresponding voiceless fricative: for example, *witan* "know," preterite *wissa; þaurban* "need," preterite *þaurfta; magan* "be able," preterite *mahta*. Contrast the "normal" pattern seen in *munan* "think," preterite *munda; satjan*, preterite *satida;* etc. These alternations reflect the special treatment of dental + dental clusters in Proto-Indo-European, and the failure of voiceless stops to undergo the Germanic Consonant Shift (see §3.6.1) when preceded by an obstruent.

3.5.5   **Clitic-related effects**

Word-final *-s* usually becomes *-z-* before vowel-initial enclitics, especially *-(u)h* "and" and the relativizing particle *-ei*: e.g., *ƕazuh* "each" < nominative singular masculine *ƕas* "who" + *-uh* (cf. Lat. *quisque*), where the final *-s* is a devoiced etymological *-z*; and *þizei* "whose" < genitive singular masculine *þis* "his" + *-ei*, where the *-z* is analogical. Similar effects are seen in the behavior of prefixes; compare the variant forms in *us-hafjan* "lift up," *uz-anan* "breathe out," and *ur-reisan* "arise." The final *-h* of *-(u)h* sometimes assimilates to a following *-þ-*, as in *wesunuþþan* (= *wesun-uh-þan*) "but there were," *sumaiþþan* (= *sumai-h-þan*) "but some," etc.

3.6   Diachronic developments

3.6.1   **Grimm's Law**

As a Germanic language, Gothic shared in the characteristic phonological developments that set Germanic apart from the rest of the Indo-European family. The most conspicuous sound change in the prehistory of Germanic was *Grimm's Law* or the *Germanic Consonant Shift*, which took place in three steps:

(4)   A. PIE voiceless stops *p, *t, *k̂ (+ *k),[1] *kʷ became the voiceless fricatives *f, *þ, *x (> h), *xʷ (> *hʷ) when not preceded by an obstruent

       B. PIE voiced stops *b (rare), *d, *ĝ (+ *g), *gʷ became the voiceless stops *p, *t, *k, *kʷ

       C. PIE voiced aspirated stops *bʰ, *dʰ, *ĝʰ (+ *gʰ), *gʷʰ became the voiced fricatives *ƀ, *đ, *g̥, *gʷ, which further developed to voiced stops in some environments

Examples are legion: compare (A) Go. *fotus* (Eng. *foot*), *þrija* (Eng. *three*), *haurn* (Eng. *horn*), *ƕata* (Eng. *what*) beside Lat. *pēs, trēs, cornu, quod*; (B) Go. *tunþus* (Eng. *tooth*), *kaurn* (Eng. *corn*), *qius* (Eng. *quick*) beside Lat. *dēns, grānum, uīuus* (< *g^wīwos*); (C) Go. *beitan* (Eng. *bite*), *(ga)-daursan* (Eng. *dare*), *gaits* (Eng. *goat*), *warmjan* (Eng. *warm*, with *w-* < *g^w-*) beside Skt. *bhid-* "split," *dhrs-* "be bold," Lat. *haedus* (< *x-* < *k^h-* < *$\hat{g}^h$-*), Skt. *gharmá-* (< *g^{wh}-*) "hot drink."

The voiceless stops, however, remained unchanged after *s* (cf. Go. *steigan* "climb" beside Gk. στείχω (*steík^{h}ō*) "id.") or when preceded by another stop (cf. Go. *-hafts* "having, having taken" beside Lat. *captus* "taken").

3.6.2 Verner's Law

The Germanic Consonant Shift applied both word-initially and word-internally (Proto-Indo-European word-final stops were lost). In word-internal position, however, the voiceless fricatives produced by the shift, together with the inherited sibilant fricative *s*, were potentially subject to *Verner's Law*. The effect of this rule was to convert *f*, *þ*, *x*, *x^w*, and *s* to the corresponding voiced fricatives *ƀ*, *đ*, *ǥ*, *$ǥ^w$*, and *z* when the preceding vowel *did not* bear the pre-Germanic (equivalent to the Proto-Indo-European) movable accent. Thus, the Proto-Indo-European word for "father," which was accented on the second syllable (cf. Skt. *pitár-*, Gk. πατήρ (*patér*)), gave *faþér* by Grimm's Law and *fađér* (> Go. *fadar*) by Verner's Law, while the word for "brother," which had initial accent (cf. Skt. *bhrátar-*, Gk. φράτηρ (*p^{h}rátēr*)), became *bróþēr* by Grimm's Law and retained its voiceless *-þ-* in Gothic (*broþar*). Following the operation of Verner's Law, the pre-Germanic system of "free" accent was replaced by the attested Germanic system of fixed initial stress (see §3.3), so that the original condition for the voicing of word-internal fricatives can no longer be detected synchronically in Gothic or in any other Germanic language.

3.6.3 Further obstruent developments

The obstruent system that emerged from the operation of Grimm's and Verner's Laws was subject to further changes within the Germanic period, notably the following:

1. The weakening of *x* and *x^w* to *h* and *h^w*.
2. The "strengthening" of *ƀ*, *đ*, *ǥ*, and *$ǥ^w$* to stops after nasals and, at least in the case of *ƀ* and *đ*, word-initially.
3. The development of the fricative *$ǥ^w$* to *w* in most remaining environments (though *$ǥ^w$* was dissimilated to *ǥ* before a following *u*; note the Gothic pair *magus* "boy" < *mag^wuz* vs. *mawi* "girl" < *mag^wī*).
4. The change of *s* to *z*, regardless of the original position of the accent, in absolute final position.

The resulting Proto-Germanic system was hardly modified in Gothic at all, save by the introduction of final devoicing and by the substitution of [b], [d], [g] for [ƀ], [đ], [ǥ] after non-nasal consonants (*waurd*, etc.; see §3.4.1).

3.6.4 Sonorant developments

The Proto-Indo-European consonant system also included the liquids *r* and *l*, the nasals *m* and *n* (the latter with a velar allophone [ŋ]), the glides *y* and *w*, and the three so-called laryngeals *h_1*, *h_2*, and *h_3*, of uncertain phonetic value. The liquids were preserved unchanged in Germanic and Gothic. This was also true of the nasals except before *h* and in absolute final position, where *-m and *-n fell together and eventually disappeared. But the fate of the glides *y and *w was more complicated. Word-initially and postconsonantally, *y and *w were preserved as Germanic *j and *w, respectively (cf. Go. *juk* [Eng. *yoke*], *winds* [Eng. *wind*] beside Lat. *iugum, uentus*). After vowels, however, there were two basic treatments:

1. Germanic *-Ø- and *-w-, respectively (cf. Go. *bau-an* "dwell" < *bhū-ye/o-; *aiws* "age, time" beside Lat. *aeuom*). A specifically Gothic change subsequently deleted *-w- after the rounded vowel *o* (cf. *stojan* "judge" < *stōwjan, pret. *stauida* < *stōida* < *stōwida*).

2. Germanic *-jj- and *-ww-, respectively, whence Gothic -ddj- and -ggw-, respectively: e.g., Gmc. *twajjōn* "of two" (gen.), Go. *twaddje* (cf. Skt. *dvayoḥ* "id."); Gmc. *trewwaz* "true," Go. *triggws* (cf. Old Prussian *druwīt* "believe"). The seemingly irregular doubling or *Verschärfung* of *-y- and *-w- to *-jj- and *-ww- is now thought to reflect the original presence of a Proto-Indo-European laryngeal after the glide.

Apart from their role in *Verschärfung*, laryngeals had much the same treatment in Germanic as in the other Indo-European languages; their typical fate was to disappear with compensatory lengthening of an immediately preceding vocalic element in the same syllable. The vocalic element in question might be a vowel proper (*e, *a, etc.) or a syllabic liquid (*r̥, *l̥) or nasal (*m̥, *n̥) – the syllabic liquids or nasals being non-contrastive sounds which served in Proto-Indo-European as allophones of consonantal *r, *l, *m, *n.

3.6.5 Vocalic developments

3.6.5.1 *Proto-Indo-European*

Following the loss of laryngeals, the Proto-Indo-European dialect ancestral to Germanic had five short and five long vowels:

(5)

	Short		Long	
	Front	*Back*	*Front*	*Back*
High	i	u	ī	ū
Mid	e	o	ē	ō
Low	a		ā	

(It is no longer customary to include a central mid vowel *ə in the inventory of Proto-Indo-European short vowels. The sound denoted by this symbol in older handbooks was a subphonemic support vowel; cf., e.g., *ph₂tér* [pₐh₂té:r], which was eventually phonologized as /a/ in most Indo-European languages.) In addition, there were four short and four long syllabic liquids and nasals:

(6)   r̥, l̥, m̥, n̥   r̥̄, l̥̄, m̥̄, n̥̄

and six short and six long *i*- and *u*-diphthongs:

(7)   ei   ai   oi   ēi   āi   ōi
      eu   au   ou   ēu   āu   ōu

This is the inventory of syllabic nuclei that must be taken as the point of departure for the history of the Proto-Indo-European vowel system in Germanic.

3.6.5.2 *Proto-Germanic*

The number of vowels and vowel-like elements was greatly reduced over the course of the three millennia or so that passed between dialectal Proto-Indo-European and

Proto-Germanic. An early development was the shortening of the long diphthongs and the long syllabic liquids and nasals, which merged with their short counterparts; syllabic liquids and nasals were subsequently eliminated altogether by the change of *$r̥$, *$l̥$, *$m̥$, *$n̥$ to the vowel + consonant sequences *ur, *ul, *um, *un: e.g., Gothic *fulls* "full" < *$fulnaz$ < *$pl̥nós$ < *$pl̥h_1$-$nó$-s; *hund* "100" < *$hundan$ < *$k̑m̥tóm$; *haurn* "horn" < *$hurnan$ < *$k̑r̥nóm$. Among the vowels proper, the *a : *o distinction was lost in both the long and short subsystems, the longs merging as *$ō$ (cf. Go. *broþar*, *bloma* "flower" beside Lat. *frāter*, *flōs*) and the shorts as *a (cf. Go. *akrs* "field," *ahtau* "eight" beside Lat. *ager*, *octō*). (It is interesting to note that a similar confusion of *a*- and *o*-vowels occurred in the neighboring Indo-European languages, Celtic and Balto-Slavic.) There was also a change of short *e to *i in certain environments: for example, before nasal clusters (*-*nt*-, *-*mb*-, etc.), and before an *i in the next syllable (cf. Old High German *bintan*, Gothic *bindan* "bind" < *$b^hénd^honom$; OHG *ist*, Go. *ist* "is" < *$ésti$; but OHG *geban*, Go. *giban* "give" < *$g^héb^honom$; forms are cited from Old High German to show the still recoverable difference between Germanic *e and *i, which was effaced entirely in Gothic). These developments were paralleled in the treatment of the diphthongs: *ai and *oi merged as *ai; *au and *ou merged as *au; *ei gave *$ī$ (i.e., /ii/, spelled <ei>; cf. Go. *steigan* [OHG *stīgan*] beside Gk. στείχω (*steík^hō*)); and *eu gave the new diphthong *iu before an *i in the following syllable (cf. OHG 3rd sg. *biutit* "offers" < Gmc. *$biudiþ$, but inf. *beotan*, *biotan* < Gmc. *$beudan$). Within the long vowel subsystem, *$ē$ was phonetically lowered to approximately the sound heard in English *sad* (i.e., [æ]), while the phonetic place of the old *$ē$ was taken over by a new vowel *$ē_2$, of obscure origin.

The result of the foregoing, in the end, was the vowel system reconstructible for Proto-Germanic:

(8) Proto-Germanic monophthongs

	Short		Long	
	Front	*Back*	*Front*	*Back*
High	i	u	ī	ū
Mid	e	[o]	$ē_2$	ō
Low	a		ǣ	

Some authorities set up a secondary short *o for Proto-Germanic, but there is no evidence for such a vowel in the prehistory of Gothic, and it can equally well be explained as a common innovation of the North and West Germanic dialects. The low vowel *$ǣ$ is commonly also written *$ē$ or *$ē_1$.

(9) Proto-Germanic diphthongs

    ai   au
          eu
          iu

In addition, there were also nasalized *$ā^N$, *$ī^N$, *$ū^N$, and probably – at least in final syllables – other nasalized vowels as well. All were purely allophonic.

3.6.5.3 Gothic

The main Gothic innovations in the treatment of the Germanic short vowels were the complete merger of *e and *i as *i (cf. Go. *giban* beside OHG *geban*, etc.) and the subsequent creation of new low-mid vowels by "breaking" before -*r*, -*h*, and -*hv* (see §3.4.2). The long vowels were somewhat more extensively restructured, with **ǣ* and **ē₂* falling together as the high-mid vowel written *e* (cf. Go. *her* "here" [OHG *her, hiar*] < **hē₂r*, identical in vocalism with first plural preterite *gebum* "we gave" [OHG *gābum*] < **gǣbum*), and a new *ā* joining the system through the denasalization of **ā^N*. Here as in the shorts, the system was expanded by the addition of new low-mid vowels – this time through the monophthongization of **ai* and **au* (cf. §3.4.2). As a byproduct of the general shift of short **e* to **i*, the two remaining diphthongs, **eu* and **iu*, fell together as **iu* in Gothic (cf. -*biudan*, -*biudiþ* beside OHG *biotan, biutit*).

Gothic shows major changes vis-à-vis Proto-Germanic in its treatment of final syllables. Proto-Germanic generally preserved the vowels of late Proto-Indo-European final syllables intact; thus, for example, the *o*-stem nominative singular in **-os* was still **-az* in Proto-Germanic (cf. Runic Norse -*aR*; and see Ch. 10, §2.1), and the first singular present in **-ō* (< **-oh₂*) remained as **-ō*. In addition to normal long and short endings, however, Proto-Germanic also had final syllables with hyperlong or "trimoric" long vowels; these mainly arose from prehistoric sequences of two vowels in hiatus (e.g., PGmc. **galīkō̃* "similarly," with trimoric or "circumflex" **-ō̃* from PIE **-o-h₂ad*). Gothic is often said to have undergone a "law of three moras" or *Dreimorengesetz*, under which short vowels were lost (cf. nom. sg. *dags* "day" < **dagaz*) in final syllables, normal (bimoric) long vowels were shortened (cf. 1st sg. *nima* "I take"), and trimoric long vowels became bimoric longs (cf. *galeiko*). But this generalization is not completely valid: **-u(-)* was never lost at all (cf. *sunus* (< **-uz*) "son," *faihu* (< **-u*) "cattle"), and even bimoric long vowels retained their length before **-z* (acc. pl. *gibos* "gifts" < **-ōz* < late PIE **-ās* < **-ah₂(m)s*). As in every other Germanic language, the *Auslautgesetze* of Gothic still present many problems.

4. MORPHOLOGY

4.1 Nominal morphology

From a morphological point of view, Gothic is an averagely conservative older Indo-European language, similar in overall complexity to, e.g., Old Church Slavonic. Nouns come in three genders (masculine, feminine, neuter) and distinguish five cases (nominative, vocative, genitive, dative, accusative). There are singular and plural forms, but no dual (though the dual survives in personal pronouns; see §4.1.4). A number of features familiar from other Indo-European languages, such as the identity of the nominative and accusative cases in the neuter, and the identity of the nominative and vocative in the plural, appear in Gothic as well.

4.1.1 Nominal case development

Proto-Indo-European had eight cases: nominative, accusative, instrumental, dative, ablative, genitive, locative, and vocative. Of these, the ablative was lost in Germanic (it survives in adverbs like Gothic *galeiko* "similarly"; see §4.3), and the dative and the locative merged to form the synchronic dative. The instrumental, which was still a separate case in Proto-Germanic, was absorbed by the dative in the post-Germanic history of Gothic; thus, a form which patterns as a dative in Gothic may in principle go back to a Proto-Indo-European dative, locative, or instrumental.

4.1.2   Nominal stem-classes

Gothic declensions are conveniently classified according to the original stem-final element, which is usually best preserved in the dative plural and/or accusative plural. The most important types, as in the other Germanic languages, are (i) *a*- and *ja*-stems; (ii) *ō*- and *jō*-stems; (iii) *i*-stems; (iv) *u*-stems (collectively termed *strong*); and (v) *n*-stems (traditionally termed *weak*). The basic paradigms are given in Table 9.2.

In the *ja*-stems, the difference between *hairdeis* and *harjis* is due to Sievers' Law (see §3.5.3). The endings of *i*-, *u*-, and *n*-stems show traces of stem-final ablaut: *anstim* : *anstais* : *ansteis* (< *-**ey**-es*); *sunum* : *sunaus* : *suniwe* (< *-**ew**-ǫ̃m*); *guma* (< *-**ō(n)**)) : *gumins* : *gumans*; and *namō̃* (< *-**ō̃(n)**)) : *namins* : *namna*. Minor declensional types include relics of other consonant-stem classes, especially *r*- and *nt*-stems (e.g., *broþar*, gen. *broþrs*, nom. pl. *broþrjus*; *nasjands* "savior," gen. *nasjandis*, nom. pl. *nasjands*).

4.1.2.1   Ablaut and accent patterns

Proto-Indo-European nouns, with the exception of *o*-stems (> Gmc. *(j)a*-stems) and *ā*-stems (> Gmc. *ō*-stems), were characterized by complex alternations of ablaut and accent which affected the root, the derivational suffix that optionally followed the root, and the grammatical ending proper or *desinence*. Four or five such ablaut/accent patterns can be reconstructed for stems containing a suffix (e.g., *-t(e/o)r-*, *-(e/o)n-*, *-w(e/o)nt-*, *-t(e/o)i-*, etc.). Thus, for example, the oldest recoverable declension of the Proto-Indo-European word for "father" (Go. *fadar*) was of the *hysterokinetic* type, with nominative singular *ph_2-tḗr* (zero-grade root, accented *ē*-grade suffix, zero desinence), accusative singular *ph_2-tér-m̥* (accented *e*-grade suffix, invariant desinence), and genitive singular *ph_2-tr-és* (zero-grade suffix, accented *e*-grade desinence). Quite different from this was the declension of the word for "sowing, seed" (Go. *seþs*; *i*-stem), which was *proterokinetic*, with nominative singular *$séh_1$-ti-s*, accusative singular *$séh_1$-ti-m* (accented *e*-grade root, zero-grade suffix, invariant desinence), and genitive singular *sh_1-téi-s* (zero-grade root, accented *e*-grade suffix, zero-grade desinence). Root nouns – nouns lacking a derivational suffix – displayed comparable inner-paradigmatic allomorphy, as in the Proto-Indo-European word for "foot" (Go. *fotus*): nominative singular *pṓd-s* (*ō*-grade root, invariant desinence), accusative singular *pód-m̥* (*o*-grade root, invariant desinence), genitive singular *péd-s* (*e*-grade root, zero-grade desinence).

Little remains of this complexity in Germanic and Gothic. Root ablaut was almost completely abandoned within paradigms (*seþs* and *fotus* generalized the vocalism of the nominative singular), and suffixes and desinences fused to form what can be described synchronically as "*i*-stem endings," "*u*-stem endings," "*n*-stem endings," etc. Only the *n*-stems, which underwent a period of great expansion in Germanic, retain something of the variety of Indo-European ablaut patterns, as can be seen by comparing the morphological differences between *guma*, *hairto*, and *namo* (see Table 9.2; the feminine *n*-stem types – *qino* and *managei* – are entirely a Germanic innovation).

4.1.2.2   Gothic ō- and jō-stems

The Proto-Indo-European *o*- and *ā*-stems (i.e., thematic and *eh₂*-stems respectively) lacked the ablaut alternations of the other stem-types – a fact no doubt partly responsible for their frequency and productivity around the family. In Gothic the *ō*-stems (< *ā*-stems) in particular retain a fairly transparent declension, with the historical desinences added to the still-preserved stem-vowel (e.g., dat. sg. *gibai* < *-ā̃i* < *-eh₂-ei*; nom. pl. *gibos* < *-ā̃s*

Table 9.2   Gothic nominal stems

a- and *ja*-stems (*hlaifs* [masc.] "bread," *waurd* [neut.] "word," *hairdeis* [masc.] "shepherd," *harjis* [masc.] "army," *kuni* [neut.] "race"):

Sg.	nom.	hlaifs	waurd	hairdeis	harjis	kuni
	voc.	hlaif	waurd	hairdi	hari	kuni
	gen.	hlaibis	waurdis	hairdeis	harjis	kunjis
	dat.	hlaiba	waurda	hairdja	harja	kunja
	acc.	hlaif	waurd	hairdi	hari	kuni
Pl.	nom.	hlaibos	waurda	hairdjos	harjos	kunja
	gen.	hlaibe	waurde	hairdje	harje	kunje
	dat.	hlaibam	waurdam	hairdjam	harjam	kunjam
	acc.	hlaibans	waurda	hairdjans	harjans	kunja

ō- and *jō*-stems (*giba* [fem.] "gift," *bandi* [fem.] "bond," *mawi* [fem.] "girl"):

Sg.	nom.	giba	bandi	mawi
	voc.	giba	bandi	mawi
	gen.	gibos	bandjos	maujos
	dat.	gibai	bandjai	maujai
	acc.	giba	bandja	mauja
Pl.	nom.	gibos	bandjos	maujos
	gen.	gibo	bandjo	maujo
	dat.	gibom	bandjom	maujom
	acc.	gibos	bandjos	maujos

i- and *u*-stems (*gasts* [masc.] "guest," *ansts* [fem.] "favor," *sunus* [masc.] "son"):

Sg.	nom.	gasts	ansts	sunus
	voc.	gast	ansts	sunau, -u
	gen.	gastis	anstais	sunaus
	dat.	gasta	anstai	sunau
	acc.	gast	anst	sunu
Pl.	nom.	gasteis	ansteis	sunjus
	gen.	gaste	anste	suniwe
	dat.	gastim	anstim	sunum
	acc.	gastins	anstins	sununs

n-stems (*guma* [masc.] "man," *hairto* [neut.] "heart," *namo* [neut.] "name," *qino* [fem.] "woman," *managei* [fem.] "multitude"):

Sg.	nom.	guma	hairto	namo	qino	managei
	voc.	guma	hairto	namo	qino	managei
	gen.	gumins	hairtins	namins	qinons	manageins
	dat.	gumin	hairtin	namin	qinon	managein
	acc.	guman	hairto	namo	qinon	managein
Pl.	nom.	gumans	hairtona	namna	qinons	manageins
	gen.	gumane	hairtane	namne	qinono	manageino
	dat.	gumam	hairtam	namnam	qinom	manageim
	acc.	gumans	hairtona	namna	qinons	manageins

< *-eh₂-es; etc.). The *jō*-stems mostly follow the same pattern, but include the significant subtype represented by *mawi*, which historically contains an ablauting proterokinetic suffix *-ī-/-yā- < *-ih₂-/-yeh₂-* (nom. sg. -i < *-ih₂, gen. sg. -jos < *-yeh₂-s; cf. Sanskrit nom. *devī* "goddess," gen. *devyās*; Greek nom. τράπεζα, gen. τραπέζης, see Ch. 2, §4.1.1.1).

4.1.2.3 Gothic a- *and* ja-*stems*

The *a*- and *ja*-stems (continuing the Proto-Indo-European thematic stems) show greater phonetic erosion than the *ō*- and *jō*-stems, especially in the singular; thus, for example, the accusative singular in Germanic, *-an (< PIE *-om)*, was reduced to zero (Go. *dag*), while the corresponding sequence *-(i)jan (< *-(i)yom)* was reduced to -i (*hari, hairdi*). In the genitive singular, Gothic *-is (-jis, -eis)* is a late borrowing from the pronominal declension (cf. gen. sg. *þis, hvis* < PIE *tes(y)o, *kʷes(y)o*); the other Germanic languages have forms pointing to *-os(y)o*.

4.1.3 Nominal endings

The historical endings proper show considerable phonetic reduction in Gothic: PIE *-es* gave -s in the nom. pl. *sunjus* (< *-ew-es); PIE *-i* (locative) gave zero in the dative singular *gumin* (< *-en-i); PIE *-m* gave zero in the masculine and feminine accusative singular of all stem-classes.

The endings of the dative plural and genitive plural call for special comment. The Gothic dative plural in -m continues the Proto-Germanic instrumental plural in *-mi(z), which has close counterparts in Baltic (Lithuanian -mi) and Slavic (Old Church Slavic -mi), but contrasts with forms in *-bʰi(s) in the other Indo-European languages. The origin of the masculine and neuter genitive plural in -e is a mystery. Most feminines form their genitive plural in -o < *-õn < *-õm, and *-õm is the ending for all three genders in the other Germanic languages (cf. Old High German -o, Old Saxon -o, Old English -a, Old Icelandic -a) and elsewhere in Indo-European (cf. Latin -um, Greek -ων, etc.). The e-colored Gothic ending, presumably from *-ẽn, is an unexplained innovation.

4.1.4 Pronouns

Demonstrative and interrogative pronouns show points of contact with *a*- and *ō*-stem nouns, but with a great many idiosyncrasies (see §4.1.4.1). Below are given the paradigms of *sa* (masc.), *so* (fem.), *þata* (neut.) "this; the" (definite article) and *hvas, hvo, hva* "who, what." Note the existence of a special instrumental form in the interrogative.

(10)		Masc.	Fem.	Neut.	Masc.	Fem.	Neut.
Sg.	*nom.*	sa	so	þata	hvas	hvo	hva
	gen.	þis	þizos	þis	hvis	*hvizos	hvis
	dat.	þamma	þizai	þamma	hvamma	hvizai	hvamma
	acc.	þana	þo	þata	hvana	hvo	hva
	instr.				(= dat.)	(= dat.)	hve
Pl.	*nom.*	þai	þos	þo			
	gen.	þize	þizo	þize			
	dat.	þaim	þaim	þaim			
	acc.	þans	þos	þo			

Based on these are the more emphatic demonstrative *sah, soh, þatuh* "this ... here" and the indefinite *hvazuh, hvoh, hvah* "each," which consist of the forms of *sa* and *hvas* followed by

-*(u)h* "and" (see §3.5.5). In lieu of a separate relative pronoun, Gothic uses *sa* with the conjunction *ei* "that" (nom. *saei, soei, þatei*, gen. *þizei, þizozei*, etc.). Other demonstratives, interrogatives, and indefinites, including *jains* "that ... there," *ƕarjis* "which," and *ƕarjizuh* "each," are declined as strong adjectives (see §4.1.5).

The personal pronoun of the third person is a weakened demonstrative with separate masculine, feminine, and neuter forms; the declension is similar to that of *sa* and *ƕas*. The first- and second-person pronouns, on the other hand, are morphologically unique. Here and here alone in Gothic declension, there are separate dual forms.

(11)

		"he"	"she"	"it"	"I"	"you"
Sg.	nom.	is	si	ita	ik	þu
	gen.	is	izos	is	meina	þeina
	dat.	imma	izai	imma	mis	þus
	acc.	ina	ija	ita	mik	þuk
Du.	nom.				wit	jut (?)
	gen.				ugkara	igqara
	dat.				ugkis	igqis
	acc.				ugkis	igqis
Pl.	nom.	eis	ijos	ija	weis	jus
	gen.	ize	izo	ize	unsara	izwara
	dat.	im	im	im	uns, unsis	izwis
	acc.	ins	ijos	ija	uns, unsis	izwis

There is also a third-person reflexive pronoun, indifferent to gender and number, with gen. *seina*, dat. *sis*, and acc. *sik*.

4.1.4.1   *Pronominal idiosyncrasies*

Although many of the Proto-Indo-European demonstrative and interrogative pronouns also had stems in *-o- (masculine and neuter) and *-ā- (feminine), their declension was marked by a number of idiosyncratic features. Thus, the Gothic pronominal dative plural in -*aim* (*þaim*, etc.) shows the normal dative plural marker -*m* (see §4.1.3) added to an augmented stem form *þai*-, which otherwise surfaces without a case ending as the nominative plural masculine form. Other stem-extending elements in the Gothic pronominal system are -*mm*- < *-zm- (dat. sg. masc./neut. *þamma*; cf. Sanskrit *tasmai*) and -*z*- (gen. sg. fem. *þizos*, dat. sg. fem. *þizai*, gen. pl. masc./neut. *þize*; cf. Sanskrit *tasyās, tasyai, teṣām*). The accusative singular masculine in -*ana* (*þana*, etc.) shows the addition of a particle -*a* < *-ō to the old accusative in *-n. The peculiar nominative singular forms *sa* (masc.) and *so* (fem.) go back to a defective stem *so-, fused into a single paradigm with *to- since Indo-European times. The use of a suppletive stem in the nominative singular of the unmarked Proto-Indo-European demonstrative recalls the contrast between *ik* versus *mik, mis, meina*, or *weis* versus *uns(is), unsara* in the personal pronouns.

4.1.5   Adjectives

Gothic shares with the other Germanic languages the peculiarity of declining adjectives in two ways. The *weak* declension is used with the demonstrative/article *sa*; the forms are the same as those of the masculine, feminine, and neuter *n*-stem nouns *guma*, *qino*, and *hairto* (see Table 9.2): for example, *sa blinda magus* "the blind boy," genitive *þis blindins magaus*, etc.; *so blindo mawi* "the blind girl," genitive *þizos blindons maujos*, etc. The *strong* declension appears in all other environments. The endings are basically those of ordinary *(j)a-* and *(j)ō-*stems, but with a heavy admixture of pronominal forms:

(12)

		Masc.	*Fem.*	*Neut.*
Sg.	nom.	blinds	blinda	blind, blindata
	gen.	blindis	blindaizos	blindis
	dat.	blindamma	blindai	blindamma
	acc.	blindana	blinda	blind, blindata
Pl.	nom.	blindai	blindos	blinda
	gen.	blindaize	blindaizo	blindaize
	dat.	blindaim	blindaim	blindaim
	acc.	blindans	blindos	blinda

The strong:weak distinction between adjectives is one of the most characteristic features of Germanic. The strong adjectives continue the basic type, inherited from Proto-Indo-European. Their declension, originally no different from that of *(j)a-*, *(j)ō-*, *i-* or *u-*stem nouns, was heavily influenced by the demonstrative pronouns before the breakup of Proto-Germanic. The weak adjectives, on the other hand, are a completely new category. The suffix *-*(e/o)n-* originally served to form "individualized" derived nouns of the type Latin *Cato*, gen. *-ōnis*, literally "Smarty," or Greek Στράβων (*Strábōn*), gen. -ωνος (*-ōnos*), literally "Squint-eyes," from *o*-stem adjectives (cf. *catus* "smart," στραβός (*strabós*) "squint-eyed"). The pre-Germanic ancestor of a phrase like Gothic *sa blinda magus* thus probably once meant something like "the blind person, a boy." But by late Proto-Germanic and Gothic, the distribution of the two types had become completely grammaticalized, the weak form being *de rigueur* after the definite article and the strong form being almost mandatory elsewhere.

In principle, most adjectives also form a comparative and a superlative. The comparative is always declined according to the weak paradigm; it is marked by a suffix *-iza* (nom. sg. masc.; fem. *-izei*, neut. *-izo*) or, less frequently, *-oza* (*-ozei*, *-ozo*). The superlative ends in *-ists* or *-osts* and is declined both strong and weak: for example, *manags* "much": comparative *managiza* : superlative *managists*; *arms* "miserable" : **armoza* : *armosts*. A few common adjectives have suppletive comparative and superlative forms, e.g., *goþs* "good" : *batiza* "better" : *batists* "best"; *mikils* "large" : *maiza* "larger" : *maists* "largest."

4.2 Verbal morphology

The Gothic verbal system is similar to that of the other Germanic languages, but with a number of conspicuously archaic features. In addition to the singular and plural, there are special dual forms in the first and second persons. The only tenses are the present and preterite; to express future time Gothic uses the simple present rather than a periphrastic construction like English *I will go* or German *ich werde gehen*. No purely morphological distinction is made between forms meaning "I went" and "I was going/used to go," or between "I went" and "I have gone." The active : passive distinction, marked periphrastically in the other early Germanic languages, is expressed in Gothic, at least in the present tense, with the aid of a special inflected passive. There are three moods – indicative, optative, and imperative; the imperative is remarkable for having third- as well as second-person forms. The nonfinite forms of the verb, consisting of an infinitive, a present active participle, and a past passive participle, conform to the Germanic standard.

4.2.1   Strong versus weak

As in the declensional system (see §§4.1.2, 4.1.5), most verbs can be classified as *strong* or *weak*. The terms are traditional, going back to Jakob Grimm in the early nineteenth century. (As used by Grimm, "strong" referred to vowel-stem nouns and vowel-changing verbs, while "weak" referred to consonant-stem [typically *n*-stem] nouns and consonant-suffixing verbs). Formally, verbs are distinguished as strong or weak depending on how they form their preterite and past participle. Strong verbs, which are almost always primary, are characterized by a participle in -*an(a)*- (nom. sg. masc. -*ans*) and by ablaut or reduplication (occasionally both) in the preterite. Weak verbs, typically denominative or derived from another verb, are marked everywhere outside the present by a dental suffix, normally -*d*-.

To generate the complete paradigm of a normal strong or weak verb, it is necessary to know four potentially different stem-forms, corresponding to the four *principal parts* of traditional grammars:

1.   The *infinitive* (e.g., *niman* "take," *satjan* "set"), reflecting the stem of the present indicative and optative (active and passive), and of the imperative and present participle;
2.   The *first singular preterite* (e.g., *nam, satida*), underlying the rest of the preterite singular;
3.   The *first plural preterite* (e.g., *nemum, satidedum*), underlying the rest of the preterite plural and dual, along with the preterite optative;
4.   The *past participle* (e.g., *numans, satiþs* [stem *satida*-]).

4.2.2   Strong verbs

The principal parts of strong verbs fall into seven well-defined patterns or classes. The first six are characterized by ablaut:

(13) Class

Class	Infinitive		1st sg. pret.	1st pl. pret.	Past part.
I	beitan	"bite"	bait	bitum	bitans
II	-biudan	"offer"	-bauþ	-budum	-budans
III	bindan	"bind"	band	bundum	bundans
	wairþan	"become"	warþ	waurþum	waurþans
IV	niman	"take"	nam	nemum	numans
	bairan	"bear"	bar	berum	baurans
V	giban	"give"	gaf	gebum	gibans
VI	faran	"go"	for	forum	farans

(*wairþan, waurþans*, etc.; *bairan, baurans*, etc. show the breaking of *i* to *ai* and *u* to *au*; see §3.4.2).

Class VII is reduplicated, usually without ablaut; the reduplication vowel is -*ai*- (= short /ɛ/; see §3.2.1):

(14) VII	skaidan	"separate"	skaiskaiþ	skaiskaidum	skaidans
	aukan	"increase"	aiauk	aiaukum	aukans
	letan	"let"	lailot	lailotum	letans
	ƕopan	"boast"	ƕaiƕop	ƕaiƕopum	ƕopans

A very few strong verbs have infinitives in -*jan* or -*nan*, which affects their conjugation in the present but not in the preterite or past participle: for example, *bidjan – baþ – bedum – bidans* "request"; *hafjan – hof – hofum – hafans* "lift"; *fraihnan – frah – frehum – fraihans* "ask" (note also *standan – stoþ – stoþum*, with infixed *-n-* in the present stem).

The class membership of a given strong verb is generally predictable from the vocalism and root structure of the infinitive. Note that classes III–V are in complementary distribution: in class III the root ends in a nasal + obstruent or liquid + obstruent cluster; in class IV it ends in a single liquid or nasal; in class V it ends in a stop or fricative. Class VII includes all strong verbs with *ai, au, e* (cf. also *saian* "sow" < **sean* [see §3.4.3], pret. *saiso*) or *o* in the infinitive.

4.2.3   Weak verbs

The weak verbs are likewise traditionally grouped into classes:

(15)

Class	Infinitive		1st sg. pret.	1st pl. pret.	Past part.
I	satjan	"set"	satida	satidedum	satiþs
II	salbon	"anoint"	salboda	salbodedum	salboþs
III	haban	"have"	habaida	habaidedum	habaiþs
IV	fullnan	"become full"	fullnoda	fullnodedum	—

A small number of weak verbs with infinitives in *-jan*, such as *waurkjan*, pret. *waurhta* "make" and *þagkjan*, pret. *þahta* (< **-anh-*) "think," lack the union vowel *-i-* in the preterite and past participle. Class I weak verbs with a heavy first syllable (e.g., *hausjan* "hear") or more than one syllable before the infinitive ending (e.g., *mikiljan* "magnify") substitute *-ei-* for *-ji-* in the present, exactly as in *ja*-stem nouns (3rd sg. *hauseiþ, mikileiþ*). Class IV weak verbs in *-nan*, which are intransitive, lack past participles; their inflection is like that of *niman* in the present but like that of *salbon* in the preterite (see Table 9.3). The mood sign of the optative is /i:/, which appears as *-ei-* in the preterite and contracts with the preceding stem vowel to give *-ai-* (*nimai-, satjai-*, etc.) or *-o-* (*salbo-*) in the present.

4.2.4   Preterito-presents

By far the largest class of irregular verbs are the so-called *preterito-presents* – verbs whose presents resemble strong preterites and whose synchronic preterites are weak. Given below are representative forms of *witan* "know," *munan* "think," *magan* "be able," and *þaurban* "need":

(16)

Pres. indic. sg.	*1*	wait	man	mag	þarf
	2	waist	mant	magt	þarft
	3	wait	man	mag	þarf
pl.	*1*	witum	munum	magum	þaurbum
	2	wituþ	munuþ	maguþ	þaurbuþ
	3	witun	munun	magun	þaurbun
opt. sg.	*2*	witeis	muneis	mageis	þaurbeis
	3	witi	muni	magi	þaurbi
part.		witands,	munands,	magands,	þaurbands,
		fem. -ei	*fem.* -ei	*fem.* -ei	*fem.* -ei
Pret. indic. sg.	*1*	wissa	munda	mahta	þaurfta
pl.	*1*	wissedum	mundedum	mahtedum	þaurftedum

Also irregular are *wisan – was – wesum* "be," with a suppletive and anomalous present (sg. *im, is, ist*, pl. *sijum, sijuþ, sind*; opt. *sijai-*), and *wiljan – wilda – wildedum* "want," which

Table 9.3			Gothic strong and weak verb paradigms			
			Active			
Pres. indic.	sg.	1	nima	satja	salbo	haba
		2	nimis	satjis	salbos	habais
		3	nimiþ	satjiþ	salboþ	habaiþ
	du.	1	nimos	satjos	salbos	habos
		2	nimats	satjats	salbots	habats
	pl.	1	nimam	satjam	salbom	habam
		2	nimiþ	satjiþ	salboþ	habaiþ
		3	nimand	satjand	salbond	haband
Pres. opt.	sg.	1	nimau	satjau	salbo	habau
		2	nimais	satjais	salbos	habais
		3	nimai	satjai	salbo	habai
	du.	1	nimaiwa	satjaiwa	salbowa (?)	habaiwa
		2	nimats	satjats	salbots	habats
	pl.	1	nimaima	satjaima	salboma	habaima
		2	nimaiþ	satjaiþ	salboþ	habaiþ
		3	nimaina	satjaina	salbona	habaina
Pres. impv.	sg.	2	nim	satei	salbo	habai
		3	nimadau	satjadau	salbodau	habadau
	du.	2	nimats	satjats	salbots	habats
	pl.	1	nimam	satjam	salbom	habam
		2	nimiþ	satjiþ	salboþ	habaiþ
		3	nimandau	satjandau	salbondau	habandau
Pres. part.			nimands, f. -ei	satjands, f. -ei	salbonds, f. -ei	habands, f. -ei
Pres. inf.			niman	satjan	salbon	haban
Pret. indic.	sg.	1	nam	satida	salboda	habaida
		2	namt	satides	salbodes	habaides
		3	nam	satida	salboda	habaida
	du.	1	nemu	satidedu	salbodedu	habaidedu
		2	nemuts	satideduts	salbodeduts	habaideduts
	pl.	1	nemum	satidedum	salbodedum	habaidedum
		2	nemuþ	satideduþ	salbodeduþ	habaideduþ
		3	nemun	satidedun	salbodedun	habaidedun
Pret. opt.	sg.	1	nemjau	satidedjau	salbodedjau	habaidedjau
		2	nemeis	satidedeis	salbodedeis	habaidedeis
		3	nemi	satidedi	salbodedi	habaidedi
	du.	1	nemeiwa	satidedeiwa	salbodedeiwa	habaidedeiwa
		2	nemeits	satidedeits	salbodedeits	habaidedeits
	pl.	1	nemeima	satidedeima	salbodedeima	habaidedeima
		2	nemeiþ	satidedeiþ	salbodedeiþ	habaidedeiþ
		3	nemeina	satidedeina	salbodedeina	habaidedeina
			Passive			
Pres. indic.	sg.	1	nimada	satjada	salboda	habada
		2	nimaza	satjaza	salboza	habaza
		3	nimada	satjada	salboda	habada
	pl.	1–3	nimanda	satjanda	salbonda	habanda
Pres. opt.	sg.	1	nimaidau	satjaidau	salbodau	habaidau
		2	nimaizau	satjaizau	salbozau	habaizau
		3	nimaidau	satjaidau	salbodau	habaidau
	pl.	1–3	nimaindau	satjaindau	salbondau	habandau
Pres. part.			numans, fem. -a	satiþs, fem. -da	salboþs, fem. -da	habaiþs, fem. -da

inflects in the present like a preterite optative (*wiljau, wileis*, etc.). Note, too, the irregular preterite *iddja*, pl. *iddjedum*, suppleting *gaggan* "go."

4.2.5   Verb endings

The inflection of the individual moods and tenses in Gothic conforms closely to what would be expected in an archaic Germanic language. In the present system, both strong and (class I) weak verbs preserve the inherited distribution of the thematic vowel (*-i-* in *nimis*, *nimiþ*; *-a-* in *nimam, nimand*, part. *nimands*; *-a* < **-ō* (< **-o-h₂*) in 1st sg. *nima*). The only athematic present to survive in Gothic was the verb meaning "to be," which preserves a trace of the athematic ending **-mi* in the first singular form *im* (on Indo-European thematic and athematic morphology see Appendix 1, §3.4). The optative of an athematic present underlies the paradigm of *wiljan* (see §4.2.4).

The verb endings themselves are well anchored in Indo-European comparative grammar, including those of the present optative, which differ in part from the terminations of the indicative (e.g., 1st sg. *nimau* < **-oih₁-m̥*, 3rd sg. *nimai* < **-oih₁-t*, with the Proto-Indo-European *secondary* endings). In the other Gothic modal category, the imperative (no trace of the Indo-European subjunctive survives in Gothic), the second singular and second plural go back to well-established preforms in **-e* and **-ete*, while the third-person forms in *-adau* and *-andau* have close, though not exact, counterparts in Sanskrit and Hittite. The special passive forms *nimada* (3rd sg., extended to the 1st sg.), *nimaza* (2nd sg.), and *nimanda* (3rd pl., extended to the 1st, 2nd pl.) continue earlier middles in **-toi*, **-soi*, and **-ntoi*, with exact equivalents in Greek and Sanskrit. A significant innovation of the passive in Gothic and Germanic was the generalization of the *a*-colored variant of the thematic vowel throughout the paradigm.

All preterites are inflected alike outside the indicative singular. The plural (and dual) endings contain the vowel *-u-*, which arose by regular sound change in the third plural (*-un* < **-n̥t*) and was morphologically extended as a union vowel. In the singular, strong preterites and preterito-presents have the reduced endings of the Proto-Indo-European perfect (1st sg. **-a* (< **-h₂a*), 2nd sg. **-t(h)a* (< **-th₂a*), 3rd sg. **-e*). The singular of the weak preterite has special endings, of which only the first-person form in **-(d)ōn* is wholly uncontroversial.

4.2.6   Diachrony of the Gothic verb

The Gothic verbal system retains a number of significant archaisms vis-à-vis the other Germanic languages, such as the inflected passive, the third-person imperative, and the special dual forms of the first and second person. Yet in comparison with the Indo-European parent language, Gothic shares the characteristic Germanic features of *reduction* and *regularization*: reduction in the number of grammatical categories, and regularization in the number of ways that these categories can be expressed.

4.2.6.1   Tense-aspect

The Proto-Indo-European tense-aspect system included three preterite-like formations: (i) the *imperfect*, built to the present stem and sharing its imperfective (iterative, durative, etc.) nuance; (ii) the *aorist*, formed from a distinct stem and denoting a punctual action or process; and (iii) the *perfect*, likewise formed from its own stem and properly denoting the state resulting from a process. Proto-Germanic reduced this system more drastically than most of the other early Indo-European languages, completely eliminating the imperfect and aorist and converting the perfect into a simple preterite.

4.2.6.2   Strong verbs

The past tense which arose from the Indo-European perfect was the Germanic and Gothic *strong preterite*, which betrays many traces of its origin. The perfect in Proto-Indo-European was characterized by reduplication with *-e-, special endings, and *o* : zero ablaut; the accent was on the *o*-grade root in the indicative singular and on the endings elsewhere. In general, Germanic gave up reduplication in verbs where ablaut was preserved, but retained reduplication in the minority of cases where ablaut distinctions were impossible. The strong preterites of classes I–III illustrate the typical treatment:

(17) Class   PIE (sg./pl.)   Germanic   Gothic

	Class	PIE (sg./pl.)	Germanic	Gothic
	I	*bʰebʰóid-/*bʰebʰid-ʹ	*bait-/*bit-	bait/bitum
	II	*bʰebʰóudʰ-/*bʰebʰudʰ-ʹ	*baud-/*bud-	bauþ/budum
	III	*bʰebʰóndʰ-/*bʰebʰn̥dʰ-ʹ	*band-/*bund-	band/bundum
		*wewórt-/*wewr̥t-ʹ	*warþ-/*wurd-	warþ/waurþum

There is a complication in classes IV (*niman, bairan*) and V (*giban*), where the singular has the regular *o*-grade (*nam, bar, gaf < *(ne)nóm-, *(bʰe)bʰór-, *(gʰe)gʰóbʰ-*), but the plural, which would have been inconvenient or unpronounceable with the expected zero-grade (*nmum, *brum, *gbum), inserts an -*ǣ- of uncertain origin (*nemum, berum, gebum*). Class VI is deviant; the nucleus consists of verbs which had Proto-Indo-European *-a- in the present and made their perfects by lengthening *-a- to *-ā- (cf. Go. *skaban* "scrape," pret. *skof, skobum*, matching Lat. *scabō* "scratch," perf. *scābī*). Class VII, with retained reduplication, is largely composed of verbs which were incapable of ablaut, or whose vocalism in the perfect fell together with their vocalism in the present (*skaidan – skaiskaiþ, aukan – aiauk*, etc.). Ablaut and reduplication aside, a peculiarity of the strong preterite in Gothic is the elimination of inherited *grammatischer Wechsel* (see §3.5.1) between singular and plural. Note the contrast between, on the one hand, Gothic *warþ – waurþum*, with -*þ*- in both singular and plural, and, on the other, Old English *wearþ – wurdon*, with etymological *-d- in the plural.

The regularization and regimentation characteristic of the preterite are equally typical of the present (and of the derived present infinitive, which continues a Proto-Indo-European verbal noun in *-ono-; Go. *bairan* = Skt. *bháraṇam* "(act of) carrying"). Of the numerous ways that roots could form presents in Proto-Indo-European, one was greatly extended at the expense of the others in Germanic – the *primary thematic* type, marked by accented *e*-grade of the root and the suffix-like thematic vowel *-e/o- (*-e- before obstruents, *-o- elsewhere). Thus, the standardly cited examples *beitan* (< *bʰéide/o-), -*biudan* (< *bʰéudʰe/o-), *bindan* (< *bʰéndʰe/o-), *niman* (< *néme/o-), and *giban* (< *gʰébʰe/o-) all go back to *e*-grade thematic preforms; the comparative evidence, however, indicates that at least *bʰeidʰ- "split" and *bʰeudʰ- "awake" formed their presents differently in Proto-Indo-European (cf. Lat. *fi-n-dō*, Skt. *budh-ya-te*). In classes I–V the monotony of the usual pattern is broken only by a handful of old *ye/o-* and *ne/o-*presents like *bidjan* and *fraihnan* (see §4.2.2). Even the more seriously aberrant classes VI and VII, consisting of inherited *o*-grade presents (e.g., *faran*) and verbs with inherent *a*-vocalism (*skaban*, etc.), have been considerably normalized.

The past participle of strong verbs goes back to a zero-grade verbal adjective in *-ana- < *-onó-, which was generalized at the expense of the competing participial suffix *-tó-. Classes I–III thus show the same vocalism in the participle as in the preterite plural (*bitans, -budans, bundans, waurþans*). In classes IV and V, where the vocalism of the preterite plural is an innovation (Go. *nemum, gebum*, etc.), the vowel of the participle is secondary as well (*numans, gibans*). The pattern of the non-ablauting verbs of class VII, which have the same vowel in the participle as in the present (*skaiþans*, *haitans*, etc.), was copied in class VI (*farans*).

4.2.6.3   Weak verbs

The two most important classes of weak verbs, represented by *satjan* (class I) and *salbon* (class II), go back to Proto-Indo-European presents in **-eye/o-* and **-āye/o-* (earlier **-eh₂ye/o-*), respectively. The suffix **-eye/o-* made causatives and denominatives in the parent language; typical Gothic reflexes are *satjan* itself (< **sod-éye/o-*) and *fulljan* "fill (tr.)." Proto-Indo-European **-āye/o-* made both denominatives like *salbon* itself (< *salba* "unguent") and iteratives of the type *ƕarbon* "walk back and forth" (< *ƕairban* "walk").

Since derived verbs had no perfects in Proto-Indo-European, they lacked ablauting or reduplicated preterites in Germanic. New preterites were therefore needed, and these were of a characteristic innovated type, marked by an added dental element. The origin of this formation, the *weak preterite*, is the most widely discussed morphological problem in Germanic. Although there is no solution that is generally agreed upon, many arguments favor the old view that the weak preterite goes back to a periphrastic formation involving the verb "to do" (Gmc. **dōn*, pret. **ded-/*dǣd-*). Particularly striking is the resemblance of the Gothic plural forms in *-dedum*, *-deduþ*, *-dedun* to the Old High German free-standing preterite plural *tātum*, *tātut*, *tātun* "we, you, they did." The "long" endings *-dedum*, *-deduþ*, and so forth are a Gothic specialty; the other Germanic languages simplified **-dǣd-* to **-d-* under the influence of the singular.

The **-da-* of the weak past participle goes back to PIE **-tó-*, which was favored over **-ana-* < **-ono-* because of its resemblance – probably originally accidental – to the preterite marker **-d(ǣd)-*. The vowel that preceded the participial suffix was extracted from the stem of the (pre-Germanic) present: class I presents in **-eye/o-* were given participles in **-e-tó-* (Go. *satiþs* < **satidaz* < **sod-e-tó-*) and class II presents in **-āye/o-* were given participles in **-ā-tó-* (Go. *salboþs* < **salbōdaz* < **solp-ā-tó-*). The pattern of employing **-e-* (> Gmc. **-i-*) and **-ā-* (> Gmc. **-ō-*) as "linking vowels" before the dental of the participle eventually became characteristic of the preterite proper as well (cf. Go. *satida*, *satidedum* and *salboda*, *salbodedum*).

The stage was thus set for two further developments:

1. The weak verbs of class III, which were marked by an etymologically obscure diphthong **-ai-* in some of their present forms (cf. Go. *habaiþ* "has"), extended this element to the preterite and past participle (cf. Go. *habaiþ – habaida – habaiþs*).
2. The preterito-presents (see §4.2.4) – old stative perfects that escaped the normal Germanic development of the perfect to a preterite – were provided with weak preterites based on their inherited participles in **-tó-* (cf. Go. *witan*, part. **wissa-* (< **wid-tó-*), pret. *wissa*; *þaurban*, part. *þaurfts*, pret. *þaurfta*).

4.3   Adverbs

Gothic adverbs are productively made from adjectives by means of the suffixes *-ba*, of obscure origin (e.g., *bairhtaba* "brightly" from *bairhts* "bright") and *-o*, historically the ending of the *a*-stem ablative singular (e.g., *galeiko* "similarly" from *galeiks* "similar"). Adverbs of location are commonly associated in semantically related groups, as, for example, *þar – þadei – þaþro* "there" – "thither" – "thence"; *inna – inn – innaþro, innana* "within" – "to within" – "from within." Like adjectives, adverbs can have comparatives and superlatives;

the comparative form ends in *-is* (e.g., *airis* "earlier," *hauhis* "higher"), showing a more archaic variant of the suffix (from PIE *-yes-/-yos-/-is-*) than the *n*-extended form found in adjectives (see §4.1.5).

4.4 Numerals

The *numerals* in Gothic present a characteristic mixture of inflected and invariant forms. The numbers from 1 (*ains*) to 3 (*þreis*) are adjectives with masculine, feminine, and neuter forms; 2 (*twai*) has the notable genitive form *twaddje* (< *twajj-*), apparently the replacement of an old genitive dual. From 4 (*fidwor*) onwards there are no gender distinctions and only optional inflection for case. Noteworthy among the higher numerals are the decades from 20 to 60, which incorporate the *u*-stem noun *tigus* (cf. *taihun* "10") "a tenfold" (e.g., *twai tigjus* "20," etc.). Both 100 (*hund*) and 1,000 (*þusundi*) are nouns.

5.   SYNTAX

5.1   Syntax and the Greek text

Because almost the whole Gothic corpus is a literal translation from the Greek, it is extremely difficult to tell how much of Wulfila's syntax is authentically Gothic and how much is Greek in Gothic disguise. Thus, for example, the supposed dative absolute construction seen in the recurrent phrase *(at) andanahtja waurþanamma* "when evening had come on" has often been dismissed as artificial because the dative absolute in Gothic invariably translates a similar construction – the genitive absolute – in Greek (οψίας γενομένης).

Relatively safe conclusions can be drawn, on the other hand, about the placement of enclitic particles and pronouns, which frequently pattern quite differently in the two languages. In Mark 8.23, for example, where the Greek reads

(18) ἐπηρώτα   αὐτόν   εἴ   τι   βλέπει
      he was asking him   if   anything he sees
      "He asked him whether he saw anything"

the Gothic has

(19) frah ina ga-u-ƕa-seƕi

with both the question particle *-u* (here = "whether") and the indefinite/interrogative pronoun *ƕa* (here = "anything") infixed into the compound verb *ga-saiƕan* "see" (perfective). Such *tmesis*, or "cutting," of a compound is an Indo-European feature that was lost from New Testament Greek, but remains fairly common in Gothic, especially when the inserted element is *-uh* "and" (cf. *uz-uh-hof* "and he raised" < *us-hafjan* "raise").

5.2   Word order

Larger-scale questions about word order are harder to answer. The best evidence comes from cases where a word-for-word translation was simply impossible. Thus, in II Timothy 3.12, the Greek mediopassive verb διωχθήσονται "they will suffer persecution" could only be rendered by a two-word sequence in Gothic, with separate words for "will suffer" (*winnand*) and "persecution" (*wrakos*). Here and in similar cases, Wulfila put the object before the verb (*wrakos winnand*); when the object was a pronoun, on the other hand, he put the verb first (cf. Matthew 27.5 ἀπήγξατο "he hanged himself," rendered *ushaihah sik* in Gothic). Occasional details like these, gleaned from a minute comparison of the Greek and Gothic texts, provide our safest points of reference for the study of Gothic syntax.

5.3 Prepositions

Gothic has a full complement of *prepositions*, some of which govern the dative (e.g., *miþ* "with," *us* "out of," *fram* "from"), some the accusative (e.g., *faur* "for," *and* "along," *þairh* "through"), and some more than one case, including the genitive (e.g., *ana* "at" [+ dat.], "to" [+ acc.]; *in* "in" [+ dat.], "into" [+ acc.], "on account of" [+ gen.]).

As in most early Indo-European languages, the inventory of prepositions overlaps considerably with the set of *preverbs* – preposition-like elements optionally prefixed to verbs to form compounds (e.g., *ana-biudan* "command," *faur-biudan* "forbid"; *af-niman* "take away," *and-niman* "receive"). Although prepositions and preverbs can be traced historically to a single category, the two are synchronically quite distinct in Gothic; thus, for example, the common preverbs *fra-* (sometimes meaning "away, forth") and *ga-* (sometimes meaning "together" and sometimes merely perfectivizing) lack prepositional counterparts. As in the oldest Greek and Sanskrit, verbal compounds in Gothic sometimes display *tmesis* – the interposition of a restricted range of words and particles between the verb and prefix: for example, *ga-u-ƕa-seƕi* "whether he might have seen anything" (*ga-saiƕan* "see" [perfective], *-u* = question particle, *ƕa* = indefinite/interrogative pronoun); *uz-uh-hof* "and he raised" (*us-hafjan* "raise," *-uh* "and"). Phrase-internal facts like these are among our safest points of reference for the study of Gothic syntax.

5.4 Conjunctions

Gothic retains the inherited enclitic *-(u)h* (PIE **-kʷe*) "and"; the normal free-standing word for "and" is *jah* (< *yo-kʷe), with cognates elsewhere in Germanic. The ubiquitous subordinating conjunction is *ei*, which in isolation introduces purpose clauses and which combines with other words to form complex conjunctions of the type *þatei* "that," *akei* "but," *faurþizei* "before," *miþþanei* "while," and so forth. Other common conjunctions include *aiþþau* "or," *auk* "for," *iþ* "but," and *unte* "until," *swe* "as," and *þau* "than," all inherited or composed of inherited materials.

Note

1. Germanic belongs to the *centum* division of IE languages, in which the PIE "palatals" *k̂, *ĝ, *ĝh and the less common "velars" *k, *g, *gh fell together into a single velar series.

Bibliography

Bammesberger, A. 1986–1990. *Untersuchungen zur vergleichenden Grammatik der germanischen Sprachen*. Heidelberg: Carl Winter.

Bennett, W. 1980. *An Introduction to the Gothic Language*. New York: Modern Language Association of America.

Braune, W. and E. Ebbinghaus. 1981. *Gotische Grammatik* (19th edition). Tübingen: Niemeyer.

Jasanoff, J. 1994. "Germanic." In F. Bader (ed.), *Langues indo-européennes*. Paris: CNRS Editions.

Krahe, H. and E. Seebold. 1967. *Historische Laut- und Formenlehre des Gotischen* (2nd edition). Heidelberg: Carl Winter.

Krahe, H. and W. Meid. 1967–1969. *Germanische Sprachwissenschaft* (7th edition). Berlin: De Gruyter.

Krause, W. 1968. *Handbuch des Gotischen* (3rd edition). Munich: Beck.

Lehmann, W. 1986. *A Gothic Etymological Dictionary* (based on third edition of S. Feist, *Vergleichendes Wörterbuch der gotischen Sprache*). Leiden: Brill.

Mossé, F. 1956. *Manuel de la langue gotique: grammaire, textes, notes, glossaire* (2nd edition). Paris: Aubier.

Robinson, O. 1992. *Old English and its Closest Relatives.* Stanford: Stanford University Press.

Seebold, E. 1970. *Vergleichendes und etymologisches Wörterbuch der germanischen starken Verben.* The Hague/Paris: Mouton.

Streitberg, W. 1965. *Die gotische Bibel. I. Teil: Text* (5th edition). Heidelberg: Carl Winter.

CHAPTER 10

Ancient Nordic

JAN TERJE FAARLUND

1. HISTORICAL AND CULTURAL CONTEXTS

Germanic languages prior to AD 500 are attested in two major types of documents, the Gothic Bible translation and runic inscriptions. The bulk of the runic inscriptions are in a language different from Gothic. Most of them are found in Scandinavia, but there is some controversy as to whether the language represents a common Northwest Germanic stage or a separate North Germanic variety (see §1.2). Without further implications and without prejudice in favor of one or the other view, I will henceforth refer to this language as *Ancient Nordic*.

1.1 Prehistory

There is considerable controversy over the absolute chronology of the Indo-European settlement of Northern Europe and of the development of a separate branch of Germanic languages. But most archeologists and historical linguists seem to have reached the consensus that southern Scandinavia and northern Germany were inhabited by speakers of an Indo-European language by the beginning of the third millennium BC (Østmo 1996), and that a distinct branch of Indo-European had evolved by *c.* 500 BC. From this region the Germanic-speaking people spread north into Sweden and Norway and south into the European continent.

The Germanic area was never politically unified; there has never been a Germanic nation (Haugen 1976:100). The Germanic-speaking people were farmers and cattle-herders organized in loosely knit bands of extended families and clans. During the late Roman period, pre-Christian Scandinavia was a stable society with a strict social hierarchy. Marriage, funerals, and inheritance were conducted according to fixed laws and regulations (Grønvik 1981).

The earliest known group to have left the Germanic homeland was that of the Goths, who moved south and east, their dialect(s) becoming the East Germanic group of languages, of which the Gothic language of Wulfila's Bible translation is the best-known and most completely attested variety (see Ch. 9). After the departure of the Goths, the other Germanic tribes stayed in contact for some hundred years still, until the dialects spoken on the continent (West Germanic) began to develop features that would separate them from the more conservative dialects spoken in Scandinavia (North Germanic).

1.2 North or Northwest Germanic?

As for the actual identity of the language of the runic inscriptions, four main views can be identified in the literature:

1.   Ottar Grønvik argues, mainly on the basis of the development of the vowel systems, that North and West Germanic must have split off from each other during the first couple of centuries of our era. Since the inscriptions are Scandinavian, the language is distinctly North Germanic.

2.   Hans Kuhn (followed by Haugen and others) finds that the runic language also has so many "Western" features that it is most probably the common ancestor of North and West Germanic. According to this view, the Northwest Germanic unity was maintained until the Anglo-Saxon settlement of England in the fifth century.

3.   Elmer Antonsen agrees with Grønvik that the split between North and West Germanic took place before AD 500 (200–300 according to Antonsen), but asserts that the split consisted only in innovations in West Germanic. The Scandinavian dialects maintained the archaic form of the common parent language, which is what we find in the runic inscriptions.

4.   E. A. Makaev (followed by Krause and Kufner) considers the runic inscriptions to have been written in some kind of *koine*, a common ritual pan-Germanic language.

1.3 Language variation

Many scholars have remarked on the homogeneity of the language of the inscriptions, and it is this homogeneity which has led to the theory of a koine (see §1.2). The chief problem with the koine scenario is the absence of a unifying social and political organization that would support scribal education and language codification. Moreover, it seems that the linguistic homogeneity of the inscriptions may simply be due to a common geographic origin (Southern Scandinavia).

On closer inspection, however, the language may not be as uniform as previously assumed. The number of securely interpreted forms is very limited, and there may well have been dialect differences between, for instance, East and West Scandinavian, as well as historical differences, that are not reflected in the attested material. In addition, it must be kept in mind that part of our assumed knowledge of Ancient Nordic comes from reconstruction based on other Indo-European languages and younger stages of Germanic. In many cases the results of this reconstruction have favored certain readings over others. This has no doubt made the language appear more uniform than it actually is. There are no securely interpreted forms in the total body of inscriptions that would preclude a certain amount of dialect variation. There is, in other words, no reason to assume that the rune carvers did not write on the basis of their own spoken language.

1.4 The documents

All of the extant material in Ancient Nordic consists of inscriptions in the older runic alphabet (the *older futhark*). None of the inscriptions refer directly to historical persons or events, therefore an absolute chronology based on the linguistic documents alone is impossible. The dating of the inscriptions is partly based on archeological findings, and partly on relative chronology of linguistic forms. The oldest inscriptions can be dated to the end of the second century AD; towards the eighth century the older futhark was replaced by the *younger futhark* and eventually by the Latin alphabet. Standard corpora of inscriptions in the older futhark (Krause and Jankuhn 1966, Krause 1971, Antonsen 1975) consist of some 120–130 items. Of these, between 100 and 105 (depending on the dating and interpretation) can be said to be written in Ancient Northwest or North Germanic. The rest either belong to a later stage of the language (sixth and seventh centuries), or have a distinctly East Germanic (Gothic) form.

Through the entire period, inscriptions were made on movable artifacts such as spear-heads, arrow shafts, swords, shields, combs, buckles, clasps, and rings. From the last part of the period we have bracteates, a kind of gold medallion, with inscriptions. From the fourth century on, there are inscriptions on stone, usually gravestones and memorial monuments. This custom seems to have originated in Norway and spread to Sweden and Denmark. No inscription on stone in the older runic alphabet has been discovered outside of Scandinavia.

All of the inscriptions are short, varying from a single rune to the five-line inscription of fifteen words on the Tune stone. The content may be a short description (one word) of the object carrying the inscription, or of the owner. The stone carvings usually contain the name of the person commemorated, or the name of the person who erected the stone, or both, often in the form of a complete sentence or phrase. Some inscriptions seem to have a metrical form.

Many of the inscriptions are uninterpretable. Some contain just a few runes, which, although identifiable, do not make sense. Others may be longer, but contain so many unclear runes that an interpretation hardly amounts to more than guesswork.

1.5 Corpus and transliteration

The present survey of Ancient Nordic is based on a corpus consisting of the runic inscriptions from *c.* AD 500 and earlier. Those inscriptions which runologists have not been able to interpret are omitted from my corpus, as are those which have engendered widely differing interpretations by experts. For the remaining inscriptions, I have followed accepted readings as presented by Krause (1971) and Antonsen (1975).

By convention, runes are transliterated by boldface lower case letters. This has been done in the present work mainly in the phonology section, where the original spelling is relevant. In the morphology and syntax sections, Ancient Nordic forms are printed in italics. Vowel length is not indicated in the runic alphabet (see §3.1). In forms given in italics below, vowel length will be indicated (by a macron) only in grammatical morphemes and only in the morphology section. Although proper names often have a transparent meaning, they are generally not glossed, but their gender is indicated as PNm (masculine) or PNf (feminine).

An Ancient Nordic inscription is traditionally identified by the name of the place where it is found. This name is given in parentheses after each cited form.

2. WRITING SYSTEM

2.1 The runes and the futhark

The symbols used to write Ancient Nordic are called *runes*. There are twenty-four runes, at least twenty-two of them representing phonemes of the language. The runes were organized in a specific order, like an alphabet; such a runic alphabet is called a *futhark*, from the values of the first six runes. Although there was some individual variation, the futhark was remarkably uniform throughout the area and through the four centuries of use.

Table 10.1 The Northwest Germanic futhark

ᚠ	ᚢ	ᚦ	ᚨ	ᚱ	ᚲ	ᚷ	ᚹ	ᚺ	ᚾ	ᛁ	ᛃ	ᛈ	ᛇ	ᛉ	ᛊ	ᛏ	ᛒ	ᛖ	ᛗ	ᛚ	ᛜ	ᛞ	ᛟ
f	u	þ	a	r	k	g	w	h	n	i	j	p	ė	z	s	t	b	e	m	l	ŋ	d	o

The order of the runes is known from several inscriptions containing the full list. Their value can be deduced from their use in identifiable words, and from their correspondence with letters in the Mediterranean alphabets. In addition, each rune has its own name, beginning with the sound that it represents. The twenty-four runes are organized into three groups of eight runes each. The groups are called *ættir* (sg. *ætt* "family," or the word may also be related to *átta* "eight").

There is a close correspondence between what may be assumed to be the phonetic value of the runes and the reconstructed phonological system of the language. The only real uncertainty resides in ᚫ, which probably represents a long, low unrounded vowel, contrasting in Proto-Germanic with a long, low rounded vowel (Antonsen 1975:2f.). This is a contrast that does not exist in the short vowel system of Proto-Germanic, where /a/ is the only low vowel. The rune eventually became superfluous through phonological development, which explains why it is found almost only in the futharks, and hardly in any complete word (with one possible exception). One other rune which may not have represented a separate phoneme is ᛜ.

The reflex of Germanic /z/ (from /s/ by Verner's Law) is written ᛦ. This letter was earlier considered to represent a palatalized /ř/, since it later merged with /r/. It could not be /z/, it was assumed, since it did not undergo final devoicing (as its Gothic equivalent did: Gothic *dags* "day" vs. Old Norse *dagr*). But since there is no other reason to posit a transitional stage between /z/ and /r/, we will follow Antonsen (1975), among others, in transcribing it <z> and considering it a voiced sibilant.

The writing is usually from left to right, but the opposite direction and bidirectional writing (*boustrophedon*) are also used. Words are usually not spaced.

2.2 Origin

The futhark is a phonologically based writing system of the same type as the Greek and Latin alphabets. Many of the symbols have a clear Latin or Greek base, such as ᚠ, ᛒ, <, |, ᛉ, ᛏ, ᛗ. In addition, ᚱ and ᚺ can have a Latin, but not a Greek, origin. Conspicuously, runes that represent phonemes not found in Latin show no similarity to Latin or Greek letters: ᚦ, ᚹ, ᚫ, ᛜ. The most likely root of the runic script may therefore be the Latin alphabet, combined with the creativity and ingenuity of its inventor (notice that the runic script, unlike the Latin alphabet, distinguishes between /i/ and the semivowel /j/, and between /u/ and the semivowel /w/), who also found inspiration in the Greek alphabet and perhaps in North Italian writing systems.

Who the inventor was and when and where s/he lived, we of course do not know. The date of invention must be prior to AD 150, but perhaps not much earlier, since this is the earliest date of a securely identified inscription (the Meldorf Fibula from before the middle of the first century AD may contain runes; in which case the date of the first appearance of runic inscriptions has to be pushed back more than a century). On the other hand, it is not unlikely that the runes were first exclusively written on wooden objects that are now lost, as the angular shape of the runes may indicate that they were originally designed for carving in wood. Their inventor must have been a Germanic-speaking person, since the futhark is particularly well suited for representing an early Germanic phonological system. If the invention took place not too long before the earliest inscriptions, it is plausible that the locale was somewhere near the center of their greatest diffusion, namely Denmark (as claimed by Moltke [1985:64]). It is clear, however, that the runes could not have been invented by someone who did not have contact with the classical cultures of the Mediterranean. On the other hand, it is not likely that the futhark would have been invented in the immediate vicinity of the Latin or the Greek world, since in that case one could simply have adopted the Latin or the Greek alphabet, which in fact the High Germans and Wulfila the Goth did.

3. PHONOLOGY

3.1 Vowels

The runic alphabet contains five vowel symbols (plus the ambiguous **è**). These correspond exactly to the Ancient Nordic vowel system with the five canonical vowels /i, u, e, o, a/. In addition there is a length contrast, which is not indicated by the runic letters, but which can be reconstructed on a comparative basis. Each short vowel except /e/ has a long counterpart. In accented syllables, reflexes of Proto-Germanic */e:/ have become /a:/. The vowel system of Ancient Nordic can therefore be represented thus:

(1)

	i	*i:*	*u*	*u:*	*e*	*o*	*o:*	*a*	*a:*
HIGH	+	+	+	+	−	−	−	−	−
LOW	−	−	−	−	−	−	−	+	+
ROUND	−	−	+	+	−	+	+	−	−
LONG	−	+	−	+	−	−	+	−	+

Redundancy rule: [+ ROUND] > [+ BACK] (i.e., all rounded vowels are back vowels).

There are three diphthongs, /ai/, /au/, /iu/; in addition, a fourth attested diphthong, *eu*, is probably an allophonic variant of /iu/.

3.1.1 Vowels in unaccented syllables

Ancient Nordic has already acquired the common Germanic accentual pattern, whereby the accent falls on the root syllable of words, while affixes remain unaccented. As a result of this fixed accent, Ancient Nordic has a different vowel inventory in accented and unaccented syllables: /i/ and /e/ have merged and are written **i**, and there is no short /o/ in unaccented syllables (the short /o/ in accented syllables is the result of *a*-umlaut).

Among unaccented long vowels, there is a contrast *u/o*, but the /a:/ has been fronted and is written **e**. The diphthong /ai/ is monophthongized in unaccented syllables and is also represented by **e**. There is no attestation of /au/ in unaccented syllables, but there is probably a reflex of /eu/ in *Kunimundiu* (PNm; Tjurkö).

In unaccented open final syllables of original Indo-European bisyllabic words, short vowels (except /u/) were lost prior to attested Ancient Nordic. This is shown by the first- and third-person singular preterite of strong verbs, *unnam* "undertook" (Reistad), *was* "was" (Kalleby); and by the third-person singular present form of "be": *ist* (Vetteland).

An epenthetic vowel /a/ is sometimes inserted in consonant clusters containing a liquid: **worahto** (= *worhto* "wrought"; Tune), **harazaz** (= *Hrazaz* PNm; Eidsvåg), **harabanaz** (= *Hrabnaz* "raven," PNm; Järsberg), **witadahalaiban** (= *witandahlaiban* "bread-ward"; Tune). This was probably a synchronic process which became nonproductive, as these forms have not been passed down to later stages of Nordic; compare Old Norse *orta, hrafn*. Contemporary forms without the epenthetic vowel are also found: **hrazaz** (Rö). In later inscriptions an epenthetic vowel is also used in certain other consonant clusters.

3.2 Semivowels

The semivowels, or glides, are /j/ and /w/. The former is sometimes written **ij**. This is always the spelling in the case of a three-moraic rhyme: **raunijaz** "tester, prober" (Øvre Stabu), **holtijaz** "son of Holt" (Gallehus), **þirbijaz** (PNm; Barmen). After one or two morae, both forms occur: **harja** (PNm; Vimose comb), **auja** "luck" (Sjælland), **bidawarijaz** (PNm; Nøvling), **gudija** "priest" (Nordhuglo).

3.3 Consonants

Ancient Nordic's consonant inventory is comprised of stops, fricatives, nasals, and liquids.

3.3.1 Obstruents

The runic alphabet has nine letters representing obstruents. As with vowels, this matches the phonological contrasts exactly. The obstruents (stops and fricatives, voiced and voiceless) have three contrasting points of articulation: labial, dental, and velar. Among the voiced obstruents, stops and fricatives occur as allophonic variants (each allophonic pair being spelled with the same runic symbol).

(2)

	LABIAL			*DENTAL*			*VELAR*		
	b	**p**	**f**	**d**	**t**	**þ**	**g**	**k**	**h**
VOICE	+	−	−	+	−	−	+	−	−
STOP		+	−		+	−		+	−

Thus, **d** is seen to alternate with **þ** in the same morpheme in different environments: **laþodu** (Trollhättan) versus **laþoþ** (Halskov) "invitation (acc.)," where the alternating consonant is a fricative in both cases, but with voicing alternation (voiced and voiceless respectively). In summary, **b**, **d**, and **g** represent a voiced stop word-initially, after nasals, and after /l/; but a voiced fricative intervocalically, after /r/, and perhaps word-finally. The **p** is very rare, and does not occur in any full word in the inscriptions from our period.

There also exists a pair of dental sibilants: unvoiced /s/ and voiced /z/. The voiced sibilant never occurs word-initially; it eventually merged with /r/.

3.3.2 Sonorants

As with the obstruents, there is a series of nasals with three points of articulation: /m/, /n/, /ŋ/. The phonemic status of /ŋ/ is not quite clear; it may be an allophonic variant of /n/ before velars. In addition there occur liquids, /l/ and /r/. See also the above discussion of glides (§3.2).

4. MORPHOLOGY

Ancient Nordic is a typical archaic Indo-European language in that it has a rich inflexional morphology. Grammatical categories are to a large extent expressed by means of suffixation. Apart from the inherited ablaut system, there is little morphophonological variation. The complex morphophonology of younger Nordic languages is due to sound changes such as umlaut and syncope, which took place after AD 500. Ancient Nordic therefore appears to have a more agglutinative character than its descendants.

4.1 Nominal morphology

Nouns, adjectives, pronouns, and determiners are inflected for gender, number, and case.

4.1.1 Nominal stem-classes

Ancient Nordic nouns and adjectives belong to several declensional classes; the class is determined by the stem suffix (a stem consisting of a root plus [optionally] one or more suffixes, to which an ending is then attached [see below], in typical Indo-European fashion). Three stem-types can be identified: (i) vowel; (ii) vowel + *n*; (iii) zero (consonant stems). Four different vowel stems occur, *a*-, *ō*-, *i*-, and *u*-stems; and two different n-stems, *an*- and *ōn*-stems.

There are three genders, marked, to a degree, by the stem-vowel: *a*-stems and *an*-stems are masculine or neuter; *o*-stems and *on*-stems are feminine; *i*-stems are masculine or feminine; *u*-stems are masculine, feminine, or neuter; consonant-stems are masculine or feminine.

The stem suffix is followed by an ending indicating number and case. As in other Indo-European languages, the two categories can be expressed by a single morpheme. The number/case morpheme varies according to gender and partly according to stem-class. There is a singular/plural distinction, and at least four cases are marked: nominative, accusative, dative, and genitive. Already at the stage of Ancient Nordic, the stem-vowel and the number/case ending may have coalesced, so that the stem-vowel is not always identifiable synchronically.

No single noun or adjective is attested in all its number/case forms in the runic corpus. By comparing different words in different forms, however, it is possible to establish complete paradigms for some declensional classes. Most of the remaining lacunae can be filled in on the basis of comparison with Gothic and with later stages of Nordic and West Germanic; see Table 10.2, in which vowel length is indicated for the endings only:

Table 10.2	Ancient Nordic nominal stems			
	Nominative	Accusative	Dative	Genitive
a-stems: masculine				
Sg.	eril-az[†]	stain-a "stone"	Wodurid-ē PNm hanh-ai "horse"	Godag-as PNm
Pl.	*-ōz	*-an	*-amz/-umz	*-ō
a-stems: neuter				
Sg.	lin-a "linen"	horn-a "horn"	-kurn-ē "grain, corn"	*-as
Pl.	hagl-u	*-u	*-amz/-umz	*-ō
o-stems: feminine				
Sg.	laþ-u "summons"	run-ō "rune"	Birging-ū PNf	*-ōz
Pl.	*-ōz	runōz	*-amz/-umz	*-ō
i-stems: masculine and feminine				
Sg.	-gast-iz "guest"	hall-i "stone"	win-ē "friend"	ungand-īz "unbeatable"
Pl.			*-amz/-umz	*-o

(cont.)

Table 10.2 *(cont.)*				
	Nominative	Accusative	Dative	Genitive
u-stems: masculine and feminine				
Sg.	Haukoþ-uz	mag-u	Kunimundiu	mag-ōz
	PNm	"son"	PNm	
Pl.	*-iuz	*-un	*-umz	*-ō
u-stems: neuters (as above but without the nominative singular -z, thus:)				
Sg.	alu			
an-stems: masculine (distinct neuter forms are not attested)				
Sg.	gudij-a	*-an	-hlaib-an	Keþ-an
	"priest"		"bread"	PNm
Pl.	*-niz	*-an	*-umz	arbij-ano
				"heirs"
on-stems: feminine				
Sg.	Bor-ō	*-ōn	*-ōn	Ingij-ōn
	PNf			PNf
Pl.	*-ōn	*-ōn	*-ōmz/-umzᵢ	*-ōno
Consonant stems: feminine				
Sg.	swestar			
	"sister"			
Pl.	dohtriz			
	"daughters"			

†The word *erilaz*, which occurs in several inscriptions, has an obscure meaning. It has been suggested that it is the name of a tribe or an ethnic group, that it means "rune-master," or that it is a proper name.

In the superlative adjective *asijostez* "dear, lovable" (Tune; see Grønkik 1981), the masculine plural nominative appears as *-ēz*, which is a specifically adjectival ending.

In a couple of inscriptions, a proper name occurs in its root form. This may be taken either as a vocative case (Krause 1971:48) or as a separate West Germanic form (Antonsen 1975:26) – nominative singular lost its ending early on in West Germanic.

Younger West Germanic dialects (Old High German, Old English) have a separate instrumental case, therefore such a case would be expected also in early Northwest Germanic, but there is no syntactic position attested in which the instrumental would be required. Consequently, we have no evidence of the possible existence of such a case form.

4.1.2   Pronouns and determiners

Only personal pronouns in the first-person singular are securely attested in the corpus. The nominative occurs several times, usually in the form *ek*, but also *ik*, which may be a West Germanic form or may reflect an unaccented pronunciation. In enclitic position the forms *-eka* or *-ika* are used. The dative form *mez* is also attested.

Determiners may have adjectival endings, as the first-person possessives *minas* (masc. sg. gen.) and *minu* (fem. sg. nom.), or they may have pronominal endings, as the first-person possessive *mininō* and the demonstrative *hinō* "this," which are both masculine singular accusative. No other determiners are securely attested.

4.2 Verbal morphology

4.2.1 Verbal stems

Though there are very few verb forms attested in the corpus, both strong and weak verbs are represented (see Ch. 9, §4.2.1). Among strong verbs, the following ablaut series and stages are attested (cf. Ch. 9, §4.2.2):

(3)		*Present*	*Preterite singular*	*Participle*
I.		writu "write"		
IV.			-nam "took"	
V.		gibu "give"		
		ligi "lie"		
			was "was"	
VI.				slaginaz "slain"

The weak verbs form their preterite by adding *-d-* to the stem (plus the person/number ending). Most of the verbs that are attested in the corpus have a stem-forming suffix *-(i)j-* added to the root. This suffix appears as a vowel *-i-* when it occurs in front of the preterite marker *-d-*: *faihidō, tawidō, satidō* (cf., with no stem-vowel, *worhtō*).

4.2.2 Finite verbs

The finite verbs are attested in the indicative present and preterite, and in the optative present. Verbs are conjugated for three persons and two numbers. No secure second-person forms seem to be attested, and no dual forms. The person/number endings that are found are illustrated in (4):

(4)

			Strong verbs		*Weak verbs*	
			Present	*Preterite*	*Present*	*Preterite*
Indicative						
Sg.	1.		writ-u "write"	-nam "took"	taw-ō "make"	tawid-ō
	3.					tawid-ē
Pl.	3.					dalid-un "prepared"
Optative†						
Sg.	2.					watē "wet"
	3.		ligi "lie"			skaþi "scathe"

†These forms are all from the Strøm whetstone, the interpretation of which is rather controversial (cf. Grønvik 1996).

One verb belonging to the reduplicating class of strong verbs is attested in the first-person singular present: *haitē* "I am called" (which derives from the old middle conjugation). The verb "to be" occurs in the third-person singular indicative present, *ist*, and preterite, *was* (according to Antonsen [1975] the word *em* [1st. sg. pres. indic. of "to be"] occurs in *ek erilaz Asugisalas em* "I am Asugisala's *erila*" [Kragehul]; but this reading is very insecure and has been challenged by Knirk [1977], among others).

4.2.3   Participles

The past participle of strong verbs has a root vowel from the relevant ablaut series, and the suffix *-in-* (plus nominal inflexion): *slaginaz*. The past participle of weak verbs is formed by means of the suffix *-d-* (plus nominal inflection): *hlaiwidaz* (cf. 4.3.2). The present participle is formed in *-and-* (plus nominal inflexion): *witanda-*.

4.3   Derivational morphology

4.3.1   Prefixation

The prefix *un-* is used to denote negation or absence of a quality: *Unwodiz* "calm, peaceful" (PNm; Gårdlösa), compare *wodiz* "furious, raging"; *Ungandiz* "unbeatable" (PNm; Nord-huglo).

4.3.2   Suffixation

Proto-Germanic had several derivational suffixes inherited from Indo-European. Some of these became unproductive before the Ancient Nordic stage and thus have been lexicalized, for example, *-s-* in *laus-* "loose" (cf. Greek λύω "I loose" and Latin *luo* "I pay, atone"). Other derivational suffixes were grammaticalized to become inflexional endings, for example, *-d-*, which formed the basis of the past participle of the weak verbs.

   The following derivational suffixes seem to be more or less productive, with an identifiable meaning in Ancient Nordic:

(5)   A.   *-j-*: agent nominal or patronymic, *raunijaz* "tester, prober" (Øvre Stabu), *holtijaz* "son of Holt" (Gallehus)
      B.   *-ing-*: (place of) origin, *iuþingaz* "from *Yd" (Reistad)
      C.   *-oþ-/-od-*: action nominal, *laþodu* "invitation" (Trollhättan)
      D.   *-san-/-son-*: diminutive, *Hariso* (PNf; Himlingøje I)

4.4   Compounding

Despite the small size of the corpus, the Ancient Nordic material offers a large number of compounds, constructed of nouns and adjectives. The first member of the compound ends in the stem-vowel: *-a-*, *-i-*, or *-u-*.

   1. *Noun + noun.* The second member is the head of the word, while the first member functions as a modifier: *walha-kurne* "Celtic corn" (i.e., "foreign gold"; Tjurkö); *widu-hundaz* "forest dog" (Himlingøje II).

   2. *Adjective + noun:*

   2A.   The noun is the head: *Wodu-ride* "furious rider" (Tune); *Hagi-radaz* "giver of suitable advice" (Garbølle), from *hag-* "suitable" + *rad-* "advice" – this example could also belong to type 2C.
   2B.   The adjective is the head: *witanda-hlaiban* "bread-ward" (Tune). The first member is an adjective (present participle) derived from a verb meaning "to see to, pay attention to," and the second member is the noun "bread."
   2C.   Headless, or exocentric, compounds, typically i-stems: *alja-markiz* "foreigner" (Kårstad), from *alj-* "other" + *mark-* "land"; *glœ-augiz* "bright-eyed" (Nebenstedt).

3. *Noun + adjective.* The second member, the adjective, is the head: *saira-widaz* "with gaping wounds" (Rö), from *sair-* "wound" + *widaz* "wide, open"; *flagda-faikinaz* "threatened by deceit" (Vetteland).

4. *Proper names.* The great majority of the nominal compounds in the corpus are proper names. Most of these were semantically transparent (which, however, does not necessarily mean that they are still interpretable), and for some (the oldest ones?), the composition is also motivated: *Woduride* "furious rider" (Tune); *Hadu-laikaz* "battle-player" (Kjølevik). Other names look more like arbitrary juxtapositions, thus several names in *-gastiz* "guest," for example, *Hlewa-gastiz* (Gallehus), from *hlew-* "lee, protection" (Ottar Grønvik [personal communication] suggests that the apparent arbitrariness of these names is due to our lack of knowledge of the ancient society; if *hlewa-*, for instance, refers to some kind of sanctuary or temple, *Hlewagastiz* might mean "priest").

5. SYNTAX

Among the inscriptions from before *c.* AD 500 which have been deciphered and interpreted in a sufficiently secure and noncontroversial way, it is possible to identify forty-three combinations of words that can be considered syntactic constructions (divided among thirty-one inscriptions). It goes without saying that it is impossible to present anything even remotely reminiscent of a full syntactic description of the language on the basis of this small corpus. The material should rather be seen as illustrative of certain syntactic features. None of the constructions in the corpus represents crucial counterevidence to what may be expected from an Indo-European language of this period (if it did, it should probably be taken as evidence that the inscription has been misinterpreted; for a discussion of a younger inscription from such a perspective, see Faarlund 1990:166). On the other hand, even this limited database gives us an indication as to which choices the grammar of Ancient Nordic has made among alternatives exploited differently by various Indo-European languages.

There is no example of a subordinate sentence or of sentence conjunction in the corpus.

5.1 Noun phrase structure

5.1.1 Noun phrase word order

In the Ancient Nordic material there are twenty-seven complex noun phrases. The dominant ordering pattern is head-dependent. This is the case in all of the examples with an adjective: *Hlewagastiz holtijaz* "H. (son) of Holt" (Gallehus); *Swabaharjaz sairawidaz* "S. with gaping wounds" (Rö). In *Owlþuþewaz ni wajemariz* "O. of no bad fame" (Thorsberg) the adjective is itself modified. Possessive and demonstrative determiners also follow the head noun: *magoz minas* "son mine" (Vetteland); *swestar minu* "sister mine" (Opedal); *halli hino* "stone this" (Strøm). A dependent genitive also usually follows its head: *erilaz Asugisalas* (Kragehul); *þewaz Godagas* "servant of G." (Valsfjord); *gudija Ungandiz* "priest of U." (Nordhuglo). In two instances, where the head noun denotes the monument bearing the inscription and the genitive the person commemorated, the genitive precedes the noun: *Ingijon hallaz* "Ingio's stone" (Stenstad); *. . . an waruz* ". . .'s enclosure" (Tomstad; all of the attested examples with genitive nouns or possessive determiners are consistent with an observation by Smith [1971] that animate heads require a following genitive and inanimate ones a preceding genitive; see also Antonsen 1975:24). The only quantifier attested precedes its head: *þrijoz dohtriz* "three daughters" (Tune).

5.1.2   Apposition

By far the most commonly occurring complex noun phrases in the corpus are appositional constructions. Most of these consist of a first-person singular pronoun + a noun phrase (NP). The second member is usually a proper name or a nominalized adjective functioning as a proper name: *ek Unwodiz* (Gårdlösa) "I U."; *mez Wage* "me W.(dat.)" (Opedal); *ek Hrazaz* (Rö). The second member can also be a complex NP: *ek Hlewagastiz holtijaz* "I H. of Holt" (Gallehus); *ek gudija Ungandiz* "I the priest of U." (Nordhuglo). In *Woduride witandahlaiban* "W. the bread-ward" (Tune) and *Boro swestar minu* "B. my sister" (Opedal), the first member of the apposition is a proper name. There are even three-member appositions, consisting of a first-person singular pronoun + a proper name + a further identification or characterization: *ek Hagustaldaz þewaz Godagas* "I H. the servant of G." (Valsfjord); *ek Wagigaz erilaz Agilamundon* (Rosseland).

5.1.3   Agreement

As can be seen from these examples, aside from dependent genitives, all dependents agree with their heads in gender, number, and case.

5.2 Prepositional phrase structure

The Ancient Nordic corpus preserves four instances of a preposition followed by an NP complement; no postpositions occur. Only two different prepositions are attested, *an(a)* "on" and *after* "after." They both govern the dative case: *ana hanhai* "on horse" (Möjbro); *an walhakurne* "on Celtic corn" (Tjurkö); *after woduride witandahlaiban* "after (i.e., in commemoration of) W. the bread-ward" (Tune).

5.3 Verb phrase structure

5.3.1   Complements

The verb *haitan* "to be called" takes a predicate complement in the nominative: *Uha haite* "(I) am called U." (Kragehul); *ek erilaz Sawilagaz hateka* "I, the *erila*, am called S." (Lindholm).

Transitive verbs take a noun phrase in the accusative as their object: *ek Hlewagastiz holtijaz horna tawido* "I H. of Holt made the horn" (literally, "horn (acc.) made"; Gallehus); *ek erilaz runoz waritu* "I the *erila* wrote the runes" (literally, "runes (acc.) wrote"; Järsberg). In addition, prepositional phrases occur as verb complements: *ana hanhai slaginaz* "slain on the horse" (literally, "on horse slain"; Möjbro); *ek Wiwaz after Woduride witandahlaiban worhto* "I Wiwa wrought in commemoration of Wodurida" (literally, "I Wiwa after Wodurida bread-ward wrought"; Tune).

In *ek Hrazaz satido staina ana . . . r . . .* "I H. set stone (acc.) on . . ." (Rö), there is a prepositional phrase (with an illegible complement) in addition to an accusative object. And *[falh] Woduride staina* "dedicated the stone to W." (literally, "dedicated Wodurida [dat.] stone [acc.]"; Tune) is a double object construction with a dative object preceding the accusative (the runes preceding **woduride** here are partly missing; Grønvik [1981] argues very convincingly for the emendation of a verb form *falh*, preterite indicative third person of **felhan* "to dedicate").

The direct object is sometimes omitted when it refers to the object bearing the inscription or to the runes themselves: *Bidawarijaz talgide* "B. carved" (Nøvling); *Hagiradaz tawide* "H. made" (Garbølle).

5.3.2   Auxiliary verbs and passive voice

In the two occurrences of a complex verb form, the auxiliary follows the main verb (supporting an OV analysis of the language; see §5.4): *flagdafaikinaz ist* "is threatened by deceit" (Vetteland); *haitinaz was* "was called" (Kalleby).

These two sentences must be interpreted as passives. The passive auxiliary may be omitted, however, as in *ana hanhai slaginaz* "slain on the horse" (Möjbro), and ... *iz hlaiwidaz þar* "...i buried here" (Amla).

There are no attested occurrences of the inflectional passive which is found in Gothic and in non-Germanic Indo-European languages (the only trace of the Indo-European middle voice is perhaps the verb *haitē* "I am called").

5.4   Word order

5.4.1   Verb position

The examples above having a single complement – be it a predicate complement, an accusative object, or a prepositional phrase – may be taken as evidence that Ancient Nordic is a verb-final (OV) language (there are, however, no postpositions in the corpus, only prepositions; note also the predominant head-dependent order in NPs [see 5.1.1]). This is by no means surprising, since this is the order which can be reconstructed for Proto-Indo-European, and since there are traces of an underlying verb-final pattern in Old Norse.

In contrast, the two sentences above with double complements (*ek Hrazaz satido staina ana ... r ...* "I H. set stone (acc.) on ..."; and *[falh] Woduride staina* "dedicated the stone to W.") appear to suggest a VO order (as do several other sentences in the corpus). It is worth noting, however, that in all the examples with a nonfinal verb, the verb is finite, and it is in first or second position. This is consistent with a rule of verb movement, shifting the finite verb into second position, as in later stages of Germanic and in all of the modern Germanic languages (except English): *ek Hagustadaz hlaiwido magu minino* "I H. buried my son" (Kjølevik).

The sentences with the verb in first position are subjectless sentences (cf. §5.4.2), except *wate halli hino horna* "wet this stone, horn!" (Strøm), where the verb is in the optative mood and perhaps fronted for emphasis.

Since we find no verb in any other position than first, second, or last, and since we find no nonfinite verb preceding its complement, it can be concluded that Ancient Nordic is V2 (verb-second) and OV (verb-final) at the same time, just like Modern German.

5.4.2   Subject position

There are eighteen sentences in the corpus having a finite verb and a nominative subject. In fifteen of these the subject is in first position, as in *Bidawarijaz talgide* "B. carved" (Nøvling) and *ek Hlewagastiz holtijaz horna tawido* "I H. of Holt made the horn" (Gallehus). More examples are provided by sentences cited above. In *wate halli hino horna* "wet this stone, horn!" (Strøm), the verb is in the optative and in first position. In *wurte runoz an walhakurne Heldaz Kunimundiu* "wrought runes on the Celtic corn, H. for K." (Tjurkö), the subject has been focused and moved to the right. In *Hariuha hait-eka farawisa* "H. I am called, the travel-wise" (Sjælland), the subject is expressed as an enclitic on the verb. And in *ek erilaz Sawilagaz hait-eka* "I, the *erila*, am called S." (Lindholm), the clitic repeats the subject in first position.

There is no doubt that the apparent regularity with regard to the position of the subject must be due to the homogeneous nature of the material, consisting solely of epigraphic texts. Ancient Nordic must have a rather free word order, like its relatives in Germanic and other Indo-European language groups.

5.5 Pro-drop?

On the basis of epigraphic material alone it is impossible to determine securely whether the language has *pro-drop* or not – that is, whether the subject can be omitted and represented by verbal inflection alone, even when it is not recoverable from the context. It is true that there is not one single occurrence of a pronoun as a subject in the corpus; all of the subject pronouns attested occur as constituents of appositional constructions (cf. §5.1.2). Moreover, we do find five occurrences of a missing subject. Four of these, however, follow immediately after other lexical material in which the subject referent is mentioned: *Hariuha haiteka farawisa gibu auja* "H. I am called, the travel-wise, give (1st per.) luck" (Sjælland). In this sentence, *gibu* is first-person present, and the subject is the same as that of *hait-*, namely *-eka* "I." In *haitinaz was* "was called" (Kalleby), the subject can be inferred from a preceding genitive noun, *þrawijan* (PNm). In the case of *Uha haite* "I am called Uha" (Kragehul), preceding is *ek erilaz Asugisalas*. The sentence *wurte runoz an walhakurne* "wrought runes on the Celtic corn" (Tjurkö) occurs together with the two names *Heldaz Kunimundiu*, in the nominative and dative, respectively, on the same stone (Grønvik 1987:151); the subject is therefore recoverable (*Heldaz*). This leaves us with one short inscription with two words: *tawo laþodu* "make (1st per.) the invitation" (Trollhättan). Bearing in mind that this is epigraphic material, we certainly have no evidence to conclude that Ancient Nordic is a language in which subject pronouns can be freely omitted.

5.6 Nonverbal sentences?

Examples have already been given of deleted auxiliaries. The question is whether this is due to the epigraphic style (comparable to modern newspaper headlines – cf. "Ten killed in car crash"), or part of the regular grammar of the language (as in, e.g., Modern Russian). The question is further complicated by apparent appositional constructions consisting of two nominative NPs (cf. §5.1.2). When these stand by themselves in an inscription, they may also be read as a copular sentence with an omitted copula: *ek Unwodiz [em]* "I am Unwodi"; *ek gudija ungandiz [em]* "I am Ungandi's priest"; and so forth.

6. LEXICON

The vocabulary in the Ancient Nordic inscriptions consists almost exclusively of inherited Germanic items. In the extant material there is no certain example of a word with a distinctly non-Germanic form, or a loanword from a non-Germanic language, although we know from later attestations that, for example, Celtic words had been adopted during the early Iron Age.

Acknowledgments

I am grateful to Ottar Grønvik, Jan Ragnar Hagland, Kathy Holman, Brit Mæhlum, and Arne Torp, who have read a previous version of this chapter and given me many valuable comments and suggestions.

Bibliography

Antonsen, E. H. 1975. *A Concise Grammar of the Older Runic Inscriptions.* Sprachstrukturen. Reihe A. Historische Sprachstrukturen 3. Tübingen: Niemeyer.

Bammesberger, A. 1990. *Die Morphologie des urgermanischen Nomens.* Heidelberg: Carl Winter.

Faarlund, J. T. 1990. "Syntactic and pragmatic principles as arguments in the interpretation of runic inscriptions." In J. Fisiak (ed.), *Historical Linguistics and Philology,* pp. 165–186. Berlin/New York: Mouton de Gruyter.

Grønvik, Ottar. 1981. *Runene på Tunesteinen.* Oslo: Universitetsforlaget.

———.1987. *Fra Ågedal til Setre.* Oslo: Universitetsforlaget.

———.1996. *Fra Vimose til Ødemotland. Nye studier over runeinnskrifter fra førkristen tid i Norden.* Oslo: Universitetsforlaget.

Haugen, E. 1976. *The Scandinavian Languages. An Introduction to their History.* London: Faber and Faber.

Knirk, J. E. 1977. Review of *A Concise Grammar of the Older Runic Inscriptions,* by E. H. Antonsen. *Maal og Minne,* pp. 172–184.

Krause, W. 1971. *Die Sprache der urnordischen Runeninschriften.* Heidelberg: Carl Winter.

Krause, W. and H. Jankuhn. 1966. *Die runeninschriften im älteren Futhark.* Göttingen: Vandenhoeck and Ruprecht.

Moltke, E. 1985. *Runes and their Origin. Denmark and Elsewhere.* Copenhagen: Nationalmuseets Forlag.

Morris, R. L. 1988. *Runic and Mediterranean Epigraphy.* NOWELE Supplement 4. Odense: Odense University Press.

Østmo, E. 1996. *The Indo-European Question in a Norwegian Perspective. A View from the Wrong End of the Stick.* Journal of Indo-European Studies Monograph 17.

Smith, J. R. 1971. *Word Order in the Older Germanic Dialects.* Ann Arbor: University Microfilms.

Syrett, M. 1994. *The Unaccented Vowels of Proto-Norse.* NOWELE Supplement 11. Odense: Odense University Press.

Indo-European

HENRY M. HOENIGSWALD AND
ROGER D. WOODARD
with a discussion of syntax by
JAMES P. T. CLACKSON

1. THEORETICAL AND HISTORICAL CONTEXTS

1.1 The comparative method

The parent language of the Indo-European linguistic family is an "ancient" language in a special sense: it is a *protolanguage*, not attested but reconstructed. Since a protolanguage is, broadly speaking, the collection of all *retentions* in the daughter languages, the ability to segregate *innovation* from retention in the latter is crucial for the reconstruction of the former. The *"comparative" method* (in the narrow, phonological sense of the term) accomplishes that segregation to a large extent (on the comparative method of historical linguistics, see also *WAL* Ch. 45). Those innovations which we classify as *sound-changes* are capable of producing homophony among morphs; they are phonemic mergers, with the algebraic form /a/ > /m/, /b/ > /m/ (further elaboration is needed for conditioned sound-changes). Owing to the "Polivanov" property of sound changes ("no split without merger"), which follows from their definition as replacements statable in purely phonological terms (without reference, that is, to particular morphs), it is the case that if one phoneme, or one phonemic component (distinctive feature specification), or one phoneme combination (diphthong, cluster, syllable, etc.) in *language A* corresponds to one phoneme or phonemic component or phoneme combination in a related *language B* in one set of morphs, and to some other phoneme (etc.) in another set of morphs, then language A has in this detail innovated. As regards other details the converse may be the case, and language B may be the innovator. If A is found to have innovated in all details and B in none, A is a descendant (or later stage) of B and B the ancestor (or earlier stage) of A. In this case, language B may be predicted to have occurred in time before language A.

The comparative method aims at the recovery of the phonological shape of morphs. When it comes to morphemics – obsolescence, neologism, semantic change, borrowing, analogic change, and so forth – what is sometimes also called the comparative method is in reality something quite different (hence the preponderance of phonological subject matter in comparative work). The methods available for morphemic retrieval are much more akin to "comparison" in the everyday meaning of the word. They tend to rely on grammatical and lexical consensus and on resemblances and differences that do not by themselves, typological considerations aside, carry any clear-cut chronological implications. Extensive use, however, is made of internal reconstruction which operates not only with phonological alternations which result from conditioned sound-changes, but also with semantic isolation of forms in morphological and syntactic paradigms and the like.

1.2 Scholarly tradition

The conceit of related languages having their descent from a no longer spoken "parent language" is old (Metcalf 1974:251). For the Indo-European languages it was memorably voiced in 1786 by Sir William Jones (1746–1794), the justly admired and influential British jurist and scholar who served in India. Though without a marked intellectual interest in language as such, Jones was riding the crest of the new-found wave of enthusiasm (an enthusiasm in the creation of which he was himself a leading spirit) about things Indic. In matters of language he argued in traditional fashion from the "perfection" of Sanskrit, Greek, and Latin. Of the sober efforts directed at the Finno-Ugric languages by Strahlenberg (1676–1647) in 1730 and Sajnovics (1733–1785) in 1770 he was unaware.

The nineteenth and twentieth centuries witnessed the unfolding of the great work of filling old metaphors with a new technical content, not necessarily acknowledged in the abstract but abundantly clear from substantive, especially polemical, endeavor. Since the days of Wilhelm von Humboldt (1767–1835) proof of "relationship" in the form of carrying out convincing reconstructions has been provided for language families as diverse as Austronesian, Afro-Asiatic (including Semitic), Dravidian, Algonquian, among others.

1.3 Internal and external relations of Indo-European

Proto-Indo-European (PIE) may well have been spoken somewhere in the Black Sea area before the middle of the fifth millennium BC. At that time the speech community began to break up in a complex, long-drawn-out, and only partly recoverable process. The main branches which survived into historical times are (to list them in the chronological order of their first documentation): Anatolian (now extinct; see *WAL* Chs. 18–23), Indo-Iranian (*WAL* Chs. 26–30), Greek (Chs. 2–3), Italic (Chs. 4–5), Celtic (Ch. 8), Germanic (Chs. 9–10), Armenian (*WAL* Ch. 38), Tocharian (extinct), Balto-Slavic, and Albanian (the three last-named being too recently attested for inclusion in the present volume). Additional Indo-European languages are attested in antiquity which do not clearly belong to any of these ten subfamilies, or whose membership is debated, such as Phrygian (*WAL* Ch. 31), Venetic (Ch. 6) and Messapic (Ch. 1, §7).

Once severed from one another, each branch went through changes that were largely but not entirely independent. Subgroupings based on the principle of shared innovation in the manner of the well-known *family tree* (German *Stammbaum*), or some other topological or geometrical scheme, will in general be discussed in the later chapters (noted above) which deal with the comparative evidence, that is, with the changes that define the descendant languages.

Proto-Indo-European is certain to have had outside connections of two kinds: (i) common descent from an anterior pre-protolanguage, and (ii) contacts recognizable from membership in areal typologies. Efforts to identify either kind have remained inconclusive.

2. PHONOLOGY

2.1 Consonants

The reconstructed consonantal inventory of Proto-Indo-European is comprised of obstruents (stops and fricatives), nasals, and sonorants (liquids and glides), as well as the so-called laryngeal consonants.

2.1.1   Obstruents

The stop phonemes of Proto-Indo-European, identified following established practice, are produced at five articulatory positions: (i) bilabial; (ii) dental; (iii) palatal; (iv) (pure) velar; (v) labiovelar. For each position, a (i) voiceless, (ii) voiced, and (iii) voiced aspirated stop is reconstructed:

(1)

	bilabial	*dental*	*palatal*	*velar*	*labiovelar*
voiceless	p	t	$\hat{k}$	k	k^w
voiced	b	d	$\hat{g}$	g	g^w
voiced asp.	b^h	d^h	$\hat{g}^h$	g^h	g^{wh}

The voiced bialabial $*b$ occurs only rarely. In the recently advocated "glottalic" view, the values of traditional $*p$, $*b$, and $*b^h$ (etc.) are $*p^{(h)}$ (aspirated, with unaspirated allophones), $*p'$ (voiceless glottalized), and $*b^{(h)}$ (etc.) respectively; see Gamkrelidze and Ivanov 1995 and, for an evaluation, Watkins 1998:38.

The labiovelar phonemes $*k^w$, $*g^w$, and $*g^{wh}$ are distinct from the sequences $*\hat{k}w$, $*\hat{g}w$, $*\hat{g}^hw$ (palatal stop + labiovelar glide) as well as perhaps from the sequences $*kw$, $*gw$, $*g^hw$ (velar stop + labiovelar glide). Still, it is remarkable that something like the geminate prohibition (see §2.3) neutralizes labiovelars and velars before [u], with outcomes that are those of the velars. This is especially visible in post-Mycenaean Greek where $*k^wa$ gives Attic [pa] but $*k^wu$ yields [ku] (see Ch. 2, §3.7.1).

On the basis of the evolutionary outcome of the Proto-Indo-European palatal, velar, and labiovelar stops, Indo-Europeanists have traditionally divided the Indo-European daughter languages into two major groups, labeled *centum* (Latin for "100") and *satem* (after Avestan *satəm* "100"; both forms from PIE $*\hat{k}mtom$). The general case is that western Indo-European (centum) languages merge the palatal and velar stops, whereas in the eastern (satem) dialects, the palatal stops exhibit distinct reflexes while the velars and labiovelars fall together (see Melchert 1987). The conspicuous exception to this distributional pattern is provided by Tocharian. Spoken far to the east in antiquity (with documentary remains surviving in the deserts of Chinese Turkestan or Xinjiang Uygur), Tocharian shows the centum treatment of back consonants.

Proto-Indo-European possessed the dental sibilant $*s$, presumably with allophones [s] and [z], the latter occurring before plain voiced and voiced aspirated obstruents. The occurrence of an interdental fricative /þ/ has long been proposed to account for that stop/fricative correspondence seen in cognates such as, for example, Greek ἄρκτος (*árktos*) and Sanskrit ŕkṣa-, "bear," but this remains problematic as another, more sophisticated solution has been proposed.

2.1.2   Sonorants

The Proto-Indo-European sonorant phonemes occur as both nonsyllabic and syllabic allophonic variants (see §2.1.4):

(2)

nasals	*liquids*	*glides*
n/n̥	r/r̥	y/i
m/m̥	l/l̥	w/u

2.1.3 Laryngeals

Those consonantal sounds identified as "laryngeal" likewise occur in nonsyllabic and syllabic forms:

(3) h_1/∂_1 h_2/∂_2 h_3/∂_3

(for other notations and other views, see Watkins 1998:40). Phonetically, these are, to judge from their comportment in conditioned sound change in the descendant languages, neutral (h_1), *a*-colored (h_2), and *o*-colored (h_3), respectively. The nonsyllabic allophones of the first two laryngeals seem to be voiceless; that of the third, voiced.

2.1.4 Vocalic versus consonantal

The full-grade vowels (see §2.2), the long vowels, the syllabic allophones of glides and laryngeals, and the diphthongs will henceforth be referred to, when convenient, as *vocalics*; nonvocalics are *consonantals*.

2.1.5 Nonsyllabic versus syllabic

In certain respects the three laryngeals resemble the sonorants. The resemblance is weakened and tends to disappear in the descendants. Very roughly, the following holds:

1.   After a full-grade vowel (see §2.2) and preceding a consonant, both the sonorants and the laryngeals appear in their *nonsyllabic* shapes, the sonorant combinations forming diphthongs and the laryngeal combinations merging in the descendants (if not earlier), for the most part, with the long vowels. Similarly, syllabic *i* and *u* with a following laryngeal generate *ī* and *ū*. The syllabic allophones of the liquids and nasals lead to different results in the descendants.

2.   Unless following a full-grade vowel, sonorants and laryngeals preceding a consonantal appear in their *syllabic* shapes. However, special provisions require certain sonorants and certain laryngeals to appear word-initially in nonsyllabic form when followed by certain nonsyllabic sonorants which are followed in turn by vowels, so as to form an initial sonorant cluster (e.g., *#[wr-]). In the descendant languages, laryngeals in their syllabic shapes end up merged with the full-grade vowels and their outcomes (*h_1 = e, *h_2 = a, *h_3 = o) – once again a process that may have commenced in Proto-Indo-European.

3.   Word-medially when occurring after the sequence short vowel + one consonant and before a vocalic (VC ___ [+ vocalic]), sonorants appear in their *nonsyllabic* shape (algebraically, ..*et[y]e*..). When occurring after the sequence vowel + two consonants, or long vowel + one consonant, and before a vocalic ({VCC or VVC} ___ [+ vocalic]), sonorants appear in their *syllabic* shape (i.e., ..*ekt[i]e*.., *Sievers' Law*). After a single word-initial consonant, syllabic and nonsyllabic shapes both occur – generalized from occurrences after a preceding word-final vowel or word-final consonant respectively (i.e., ..*#t[y]e*.., ..*#t[i]e*..).

2.2 Vowels

The Proto-Indo-European vowel inventory consisted of the "full-grade" *short* vowels *e*, *o*, and *a*, as well as *i* and *u*, the syllabic allophones of the glides *y* and *w* (see §2.1.2); and the "lengthened-grade" *long* vowels *$\bar{e}$, *$\bar{o}$, and *$\bar{a}$, plus long *$\bar{\imath}$ and *$\bar{u}$. The resulting vowel systems, short and long, were thus:

(4)

	short		long	
	front	*back*	*front*	*back*
high	i	u	$\bar{\imath}$	$\bar{u}$
mid	e	o	$\bar{e}$	$\bar{o}$
low		a		$\bar{a}$

Moreover, there occurred the automatic syllabic outcropping [$_e$] between obstruents, known as *schwa secundum* (see §2.4, 3.1).

2.3 Phonotaxis

Various phonotactic constraints limit the permissible sequences of sounds in Proto-Indo-European (see also §3.3):

1.   There are no geminates. Geminate clusters arising across morpheme boundaries were simplified: for example, *$h_1$és-si* "you (sg.) are" yields *$h_1$ési*, as in Sanskrit *ási* (though a marginal process of gemination creates hypocoristic by-forms of personal names and the like; see Watkins 1998:40). The sequence *..t-t.. was, however, analogically restored.

2.   There are no clusters (*hiatus*) of full-grade vowels, both like and unlike. Where such sequences arise at morpheme boundaries, the vowels are contracted into long vowels bearing a distinctive accent in some descendant languages (the "long diphthongs," where they are not contraction products [as in, e.g., the thematic dative singular ending, see §3.5.3], pose difficult problems).

3.   Obstruent (and *s*) sequences are entirely voiced or entirely voiceless. If a voiceless and a voiced or voiced aspirated obstruent abut at a morpheme boundary, regressive dissimilation will take place. It is likely, by the same token, that the distinction between the three manners of articulation was neutralized, phonetically in favor of voicelessness, before a word boundary (see §2.5). The word-final sequences *-ms# and *-ns# are likewise neutralized (Leumann 1977:415); this is relevant for the animate accusative plural ending; see n. 36.

4.   *Bartholomae's Law* specifies that "if the first member of an obstruent cluster is . . . aspirated, the assimilation is progressive" (see Watkins 1998:40–41).

2.4 Syllabicity

There are hints of an overarching principle governing syllabicity. This principle is accessible only in a schematically simplified and chronologically flat form which fails to convey the sliding nature of the scale along which developments took place, and which stretches from a remote past well into the era of the descendant languages. While most of the evidence is Indo-Iranian and Greek, it testifies nevertheless to a state of affairs that is essentially Indo-European. It is likely that syllabicity largely falls out in such a way as to preclude the accumulation of more than two consonantals in the flow of speech (with a *word boundary* as well as the sibilant *s* playing an uncertain role; see Beekes 1982:110) – hence, before vowels, *Sievers' Law* (*..et[y]e, ..et[r]e* but *..ekt[i]e, ..ekt[ṛ]e*; see §2.1.5) as modified by *Lindeman's Law* (which regulates word-initial obstruent + sonorant clusters; see Lindeman 1965).

There could well have existed an *Extension of Sievers' Law* before consonantals and before a pause if – as the surviving difference between Greek (Attic-Ionic) ὄφρα (*óphra*) "in order that" (with one short vowel and one consonant preceding) and ἧπαρ (*hêpar*) "liver" (with one long vowel and one consonant preceding) suggests – the allophonic notation *[r̥] stands for two quite distinguishable allophonic entities: *[r̥ₑ], with (it may be imagined) increasingly prominent syllabicity (in ὄφρα); and *[ₑr̥], with syllabicity decreasing to the rightward (in ἧπαρ).

In word-initial syllables where the determining environment is not built in, one would expect vacillation between [ra] and [ar], with a potential for mutual analogic exchanges and generalizations. This is indeed what one finds: for example, in Homeric κραδίη (*kradíē*) beside καρδία (*kardía*) "heart."

In Greek, as in other descendant languages, this *[ₑ] adjacent to liquids and nasals became phonemic by merging with some existing vowel (in Attic-Ionic with [a]). In the case of Indo-European *[y/i] and *[w/u] (these from the oldest period), and (much later) Indo-Iranian *[r/r̥] (Sanskrit...*/r* [but *[r̥] > Sanskrit *ir* before vocalics (..*aktira*..) under Sievers' Law proper; i.e., not the Sievers' Law "Extension"], Avestan ...*/ərə*), the three pairs of two positional variants are transformed into one segment each, perhaps of steady (i.e., neither increasing nor decreasing) vowel-like quality. Under similar circumstances [ₑ] in the vicinity of obstruents can end up phonemic in the descendant languages by merging with one of the existing vowels, though here the data remain shadowy. As a result of all of this, overlong syllables (short vowels with more than two consonants, or long vowels or diphthongs with two consonants before the next vowel) are rare, for example in Vedic and in Greek, until sound changes create new overlengths (see Hoenigswald 1994 for the details; lengthened grade [see §3.2] in certain formations is [still?] extremely rare in Sanskrit before consonant clusters; see Debrunner 1954:61).

The phenomena treated above militate in their own typological way in favor of the retentive nature of pitch accent and quantitative meter; see §§2.6, 2.7.

2.5 Word boundaries

Word boundaries (i.e., seams between so-called minimum free forms; see Hoenigswald 1992) loom large as conditioning factors in sound changes. So far from indicating, however, that all word boundaries are phonologically marked and contrast with Ø in *word-interior* position (note §2.4 on phonetic conditioning across a word boundary), word boundary is best considered an analogical development made possible by the circumstance that *pause* (the absence of sound which contrasts with the presence of sound, a universal condition) is an option at word boundaries. Post-pausal and ante-pausal allophony was generalized and turned into apparent word-initial and word-final phonology, each contrasting with word-interior phonology. The descendant languages differ somewhat in the extent to which this analogic change is carried through. Where analogic generalization is complete, utterances may indeed be treated as "composed of" (rather than "analyzed into") words in *external sandhi* (some of the sandhi phenomena of Insular Celtic may be relevant survivals – see Russell 1995; sandhi phenomena were, however, created again and again in the separate branches).

2.6 Accent

The fragmentary character of the scripts in which the texts of the descendant languages are recorded, combined with the neglect of relevant phenomena despite their syntactic centrality, have prevented deciding whether *phonemic stresses* forming stressed morphs existed, let alone reconstructing them. For some daughter languages metrical indications are available but have scarcely been exploited. Such a determination would be of paramount importance for syntax. Much of syntax is customarily discussed, *faute de mieux*, in terms of *word order*. In many languages, however, word-order phenomena (recognizable in the texts) are correlated with, or even dependent on, stress phenomena (ignored in the texts); see Hoenigswald 1980.

A lexical *word accent* (/ ́/) – likely a *pitch* accent – contrasted with the absence of accentuation. Such an accent may be reconstructed from Vedic Sanskrit, Greek, Anatolian, Balto-Slavic, and from the effect it had in Germanic (*Verner's Law*; see Ch. 9, §3.6.2). Clitics were unaccented, enclitics occupying the second place in a clause (*Wackernagel's Law*; see Szemerényi 1996:81–82, with references).

Little is known about sentence intonations. It is possible, though unlikely, that the fixed high pitch of the question pronoun in Greek τίς, τί (*tís, tí*) represents the survival of an Indo-European interrogative intonation.

2.7 Meter

It is uncertain whether Proto-Indo-European meter is quantitative in nature and based on the characteristics of syllables, as it is in Sanskrit and in Greek, or whether these two daughter languages have innovated (so Watkins 1995:21). The absence of any metrical function for word accent in these two branches is often associated with quantitative meter, whether retained or innovated. Verner's Law in Germanic (see §2.6) as well as the dependence of the ablaut zero-grade (see §3.2) upon lack of accent seem to point to an original strongly "dynamic" character for word accent; see Lehmann 1952:109.

3. MORPHOLOGY

3.1 Word formation

The morphology of nouns/adjectives (including pronouns) and verbs, comprises derivation, inflection, and compounding. A single *root*, minimal or extended (see §3.3), precedes a derivational *suffix* or suffix sequence (or accommodates the *-n/ne-* infix) which, in tandem with syntactic function, define the resulting "word" (marked, as often as not, by the incidence of accent) as a *noun* or *verb*. The resulting root + affix complex is a *stem*, though in some instances the root alone can function as a stem. In compounding (always binary), noun stems combine to form more complex noun stems. Verbs are not in that sense capable of compounding. Stems in turn are followed by a single nominal or verbal *inflectional ending* which likewise contributes to syntactic identification. The paradigms that result in this synthetic structure are close-knit and, especially insofar as the endings are concerned, characterized by well-recognizable and clear-cut allomorphies.

3.2 Ablaut

Proto-Indo-European ablaut, or *apophony*, originally depended on word accent (see §2.6) in ways which are only in part transparent. The phenomenon is a pervasive, nonautomatic, morphologically conditioned alternation of the vowels of (5):

(5)	ablaut vowel	designation
	e (and infrequently a)	full-grade, or simply e-grade
	o	o-grade
	$\emptyset$	zero-grade
	$\bar{e}, \bar{o}$ (and infrequently $\bar{a}$)	lengthened-grade

In the case of the zero-grade, accumulations of obstruents tend to be relieved by $[_e]$, the so-called *schwa secundum*. Processes such as, perhaps, the internally reconstructed sound change $*..ers\# > *..\bar{e}r\#$ produce the lengthened-grade vowels; see Szemerényi 1996:115–116. If the derivative process known in Sanskrit as *vṛddhi* (see *WAL* Ch. 26, §3.4.3) goes back to the Proto-Indo-European period, it is another source of lengthened-grade vowels.

3.3 Root structure

Minimal roots consist of two consonants (i.e., phonemes other than full-grade and lengthened-grade vowels): $C_1 \ldots C_2$. Minimal roots may also be extended to form structures of three and four consonants: $C_1 \ldots C_2 \ldots C_3 (\ldots C_4)$, always subject to phonological constraints in accordance with the the the sonority of their components. Taken together with ablaut, and observing the rule that full-grade vowels (here represented by e) can occur only once within a root, the following varieties exist: (i) for $C_1 C_2$: $C_1 e C_2$; (ii) for $C_1 C_2 C_3$: (a) $C_1 e C_2 C_3$, (b) $C_1 C_2 e C_3$; (iii) for $C_1 C_2 C_3 C_4$: $C_1 C_2 e C_3 C_4$ (see Watkins 1998:53, following Benveniste 1935 *passim*; there may be a few roots with initial full-grade vowels, but many roots which appear to fall into this category are in fact to be reconstructed with an initial laryngeal). In a given root, C_1 may freely alternate with sC_1 (*s mobile*) devoid of semantic function.

In addition, the initial and the final obstruents of roots with or without extensions are subject to a set of highly compact *compatibility rules* or *root constraints*. With insignificant exceptions, the initial and the final phoneme of a root must not be the same (note that this prevents the zero-grade from creating a geminate cluster [see §2.3]; in the case of minimal roots, not even the places of articulation of C_1 and C_2 are permitted to be the same): thus, roots of the form $**nen$, $**tet$, $**tert$, $**d^hed^h$, $**d^hed$ are excluded. Voiced obstruents do not occur with one another; neither do voiceless obstruents occur with voiced aspirated obstruents ($**bed$, $**b^het$, $**ped^h$, $**perd^h$, etc.). In contrast, (i) voiceless obstruents can co-occur, (ii) as can voiced aspirates, (iii) and voiceless obstruents can occur with voiced obstruents, (iv) and voiced obstruents with voiced aspirated: thus, $*pet$, $*ped$, $*bet$, $*b^hed^h$, $*b^hed$, $*b^herd$, $*b^hend$, and so forth (but not $**ted$). For an organization of these constraints, see Hoenigswald 1954:469, n. 2.

3.4 Athematic versus thematic

Noun/adjective and verb morphology show a thoroughgoing parallelism between *athematic* and *thematic* formation. The latter exhibits a stem suffix $e \sim o$ (o before endings with $-m\ldots$) preceding the inflectional ending, whereas the former has no such vowel. Athematic formations frequently exhibit a play of ablaut in root, suffixation, and ending (associated with accent; for a critique of the classificatory schemes proposed to deal with accent in inflectional noun paradigms, see Watkins 1998:62), while the thematic vowel tends to freeze accent and ablaut.

3.5 Nominal morphology

Under this heading can be treated both nouns and adjectives, as well as pronouns. As one goes back in history, the difference between noun and adjective tends to lessen. A noun has one gender as an inherent characteristic. A given adjective, on the other hand, aside from its syntactic and semantic standing as attribute or predicate and as a counter for the rules of grammatical agreement, is defined, in most of the descendant languages at least, by the fact that it occurs in all three genders. For example, derivative suffixation, as it serves to create feminines (once these are established) from some masculines, becomes a part of the paradigm for any adjective.

3.5.1   Derivation

Nominal (noun/adjective) derivation by means of suffixes (see §3.1), including simply the thematic vowel itself, is either *primary* (directly from the root) or *secondary* (from a stem). Nominal suffixes range from (i) athematic (including -Ø-, in the case of root nouns, with inflectional endings attached directly to the root, which thus serves as the stem); to (ii) thematic suffixes (i.e., suffixes ending in the thematic vowel; see §3.4); to (iii) the suffix *-eh₂* (and the ablauting *-yeh₂* [e-grade], *-ih₂* [zero-grade]) which became completely recast as the sign of feminines and collectives in the descendants. Stems formed with athematic suffixes have been traditionally classified by the final segment of the suffix, for example:

(6)
stem-class	*nominative singular*	*genitive singular*	
t-stems	*nókʷ-t-s	*nékʷ-t-s	"night"
r-stems	*ph₂-tér	*ph₂-tr-és	"father"
n-stems	*tér-mņ	*tér-mņ-s	"boundary"
i-stems	*mén-ti-s	*mņ-teí-s	"mind"
u-stems	*pér-tu-s	*pŗ-teú-s	"a crossing over"

For a full discussion of derivational suffixes, see Watkins 1998:62–65.

There are two processes that compete with suffixation. One is *accent shift*; the contrast between Sanskrit *bráhman-* (neuter), the religious concept, and *brahmán-* (masculine) "singer, etc." seems to be old. The other is *compounding*.

Both compounds and secondary derivation by suffix are, on the whole, exocentric rather than simply determinative. In compounds, while the first stem may indeed be said to modify the second, the compounding itself has a derivational function: Sanskrit *bahu-* means "much" and *vrīhi-* "rice," but *bahu-vrīhi-* is not simply "much rice" but "having much rice" (see *WAL* Ch. 26, §4.4.2.3). In consequence, certain secondary suffixes indicating "having" and the compound construction are complementary to each other. In Greek terms, θεός (*tʰeós*) "god," suffixed θε-ῖ-ος (*tʰe-î-os*) "divine," but compounded θεο-ειδής (*tʰeo-eidḗs*) "having a god's appearance," and **not** **θε-ι-ο-ειδής (*tʰe-i-o-eidḗs*), on a par with πολύ-μητις ([polŭ-me:tis]) "of many counsels" (cf. Skt. *bahu-vrīhi*), even though both θεῖος (*tʰeîos*) and πολύς (*polús*) are attributive adjectives.

In secondary derivation by suffix, too, mere modification of meaning, as in diminutives, pejoratives, augmentatives, and so forth, is very rare. To continue the preceding example, Greek θεῖος (*tʰeîos*) is, in fact, typical: it refers not to some sort of "god" but to an outside person or object characterized by gods.

This relationship extends to the process of *internal derivation* by a rightward shift of word accent, which turns some athematic nouns into possessive adjectives. For example, **krétu-* "strength" yields *krtú-* "strong"; see Watkins 1998:62 and Schindler in Nussbaum 1998:14.

The secondary comparative in *-tero-*, going back to a primary suffix to express opposing attributes ("other," etc.; cf. Latin *alter* "the other of two"), which later, in some descendants, competes uneasily with primary formations, is a notable exception to the foregoing generalization.

3.5.2 The Caland System

Recognition of "Caland" suffixation represents an insight of an unusual kind. A set of suffixes is distributed in such a way that the presence of one (in one semantic function) implies, almost to the point of predictability, the existence of some or all other members of the set (in other semantic functions). Thus, in Greek, adjectives in *-(e)ró-s* (e.g., κυδ-ρός (*kud-rós*) "famous"; κρατ-ερός (*krat-erós*) "powerful") or *-ú-s* (e.g., κρατύς (*kratús*) "strong") go together with neuter nouns in *-es/-os* (κάρτ-ος (*kárt-os*) "strength"; κῦδ-ος (*kûd-os*) "fame," etc.); with the primary comparatives; with first compound members in *-i-* (κυδι-άνειρα (*kudi-áneira*) "of famed men" fem.); and so forth. On the Caland System, see Risch 1974:65–97; 208.

3.5.3 Nominal endings

Noun/adjective stems are followed by declensional endings in which the categories of (i) *number* (singular, dual, plural) and (ii) *gender* (once animate and neuter; then masculine, feminine, and neuter) – these two being really derivational – as well as (iii) *case* (eight in number; see Table A.1) are fused, with few or no hints at a more agglutinating prehistory (the animate accusative plural ending, *-ns*, perhaps was built from accusative *-m* [as in the singular] plus the plural *-s*). These endings, insofar as they can be retrieved with any assurance, are presented in Table A.1 (cf. Watkins 1998:66):

Table A.1	Proto-Indo-European nominal endings	
	Athematic	Thematic
Nominative	*-s	*-o-s
Vocative	*-Ø	*-e
Accusative	*-m	*-o-m
Nom./Acc. neuter	*-Ø	*-o-m
Genitive	*-es/-os/-s	*-o-s/-o-s(y)o
Ablative	*-es/-os/-s	*-o-h₂ed
Dative	*-ei	(*-o-ei>) *-ōi
Locative	*-i; *-Ø	*-e/o-i
Dual		
Nom./Acc.	*-h₁	*-o-h₁
Plural		
Nom./Voc.	*-es	(*-o-es>) *-ōs
Accusative	*-ms	(*-o-ms>) *-ons
Nom./Acc. neuter	*-h₂	*-e-h₂
Genitive	*-om	(*-o-om>) *-ōm
Dat./Abl.	*-bʰ(y)os; *-mos	*-o-bʰ(y)os; *-o-mos
Locative	*-su	*-oisu
Instrumental	*-bʰis; *-mis	*-ōis

3.5.4 Pronouns

Pronouns may be classified superficially into (i) personal pronouns and (ii) the various pronominal adjectives and adverbs that form well-integrated derivational and inflectional paradigms.

Among the *personal pronouns* it seems possible to reconstruct these nominatives:

(7) $*(h_1)e\hat{g}oh_2$, $*(h_1)e\hat{g}h_2om$ "I"
      $*tuh_2$ "you" (sg.)
      $*weis$, $*h_1\underset{\circ}{n}smes$ "we"
      $*yuh_xs$, $*h_1usmes$ "you" (pl.)

The other cases have each an orthotone and an enclitic variant. There is also the much remarked-on suppletion in the first-person singular paradigm between the nominative stem and the oblique case forms with initial $*m$-. The reconstruction of all these forms is complex and problematic; see Rix 1976:177–180, Szemerényi 1996:216–218.

A *reflexive* stem $*s(w)e/o$- is used for all three persons.

Possessive pronouns are thematic derivations based upon the personal pronouns. *Demonstratives* are a mixture of indeclinable particles and adjective-like paradigms built on the latter. Limiting this presentation again to the nominative (singular) forms, the conglomerate particle $*so$ "and he" (maintained as such in Hittite) and the neuter $*to$-d (with the characteristic neuter singular ending that distinguishes pronouns from ordinary adjectives; cf. Latin neuter *aliud* "other") combined in the non-Anatolian descendants to form a suppletive thematic paradigm: masculine $*so$ (feminine $*seh_2$), neuter $*tod$, preserved, for instance, as the Attic Greek "definite article," ὁ (*ho* – without a nominative ending!; feminine ἡ (*hē*)), τό (*tó*). The *interrogative* stems are $*k^wo$- and $*k^wi$- (it is a characteristic of pronominal inflection that thematic stems and *i*-stems can exist side by side); when enclitic, these serve as indefinites. In the *relative* function, $*k^wo$-/$*k^wi$- competes with $*(h_1)yo$- which is possibly derived from the demonstrative $*h_1i$- (as in Latin *is* "that one").

3.6 Verbal morphology

3.6.1 Derivation

Verb-stems carry derivational affixes – often governed by *principles* which duplicate the corresponding processes in noun formation (see §3.5.1; also §3.1). Affixes utilized in verb-stem formation include: (i) athematic and thematic ($*$-e/o-) suffixes; (ii) both denominative and nondenominative $*$-ye/o-; (iii) the nasal infix $*$-n/ne-; (iv) the $*$-s- of the "sigmatic aorist"; (v) the iterative suffix $*$-$s\hat{k}e/o$-; (vi) the thematic vowel itself as sign of the *subjunctive* mood; (vii) the *optative* suffix $*$-yeh_1/ih_1- (placed immediately before the ending; thus in athematic paradigm after the thematic vowel: 3rd sg. pres. act. $*b^hér$-o-yh_1-t > Gk. φέροι (*phéroi*) "may (s)he carry," matching the indicative φέρει (*phérei*)); (viii) the thematic $*$-se/o- of some futures (a doubtful case for the parent Indo-European language, but so used among daughters); (ix) as well as reduplication; and (x), in athematic subparadigms, the play of ablaut.

These affixations are distributed over the *voices* (active and middle), *tenses* (non-perfect and perfect), *moods* (indicative, subjunctive, optative, injunctive, imperative), and *persons* (first, second, and third; with *numbers*, singular, dual, plural) of finite verbs in complicated but well-delineated patterns. In some of the more conservative descendants a given verb appears with paradigmatically predictable forms in (nearly) all the intersections of the categories named (e.g., "2nd-person plural, subjunctive, present, middle..."). The protolanguage is not like that. Seen from that more familiar standpoint, only certain particular portions of the paradigm seem filled – in ways, however, that lend themselves to coherent and convincing internal reconstruction.

3.6.2 Verb endings

Verbs are inflected for the categories named above. In main clauses verbs are enclitic; in dependent clauses and under certain other conditions they are orthotone. Some of the *active* personal endings (personal endings being what makes these constructs "finite" forms, as distinct from participles – infinitives developing only in the descendant languages) are given in (8)–(10), for singular and plural only, and with the added category of *secondary* (unmarked) versus *primary*, the latter perhaps with an added morph, *-i, the so-called *hic et nunc* particle (see Watkins 1998:60–62; "secondary" and "primary" endings are to be distinguished from secondary and primary affixation in noun derivation [see §3.5.1]; the homonymy is unfortunate). More loosely attached is the so-called augment *h_1e-, optionally prefixed to past tense indicatives, which survives in a number of descendants:

(8)

		Athematic		Thematic	
		Primary	Secondary	Primary	Secondary
Singular	*1.*	-mi	-m	-o-$h_2$ei	-o-m, -o-h_2e
	2.	-si	-s	-e-si	-e-s
	3.	-ti	-t	-e-ti	-e-t
Plural	*1.*	-me	-me	-o-me	-o-me
	2.	-te	-te	-e-te	-e-te
	3.	-enti	-ent	-o-nti	-o-nt

The athematic inflection appears to have exerted a strong influence on the thematic. A first-person singular primary thematic *-o-mi can also be reconstructed for a common Indo-European stage. In addition, for the thematic inflection, earlier second- and third-person singular forms have been reconstructed:

(9)

		Primary	Secondary
Singular	*2.*	-e-(th$_2$e)i	-e-(th$_2$e)
	3.	-e-i	-e

Distinct endings for the active *imperative* are reconstructed as follows:

(10)

		Athematic	Thematic
Singular	*2.*	Ø, -d^{h}i	-e-Ø
	3.	-tu	-e-tu
Plural	*3.*	-entu	-o-ntu

A similar array may be assembled for the *middle* voice, though there is considerable uncertainty regarding the forms of the first and second plural in the protolanguage:

(11)

		Athematic		Thematic	
		Primary	Secondary	Primary	Secondary
Singular	*1.*	-h$_2$ei	-h$_2$e	-o-h$_2$ei	-o-h$_2$e
	2.	-th$_2$ei, -soi	-th$_2$e, -so	-e-soi	-o-th$_2$e, e-so
	3.	-oi, -toi	-o, -to	-o-i, e-toi	-o, -e-to
Plural	*3.*	-ontoi	-onto	-o-ntoi	-o-nto

The *perfect* has no distinction of voice. It is largely reduplicated; its endings, insofar as they can be clearly reconstructed, are as follows:

(12)	*Singular*	*1.*	-h$_2$e
		2.	-th$_2$e
		3.	-e
	Plural	*1.*	-me
		2.	-e
		3.	-r

Two examples must suffice to illustrate some of the inflectional processes at work.

1. The verb "to go" is an athematic root present (i.e., the root itself serves as the present tense stem, without a suffix attached; see §3.6.1) with ablaut. Its constructs for the singular and plural of the indicative are _*(h$_1$)éi-mi_, _*(h$_1$)éi-si_, _*(h$_1$)éi-ti_; _*(h$_1$)i-més_, _*(h$_1$)i-té_, _*(h$_1$)i-énti_.
2. The verbs _*l(e)ik^w-_ "leave" and _*p(e)uh$_2$-_ "purify" form an indicative present from their zero grade with the ablauting nasal infix _*-n(é)-_: thus, third singular active _*li-né-k^w-ti_, _*pu-né-h$_2$-ti_; third plural _*li-n-k^w-énti_, _*pu-n-h$_2$-énti_ (giving Vedic Sanskrit *riṇákti*, *punā́ti*; *riñcánti*, *punánti*; see Watkins 1998:57).

3.6.3 Participles

There are four participles or participle-like verbal adjectives: one mostly primary, formed in _*-tó-_ (generally middle in meaning; e.g., Gk. κλυ-τό- (*klu-tó-*) "famous"), and three mostly secondary: (i) active, formed in _*-nt-_ (e.g., Gk. δό-ντ- (*dó-nt-*) "giving," φέρ-ο-ντ- (phér-o-nt-) "carrying"); (ii) middle, in _*-mh$_1$n-o-_ (*[mə$_1$no-], *[-m̥h$_1$no-]; e.g., Gk. φερ-ό-μεν-ο- (*p^{h}er-ó-men-o-*) "being carried"); and (iii) perfect, in _*-w(o)s-_ (e.g., Gk. nom. masc. πε-ποιθ-ώς (*pe-poit^h-ṓs* < earlier _*pe-poit^h-wṓs_), fem. πε-ποιθ-υῖα (*pe-poit^h-uî-a* < earlier _*pe-poit^h-us-ya_) "trusting").

3.7 Adverbs

Adverbs may be primary, even unanalyzable, or else derived – most typically from adjective stems. The forms more often known from some descendant languages in their function as prepositions or postpositions were adverbs that occurred in close syntactic construction with nouns/adjectives and verbs. They enter into compounds – *bahuvrīhi* compounds (see §3.5.1) – as first members, very much on a par with noun stems. A bit of derivational paradigm from Greek will illustrate not only their formal and semantic properties but also those of a number of prefixes such as the negative _*h$_1$n-_ (Gk. ἀ- (*a-*), ἀν- (*an-*)), zero-grade of the sentence negation _*h$_1$né:_ πολύ-θεος (*polú-t^{h}eos*) "belonging to many gods"; ἔν-θεος (*én-t^{h}eos*) "having the god within, inspired"; ἄ-θεος (*á-t^{h}eos*) "without a god."

4. SYNTAX

The twentieth century saw a fundamental revision of the reconstructed phonology and morphology of Proto-Indo-European, but much of the nineteenth-century scholarship on reconstructed syntax, notably Delbrück (1893–1900) and Wackernagel (1926), is still standardly cited in books and articles, including this one, and their work is the starting point for much current research – witness the volumes edited by Eichner and Rix (1990) and Crespo and García Ramón (1997). Although some writers take the resilience of Delbrück and Wackernagel's work as an indictment of more recent, and more transient, scholarship, it rather shows widespread agreement over many of the fundamentals of reconstructed syntax. Much of what we know about Indo-European syntax is tacitly assumed in morphological reconstruction: there were three numbers – singular, dual, and plural (on the "collective" see further below); adjectives show concord in number, gender, and case with their head noun; subject pronouns are not obligatorily present, but are encoded in the verbal inflections; case inflections marked both grammatical roles and local relations; and verbs are marked for mood and voice as well as tense (with certain restrictions, see §3.6 above).

Indeed, the reconstruction of any morphological category makes tacit assumptions about the syntax. Thus, the postulation of a nominative-accusative case system entails the reconstruction of nominative-accusative syntax. Since the end of the last century, many scholars have wondered whether the Proto-Indo-European verb might not in fact have had ergative syntax and have consequently relabeled the reconstructed nominative case "ergative" and the accusative "absolutive" (see the bibliography in Szemerényi 1996:331–332). The principal argument in support of this hypothesis is the syncretism of nominative and accusative in all numbers of neuter nouns, anomalous in terms of accusative syntax, but explainable if neuter nouns originally only occurred in the absolutive. However, despite a number of ingenious morphological arguments, there is no widely agreed route by which the ergative syntax and morphology could have given the nominative-accusative morphology as reconstructed in §3.5, and if Proto-Indo-European did have an "ergative phase," it may have been earlier than we can reach using the standard methods of reconstruction.

Much as anomalous morphological reconstructions have led to theories of Proto-Indo-European syntax, so anomalous syntactic constructions in Indo-European languages have led to revisions in the morphology. A striking case in point is an apparent breach of the concord rules of subject noun and verb. In Greek prose, neuter plural subjects take a singular verb:

(13) τὰ   ζῷα   τρέχει
      the-NEUT.PL.   animal-NEUT.PL. run-PRES.3RD.SG.
      "The animals run"

The same rule applies in Hittite and Gathic Avestan. The agreement of such an unusual syntactic rule across three of the earliest attested Indo-European languages can only represent the survival of an archaism. However, it is now generally accepted that the apparent concord of a plural subject and singular plural is a reflection of the fact that the neuter plural was originally a collective, formed with a suffix $*-h_2$, which was later incorporated into a full paradigm. Consequently, we cannot set up a special syntactic rule of concord for Proto-Indo-European, but have rather to reconstruct a new morphological category – the collective.

Since Delbrück, the major work on reconstructing syntax has been done in two broad areas: word order studies and hypotaxis, particularly the syntax of relative clauses. Any acount of Proto-Indo-European word order must begin with a statement of *Wackernagel's Law*, already mentioned in §2.6: enclitics occupy second position in the clause.

The case for the validity of Wackernagel's Law as an Indo-European phenomenon has been supported by the decipherments of Hittite and Mycenaean Greek, which show more rigorous applications of the law than Homeric Greek or Vedic Sanskrit. However, in recent years scholars have paid closer attention to the law's shortcomings (see especially Hale 1987, Krisch 1990, Adams 1994). In Wackernagel's original article on the law (Wackernagel 1892), he envisaged "enclitics" to cover three separate categories of unaccented words: (i) sentence particles (these may be further categorized, see Hale 1987:19–20); (ii) enclitic forms of personal pronouns; and (iii) accentless verbal forms. Although difficulties of script and interpretation mean that we do not always have a clear idea of which words were truly clitics in early Indo-European languages, it appears that Wackernagel's Law is best observed (given certain modifications) with enclitics of class (i), while pronouns also show a tendency to associate with the verb phrase. The behavior of accentless verb forms is more complicated. In Vedic Sanskrit, verbs are usually accented in subordinate clauses but unaccented in main clauses, and Wackernagel saw an exact parallel to this in the Modern German verb-second order of main clauses, but verb-final order in subordinate clauses (1892:427). However, this correspondence appears to be fortuitous, and since Delbrück (1900:82), scholars have argued that only the copula verb was truly an enclitic.

It seems likely that Proto-Indo-European did not have fixed word order, and the attempt to fit Proto-Indo-European syntax into the straitjacket of typological universals has now largely been superseded by more nuanced assessments of word placement (see in particular the criticisms of Lehmann 1974 in Watkins 1976). The unmarked order appears to have been head-final, although pragmatic and prosodic factors may have played an important role. Note, for example, that Vedic Sanskrit, Greek, and Hittite all allow constituents to be fronted to a TOPIC position to the left of the sentence proper (Hale 1987:14f.).

The reconstruction of subordination and embedding for Proto-Indo-European continues to provoke debate. Even the reconstruction of relative clauses is controversial. Most of the Indo-European languages mark relative clauses with the reflex of either *yo- (Greek, Sanskrit, Celtic, etc.) or *kʷo-/*kʷi- (Hittite, Latin, Tocharian, etc.). Although some scholars have argued that the use of two different markers shows that Proto-Indo-European did not have relative clauses of any type, others reconstruct both relative pronouns for the parent language, with an original distinction between *kʷo-/*kʷi-, functioning as a restrictive or defining relative, and *yo- as an appositional or descriptive relative (see Hettrich 1988 for discussion).

Those who deny the existence of any relative pronouns in Proto-Indo-European envisage a development of relatives, and other subordinate clause types, in the daughter languages from earlier paratactic structures. Indeed, Kiparsky (1995) argues that the difficulty of reconstructing any complementizers for Proto-Indo-European implies that there was no complementation at all. However, the reconstruction of participles (§3.6.3), and compounding (§3.5.1), suggests that some forms of syntactic embedding were possible, and further research in this area is needed.

5. READING LIST

Fundamental and classic works on Proto-Indo-European grammar include Brugmann 1930, and the shorter Brugmann 1902–1904; Hirt 1921–1937; and Meillet 1964. On the Proto-Indo-European lexicon, an invaluable, if somewhat outdated, source is Pokorny 1973. A recent reworking of the lexicon is Rix 2001. For a valuable and up-to-date treatment of the Proto-Indo-European roots of English vocabulary, see Watkins 2000. More recent presentations of Proto-Indo-European phonology and morphology include Meier-Brügger 2002, Szemerényi 1996, Beekes 1995 (each with helpful bibliography), Cowgill and Mayrhofer 1986, Watkins 1969, and Kuryłowicz 1968. Surveys of various Indo-European daughter languages can be found in Bader 1994, Ramat and Ramat 1998, and Baldi 1983. A survey of Indo-European linguistic laws is presented in Collinge 1985.

The authors wish to express their indebtedness to the many scholars cited herin, as well as to Sara Kimball and Jochem Schindler. Most especially we are indebted to Calvert Watkins.

Bibliography

Adams, J. 1994. *Wackernagel's Law and the Placement of the Copula esse in Classical Latin.* Cambridge: Cambridge Philological Society.

Bader, F. 1994. *Langues indo-européennes.* Paris: CNRS Editions.

Baldi, P. 1983. *An Introduction to the Indo-European Languages.* Carbondale, IL: Southern Illinois University Press.

Beekes, R. 1982. Review of M. Peters, *Untersuchungen zur Vertretung der indogermanischen Laryngale im Griechischen. Kratylos* 26:6–15.

———. 1995. *Comparative Indo-European Linguistics.* Amsterdam: John Benjamins.

Benveniste, E. 1935. *Origines de la formation des noms en indo-européen.* Paris: Adrien-Maisonneuve.

Brugmann, K. 1902–1904. *Kurze vergleichenden Grammatik der indogermanischen Sprachen.* Strasburg: Trübner.

———. 1930. *Grundriss der vergleichenden Grammatik der indogermanischen Sprachen* (2nd edition). Berlin and New York: de Gruyter.

Collinge, N. 1985. *The Laws of Indo-European.* Amsterdam: John Benjamins.

Comrie, B. 1998. "The Indo-European language family: genetic and typological perspectives." In Ramat and Ramat 1998, pp. 74–97.

Cowgill, W. and M. Mayrhofer. 1986. *Indogermanische Grammatik I/1–2. Lautlehre.* Heidelberg: Carl Winter.

Crespo, E. and J. Garcia Ramón. 1997. *Berthold Delbrück y la sintaxis indoeuropea hoy: Actas del Coloquio de la Indogermanische Gesellschaft, Madrid, 21–24 de septiembre de 1994.* Madrid: Ediciones de la Universidad Autónoma de Madrid.

Debrunner, A. 1954. *Die Nominalsuffixe.* (= J. Wackernagel, *Altindische Grammatik*, vol. II, part 2). Göttingen: Vandenhoeck and Ruprecht.

Delbrück, B. 1893–1895. *Vergleichende Syntax der indogermanischen Sprachen.* (= K. Brugmann and B. Delbrück, *Grundriss der vergleichenden Grammatik der indogermanischen Sprachen*). Strasburg: Trübner.

Eichner, H. and H. Rix. 1990. *Sprachwissenschaft und Philologie: Jacob Wackernagel und die Indogermanistik heute: Kolloquium der Indogermanischen Gesellschaft vom 13. bis 15. Oktober 1988 in Basel.* Wiesbaden: Dr. Ludwig Reichert.

Gamkrelidze, T. and V. Ivanov. 1995. *Indo-European and the Indo-Europeans.* Berlin: Mouton de Gruyter.

Hale, M. 1987. "Studies in the comparative syntax of the oldest Indo-Iranian languages." Ph.D. dissertation, Harvard University.

Hettrich, H. 1988. *Untersuchungen zur Hypotaxe im Vedischen.* Berlin: de Gruyter.

Hirt, H. 1921–1937. *Indogermanische Grammatik.* Heidelberg: Carl Winter.

Hoenigswald, H. 1954. Review of *Proto-Indo-European Phonology*, by W. Lehmann. *Language* 30:468–474.

———. 1980. "Notes on reconstruction, word order and stress." In P. Ramat (ed.), *Linguistic Reconstruction and Indo-European*, pp. 69–87. Amsterdam: John Benjamins.

———. 1992. "Minimum freedom and the sentence." In S. Hwang and R. Merrifield (eds.), *Language in Context: Essays for Robert E. Longacre*, pp. 531–536. Arlington, TX: Summer Institute of Linguistics.

———. 1994. "Meter and phonology: the chronological interpretation of idealized reconstructions." In G. Dunkel, G. Meyer, S. Scarlata, *et al.* (eds.), *Früh-, Mittel-, Spätindogermanisch – Akten der IX. Fachtagung der Indogermanischen Gesellschaft vom 5. bis 9. Oktober 1992 in Zürich*, pp. 135–148. Wiesbaden: Dr. Ludwig Reichert.

Kiparsky, P. 1995. "Indo-European origins of Germanic syntax." In A. Battye and I. Roberts (eds.), *Clause Structure and Language Change*, pp. 140–169. New York/Oxford: Oxford University Press.

Krisch, T. 1990. "Das Wackernagelsche Gesetz aus heutiger Sicht." In Eichner and Rix 1990, pp. 64–81.

Kuryłowicz, J. 1968. *Indogermanische Grammatik ii. Akzent, Ablaut.* Heidelberg: Carl Winter.

Lehmann, W. 1952. *Proto-Indo-European Phonology.* Austin: University of Texas Press.

———. 1974. *Proto-Indo-European Syntax.* Austin: University of Texas Press.

Leumann, M. 1977. *Lateinische Laut- und Formenlehre.* Handbuch der Altertumswissenschaft. Munich: Beck.

Lindeman, F. 1965. "La loi de Sievers et le début de mot en indo-européen." *Norsk Tidsskrift for Sprogridenskap* 20:38–108.

———. 1997. *Introduction to the Laryngeal Theory.* Innsbruck: Institut für Sprachwissenschaft der Universität Innsbruck.

Meier-Brügger, M. 2002. *Indogermanische Sprachwissenschaft* (8th edition). Berlin/New York: de Gruyter.

Meillet, A. 1964. *Introduction à l'étude comparative des langues indo-europénnes* (8th edition). Tuscaloosa: University of Alabama Press.

Melchert, C. 1987. "Proto-Indo-European velars in Luvian." In C. Watkins (ed.), *Studies in Memory of Warren Cowgill*, pp. 182–204. Berlin/New York: de Gruyter.

Metcalf, G. 1974. "The Indo-European hypothesis in the sixteenth and seventeenth centuries." In D. Hymes (ed.), *Studies in the History of Linguistics. Traditions and Paradigms*, pp. 233–257. Bloomington: Indiana University Press.

Nussbaum, A. 1998. *Two Studies in Greek and Homeric Linguistics. Hypomnemata 120.* Göttingen: Vandenhoeck and Ruprecht.

Pokorny, J. 1973. *Indogermanisches etymologisches Wörterbuch.* Berlin/New York: de Gruyter.

Ramat, A. and P. Ramat (eds.). 1998. *The Indo-European Languages.* London/New York: Routledge.

Risch, E. 1974. *Wortbildung der homerischen Sprache* (2nd edition). Berlin/New York: Walter de Gruyter.

Rix, H. 1976. *Historische Grammatik des Griechischen.* Darmstadt: Wissenschaftliche Buchgesellschaft.

———. 2001. *Lexikon der indogermanischen Verben: Die Wurzeln und ihre Primärstammbildungen.* Wiesbaden: Dr. Ludwig Reichert.

Russell, P. 1995. *An Introduction to the Celtic Languages.* Harlow: Longman.

Szemerényi, O. 1996. *Introduction to Indo-European Linguistics.* Oxford: Clarendon Press.

Wackernagel, J. 1892. "Über ein Gesetz der indogermanischen Wortstellung." *Indogermanische Forschungen* 1:333–436.

———. 1926. *Vorlesungen über Syntax.* Basel: Birkhäuser. Reprint 1950.

Watkins, C. 1969. *Indogermanische Grammatik III/1. Verbalflexion.* Heidelberg: Carl Winter.

———. 1976. "Towards Proto-Indo-European syntax: problems and pseudo-problems." In S. Steever, C. Walker, and S. Mufwene (eds.), *Papers from the Parasession on Diachronic Syntax*, April 22, 1976, pp. 305–326. Chicago: Chicago Linguistic Society.

———. 1995. *How to Kill a Dragon.* New York/Oxford: Oxford University Press.

———. 1998. "Proto-Indo-European: comparison and reconstruction." In Ramat and Ramat 1998, pp. 25–73.

———. 2000. *The American Heritage Dictionary of Indo-European Roots* (2nd edition). Boston: Houghton Mifflin.

Full tables of contents from *The Cambridge Encyclopedia of the World's Ancient Languages,* and from the other volumes in the paperback series

Table of contents of *WAL*

Table of contents of *The Ancient Languages of Asia Minor*

Table of contents of *The Ancient Languages of Asia and the Americas*

Table of contents of *The Ancient Languages of Mesopotamia, Egypt, and Aksum*

Table of contents of *The Ancient Languages of Syria-Palestine and Arabia*

Index of general subjects

Index of grammar and linguistics

Index of languages

Index of named linguistic laws and principles